# CULTURE AND VALUE

# CULTURE
*and*
# VALUE

TOURISM, HERITAGE,

*and*

PROPERTY

INDIANA UNIVERSITY PRESS

REGINA F. BENDIX

*This book is a publication of*

Indiana University Press
Office of Scholarly Publishing
Herman B Wells Library 350
1320 East 10th Street
Bloomington, Indiana 47405 USA

iupress.indiana.edu

*Manufactured in the
United States of America*

Cataloging information is available from
the Library of Congress.

ISBN 978-0-253-03567-7 (cloth)

ISBN 978-0-253-03566-0 (paperback)

ISBN 978-0-253-03568-4 (ebook)

1 2 3 4 5  23 22 21 20 19 18

CONTENTS

*Culture and Value: An Introduction*   1

Section I
Introduction: Creating, Owning, and Narrating within
Tourist Economies   17

1. Tourism and Cultural Displays: Inventing Traditions
   for Whom?   23

2. On the Road to Fiction: Narrative Reification in Austrian
   Cultural Tourism   44

3. Fairy-Tale Activists: Narrative Imaginaries along a German
   Tourist Route (with Dorothee Hemme)   61

4. Capitalizing on Memories Past, Present, and Future: Observations
   on the Intertwining of Tourism and Narration   74

Section II
Introduction: Heritage Semantics, Heritage Regimes   96

5. Heredity, Hybridity, and Heritage from One *Fin de Siècle*
   to the Next   104

6. Heritage between Economy and Politics: An Assessment from
   the Perspective of Cultural Anthropology   123

7. Inheritances: Possession, Ownership, and Responsibility   146

8. The Dynamics of Valorizing Culture: Actors and Shifting
   Contexts in the Course of a Century   170

Section III
Introduction: Culture as Resource, Culture as Property   196

 9. Expressive Resources: Knowledge, Agency, and
    European Ethnology   201

10. Daily Bread, Global Distinction? The German Bakers' Craft and
    Cultural Value-Enhancement Regimes   217

11. TK, TCE, and Co.: The Path from Culture as a Commons to a
    Resource for International Negotiation   236

12. Patronage and Preservation: Heritage Paradigms and Their
    Impact on Supporting "Good Culture"   254


    *Index*   273

# CULTURE AND VALUE

# Culture and Value: An Introduction

Q uestions of value permeate tourism, heritage, and cultural
property, but they reached their present, prominent place in
cultural scholarship quite slowly. This is true of my own contributions to
these fields of research as well: only in the past decade have I been able to
see more clearly the constant undercurrent of issues revolving around the
(e)valuation, distinction, and individual and social economic, ideational,
and scholarly value inherent to these interconnected parts of my work.
Thinking about how best to frame the articles gathered in this volume, it
seemed most useful to trace the change in scholarly attention and attitude
toward value regimes involving culture, folklore, or tradition during the
time since I trained in the fields of folkloristics and cultural anthropology
in Switzerland and the United States in the late 1970s and 1980s. In hindsight, three overlapping steps are clearly recognizable. Cultural scholarship
moved first from a negative, even outraged witnessing of marketed, ideologically deployed, and adulterated expressive forms in nation-building
and commerce, toward examining (and occasionally supporting and celebrating) cultural representations as opportunities to uphold identities
in increasingly diverse, globalized worlds, to finally acknowledging and
occasionally advocating efforts to claim ownership of culture as property.

Obviously, scholars do not speak with a unified voice: each of these
stances finds support, depending on the location and the sociopolitical and economic context within which cultural actors and scholarship

about them is situated. These are, however, the layers I can make out as influential for my development as a cultural researcher. Each of these steps bore increasing marks of the constructivist turn which, in its unfolding, endowed me with a particular gaze not just on phenomena to study but also on those who study them. This reflexive move in cultural scholarship, so beautifully captured in *Observers Observed*, one of George W. Stocking Jr.'s many important volumes on the history of anthropology, has accompanied me throughout my professional life. In situating the present collection, it seems fitting to sketch these three takes on culture and value. I am not aiming for an overarching, four-decade-long historiography of neighboring disciplines; rather, I seek to point to some contexts and works that I encountered and that contributed to the questions I chose to pursue. I trained first in German-speaking Europe, and then in the United States; I taught for more than a decade in the latter before moving back to Europe and teaching for many years now in Germany. There is thus a certain amount of serendipity regarding which conversations and controversies I read and participated in, and which ones bypassed me or reached me in circuitous ways. Many were not part of my training and had to be absorbed along the way.[1] The networks and interests of our mentors, colleagues, and doctoral students manifest themselves in how and where our thinking turns—the lacunae that arise are, as one is wont to state, entirely my own fault.

Folklore and nationalism emerged as a topic of scholarly inquiry in the early 1970s, as concern over the economic uses of expressive forms had already arisen in the early 1960s. Both were, arguably, concerned with ways of marking and enhancing the value of excerpts of culture. Heightened attention to "tradition" linked to both these trajectories as of 1983. That year saw the publication of Eric Hobsbawm and Terence Ranger's *The Invention of Tradition* and Benedict Anderson's *Imagined Communities*. Each in their own manner expedited the intertwined discussion of nationalism's codification and the role of marking tradition, culture, and shared sets of knowledge facilitated through new forms of communication. To a graduate student, the unfolding of these academic discussions was at once puzzling and intriguing. They seemed to be next to, or outside of, the heart of the subject matter that really was the focus of folklore studies and anthropology, that is, outside of the cultures lived and expressive forms performed in everyday life within the milieus—however homogeneous or heterogeneous. During my training, I conducted fieldwork on year-cycle rituals and lay-theater productions in Switzerland, but on the margins, I kept encountering the intermeshing of my topics with tourism in local economies, nationalism, mass cultural distribution, and the building up of heritage sentiment in newly founded institutions. These developments were part of the local scene, debated controversially but ultimately also intertwined with everyday lives, and I included them in my ethnographic documentation.

During the 1980s, most scholars in the disciplines I studied still made an effort to separate such phenomena from the core concerns of research. Folklorismus and fakelore, political manipulation from the right and the left, invention and commoditization were studied as irritating phenomena, as scholars of culture perceived them as spoiling the "actual culture" ethnographers set out to study.[2] Yet if one took field consultants seriously, it was hard to separate their actions and productions in acceptable and inacceptable varieties, and hence I found myself perplexed by such scholarly formulations and was immensely grateful to discover Hermann Bausinger's "critique of Folklorismus critique" (1966). It was not up to scholars to herd culture into an ever-smaller corral. And while Arjun Appadurai had not yet published his groundbreaking *Modernity at Large* (1996), the notions of disjuncture and difference theorized by Appadurai were already in Bausinger's early work, which noted the impact of technology and media on cultural worlds that never were closed off, and actors who navigated between old and opening horizons (1990 [1961]).

Further helpful tangents moving the question of culture and value to the second perspective that sought to understand the marking of culture and tradition came from inquiries in the field of travel and culture. Questions of encounter, captured in such a prescient formulation as "the fourth world" by Nelson Graburn (1976), were, for obvious reasons, central to the anthropology of tourism. Yet, this subfield initially struggled to gain acceptance within cultural research, as tourism was perceived as an agent undermining "intact" cultures. The critical, reflexive turn toward ethnographic practice (Clifford and Marcus 1986), and the broadening of cultural historical research to colonial encounter and its critique, assisted in shifting perspectives. Along with the rise of postcolonial work, conceptualizations of whole cultures were hard to maintain. New understandings were put forward for how culture as lived, habitual practice could turn into "culture" as different, other, and marked within the contact zone (Pratt 1992), or as Edward Bruner perhaps more aptly formulated, within the "border zone" (2004, 192), given that bordering and gaining awareness of one another does not necessarily make for contact.

However, these shifts in perspective were slow in coming. In 1989, I was asked by the department chair of a small college to change my adjunct course topic away from the anthropology of tourism to "proper" anthropology, because the college president had taken offense at my course announcement. My own fieldwork had not been in a "pristine" area but rather in Switzerland, one of the cradles of tourism where cultural encounter and performances were early on employed to market regions. Perhaps this is why scholarly debates about fakelore irritated me, in particular for the absoluteness with which some scholars claimed not just the capability but also the authority to separate the wheat from the chaff. Relying on both latent and overt arguments concerning all kinds of value except for the economic one, they insisted on scholars' and scholarship's importance in delineating boundaries between the authentic and the fake. In my monograph *In Search of Authenticity* (1997), I sought to show the roots and reasons for this dichotomous vision that continuously lapsed into categories separating the real from the adulterated, proclaiming the expert's instrumental role to detect and circumscribe essence, purity, and thus appropriate values of phenomena vis-à-vis muddied and cheapened manifestations. It was possible to delineate the proclivity toward such dichotomous sorting in over two centuries of scholarship, during which text- and ethnography-based disciplines on culture emerged, disciplines that furthermore complicated a bourgeois notion of culture as a civilizational achievement of the West.[3]

Looking back beyond my irritation at fakelore accusations and my struggle to undo authenticity's hold in cultural scholarship, I can now appreciate what motivated critics beyond enlarging the scholarly expert's role in debates about culture, genuine and spurious. Genuine culture is what ethnographically working researchers thought they themselves were revealing far into the post–WWII years; they made graspable what Pierre Bourdieu (1977) would term habitus, and reveled in understanding the difference of cultures conceptualized as wholes. The very value of culture was its genuineness, and the contribution, and thus value, of ethnographic scholarship lay in documenting and testifying to it. The "spurious" was evidence of forces other than scholarship meddling with cultures and thus threatening cultures' very wholeness. While certainly not all cultural researchers conceptualized their work in this manner, this was an ethos guiding a great deal of ethnographic training and work. Recognizing a disturbance to this disciplinary matrix might be likened to Karl Marx's take on industrialization more than a century before. Marx considered the worker as alienated from the fruits of his labor within the capitalist process of production. To some ethnographers, commoditized culture threatened to bring about a people's alienation from their very way of being. If Marx conceived of self-determined work as defining human selfhood, how much worse, then, was the alienation of an entire people from its culture! Throughout the last decades of the twentieth century, however, the rising actor-centered perspective forced scholars to reflect on their own role in constructing cultural wholes, and, more important for the interests reflected in this collection of articles, to acknowledge social actors' own interests in assigning diverse kinds of value to aspects of culture.

This second step toward theorizing culture and value was situated not just within the turn to a transcultural perspective but also within the larger turn toward agency and the growing interest in how actors themselves worked with folklore and culture in diverse settings and the role scholarship had in enhancing culture's value on the ground. In the course of the late 1980s and 1990s, critiques of cultural essentialism in nation-building broadened toward understanding representational formats—festivals, exhibits, museums—and the kinds of goals and desires pursued and fulfilled within and through them (e.g., Cantwell 1993; Welz 1996). This does not mean that reservations regarding cultures' ideological availability were laid to rest, but an understanding for actors' motivations grew.

For many social actors, economic value is not separate but intertwined with other kinds of value. This third perspective unfolded through the turn toward the material. Influential for me was the group of scholars brought together by Arjun Appadurai who investigated *The Social Life of Things* (1988). They began to pay attention to these dynamics across time with critical ethnographic and historical curiosity rather than employing such

analysis aiming strongly toward cultural critique, as had been the case
with the Frankfurt School. In subsequent work, Appadurai formulated an
analytic framework—most poignantly so under the heading "global flows"
(1996, 27–85)—that allows for an understanding of the confluence of historical, sociopolitical, and financial developments, as well as media within
which actors see fit to materialize and scrutinize aspects of their culture
and tradition in a range of values. My bridge into this realm remained
authenticity—a concept whose social life seemingly never ends. In its
constructed and often arbitrary nature, authenticity is a value designa-
tor. It surfaces, along with further denotations of value: uniqueness and
exclusivity, age and quality turn into markers of authenticity in tourism,
heritage, as well as many kinds of commodities ranging from food to fashion to pharmaceuticals. It was such growing circulation of commoditized
cultural expressions or folklore that pushed a third take on culture's value
into the foreground: could cultural expressions and traditional knowledge
be considered a form of intellectual property? Was it possible to hold ownership of cultures or components of culture?

The forums where these questions entered the debate were—for the
reasons just outlined—not scholarly. Questions of cultural property were
brought into courts of law and international organizations. Stakeholders
from communities offended by outsiders marketing and profiting from
what they considered their culture brought forth their concerns (Brown
2003). The United Nations' World Intellectual Property Organization
(WIPO) was established in 1967 to address issues of copyright and patent law, following on the earlier United International Bureaux for the
Protection of Intellectual Property, founded in 1893. WIPO became one
of the major negotiating bodies for cultural property issues, officially
starting a special, still-ongoing Intergovernmental Committee in 2001 to
understand the scope of the questions that cultural property might entail
(see, for example, Hafstein 2004; Bendix and Hafstein 2008).

This arose parallel to the thickening of practices and interests surrounding UNESCO's heritage conventions—with the Convention for
Intangible Cultural Heritage proclaimed in 2003. Much as in WIPO's
deliberations on economic rights, communal traditional knowledge and
traditional cultural expressions were to be nominated for celebratory and
safeguarding purposes—opening a door toward claiming ownership

rights as well. WIPO seeks to legally accommodate individual property rights to the concerns of communities and collectives. The definitional problems of how to achieve this have kept WIPO's intergovernmental committee busy for close to two decades; UNESCO has taken up "community" as a respectable category as well, setting in motion definitional discourses about just what community should be policy-making bodies (Hertz 2015). As of 2004, I searched for ways to research and understand the seemingly irreconcilable issues brewing in these new developments. Copyright and culture, the cultural commons versus restricted ownership in capitalist economies, and ever-increasing parceling of valuable morsels of culture from the rest, required more than ethnographic attention. At Göttingen University, where I have been teaching since 2001, I found colleagues in institutional and agricultural economics and international and institutional law interested in working together with cultural and social anthropology on issues of cultural property. Working in a field of cultural research, I had realized that our discipline's stance toward the question of ownership and value was, for one, shaped by intellectual traditions and methods different from law and economics. For another, such normative disciplines link rather directly into policy and governance, whereas the hermeneutic disciplinary ethos guiding ethnography and history rarely has access to policy forums—and generally has not sought such access. Applied variants of such fields, as well as public folklore and anthropology, are differently poised, of course, and the rise of the heritage regime has given practitioners in such settings more opportunities to implement programs ascertaining the value of vernacular arts and the communities bringing them forth through public sponsorship (Baron and Spitzer 2008). Ownership rights, however, as pushed forward by WIPO's deliberations, were hardly evident in public presentation endeavors beyond an ideational association between expressive forms and communities (see Noyes 2016, 17–94). The link between the politics and economics of a community's overt interests in aspects of its culture needed theoretical attention (Noyes 2016, 337–70); but platforms for bringing cultural theorizing into policy frameworks still need to be established. From 2008 to 2014, I led our research group on "The Constitution of Cultural Property: Actors, Discourses, Contexts, Rules," funded by the German Research Foundation (Interdisziplinäre Forschergruppe 2017). Property is intrinsically connected with questions of value, and we had chosen to work in this interdisciplinary configuration in an attempt to allow our very diverse disciplinary perspectives to shed light on what I consider an important, global concern with culture and its value.

Our group's work proved a challenge beyond the research questions at hand, as working in an interdisciplinary configuration demands investments not only in precious time but also in understanding divergent disciplinary habits (Bendix, Bizer, and Noyes 2017). The integrity of one's own professional home is challenged, and it takes effort to experience this not as a devaluation, but rather as an enrichment and a broadening of intellectual and social possibilities. The experience proved wholesome in many ways. For me as a cultural researcher, it was important to recognize how small an issue the rise of traditional knowledge as potential property appears to be from the vantage point of disciplines involved in regulating questions of property and economic advance in state and global contexts. Indeed, the outcry concerning culture's commoditization and folklore's ideological use, which had accompanied my training in ethnographic fields, was evaluated soberly or sometimes even enthusiastically in these normative disciplines. The task at hand for cultural research remains twofold: to infuse more ethnographic, hermeneutically guided knowledge into these fields—which have so much greater access to policy—and simultaneously to understand, free of judgment, the resource nature of marked and foregrounded culture, particularly for sites and milieus that have few other resources to bring to market.[4] There are ethnic, indigenous, tribal, and aboriginal anthropologists and folklorists, but there are—just as in universities—more ethnic, indigenous, tribal, and aboriginal lawyers and economists who assist their communities in finding ways to sustain their way of life. Construing culture as property is one such option, delineating exclusive and inclusive rights along the way. The value of culture and the culture of value remain dynamic in globalized, heterogeneous settings operating in all channels of communication.

*****

This volume assembles articles, essays, and conference papers published or delivered between 1989 and 2015. Some of them have been translated from German and appear in English for the first time. Most chapters have been lightly reedited, but remain true to the moment in time they were published initially. Some bibliographic additions have been made, but I have written the short introductions for each section with an eye toward bringing into the discussion new research as well as tangents of scholarship previously not considered. All web pages referenced in the individual papers were checked and, when necessary, replaced with more current ones.

The papers are grouped into three sections, which by necessity overlap, as the phenomena examined are not and should not be separated. The first section emphasizes tourism, in particular the ways in which a seemingly immaterial practice—narration—materializes in tourist economies. The second section assembles contributions that theorize heritage practices, drawing attention to language use, the kinds of semantics facilitated through them, and the governance emerging as a result thereof. The papers in the third section, finally, emphasize the need to consider value-making practices outside of sub- and sub-sub-disciplines, search for ways to integrate heritage and other value-creating regimes in cultural analysis at large, and consider bringing our insights to settings between disciplines and beyond the academic. Readers who choose to read the articles consecutively will note that I took my own sweet time to appreciate social actors' economic interests. In particular, the confrontation with heritage-making has been an instructive lesson: if you have few or no other resources, history and culture prove to be an asset. Social, political, personal, and emotional investment in one's cultural legacy need not be seen as dirtied by economic transactions, and cultural researchers do well in expanding their repertoire from critic to, if desired at all, advisor. Working in the expanding realms of heritage scholarship and critical heritage studies, I have been impressed by colleagues both in small countries and in countries with a huge surplus of ethnologists with doctorates and a dearth of academic positions. The latter has forced many scholars intent on research to take temporary and long-term positions within the heritage machinery. Their interest to keep up an intertwined, reflexive attention to applied and intellectual contributions, and to simultaneously participate in heritage consulting and heritage scholarship has benefited both. This has also contributed to a more consistent acknowledgment and positive reception of cultural researchers' contribution to policy in this area.[5]

Readers will notice my struggle with terms. I live and work in and between German and English, and the semantic reach of the English noun "value" is neither completely identical to that of the German "Wert," nor is it possible to render in English some of the nice German compounds containing "Wert." This does not even begin to address the specificity of value-related terminology in English or German economics, some of which have crept into cultural scholarship on heritage conceptualized as industry. After nearly a decade of collaborating with or at least witnessing economists addressing cultural phenomena, my grasp of the terminology has not appreciated by much, but I have overcome some of the disciplinary prejudices; economists, too, include social and moral values in their thinking, but their discipline asks for abstraction and reduction of complexity.[6] I also work in between folklore studies and cultural anthropology, drawing from European and American research traditions, sometimes trying to serve as an interlocutor, and sometimes finding myself dumbfounded at gaps and different circuits of concepts in either one or the other, as well as (more prominently) blank spots in my training and subsequent reading.

Looking through one's own work is a rather humbling experience. In rereading and slightly revising the articles, I was reminded of a somewhat bemused observation made in the late 1980s by my father-in-law, Reinhard Bendix. Going through his own offprints while clearing out his offices at the University of California in Berkeley, he said, "I think I have had the same idea over and over again." This certainly is my plight as well. I appear to have been motivated, time and again, by the role cultural scholarship itself has played in marking folklore, tradition, cultural expression, and heritage as recognizable and usable categories. As indicated earlier, this is not least due to my coming of age academically during a time when folklorists and anthropologists reflexively turned inward and applied the constructivist tool kit to their own disciplines. It left me with a permanent double vision, grasping a phenomenon at hand and asking myself how scholarly concepts and knowledge transfer might have affected it. The present introductory outline of paradigmatic shifts in cultural research that informed these chapters points to some of these moments. The reader will repeatedly encounter my interest in the intertwining of the history of cultural scholarship and practices of bestowing value on excerpts of culture. Lingering behind this observation is another enduring question that ought to be addressed more prominently in the future: how is it that some scholarly concepts are successfully transferred into public discourse,

while others remain hidden? Particularly in a time when anti-intellectu-
alism is part of numerous, populist governments and aspiring political
platforms, understanding and mending the processes by which knowledge
turns expertise and then, perhaps, policy, seems to be vital.

"Bestowing value is at the core of culture. It takes culture to value
culture—the question is then what causes, motivates, legitimizes bestowing value," Johannes Fabian wrote in the margins of a talk I had sent him
for comment in spring 2013. It is a comment that creates research opportunity beyond this volume, and it stands for perspectives that seek to grasp
the intertwining of multiple, dissenting actors.[7] Next to the celebration of
ethnicity and diversity, and next to the ways in which such highly valued
cultural excerpts are brought to market, it remains important to firmly
keep in view the demonizing of an essentialized other. The opposite of
valuing is devaluation, and cultural scholarship has perhaps been overly
busy with decrying the economic enhancement of culture and more reluc-
tant in giving prominence and analyzing the ways in which culture and
folklore are marked to denigrate. In this, the second decade of the twenty-
first century, a time tending toward populism and the rebirth of fascism,
this would seem to be an urgent complement to our studies of culture and
value.[8] In teaching, I developed a course pairing the terms *xenophobia* and
*xenophilia* that allowed students to explore the proximity of aggression
toward and appropriation of essentialized cultural difference and expressive morsels, ranging from music to foodways to war propaganda, further
developing the ideational power of Othering, which folklorists have long
noted (e.g., Bauman and Abrahams 1981).[9] In putting together this volume
of essays on culture and value in society and scholarship, I realize that it is
urgent to pay equal, interdisciplinary attention to the devaluing of culture
in society and policy.

*****

A first push to bring together this book was made during a sabbatical in
2011–12; sadly—or fortunately—the time was not quite sufficient to complete the work, so that it took until now, summer of 2017, to put together the
introductory texts for each section and adjust remaining matters, as well
as include a few more recent pieces. In addition to the intellectual debts
expressed at the time of initial publication with each paper, I owe gratitude

to Göttingen University for awarding me a sabbatical with replacement in 2011–12, and to the Lichtenberg Kolleg Göttingen for an affiliation during the same year. Both awards were supported by funds from the German Research Foundation (DFG), as was a further semester of leave in 2012–13. In the fall of 2012, I enjoyed an all-too-brief month at the Institute of Social Anthropology at the Academy of Sciences in Vienna, and I thank its team for the hospitality extended to me there. The idea to bring together these particular articles germinated within the context of the interdisciplinary DFG research unit 772 on the constitution of cultural property, which I led from 2008 to 2014. Working with the project and team members of this group has been a privilege, and I thank them all for many stimulating discussions and workshops.

Throughout these last years, Birgit Abels, Roger Abrahams†, Kilian Bizer, Hartmut Bleumer, Tobias Brandenberger, Don Brenneis, Charles Briggs, Johannes Fabian, Michaela Fenske, Brigitte Frizzoni, Andre Gingrich, Stefan Groth, Rebekka Habermas, Valdimar Hafstein, Lee Haring, Galit Hasan-Rokem, Dorothee Hemme, Ellen Hertz, Frank Kelleter, Wolfgang Knöbl, Ullrich Kockel, Orvar Löfgren, Sabina Magliocco, Ulrich Marzolph, Kirin Narayan, Máiréad Nic Craith, Martha Norkunas, Dorothy Noyes, Marie Sandberg, Brigitta Schmidt-Lauber, Mary Beth Stein, Markus Tauschek, Janet Theophano, Bernhard Tschofen, and Simone Winko have been intellectual companions, supportive interlocutors, as well as good friends in the increasing thicket of the corporatizing university. I am grateful to all of them for the different kinds of stimulation and distraction received. Past and present colleagues at the Göttingen University Institute of Cultural Anthropology/European Ethnology have offered an amiable context for pursuing old and new interests since 2001. Finally, many thanks go to former student assistants Nathalie Knöhr, Nora Kühnert, and Ute Seitz, who each helped with all manner of tasks associated with preparing the manuscript. And last but not least, I am grateful to Janice Frisch and her team at Indiana University Press for the interest and support, as well as to Rachel Rosolina, Anna Francis, Russell J. Santana, Jayanthi Dinesh, and team for their help with the careful production of this book.

Not to be omitted is a note on the cover image, with thanks to Roland Inauen, Appenzell, who put me in touch with the foundation Haus

Appenzell, led by Ernst Hohl, who made available the paper cut "Das traditionelle Appenzellerland" ("The Traditional Appenzell Region"). Artist Hua Yue Xiu, born in 1968, is renowned in her native China for her highly detailed paper cuts. She used her impressions from a visit to the Appenzell region to fashion a paper cut that measures nearly 8 meters in length and 1.5 meters in width, and interweaves scenes of Appenzell life reminiscent of the naïve art I am very familiar with from the Appenzell village where I did my first fieldwork. In appropriating the motives, the artist fuses these Swiss contours with forms and expressions of her own cultural background. The work is a wonderful testament to the circulation and dynamic aesthetic alteration of cultural goods. Like many other types of intangible heritage, paper cutting is a craft and art form found in many places, putting claims of cultural property in question—but allowing us to appreciate and celebrate individuals who master them.

I dedicate this volume to my mother, Gertrud Flückiger-Scheidegger†, and my aunts, Hildi Scheidegger† and Greti Lanz-Flückiger. These were the women who contributed to shaping who I am, not as a researcher, but as a human being. Deeply embedded in their social contexts, each taught me the beauties and the abysses of everyday life. Few of the concerns dealt with in this book would be of relevance to them, yet I am immensely grateful for the everyday skills learned from them, from cooking jam to telling neighborhood and family stories to appreciating the beauty of felines in one's life.

*Prospect Harbor, Maine, July 2017*

### NOTES

Names that are followed by a † symbol indicate that the person is deceased.

1. The most glaring example in this regard is probably Pierre Bourdieu's essay on different kinds of capital (1983), which came across my desk neither in graduate school nor in subsequent years of teaching in the United States. In teaching in Germany since the early 2000s, I encountered it as a core text in the introduction to the field and in the required culture theory course. Every time I teach it, I marvel at how an actor- and field-centered perspective cuts through the laborious grappling with the culture and value matrix I have worked with. Bourdieu, in turn, seemed peculiarly devoid of emotion and some of the impassioned contributions of Anglo-American colleagues continue to resonate with me. Michel Foucault and Pierre Bourdieu, as well as several historians and sociologists, were crucial ingredients in my German colleagues' teaching and research tool kit. In the background there was a smidgen of critical theory where I found at least some overlap with the representatives of cultural studies, such as

Raymond Williams and Stuart Hall, whom I had encountered in the States. Conversely, the ethnolinguistic- and performance-focused work I had absorbed was practically nonexistent among my German colleagues.

2. Many scholars have grappled with these issues, though I encountered them only later in my professional life. The Finnish scholar Lauri Honko, for instance, theorized what he called the "folklore process" and asked that one distinguish the second life of folklore from the first (e.g., Honko 1990, 185). The Croatian folklore theorist Dunja Rihtman-Augustin was less negative and far more integrative in her understanding of the historical processes in which expressive forms could come to play a new, ideologically marked role—evident in a collection of her earlier essays published in 1989. Hector Garcia Canclini placed greater emphasis to the forces of mass cultural production and their intertwining with vernacular forms (1995, the Spanish original appeared in 1990).

3. Kwame Anthony Appiah (2016) beautifully disentangled this problematic entwining of anthropological and bourgeois, Western culture concepts. In some chapters of this book, I have tried to mark this difficult yet very powerful distinction with the following formulation. I used "culture with a big C" for the Western claim for its civilizational primacy and the attendant canon of works and institutions, and "culture with a small c" for the everyday life phenomena, which are ultimately far more powerful and far reaching than the exclusive big C phenomena, which themselves arose out of centuries of class-based practices and appropriations.

4. While remarking on their own initial irritation at culture on the market, John and Jean Comaroff in their *Ethnicity, Inc.* (2009) have gone a long way in that direction.

5. The Respatrimoni (2017) network informs about many ongoing activities in this area of research and practice.

6. Hann and Hart reflect quite pessimistically on working together with economists: "Anthropologists who master the basics of game theory and have access to a brain scanner may once again be granted space in economics journals for an elegant demonstration that 'culture matters' in the economy. We have rejected such approaches in favour of working with the corpus of ethnographic and historical research. The method of controlled experiment is unlikely to reveal the values and motivations of the human economy, which are best studied in the flesh-and-blood contexts of living society" (2011, 173). In our research group, we had the pleasure of working with economists who participated in our interdisciplinary work, even though for most of the work they contributed they were not receiving appreciation in their own discipline. While it was hard to tackle conceptual discussions on terms such as "social identity," it was nonetheless instructive to see the thickness of ethnographic description whittled down to rules of the game.

7. An earlier, interpretivist anthropology was interested in understanding value-regimes that establish a normative framework for moral conduct, which in turn guides social conduct, elaborating in the process on concepts such as worldview and ethos (Geertz 1973, 124–39).

8. Gingrich and Banks (2006) offer important case studies to build on further.

9. The intellectual lineage of formulations of "group" and "other" has been traced and refined by Noyes (2012); in Abrahams's collected essays, one finds his own deepening of notions such as borders and zones (2005, 127–74). In the German cultural, anthropological, and European ethnological context within which I have been working since 2001, these explorations have had on the one hand (influenced as they are by cultural studies) a far more class-based theoretical underpinning. On the other hand, there has been a great deal of work on what is conceptualized as new and institutionalized racism, particularly in the realm of

the governance of migration. This is not the place to explore my profound discomfort with the resurgence of race as an analytic concept—albeit in the negative—that, at least for a while, seemed overcome in Anglo-American anthropology. The layers of constructing, excluding, and dominating Other and foregrounding, and valuing Own seem to be fueled by so many facets of both historically situated and newly generated political and economic practice, that reducing it all to race seems like a shorthand useful for political agency, yet deserving of continuous, scholarly disentanglement.

### REFERENCES

Abrahams, Roger D. 2005. *Everyday Life: A Poetics of Vernacular Practices.* Philadelphia: University of Pennsylvania Press.
Anderson, Benedict. 1983. *Imagined Communities: Reflections on the Origins and Spread of Nationalism.* London: Verso.
Appadurai, Arjun. 1996. *Modernity at Large.* Minneapolis: University of Minnesota Press.
Appadurai, Arjun, ed. 1988. *The Social Life of Things. Commodities in Cultural Perspective.* Cambridge: Cambridge University Press.
Appiah, Kwame Anthony. 2016. "There is no such Thing as a Western Civilization," *Guardian,* November 9. https://www.theguardian.com/world/2016/nov/09 /western-civilisation-appiah-reith-lecture?CMP=share_btn_fb.
Baron, Robert, and Nick Spitzer, eds. 2008. *Public Folklore.* Jackson: University Press of Mississippi.
Bauman, Richard, and Roger D. Abrahams, eds. 1981. *"And Other Neighborly Names." Social Process and Cultural Image in Texas.* Austin: University of Texas Press.
Bausinger, Hermann. 1990. *Folk Culture in a World of Technology.* Translated by Elke Dettmer. Bloomington: Indiana University Press.
———. 1966. "Zur Kritik der Folklorismuskritik." In *Populous Revisus,* edited by H. Bausinger, 61–75. Tübingen: Tübinger Vereinigung für Volkskunde.
Bendix, Regina. 1997. *In Search of Authenticity. The Formation of Folklore Studies.* Madison: University of Wisconsin Press.
Bendix, Regina F., Kilian Bizer, and Dorothy Noyes. 2017. *Sustaining Interdisciplinary Collaboration. A Guide for the Academy.* Urbana: University of Illinois Press.
Bendix, Regina, and Valdimar Hafstein. 2009. "Culture and Property: An Introduction." *Ethnologia Europaea* 39: 2.
Bendix, Regina, and Gisela Welz, eds. 1999. *Cultural Brokerage and Public Folklore: Forms of Intellectual Practice in Society.* Special Issue of *Journal of Folklore Research* 36, no. 2/3.
Bourdieu, Pierre. 1977. *Outline of a Theory of Practice.* Cambridge: Cambridge University Press.
———. 1983. "Economic Capital, Cultural Capital, Social Capital." *Soziale Welt* no. 2: 183–98.
Brown, Michael F. 2003. *Who Owns Native Culture?* Cambridge: Harvard University Press.
Bruner, Edward. 2004. *Culture on Tour.* Chicago: University of Chicago Press.
Canclini, Hector Garcia. 1995. *Hybrid Cultures: Strategies for Entering and Leaving Modernity.* Minneapolis: University of Minnesota Press.
Cantwell, Robert. 1993. *Ethnomimesis. Folklife and the Representation of Culture.* Chapel Hill: University of North Carolina Press.

Clifford, James, and George E. Marcus, eds. 1986. *Writing Culture. The Poetics and Politics of Ethnography*. Berkeley: University of California Press.

Comaroff, John L., and Jean Comaroff. 2009. *Ethnicity Inc*. Chicago: University of Chicago Press.

Geertz, Clifford. 1973. *The Interpretation of Culture*. New York: Basic.

Gingrich, Andre, and Marcus Banks, eds. 2006. *Neo-nationalism in Europe and Beyond*. Oxford: Berghahn.

Graburn, Nelson, ed. 1976. *Ethnic and Tourist Arts: Cultural Expressions from the Fourth World*. Berkeley: University of California Press.

Hafstein, Valdimar, tr., 2004. "The Making of Intangible Cultural Heritage: Tradition and Authenticity, Community and Humanity." PhD diss., University of California, Berkeley.

Hann, Chris, and Keith Hart. 2011. *Economic Anthropology*. London: Polity Press.

Hertz, Ellen. 2015. "Bottoms. Genuine and Spurius." In *Between Imagined Communities and Communities of Practice*, vol. 8, edited by N. Adell, R. F. Bendix, C. Bortolotto, and M. Tauschek, 25–57. Göttingen: Studies in Cultural Property.

Hobsbawm, Eric, and Terence Ranger, eds. 1993. *The Invention of Tradition*. Cambridge: Cambridge University Press.

Honko, Lauri, ed. 1990. *Religion, Myth, and Folklore in the World's Epics. The Kalevala and its Predecessors*. Berlin: De Gruyter.

Interdisziplinäre Forschergruppe zu Cultural Property. 2017. Accessed June 27. http://cultural-property.uni-goettingen.de/.

Noyes, Dorothy. 2012. "The Social Base of Folklore." In *A Companion to Folklore*, edited by R. F. Bendix and G. Hasan-Rokem, 13–39. Oxford: Wiley Blackwell.

Noyes, Dorothy. 2016. *Humble Theory*. Bloomington: Indiana University Press.

Pratt, Marie Louise. 1992. *Imperial Eyes. Travel Writing and Transculturation*. London: Routledge.

Respatrimoni. 2017. Network of Researchers on Heritagisations/Réseau des chercheurs sur les patrimonialisations. Accessed July 18. https://respatrimoni.wordpress.com/.

Rihtman-Augustin, Dunja. 1989. *Folklore and Historical Process*. Zagreb, Croatia: Institute of Folklore Research.

Stocking, George W. Jr., ed. 1983. *Observers Observed. Essays on Ethnographic Fieldwork*. Madison: University of Wisconsin Press.

Welz, Gisela. 1996. *Inszenierungen kultureller Vielfalt. Frankfurt am Main und New York City*. Berlin: Akademie.

———. 2015. *European Products. Making and Unmaking Heritage in Cyprus*. Oxford: Berghahn.

# Section I

~~~~~~~~~~~~~~~~~~~~~~~~ ✍ ~~~~~~~~~~~~~~~~~~~~~~~~

## Introduction: Creating, Owning, and Narrating within Tourist Economies

Tourism was once a neglected if not scorned area of cultural research. The development of tourism itself is the major cause for this delayed interest, as it opened a privileged experience to the middle and lower classes. If pilgrimage had been a path to absolution, paving the way to an afterlife in heaven, travel was the enlightened road to knowledge. The late medieval traveling scholar transformed into the early modern academic, whose suitability, distinction, and hence value as a university professor derived not least from the firsthand insight gained through travel (Kamp and Sing 2001; Stagl 2006). The close connection between such learning and conquest lay a foundation for the sense of entitlement that was inherent to colonization, and remains present in touristic endeavors (Pratt 1992). The children of nobility and of the growing bourgeoisie completed their preparation for lives of importance through what came to be known as the "Grand Tour" (Babel 2005; Berghoff 2002; Brilli 1995), relying on learned instructions on how to travel and—in some cases—producing literary reports on what they themselves had witnessed. Along with the development of new techniques of documentation—from paint and brush to the camera—they contributed to the construction of how cultures were to be witnessed (Hanley 2010; Urry 2002). Health entered the repertoire of motivations for travel, with sea baths and mountains as sites promising cure from ailments (e.g., Barton 2008); rest from the taxing demands of industrial labor was the major argument for opening opportunities for leisure and, eventually, travel for the working class (Barton 2005; Löfgren

1999). The road toward vacations (preferably away from home) as a modern institution was paved with class struggle. The split into tourists and travelers emerged from these alternate lineages through which members of different social classes attained their right to travel, and it was at once mocked and performed in cultural practice and literature alike (Buzard 1993). Finally, affordable means of transport facilitating mass mobility and the seemingly never-ending growth of tourism infrastructures worldwide have rendered travel and leisure away from home into a highly differentiated industry that is, in size, second to none. The dichotomy between individualistic travelers and mass tourists is maintained as a lucrative construct, as it provides individuals desirous of distinction with a means to perceive themselves as successors of enlightened or romantic revelers in search of inner betterment.

It is this dichotomous view onto types of travel and leisure which kept cultural researchers from embracing tourism as a field worthy of scholarly investigation. While economists logically devoted attention to this growth sector, it took a work such as Dean MacCannell's *The Tourist* (1976) to awaken scholarly interest in anthropology and folklore. MacCannell linked his portrait of the tourist as the quintessential modern individual to classic sociological theory on leisure and social class, and in the same year, anthropologist Nelson Graburn (1976) published the first serious collection of ethnographically based work on what he aptly termed "cultural expressions from the Fourth World." Such works opened both critical and productive lenses onto the change and creativity necessitated as well as facilitated by touristic encounter. The stages of development from pilgrimage to resort tourism are all still available within the tourist economy, and at this point the economic diversification of tourist offerings along with its consumption are part of tourism scholarship. The former neglect of scholarly attention toward tourism has turned into its reverse. The first (and evermore) interdisciplinary journal devoted to the topic, *Annals of Tourism Research*, began publication in 1973. In the second decade of the twenty-first century, there is a plethora of journals devoted to tourism, ranging from practice-oriented realms, such as hospitality and management, to questions of history, cultural change, and sustainability.[1] Shifts in the study of tourism can be traced with new key terms such as "mobilities" and "performativity" succeeding or added to interests in experience and authenticity (Cohen and Cohen 2012). Topically, the focus of cultural research keeps hosts, guests, and their interaction firmly in view, but perhaps in tandem with the broadening of the travel lens to mobility (Urry 2008),[2] interest has crept ever closer to the self and what kinds of bodily and emotional happenings are occasioned through travel, evident in conference titles such as "The Seduction of Difference," and "Emotion in Motion" (Picard and Amaral 2010; Picard and Robinson 2012).[3] Simultaneously, tourism research is at this point inextricably intertwined with the study of sustainability, postcolonialism, technology, imagination, modernity, and so forth; the breadth of tourism studies confirms the phenomenon as a *fait total* which, much like Marcel Mauss's gift exchange, entails economic and moral, legal and aesthetic, mythical and social dimensions—reflected not least in a recent conference proceedings on *Regimes of Value in Tourism* (Crossley and Picard 2016). Not surprisingly, tourism researchers have also entered (almost by necessity) the realm of heritage studies (Di Giovine 2009). Heritage sites have not just increased in numbers but are an important tourist destination; indeed, the creation of heritage sites is often connected with economic interests (see section two of this volume).

The four chapters assembled in this section engage on the one hand with the question of encounter, initiated by Graburn and carried forward in other work investigating what happens in the border zone of mutual display between groups that meet as host and guest, and as provider and consumer (Bruner 2005; Bruner and Kirshenblatt-Gimblett 1994; Kirshenblatt-Gimblett 1997). On the other hand, I am interested in the role narration takes in mediating touristic offerings and in turning into a tourist attraction itself. "Tourism and Cultural Displays: Inventing Traditions for Whom?" was written as a challenge both toward early ethnographic studies of tourism that decried the spoiling effects of this new economy on the integrity of culture and toward constructivist work following Eric Hobsbawm and Terrence Ranger's *The Invention of Tradition* (1983). As travel and tourism are hardly novel phenomena, I argued that actors within tourist economies are not necessarily at the mercy of paying guests, but rather have sufficient agency to create and experience cultural expressions that they themselves savor. Inventions, furthermore, need not be decried as inauthentic, as all tradition is continuously created and recreated so as to satisfy those who partake in and of it. Drawing on the example of various displays in the Swiss tourist destination Interlaken, the chapter illustrates how actors pursue a variety of interests beyond economic gain, and how enacting such displays enhances experiential and social values.

The two following chapters consider different aspects of the theming of landscapes through narratives such as traditional folktales and legends as well as themes and figures from children's literature and media. In "On the Road to Fiction," I examine the intersection of tourist productions and materialized fiction, such as *Märchen*, and other narrative genres in themed environments. On the backdrop of the rarely considered history of the materialization of narrative genres such as the folktale, a number of touristic sites geared toward families and children in Carinthia, Austria, are explored in terms of their aesthetic, generic, and ideological components. In the confluence of cultural commoditization, market, and touristic utopias, the tensions between an increasingly globalized tourist economy and the local aesthetic, educational and economic practices and interests become apparent. "Fairy Tale Activists" (written with Dorothee Hemme) places yet greater emphasis on the agency of local protagonists on the stage of supralocal thematic tourism. Relying on ethnography and interviews with individuals responsible for particular performances along the German Fairy Tale Street, the paper argues against the assumption that such ventures result in repetitive and devalued cultural productions. Rather, individual protagonists are shown to maintain a strong identification with their work in enacting narrative imaginaries. The success of fairytale tourism is punctual at best, but the hold of newly created institutions for its promotion in some communities documents that the active interest in valuing regional narrative need not be diminished by the simultaneous effort to turn it into a profitable resource.

"Capitalizing on Memories Past, Present, and Future," finally, argues that narratized experience has been a key ingredient in the emergence of tourism as a modern industry. Starting with published travelers' reports, narrative has shaped and structured touristic experience and, in turn, the narratized memories of travelers have stirred the desire for touristic exploits of one generation after another. Clarifying the nonindustrial nature of the tourism "industry," the chapter explores the aura of the tourist experience, the ways in which tourists seek to harness it into their narration, and how tourism providers are in turn compelled to rely on and sell potential narratable memories to travelers.

## NOTES

1. The following list of "Tourism-related journals" is made available by a consortium interested in sustainability, but offers links into all major tourism research areas in English: http://www.gdrc.org/uem/eco-tour/journals.html. Accessed May 8, 2017. If one were to enlarge the language spectrum, the number would increase dramatically.

2. The working group on tourism of the *Deutsche Gesellschaft für Volkskunde* devoted its tenth conference to mobilities and has since then changed its name to "working group for mobility regimes." Accessed May 8, 2017. http://www.d-g-v.org/kommissionen /tourismusforschung. A new journal called *Mobile Cultures Studies* has also emerged. Accessed May 8, 2017. http://unipub.uni-graz.at/mcsj.

3. The Tourism-Contact-Culture-Research Network (ToCoCu) has organized these events, continuing the work of the Center for Tourism and Cultural Change at Leeds Metropolitan University (2001–10). Accessed May 8, 2017. https://sites.google.com/site /tourismcontactculture/home.

## REFERENCES

Babel, Rainer. 2005. *Grand Tour: Adeliges Reisen und europäische Kultur vom 14. bis 18. Jahrhundert*. Ostfildern: Thorbecke.

Barton, Susan. 2005. *Working-Class Organizations and Popular Tourism, 1840–1870*. Manchester: Manchester University Press.

———. 2008. *Healthy Living in the Alps: The Origins of Winter Tourism in Switzerland, 1860–1914*. Manchester: Manchester University Press.

Berghoff, Hartmut. 2002. *The Making of Modern Tourism: The Cultural History of the British Experience, 1600–2000*. Houndmill: Palgrave.

Brilli, Attilio. 1991. *Quando viaggiare era un'arte: il romanzo del Grand Tour*. Bologna: Il Mulino.

Bruner, Edward M. 2005. *Culture on Tour: Ethnographies of Travel*. Chicago: University of Chicago Press.

Bruner, Edward M., and Barbara Kirshenblatt-Gimblett. 1994. "Maasai on the Lawn: Tourist Realism in East Africa." *Cultural Anthropology* 9 (4): 435–70.

Buzard, James. 1993. *The Beaten Track: European Tourism, Literature, and the Ways to Culture, 1800–1918*. Oxford: Oxford University Press.

Crossley, Emilie, and David Picard, eds. 2016. *Regimes of Value in Tourism*. London: Routledge.

Di Giovine, Michael A. 2009. *The Heritage-Scape: UNESCO, World Heritage, and Tourism*. Lanham, MD: Lexington.

Graburn, Nelson, ed. 1976. *Ethnic and Tourist Arts. Cultural Expressions from the Fourth World*. Berkeley: University of California Press.

Hanley, Keith. 2010. *Constructing Cultural Tourism: John Ruskin and the Tourist Gaze*. Bristol: Channel View.

Hobsbawm, Eric, and Terence Ranger, eds. 1983. *The Invention of Tradition*. Cambridge: Cambridge University Press.

Kamps, Ivo, and Jyotsna G. Singh, eds. 2001. *Travel Knowledge: European "Discoveries" in the Early Modern Period*. New York: Palgrave.

Kirshenblatt-Gimblett, Barbara. 1997. *Destination Culture: Tourism, Museums, and Heritage*. Berkeley: University of California Press.

Löfgren, Orvar. 1999. *On Holiday: A History of Vacationing*. Berkeley: University of California Press.

MacCannell, Dean. 1976. *The Tourist. A New Theory of the Leisure Class*. New York: Schocken.

Picard, David, and C. Amaral, eds. 2010. Proceedings of the TOCOCU 1st Biannual Conference. Sheffield: TOCOCU.

Picard, David, and Mike Robinson, eds. 2012. *Emotion in Motion. Tourism, Affect and Transformation*. London: Ashgate.

Stagl, Justin. 2006. *A History of Curiosity. The Theory of Travel 1550–1800*. London: Routledge.

Urry, John. 2002. *The Tourist Gaze. 2nd edition*. London: Sage.

———. 2008. *Mobilities*. Cambridge: Cambridge University Press.

# 1

⌘

# Tourism and Cultural Displays: Inventing Traditions for Whom?

In 1805, the village of Interlaken in the Swiss Alps experienced its first grandiose folklore display event. The occasion was called the *Unspunnenfest*. The emphasis at this event was the display of customs and costumes of the cowherds from the surrounding area. The audience, composed of dignitaries and many foreign guests, was treated to a display of dance, music, and song by costumed natives, and sports competitions unique to the area such as open-air wrestling (called *Schwingen*) and heaving heavy boulders as far as possible (*Steinstossen*). Madame de Staël, one of the invited guests, enthusiastically described this first "Swiss Cowherders' Festival" as an affair "pulsating with native life." She was particularly taken with the bonfires lit on the surrounding hilltops, commemorating the fires of liberty of the original Swiss confederation, and she expressed her hopes for more such display events (de Stael 1958, 287, 295). Her wish was fulfilled three years later: a second Unspunnen festival was held in 1808.

In the twentieth century, the Unspunnenfest has been commemorated and restaged five times (1905, 1946, 1955, 1976, 1981), but Interlaken has created three other events of similar magnitude: springtime processions held at the time when the cows would be herded up to the Alps (now discontinued), an open-air production of the William Tell play (staged since 1912 and still performed every summer), and a winter custom called *Harder-Potschete*, featuring supposed fertility demons and forest spirits (created in 1956 and still performed).[1]

Interlaken has a two hundred-year history of tourist development, thus providing an ideal case for examining the long-term impact of a tourist economy on a host society. The last two hundred years have also seen the emergence of numerous display events, and it is tempting to see a direct, economically motivated connection between tourism and displays.[2] This article will argue, however, that appeal to a touristic audience constitutes only a surface rationale for inventing traditions. Economic motivations are one part of the story and they constitute an important argument in the process of creating display events. But wished-for economic benefits do not sufficiently explain why such events continue for decades or even centuries. A close examination of the motivations and choices of originators, performers, and audiences of new, traditionalized displays also points toward an affirmation of local and national cultural identity in the face of seasonal mass foreign invasion.

A historically informed consideration of the case of Interlaken sheds light on the process of invention as well as on tourism's impact on expressive culture. Coined by historians, the "invention of tradition" (Hobsbawm and Ranger 1983) has fueled the older debates over "folklorismus," "fakelore," and "authenticity" in European and American folklore studies and anthropology (Bausinger 1966; Bendix 1988; Bodemann 1983; Dundes 1985; Evans-Pritchard 1987; Handler and Linnekin 1984; Kirshenblatt-Gimblett 1988; Moser 1964). While the concept of tradition received extensive treatment in light of the tradition and modernity discourse (Shils 1981), until recently "tradition has been," in Dan Ben-Amos's historiographic perception, "a term to think with, not to think about" (1984, 87).[3] But in the process of rethinking the "folk" versus "fake" and the academic versus applied dichotomy (Kirshenblatt-Gimblett 1988), folklorists have also begun to deconstruct the scholarly concept of tradition. In this context, the idea of created, negotiable tradition has been profoundly liberating. It allows for a view of cultural productions where what was previously categorized as impure and anomalous can suddenly belong to the realm of expressive culture. Furthermore, the idea of invention brings with it questions about the inventors and thus shifts the analytic focus from the event to the agency of those involved in its creation and maintenance (Giddens 1979, 49–95).

Richard Handler and Jocelyn Linnekin (1984) have also argued along those lines. Despite the long Western history of thought that sees tradition as a stable passing on of traits within a cultural system, Handler and Linnekin arrive at the conclusion that the idea of tradition is rather influenced by ideology, and thus continued reinterpretation and change (288–90). Traditions are always defined in the present, and the actors doing the defining are not concerned whether scholars will perceive a given festival or piece of art as genuine or spurious, but whether the manifestation will accomplish what they intend it to accomplish. "Inventing traditions" is thus not an anomaly but rather the rule, and it can be particularly well-studied in industrial and postindustrial nation-states exposed to extensive intercultural contact. Economists have, for obvious reasons, studied tourism extensively for over a century (e.g., Cohn 1882; Gölden 1939). Within fields of social and cultural research, touristic subjects have been regarded as worthy of serious social scientific research only since the early 1970s (Nash 1981).[4] As Davydd Greenwood noted in 1977, "a few years ago, we could lament the lack of serious research on tourism, but now, like the tourists themselves, social researchers are flocking to tourist centers" (1977, 129). Among the reasons for the delay in accepting tourism as a pervasive, intercultural phenomenon rather than scorning it as an intrusive agent destroying cultures, was the (maybe unconscious) desire to study the pristine and untouched, a desire that has its roots in the history of anthropological and folkloristic study of native peoples as well as in nineteenth-century notions of other cultures.

While tourism research has begun to flourish, the number of studies dealing with tourism and expressive culture—specifically displays of the kind discussed here—are relatively sparse. Benetta Jules-Rosette has noted that the anthropology of tourism and semiotics "overemphasize the role of image consumers [tourists] at the expense of the process of image creation that is a by-product of the tourist industry" (1984, 3). In other words, while host societies have been studied, it is not frequently in terms of their own expressive culture but more often in terms of their response to tourist pressures (see Cohen 1984). In her work with tourist art, Jules-Rosette found that the longer an artisan was in the business of producing "tourist art," the more he developed an aesthetic that satisfied his own cultural identity—a dimension acknowledged also in Nelson Graburn's (1976) seminal collection on tourist art. In the complex interplay of market, audience, and performers, the artisans eventually appropriated an externally imposed notion of authenticity, and a similar process will be illustrated with the case of Interlaken. The first staging of the Unspunnen festival in 1805 spoke directly to the romantic cravings of foreign visitors for unspoiled, "authentic" peasant and cowherder traditions; the later inventions demonstrate more and more the search on the part of natives for what they perceive to be authentic manifestations of their own culture.

## INTERLAKEN AND TOURISM

The tourist, according to Dean MacCannell, is continually in search of authentic experience (1976, 14, 91–107; see also Krippendorf 1984). The tourist industry is responding to this craving in evermore ingenious ways to let the tourist gaze at life as it is really lived in the host society. Yet no matter how far into the everyday domain a tourist is allowed to peek, the authenticity remains staged by the very fact that the tourist is looking at it.

But if authenticity in the realm of culture is difficult for the tourist to find, what kind of experience is possible? In Interlaken, in the Bernese Oberland, it is the grandiose physical environment of the Alps (Studer 1947; Winkler 1944). The landscape—unlike culture—cannot be staged, and most tourists prefer not to think about the numerous human intrusions—the carefully tended fields, the rebuilt streams, the many ski lifts and cog railways—for it is only with the aid of some of these that they can get close enough to experience the grandeur. The natural beauty is too large to spoil the impression of an authentic experience, and there would probably be no tourists in Interlaken if it were not for the village's unique geographic location between lakes and peaks.

The first tourists arrived in the Interlaken area in the second half of the eighteenth century (Kroner 1968, 22), and while an interest in native culture appeared in their travel notes, it was the Alps and nature that attracted them most (Bernard 1978; Weiss 1933). Nature was no longer the threatening antithesis to civilization, but had instead become the inspiration for cultural revitalization. The Unspunnen festivals helped to spread Interlaken's name internationally, and the number of visitors increased steadily. Interlaken responded by building housing and opening up better streets and waterways to allow the tourists to see nature up close (Gallati 1977; Spreng 1956).

A secondary interest of the early tourist was health. To satisfy this desire for health-related activities, an enterprising local artist organized the local dairy farmers to offer goat whey cures as early as the 1810s (Bourquin 1963). Survey statistics indicate that scenic beauty and personal health concerns remain the major reasons for tourists visiting Interlaken even now. Most modern tourists seek health through sports, such as skiing, hiking, tennis, swimming, horseback riding, golfing, or sailing, rather than through the goat whey cures of one hundred seventy years ago. Countless rail- and cableways allow hikers and skiers to get as close to high-altitude nature as technologically possible, and indoor saunas and hot tubs in most of the luxury hotels built around the turn of the twentieth century allow for the tourist's healthy return to civilization.

Outsiders referred to the area as Interlaken, but until the Reformation in the sixteenth century, Interlaken was only a monastery surrounded by three villages and one town. It was only in the late nineteenth century that the hotels, guesthouses, and businesses around the old monastery secured for themselves the name Interlaken (Latin for "between the lakes"). Town and village rights among the five communities remain carefully separated, with each village maintaining its own political leadership and administration. Until the advent of tourism, dairy farming was the main occupation. The number of farmers has steadily declined, following the general trend in Switzerland, and today service occupations outnumber farming and industry (Schweizerischer Alpkataster 1978). Interlaken has two thousand three hundred inhabitants (as of the 1980 census), a population swamped by the two thousand six hundred commuters who arrive there every day for work.[5] The total population of the five villages is nine thousand, and at peak tourist season, close to that many tourists can be accommodated.

## INTERLAKEN'S FOLKLORISTIC DISPLAYS

Besides relishing nature and health benefits, tourists also wish to be entertained. The foreign tourists in the nineteenth century belonged to the social elite—members of various European royal families were regular guests, and in response, classical music evenings and gambling in a specially built casino were made available (Schärli 1984). Today, for a different clientele, bars and international guest star performances are common; but as in the early days, a superb classical orchestra plays during the summer months.

Throughout the last one hundred years, however, locals, and in particular those professionals not directly involved with tourism—teachers, doctors, merchants, and lawyers—have felt that tourists should be offered representations of the local culture as well. This sentiment was repeatedly voiced in local newspapers, with the memory of Unspunnen convincing them that it was authentic cowherders' and peasant culture, which enticed visitors to come. Even though an ever-increasing proportion of area residents made their living in the tourist industry, locals nonetheless felt that Interlaken and the surrounding area did represent authentic cowherders' culture and, furthermore, that it was possible to stage, perform, or parade this emblematic culture.

## UNSPUNNEN

In 1805, the year of the first Unspunnen festival, tourism hardly existed as a concept. Travelers were inspired by the romantic notions expressed in Rousseau's and possibly Herder's writings, as well as the early literary travel reflections of Goethe and others. The turmoil of the French Revolution, and the drastic governmental changes brought about by Napoleon's occupation of most of Europe—including Switzerland—provided the backdrop. Napoleon's army stayed in Switzerland until 1802, and under his reign, the valleys surrounding Interlaken received unprecedented autonomy (Jorin 1913).

For more than six hundred years, those valleys had fought for independence from the city of Bern, and Napoleon finally granted them a separate cantonal status (Robé 1972). When Napoleon left, Interlaken and its surroundings once again fell under the government of Bern, a state which the locals did not approve of. In this situation of potential rebellion and internal war, the Bern government came up with the idea of the Cowherder's Festival in Unspunnen. Thus, the festival was anything but an innocent celebration of folk culture, but rather was instead intended as an occasion for reconciliation between the folk of the valleys and the city, nobility, and government representatives (Sammlung 1805; Spreng 1946).

As a source of international publicity (fueled by Madame de Staël and others) the Unspunnen festival was a great success. As a political move of reconciliation by the Bern government, it was a great failure. Rather than placating the various valleys, the organizers created jealousy among the folk performers from the more distant valleys who traveled to Interlaken to show their "traditions." Folk performers felt only recognition for their performance but no long-term gains from having participated, while Interlaken reaped all the long-term profits. The central government in Bern may not have been displeased by this turn of events, as it allowed them to pursue a policy of divide and rule. The second Unspunnen festival in 1808 further familiarized folk performers with the idea of displaying their traditions for foreign visitors, but then the performances ceased. The idea of restaging the festival resurfaced toward the end of the nineteenth century, the time that Hobsbawm characterized as the prime period for inventing traditions (Hobsbawm and Ranger 1983), and in 1903, preparations for the Unspunnen centennial began. One hundred years had wrought considerable change: if the first Unspunnen festival had been an occasion to parade local, alpine folk culture in front of foreign dignitaries, the twentieth-century revivals increasingly turned into displays of Swiss folk culture for fellow Swiss.

The political circumstances of the first Unspunnen staging have long been forgotten. Cultural preservationist organizations such as the Swiss Society for Folk Costume, the Swiss Association for Folk Music, and associations dedicated to organizing and preserving Swiss traditional sports have now become the sponsors of the Unspunnen revivals—not the Bern government. Many of the active performers are city dwellers who have taken courses in how to sew their regional folk costumes, or sing songs of their folk past, and they travel to Interlaken to celebrate their efforts at maintaining Swiss traditional culture. While foreign tourists vacationing in Interlaken may attend the Unspunnen revivals, it is primarily Swiss who come in droves to watch or participate.

The Napoleonic era was synonymous with the rise of nationalism, and attempts to establish images of native culture through large displays for outside consumption were common throughout Europe. Nineteenth-century industrialization brought both massive cultural changes and the disappearance of those aspects of native, pastoral, or agricultural society

celebrated by the Romantics. Regional and national societies for the preservation of "traditional" culture sprang up; it is thus unsurprising that
such groups reinterpreted Unspunnen as an original effort in cultural
preservation rather than the politically motivated display it had been.

The German historian and folklorist Hans Moser called Unspunnen
"clean folklorismus"—"folklorismus," because the event was organized
and did not take place spontaneously as a matter of tradition, and "clean"
because the performers were, in Moser's opinion, "real cowherds who
performed their sports, songs, and dances without any sense of performance routine and without reflected intent." According to Moser, the
performances were "authentic" except for the fact that they were staged
(1964, 27). This element of the early folklorismus debate well illustrates
the morass that a discussion of folklore versus folklorismus or genuine
versus spurious leads to. Having made the distinction, Moser and others then felt a need to differentiate between good and bad, or clean and
spoiled folklorismus—distinctions that, as we can see from the development of Unspunnen, were not only irrelevant to the performers but that
sidestepped the sociopolitical context of such displays.[6] Furthermore,
the quotation attests to how deeply scholars from the second half of the
twentieth century believed in the spontaneity of true tradition, rather
than recognizing the all-important role organizers or performers play in
the maintenance and alteration of cultural facts.

ALPINE PROCESSIONS

In the first decade of the twentieth century, there was an interest—once
again voiced among locals not directly linked to tourism—in creating a
tourist attraction that would properly reflect local culture, rather than just
offering services that tourists could find back home as well. The 1910s had
seen the introduction of amenities for tourists, such as horse riding stables,
tennis courts, and the modification of a little-used Catholic church into
an Anglican church for British visitors.

The question of what would be an appropriate invention was placed
in the most public forum then available, the newspaper. A call for suggestions was met by the proposal of holding a "periodically returning

alpine transhumance procession" that would display "the prettiest cattle of the area ... with yodelling cowherds and dairymen playing the alphorn, with a choir of good singers who would perform our most beautiful folk-songs, and whatever else belongs to such a native celebration" (*Oberländer Volksblatt*, May 24, 1910). Tacked onto a lengthy description was the ratio-nale that foreign guests were "tremendously interested in the customs of the cowherding folk" and few ever had a chance to see anything of the sort.

Within a week, a committee was formed to organize this display. Unlike subsequent repetitions, the 1910 event was a proper transhumance procession inasmuch as the cows did actually end up on the alp afterward (*Oberländer Volksblatt*, Jun 2, 1910). The leading organizer of this alpine procession was Carl Barbier, a local wine and beer merchant. He com-manded the respect and admiration of the local farmers and it was his appeal to their goodwill that allowed for such a rapid organization of the event. Goodwill is a rare commodity among potential folk performers in the Interlaken area. Given the segmentation of the population into five villages, and the steady presence of obviously wealthy tourists who must deposit their wealth somewhere in the area, those who are not directly working with the tourist industry have always been suspicious that the other villages may profit more from tourism than they do (Studer 1947). As much as they approve of displays of native culture, they still want to ensure that a proper price is paid. Hotel managers and others directly involved in the tourist business have remained curiously uninvolved in the planning procedures of the alpine procession.

Newspaper sources further illustrate that it was not, in fact, foreign tourists who came to see the event, but Swiss. Special train and boat rides were organized with Swiss transportation companies to bring visitors from all over northern and central Switzerland to Interlaken. The proces-sion featured not only livestock and herdsmen, but also floats decorated with wildflowers. A generic cowherders' culture was what was on display during this and later processions. Local and regional differences in cow decoration, costume, choice of music, and the like mattered little at the time, for it was cowherders in general that were featured and contrasted with foreigners and urbanites who were supposed to form the audience. From the perspective of organizers and participants, the emblematic use of cows and goats, herdsmen in costume, music, and wildflowers clearly shows the strategic use of local symbols in the face of continuous changes in the local culture due to the presence of tourism. While the first alpine procession attracted upper-class city people, later repetitions of these display events increasingly attracted farming people from near and far—people who relished the opportunity to see emblems of their folk culture displayed. The alpine processions were discontinued after the 1910s, but the next invention clearly points in this direction as well.


## THE TELL PLAY


In 1911, a group of local idealists had the idea of staging Schiller's play William Tell in Interlaken.[7] The Tell legend dates back to the fourteenth century and recounts the liberation of Switzerland. In Schiller's play of 1804 (Schiller [1804] 1980), the Swiss finally found the most convincing retelling of their national past, and the play was performed all over Switzerland throughout the late nineteenth century. William Tell embodies Swiss patriotic sentiment in a manner no other symbol has been able to, and it is not surprising that Interlaken residents came to regard the Tell play as a highly suitable attraction for their area. By 1911, Interlaken had a firm reputation as a tourist resort both inside and outside of Switzerland; the effort to stage the biggest and best Tell production was intended as a demonstration of patriotism designed to outweigh the impression within Switzerland that Interlaken catered only to foreign guests.

The wine and beer merchant, Barbier, played not only the title role, but once again managed to drum up two hundred villagers and livestock as extras. An art dealer and director of Interlaken's lay acting troupe served as director and speech coach, and a school teacher discovered the ideal open-air terrain on which to perform this play (Flückiger and Bollmann 1961). While doctors, dentists, lawyers, merchants, and bankers were willing to help organize the spectacle, there was rarely more than one hotel owner at a time on the Board of Directors.

Building a grandstand, constructing stage sets, and buying costumes required a considerable amount of money. A look at who contributed in 1911, 1930, 1950, and 1968 indicates that aside from a few larger contributions by local notables, it was mostly middle- and lower-class residents of the area who supported the Tell Play.[8] While hotel managers and owners approved of the idea and promised to send their guests, they rarely gave financial support themselves, perhaps because they could not see such a venture breaking even. This situation may strike one as peculiar, and all the more so, given the initial rhetoric surrounding the planning of the play.

In their news releases and public meetings, the original organizers emphasized that the Tell Play would be staged in late spring. This would help extend a tourist season that at the time only began in the summer, and tourists would thus bring money into the local economy earlier in the year (*Oberländer Volksblatt*, February 23, 1910). Those who benefited most from tourism should have wholeheartedly supported the venture, but there are a number of interconnected reasons why they might not have done so. One reason was that, oftentimes, the owners and managers of the most exclusive resort hotels were not natives to the area, or were immigrants who had only been there for a generation. Another reason was that guests who stayed at exclusive hotels may not have displayed a burning desire to see a theater production in antiquated German, performed by amateur actors with heavy Swiss accents. Still another reason was based on the difference in outlook between elite-oriented hotel managers and the middle-class teachers and local professionals who organized cultural life.

As with the alpine processions, it was the Swiss rather than the tourists who came to see Interlaken's William Tell. Swiss audiences rarely stayed overnight and the stage was so far from Interlaken's main tourist streets that they may not have even gotten around to buying a postcard. In fact, throughout the play's existence, tourist businesses complained that rather than furthering tourism, the Tell Play actually took business away from them.[9] It is this history that leads current performers to deny that they are participating in a tourist attraction, even if that is what an outsider might assume. Instead, they perceive what they do as a long-standing local tradition. They are generally unaware of the rocky start of the organization, the financially disastrous early seasons, the pre–World War I bankruptcy, or the abortive attempts to revive the play in the 1920s.

One of the most significant aspects regarding the sociopolitical relevance of inventing traditions was the veritable war that broke out in the late 1920s between those who wanted to revive the Tell Play and those who wanted to revive alpine processions. Both groups used the standard rhetorical argument by claiming to work in the best interests of the local economy. One informant who was alive at the time jokingly called it "the war between the Tells and the Cowherds." The Cowherds rephrased the rationale used for the alpine processions in the first decade of the century: "An attraction is to be created which will bring the foreign tourists to Interlaken in May. It should not be forgotten how deserted and silent our pre-season tends to be and how much local businesses await the arrival of tourists. It is therefore the duty of local voluntary associations to sponsor events which ... advertise our community." (*Oberländer Volksblatt*, July 9, 1925). Implied in this press release is the accusation that the Tell Play with its patriotic charter did not fulfill this mission as successfully as an alpine procession would have. In 1931, the Tell Players won, largely due to the international political situation, the growing Nazi threat, and the increasing need of the Swiss to unite behind the type of symbol that William Tell offered. However, to placate the proponents of alpine processions, the Tell Play—to this day—opens with a transhumance procession involving cows and goats. This concession toward the opposition also constitutes an admission that folkloristic symbols of the cowherding life are indeed a desirable component of Interlaken's self-image.

The Tell Play illustrates the lack of connection between the tourist economy and local interests. The organizers have maintained a theme that has been relevant and is at times crucial to their own national or local identity rather than catering to tourist tastes or interests. Schiller's play at the time of its premiere in 1804 stood as an emblem for the struggle of freedom for the Swiss, but German and Austrian tourists could have been offended at the choice, for the story it tells is that of the defeat of the Austrian empire and its tyranny, in what is often called the "Ur-Switzerland," the central cantons. The play's prodemocratic theme was cause enough for it to be banned in Germany and Austria shortly after it premiered, and it was not allowed to be performed in Germany during the Third Reich.

The Interlaken citizens clearly did not care if they offended their upper-class German or Austrian guests by putting on the play. One Interlaken editorial on the occasion of the national holiday in 1904 noted that "we cannot sufficiently remind the younger generations of the powerful figures of our history, and encourage them to emulate these men. We will always dwell on the importance of this day, in order for our foreign guests to see that we, despite the internationalizing and cultural leveling of the present, uphold our ancestors' deeds and that we are and want to remain free Swiss." (*Das Hardermannli*, 1904, 31:124). And twenty-three years later, an outraged area resident wrote: "We fully recognize the financial value of tourism and gladly grant every foreign guest the joy of looking at our wonderful mountains. But how far do we have to bend over for our guests? ... Foreign papers make fun of our benches marked 'for tourists only.' ... It is a worse matter with the motion to silence our church bells to [prolong the tourists' morning rest]. We want to at least keep our dignity and regional pride" (*Oberländer Volksblatt*, June 14, 1927).

## HARDER-POTSCHETE

The last Interlaken invention is a winter festival called Harder-Potschete, held on January 2. In 1986, this festival occurred for the thirtieth time since its invention in 1956, and the association that founded the festival issued a celebratory publication to mark the event. The booklet opens as follows: "The Harder-Potschete in Interlaken has existed for only thirty years, but we may safely say that it has become a tradition." (Wegmann and Dahler 1985, 5). The booklet is a marvelous illustration of the process of inventing a tradition. It recounts in great detail—and with quite some pride—who was responsible for the successful introduction of the Harder-Potschete. Historical documents prove that at different times the Interlaken area had midwinter celebrations that involved young men and gift-giving. In the immediate post–World War II period, this took the form of fairly wild street battles between poorly disguised groups of boys and adolescents on January 2. In 1955, one Interlaken merchant became angry watching this behavior, and decided that something ought to be done. He called up a number of friends, and sixteen men, mostly small-business owners and teachers, eventually set up a committee and designed a new celebration worthy of their village.

Winter celebrations featuring supposed forest spirits and fertility demons have enjoyed a tremendous revival in twentieth-century Switzerland (Bendix 1985), and it is not surprising that the Interlaken committee made forest spirits the central element of the Harder-Potschete. As an inspiration, they used an area legend concerning the *Hardermannli*—an unhappy soul who wandered in the nearby Harder forest (Hartmann 1910). A well-known local woodcarver was contracted to create suitable masks for this Hardermannli and his wife, and every year two additional masks are contracted for the accompanying woodspirits (called *Potsche*). The group of forest spirits in costumes made of pine forms the central part of the celebration, and on the afternoon of January 2, this group proceeds around a series of side streets of Interlaken, where most of the festival's creators have their shops. The spirits carry pig bladders and are not above charging into the sparse crowd of spectators, sometimes to hit them, sometimes to make as if they would carry them off. The celebration also features a children's costume contest, where bowls of hot Potsche-soup are sold to the freezing onlookers and participants; a brief parade with a brass band and groups of men who rhythmically swing cowbells concludes the public part of the display. Active participants then gather in a restaurant to warm up over a meal and hot drinks.

The tourist industry had no input in the festival creation. Indeed, judging from the booklet, the initiators intended this celebration for local consumption and for their own enjoyment, and the initiators themselves were also the first active participants. This display is smaller in scale than any of the others, and a rhetoric of how this festival would aid the tourist business never surfaced. Nonetheless, the Harder-Potschete brings at least as many tourists on the streets as it does natives, and it is the tourists who are fascinated by the costumes, the noise, and the emblems chosen for the display, while the locals are interested in the prizes, who wins them, and who is hidden underneath the costumes.

When asked how relevant folkloristic displays were in attracting tourists to the area, Interlaken's tourism director hesitatingly said, "It is part of our image, we may do more with it, we're thinking of offering folk music workshops" (March 13, 1986, interview). But he then quickly affirmed what the historical evidence and current survey statistics amply prove: tourists come for the Alps, for sports and health, and for entertainment. Within entertainment, folkloristic displays are but a minor offering. Indeed, the only folklore program that tourists regularly go to see, one not initiated by local interest groups, is the "Folklore Show" put on every Wednesday night at the casino. The program combines generic Swiss and German folk music and costume, with fun and games for the audience, much in the manner of a TV show; interviewed locals have nothing good to say about it.

The motivations of organizers and participants of the four display events discussed were, however, only indirectly engendered by tourism. Regional politics, cultural preservation, patriotic fervor, the pleasure of acting, a desire to stage and participate in a wintertime festival, and (in the case of some Tell Play actors who get a small remuneration for their participation) an interest in personal monetary gain, are all overt reasons for the invention and continuation of Interlaken's public displays. Symbolically, the conglomerate of communities known as Interlaken uses these displays to project a particular self-image. The cowherders' emblems used in the alpine parades and Unspunnen revivals showed pride of a (disappearing) local culture and affirmed this culture in the face of foreign tourists, attracting a largely Swiss audience. By putting on a bigger open-air Tell Play than any other Swiss community had managed thus far, local organizers hoped to reinforce a patriotic, Swiss profile for their community, and their mostly middle- and lower-class Swiss audience continues to flock to Interlaken every summer to see the play. The Harder-Potschete, finally, reverted to the narrower frame of appealing to local interest as a suitable winter custom for themselves and their children, possibly in direct response to various similar customs of somewhat earlier origin in the surrounding valleys.

CONCLUSION

In his study of a Basque festival, Greenwood discussed the "commodification of local color," which he saw as a deplorable result of tourism (1977, 130–31). Without providing data concerning the longevity of the festival, Greenwood asserts that, due to tourism, the event has been changed from a communitas-promoting occasion to a case of what he termed "culture by the pound." The locals, he felt, are being exploited, their cultural display commoditized, and "the ritual has become a performance for money. The meaning is gone" (135).[10] The participants of a colloquium on folklorismus and tourism held in Switzerland recommended that "in the future one must take care, so that *creativity*, not maximizing profit, will reign supreme. Traditions should be carried out to awaken joy, and not for vanity and greed's sake" (Friedrich 1985, 59; emphasis in original)."[11] Mentioned as responsible for this surveillance were "folklore specialists, folklore researchers and tourism specialists." Not mentioned were those who are to perform creatively rather than greedily.

Assumed in these assertions is a concept of tradition as something age-old, not to be tampered with, and existing devoid of human agency. Equally suspect is the argument that claims that meaning disappears once money is introduced as a factor in traditional performances. In the case of a culture like Switzerland's, and arguably in most other nations, money has been part of cultural endeavors for centuries, and the claim that its presence in the negotiation of cultural displays robs them of their meaning is both an overstatement and a romanticization of the "folk's" awareness of cash in their everyday lives. Utz Jeggle and Gottfried Korff (1974) have similarly argued against explanations that see only economic reasons for the commoditization of folk culture. The process of inventing traditions is always tied into the socioeconomic constellation of a community (and so is any cultural manifestation), but the choices and strategies of those doing the inventing are by far more powerful loci of analysis (55–57).

Tourism is clearly not a passing fad, and shielding cultures from touristic exploitation may be a noble but unrealistic endeavor (e.g., Kramer 1983; Mader 1985). Tourism is "more than an economic phenomenon with sociological and cultural effects; it has become a phenomenon of civilization" (UNESCO 1976, 99), and as such warrants detailed ethnographic and historical attention. The case of Interlaken illustrates that from the perspective of originators and performers, "local color," "tradition," and "folklore" are and always have been open for strategic use, and regarding tourism as the main agent of change would seem to be a misconception.[12] Cultural displays require staging and thus negotiation of some sort; even a rite of passage is newly created by active participants who decide how and when the event is to take place in ever-changing cultural conditions. Tourism and its concerns simply add a further element in the staging process. In conjunction with a tourist economy, then, it is precisely the realm of expressive culture and its strategic use by the host society that allow for a more differentiated analysis of tourism's impact on the hosts' culture, or rather, the degree of cultural resilience on the part of hosts in the face of tourism.

A host community is not only subject to its own internal dynamics but is also part of a larger regional or national culture, and tourism is merely one component contributing to the types of actions and choices made by locals. The people of Interlaken like to see their town as an important regional center, as a place steeped in area customs, and as a harbor of patriotic values. Unspunnen revivals, Harder-Potschete, and the Tell Play all aid in constructing and bolstering this self-image. The presence of a potentially interested tourist audience contributes to this process of negotiation, but it neither dominates it nor determines its outcome.[13] Much of the anthropological research of tourism has focused on Third World settings, in part because anthropology has always emphasized these cultures for ethnographic study. Yet studies of the latest frontier of tourism might benefit from insights to be garnered in First World settings. Interlaken and similar resorts with lengthy histories of tourist development are excellent research areas for learning to understand both the process of inventing traditions and the role of tourism within it. The case of Interlaken would seem to suggest that internal value systems are sufficiently resilient to cope with and confront tourism in the subtle or blatant emblems embodied in cultural displays. Interlaken and Swiss natives are no different than other host societies in their capability to realize what is happening to them, by them, for them, and around them. Their big advantage compared to host societies in Global South settings is that they have had two hundred years to find their own cultural responses to cope with touristic presence.

### NOTES

This chapter appeared originally in the *Journal of American Folklore*, 102, no. 404 (April–June, 1989): 131–46.

A version of this article was presented at the Anthropology Colloquium, University of Wisconsin, Madison, on April 15, 1988, and I would like to thank faculty and students for their lively comments. The research was conducted in 1985–86 with the support of a Foreign Language Area Studies fellowship. All translations are mine.

1. After the original publication of this article in 1989, Unspunnen was also held in 1993 and 1996; the two hundred-year jubilee of 2005 had to be shifted to 2006 due to a major flood in the Interlaken area. The community now aims for a twelve-year rhythm, with the latest installment held in 2017 (see Unspunnen 2017).

2. I define cultural displays as nonordinary, framed, public events that require participation on the part of a substantial group. They are "planned-for public occasions ... in which actions and objects are invested with meaning and values are put 'on display'" (Abrahams 1981, 303). The size of the group participating varies depending on the type of display and the nature of the separation between performers and audiences.

3. Ben-Amos's assessment of tradition in American folklore studies (1984) is well complemented by Tamas Hofer's (1984) essay on the use of the term in European research. Dorothy Noyes (2009) has provided a comprehensive survey and analysis of the concept's use.

4. *Annals of Tourism Research* began publication in 1973. Important research was carried out before then (see Cohen 1984), but one may safely say that tourism had "arrived" as a field of study once a specialized journal was established. UNESCO's continued involvement in and sponsorship of tourism research further aids the development of this research area (UNESCO 1976).

5. By the 2011 census, the population of Interlaken alone had risen to 5,468, and the five villages constituting the area numbered beyond 15,000—reflecting Switzerland's sharp increase in population, generally; the country has the highest percentage of inhabitants with foreign passports; in the Interlaken area (given its reliance on a service sector tourism economy) many of the inhabitants belong to that category as well.

6. See Bendix (1997) for a full discussion of the folklorism debate, its connection to discourses on authenticity and its hampering of reflexive scholarship that acknowledges scholars' own contribution to public enactments of "the authentic."

7. For a comparative study on two Tell Play stagings by lay actors in Switzerland, see Bendix (1989).

8. Duplicate copies of the original fund-raising letters and listings of the contributors are stored at the Tell Play office. One interviewee even admitted that it was to no small extent the speaking-role actors themselves who contributed, simply because they enjoyed participating and feared that a lack of funds might put an end to their hobby (interview March 10, 1986.

9. The stage is located in the village of Matten, and can be reached in less than fifteen minutes by foot, or in a few minutes by bus. Several participants recalled with bitter amusement one hotel owner's complaint that those guests who did go to see the play did not have time to eat (and pay for) dessert before curtain time.

10. In the revised edition of *Hosts and Guests*, Greenwood (1989, 182–85) slightly modified his stance, considering issues of middle-class culture, tourism, authenticity, and mobilization. Magliocco (2006) offers a subtler, actor-centered perspective on festival change and participant motivation.

11. The results of this colloquium sponsored by the Swiss UNESCO commission were disappointing in that two of the main contributions once again tried to delineate "good" versus "bad" forms of folklorism (Friedrich 1985, 7–21, 30–48). The summary report aptly stated: "Even if the terminology of 'genuine' and 'spurious' was circumvented or at least put in quotation marks, this still did not hide the fact that everyone avoided the actual issue, namely the problem of authenticity" (52).

12. Robert Borofsky's ethnography (1987) of the Polynesian Pukapukan islanders beautifully recasts the issue of inventing and reviving tradition as constructions of knowledge and divergent "ways of knowing" between anthropologists and natives.

13. Ann Fienup-Riordan observed that the presence of an outside film crew had much the same effect on an Alaskan community (1988, 454).

REFERENCES

Abrahams, Roger D. 1981. "Shouting Match at the Border: The Folklore of Display Events." In *And Other Neighborly Names: Social Process and Cultural Image in Texas Folklore*, edited by Richard Bauman and Roger D. Abrahams, 303–21. Austin: University of Texas Press.

Bausinger, Hermann. 1966. "Zur Kritik der Folklorismuskritik." In *Populus Revisus: Beitrage zur Erforschung der Gegenwart*, edited by Hermann Bausinger, 61–75. Tübingen: Tübinger Vereinigung für Volkskunde.

Ben-Amos, Dan. 1984. "The Seven Strands of Tradition: Varieties in Its Meaning in American Folklore Studies." *Journal of Folklore Research* 21 (2/3): 97–131.

Bendix, Regina. 1985. *Progress and Nostalgia: Silvesterklausen in Urnäsch, Switzerland.* Berkeley: University of California Press.

———. 1988. "Folklorismus: The Challenge of a Concept." *International Folklore Review* 6: 5–15.

Bernard, Paul P. 1978. *Rush to the Alps. The Evolution of Vacationing in Switzerland.* Boulder, CO: East European Quarterly.

Bodemann, Ulrike. 1983. "Folklorismus-Ein Modellentwurf." *Rheinisch-Westfälische Zeitschrift für Volkskunde* 28: 101–10.

Borofsky, Robert. 1987. *Making History: Pukapukan and Anthropological Constructions of Knowledge.* New York: Cambridge University Press.

Bourquin, Markus. 1963. *Franz Niklaus König: Leben und Werk.* Bern: Paul Haupt.

Cohen, Erik. 1984. "The Sociology of Tourism: Approaches, Issues and Findings." *Annual Review of Sociology* 10: 373–92.

Cohn, Gustav. 1882. "Die Fremdenverkehrsindustrie der Schweiz." In *Volkswirtschaftliche Aufsätze*, 635–67. Stuttgart: Cotta.

Dundes, Alan. 1985. "Nationalistic Inferiority Complexes and the Fabrication of Folklore: A Reconsideration of Ossian, the Kinder- und Hausmärchen, the Kalevala, and Paul Bunyan." *Journal of Folklore Research* 22 (1): 5–18.

Evans-Pritchard, Deirdre. 1987. "The Portal Case: Authenticity, Tourism, Traditions, and the Law." *Journal of American Folklore* 100 (397): 287–96.

Fienup-Riordan, Ann. 1988. "Robert Redford, Apanuugpak, and the Invention of Tradition." *American Ethnologist* 15 (3): 442–55.

Flückiger, A., and E. Bollmann. 1961. *50 Jahre Tellspiele Interlaken.* Interlaken (duplicated typescript available at the Tell Play Office in Interlaken).

Friedrich, Andreas, ed. 1985. *Folklore und Tourismus.* Bern: Sekretariat der nationalen schweizerischen UNESCO-Kommission.

Gallati, Rudolf. 1977. *Interlaken- Vom Kloster zum Fremdenkurort.* Interlaken: Schlaefli.

Giddens, Anthony. 1979. *Central Problems in Social Theory: Actions, Structure and Contradiction in Social Analysis.* Berkeley: University of California Press.

Gölden, Hubert. 1939. *Strukturwandlungen im Schweizerischen Fremdenverkehr um 1890–1935.* Zurich: H. Girsberger.

Graburn, Nelson, ed. 1976. *Ethnic and Tourist Arts: Cultural Expressions from the Fourth World.* Berkeley: University of California Press.

Greenwood, Davydd J. 1977. "Culture by the Pound: An Anthropological Perspective on Tourism as Cultural Commoditization." In *Hosts and Guests*, edited by Valene L. Smith, 129–38. Philadelphia: University of Pennsylvania Press.

———. 1989. "Culture by the Pound: An Anthropological Perspective on Tourism as Cultural Commoditization." In *Hosts and Guests*, rev. ed., edited by Valene L. Smith, 171–86. Philadelphia: University of Pennsylvania Press.

Handler, Richard, and Jocelyn Linnekin. 1984. "Tradition, Genuine or Spurious." *Journal of American Folklore* 97 (385): 273–90.

Hartmann, Hermann. 1910. *Berner Oberland in Sage und Geschichte*. Vol. 1. Interlaken: Benteli.

Hobsbawm, Eric, and Terence Ranger, eds. 1983. *The Invention of Tradition*. Cambridge: Cambridge University Press.

Hofer, Tamas. 1984. "The Perception of Tradition in European Ethnology." *Journal of Folklore Research* 21 (2/3): 133–47.

Jeggle, Utz, and Gottfried Korff. 1974. "Zur Entwicklung des Zillertaler Regionalcharakters." *Zeitschrift für Volkskunde* 70: 39–57.

Jorin, Ernst. 1913. "Der Kanton Oberland 1798–1803." *Schweizer Studien zur Geschichtswissenschaft* 5: 301–597.

Jules-Rosette, Benetta. 1984. *The Messages of Tourist Art: An African Semiotic System in Comparative Perspective*. New York: Plenum.

Kirshenblatt-Gimblett, Barbara. 1988. "Mistaken Dichotomies." *Journal of American Folklore* 101 (400): 140–55.

Kramer, Dieter. 1983. *Der sanfte Tourismus*. Vienna: Bundesverlag.

Krippendorf, Jost. 1984. *Die Ferienmenschen. Für ein neues Verständnis von Freizeit und Reisen*. Zurich: Orell Füssli.

Kroner, Arlinde. 1968. *Grindelwald: Die Entwicklung eines Bergbauerndorfes zu einem internationalen Touristenzentrum*. Stuttgart: Selbstverlag des Geografischen Instituts der Universität Stuttgart.

MacCannell, Dean. 1976. *The Tourist. A New Theory of the Leisure Class*. New York: Schocken.

Mader, Ueli. 1985. *Sanfter Tourismus: Alibi oder Chance?* Zurich: Rotpunktverlag.

Magliocco, Sabina. 2006. *The Two Madonnas: The Politics of Festival in a Sardinian Community*. Long Grove, IL: Waveland.

Moser, Hans. 1964. "Der Folklorismus als Forschungsproblem der Volkskunde." *Hessische Blätter für Volkskunde* 55: 9–57.

Nash, Dennison. 1981. "Tourism as an Anthropological Subject." *Current Anthropology* 22 (3): 461–81.

Noyes, Dorothy. 2009. "Tradition: Three Traditions." *Journal of Folklore Research* 46 (3): 233–68.

Robé, Udo. 1972. *Berner Oberland und Staat Bern: Untersuchungen zu den wechselseitigen Beziehungen in den Jahren 1798–1846*. Bern: Stadt- und Universitätsbibliothek.

*Sammlung aller Lieder, Gedichte und andern Schriften auf das schweizerische Alphirten-Fest zu Unspunnen im Kanton Bern*. 1805. Bern.

Schärli, Arthur. 1984. *Höhepunkt des schweizerischen Tourismus in der Zeit der "Belle Epoque" unter besonderer Berücksichtigung des Berner Oberlandes*. Bern: Peter Lang.

Schiller, Friedrich. (1804) 1980. *Die Braut von Messina. Wilhelm Tell. Die Huldigung der Künste. Schillers Werke Nationalausgabe*, vol. 10, edited by Siegfried Seidel. Weimar: Hermann Böhlaus Nachfolger.

Schweizerischer Alpkataster. 1978. *Die Land- und Alpwirtschaft im Berner Oberland, Emmental und Schwarzenburgerland*. Bern: Abteilung für Landwirtschaft des EDV.

Shils, Edward. 1981. *Tradition*. Chicago: University of Chicago Press.

Spreng, Hans. 1946. Die Alphirtenfeste zu Unspunnen. *Bernische Zeitschrift für Geschichte und Heimatkunde*, 133–88.

———. 1956. *Interlaken*. Berner Heimatbücher 64. Bern: Paul Haupt.

Staël, Germaine de. 1958. *De l'Allemagne*. 1: 280–95. Paris: Librairie Hachette.

Studer, Martin. 1947. *Die Erschliessung des Berner Oberlandes durch den Fremdenverkehr und ihre Auswirkung auf Produktion und Wirtschaftsgesinnung*. Bern: Stämpfli.

UNESCO. 1976. "The Effects of Tourism on Socio-Cultural Values." *Annals of Tourism Research* 4 (2): 74–105.

Unspunnen. 2017. "Interlaken Unspunnenfest." Accessed May 2. www.unspunnenfest.ch /de/home.html.

Wegmann, Markus, and Andre Dahler. 1985. *Harderpotschete*. Interlaken: Schlaefli.

Weiss, Richard. 1933. *Das Alpenerlebnis in der deutschen Literatur des 18. Jahrhunderts*. Horgen: Münsterpresse.

Winkler, Ernst. 1944. *Die Landschaft der Schweiz als Voraussetzung des Fremdenverkehrs*. Arbeiten aus dem Geographischen Institut der ETH Zurich 2. Zurich: Buchdruckerei an der Sihl.

# 2

────── ⁊ ──────

## *On the Road to Fiction: Narrative Reification in Austrian Cultural Tourism*

S tocked in colorful dispenser boxes at Austrian freeway rest stops, train stations, and amusement parks, Radomir Runzelschuh's folktales can be obtained for little more than candy, condoms, snacks, tampons, and similarly essential commodities typically available from sale machines in such locations. A mere twenty Austrian Schilling and a turn of the crank on the *Märchenautomat* (Folktale Automat) releases a colorful envelope whose contents can be read out loud in the car, as the family drives on to their destination. For the family on the road to a holiday destination in the south of Austria, the Runzelschuh tales are a suitable means to set the mood. They promise magic, escape, and comfort, and are but one among many strips of narrative turned material that is awaiting them. For the ethnographer in late-twentieth-century Europe, Mr. Runzelschuh and his automats are an icon representing the confluence of cultural commoditization, market, and touristic utopias.

The intersection of tourist productions and "children's tales" is a fruitful arena to consider for understanding the materialization of mentifacts, especially popular fictions. Of course, people all over the globe have always rendered narration (mythological and otherwise) in pictorials or artifacts ranging from vessels to cloths.[1] If language is at the core of how we structure and enact cultural patterns (Urban 1991), rendering visible and graspable the codes in our heads creates the material extensions of such patterns. While there are continuities in such patterns of transformation, changing social and economic circumstances also bring forth alternate ways and purposes for materializing fiction. Drawn from Austrian tourist sites, the cases I discuss show elements of a globalizing economy of cultural production intertwined with local aesthetic, educational, and economic practices. After some brief reflections on the interrelationship of material- ized fiction and the human patterning of landscape, I will turn to a discus- sion of several tourist sites in the Austrian state of Carinthia (Kärnten), and conclude by placing the case studies in the broader European context of cultural tourism and narrative materialization.

## THE MATERIALIZATION OF TALES AND THE THEMING OF LANDSCAPES

Asked about the reasons behind his innovation, Ferry Ebert (alias Radomir Runzelschuh) wrote me a letter excerpting aspects of his life history. He emphasized long periods of a kind of nomadism in search of himself. His recovery from uncertainty coincided with discovering his love for narratives and his hope for a better future based on nurturing the good in children. His tales are a mix of traditional plots and newly crafted ones, and each tale is followed with an invitation to children to write back to him and send him their tales, and he in turn promises to set them into circulation through his automats. From European narrative researchers I learned that the Runzelschuh idea germinated not only from a utopian vision of celebrating children's narrative thirst. Ebert had made a living for years in the quasi-nomadic profession of restocking the very dispensers for life's necessities next to which the *Märchenautomaten* are now sometimes stationed.[2] The automats are rectangular boxes, painted with the same pictures found along the rim of each tale. Ebert also offers cardboard varieties, fashioned like small treasure chests, which he recommends for events or locations where a more nostalgic locus of narration is called for. The only place I encountered them outside of Ebert's promotional folder was in front of Vienna's opera house, where a new tourist convey- ance was attempting to break into a market saturated with horse-drawn carriages: an upstart sedan chair operation, staffed by two young men in

medievalesque costume, tried to lure potential customers into taking a
ride. On the red plush seat sat a Runzelschuh fairy tale treasure chest, and
any one taking the service would receive a free tale envelope.[3]

The folktale has a rarely considered history of materialization;
Runzelschuh's work is but one of the more recent permutations. If it were not
for collectors who assiduously rendered narratives into texts, and texts into
handsomely bound volumes, the material appeal of textualized oral narrative might not have established itself as broadly as it has. We tend to dwell on
folktale, song, or epic's role in solidifying the nationalist *imagination*—the
scholarship on such verbal arts' ties to the national project since Herder's
time is substantial (e.g., Baycroft and Hopkin 2012; Dundes 1985; Herzfeld
1982; Hopkin 2012; Leersen forthcoming; Oinas 1978; Plochij 2012; Wilson
1976). In the process perhaps we have overlooked the very "solidity," or material presence, such reified fictions take in our lives. Rendered into books,
tales acquire an appeal to material ownership and they engage our sense of
touch and sight, especially in illustrated form. Tales have inspired not only
illustrations but also theatrical enactment (e.g., puppetry, ballet, or opera),
and more recently film and animation (e.g., Greenhill and Matrix 2010;
Greenhill and Rudy 2014; Zipes, Greenhill, and Magnus-Johnston 2016).

My special focus here, however, is how the tourism and heritage industry has taken on the job of making concrete the kind of mental connections between holiday experience and fiction that an individual might
have. Travel as a means to experience the realm of fiction and fantasy has
a considerable history (Jafari and Gardner 1991). Reaching Tibet or visiting Bali have been rendered as fulfillments or concretizations of fairyland
imaginations (Dann 1996, 124–25). Touristic promotion has also latched
onto the idea of recapturing facets of childhood, such as advertisements
promising holidays facilitating the recovery of childhood vacation experiences (Urry 1990, 102–3). Drawing on fieldwork in the Austrian state of
Carinthia in 1996, I will discuss words, visuals, and statuary that denote
the planned "theming" of landscape and built environments in a different
way: here, statuary, enactment, or perhaps most poignantly put, "things"
drawn from fiction are supplied to enhance the experience of the real.[4]

Theming is certainly not new. Certain types of gardening or landscap-
ing as practiced by nobility in the Austrian realm as well as elsewhere in
Europe deny the assumption that theming is a postmodern phenomenon.[5]

The countless calvaries (*Kalvarienberge*) in Catholic Austria are poignant evidence of mapping the twelve Stations of the Cross onto the landscape. Konrad Köstlin characterizes the architectural and enacted Stations of the Cross as a means to render the landscape cultural, and to provide special meaning and memory by impregnating regionality with religion (Köstlin 1991, 432). Enacting the Stations of the Cross thus expands a rite into a "route of passage" (436). The themed environments in Austria draw some of their layout from such religious predecessors—not because their planners intended to craft them according to the religious model, but perhaps because dotting the landscape with a sequence of related themes is a familiar pattern. However, the sources, styles, and intent of the themes are not assertions of a single (religious) dogma. They rather stem from various historical and secular layers of narration and pictorialization. The potential meaning to be gleaned from ambling through them is not overtly dogmatic and affirming of collective belief as is a calvary. Rather, as is typical of reflexive modernization, the onus of interpretation is placed on the individual. The sites promise enchantment through "experience," which in turn is the latest commoditized step in modernity's quest to achieve selfhood.[6]

Aspects of these Austrian "things" are clearly inspired by narrative-turned-theme-park in American Disneylands and Disney Worlds. Through architecture, props, and costumed staff, they "attempt to place the 'guest' into narratives" (Project on Disney 1995, 81). Yet unlike the totalizing experience aimed for by corporations like Disney and by animal experience parks such as SeaWorld (see Davis 1997) and satirized by Eco (1986) as *Travels in Hyperreality*, the Austrian examples are a great deal more fragmented—and fragmenting. Materialized narration can tell us a lot about the disjuncture between individual experience, which ultimately remains fully known only to the self, and the experience that is constructed, advertised, and purchased.

## MATERIALIZED FICTIONS IN AUSTRIAN TOURIST SITES

The tourist industry has evolved from marketing landscapes, accommodations, health, and facets of culture to the absorbing or controlling of what people purportedly wish to do and feel while being tourists.

Dean MacCannell (1976), among others, has articulated the traveler's endless effort to push beyond the touristic offering into realms of not commoditized experience. It should not surprise that the industry inevitably recognizes this demand and commoditizes it, bringing forth in turn what Feifer has called post-tourists—people at play with what they know to be staged experiences (Feifer 1985).[7] The key term in the leisure market at this point is "experience." In Carinthia, in the summer of 1996, this encompassed everything from adventure experience to taste-, Märchen-, and water-experience. The number of Carinthian sites denoting narrative is remarkable, and a special tourist credit card (the *Kärnten Card*) introduced in the 1996 season offered reduced entrance fees in almost all of them. During a stay in the region south of the Wörthersee, acquaintance with such sites and associated "theming" is almost unavoidable: aside from brochures in freeway rest stops, at information booths, reception desks, and in guest rooms, many inns and hotels have appropriated elements, however minor, as part of their decor. Driving through rural streets, garden dwarves placed ostentatiously into the front yard can be a visual indicator for available guest rooms, supporting whatever additional signage there might be. In the case of establishments geared toward families, statuary and pictorials referencing narrative are particularly numerous. At a family hotel on the shores of Rauschelesee, for instance, the house itself was painted with folktale figures, the barn with animals resembling children's books illustrations, and the extensive garden held a Snow White statue in charge of a great many more dwarves than one is accustomed to expect from the tale. The live geese were named after their literary cousins in Selma Lagerlöf's children's classic *Nils Holgersson* ([1907] 1991). Scrutiny of brochures of Carinthian guest facilities from 1996 through 1998 demonstrates that most establishments wanting to earn the designation "family hotel" make such concessions in interior and exterior décor.[8]

The mixture of source references—from nineteenth- and twentieth-century children's books to traditional popular narrative and mass-mediated narrations, such as cartoons—is characteristic of the entire Carinthian spectrum of tourist sites: some overtly focus on materialized fiction, others center on different themes. Heidi Alm Falkert, for example, can be reached by foot or by cableway, and once reaching the proper altitude, one will find plastic figurines along a trail, mapping Johanna Spyri's classic Swiss story ([1879] 1994) over what used to be an alpine pasture.

In the Gurktal, one can board a train into a Dwarf Park (*Zwergenpark*), to see everything from dwarf mythology to Batman dwarves. Elsewhere awaits the Stuffed Animal Zoo Experience (*Plüschtier Zoo Erlebniswelt*), with animals near wishing wells, stalked by cartoon protagonists Garfield and the Pink Panther. Some sites incorporate just a few referents to tale imagery, such as inflatable archetypes of a "fairy castle" and a "peasant home" to bounce on, amidst waterslides and other rides to be found at the 1. Carinthian Experience Park (*1. Kärntner Erlebnispark, Presseggersee*).

In some instances, the entire site takes its characters and scenes from fiction. A good example is the Magic Forest in the Carinthian lake valley (*Zauberwald*, Rauschelesee). A portion of the forested hillside sloping down toward the lake has been augmented from an area for recreational walking to a site filled with plywood statuary, makeshift structures intended to resemble fortresses, huts, a wishing well, and so forth. As one enters the forest, cutout heads of generic ghouls peak out from the trees, evoking no particular (and thus all kinds of) tales, legends, or myths. Mixed among them are figures from Maurice Sendak's children's book *Where the Wild Things Are*, generic witches, and Little Red Riding Hood.[9] The Magic Forest serves as a gigantic playground for children to take possession of at will. The suggested themes are fairy tales, but also—thanks to the fort and the Indian tepee—the settler-versus-Indian conflict, or medieval robber-versus-baron games. There are no guards or other safety measures in this rocky, at times steep forest; the natural terrain is part of the experience for those veering from the path.

Here resides one of the differences between these locally generated tourist sites and Disney-type environments, where safety and thus containment are writ large, and the experience—imaginary or real—is much more controlled. Another telling difference resides in the materializations themselves. Disney, perhaps more so than any other theme park enterprise, standardizes its visual images to fit within the overall Disney style and cosmos. Characters drawn from vernacular narrative appear in the look employed in animated Disney films, surrounded by enactments of cartoon animals bearing Disney looks. It is the sameness of the style in creatures, buildings, and rides that creates the ambiance. A place such as this Austrian Magic Forest, by contrast, contains a bricolage alluding to highly diverse narrative vehicles and visual inheritances. There is no effort to give all the source materials the same kind of unifying gloss. The assumption, rather, is that the glue making for the desired experience will come from the fantasy play of the children themselves, with the occasional bit of assistance from an animator.

The Keutschach tourist office in whose domain the forest is located hires a number of tale animators.[10] Their task is to facilitate more structured ways to interact with this forest. With their help, "walks in the magic forest" differ drastically depending on the animator's vision of magic, narration, and childhood. Thus one such walk was a peaceful amble through the forest, with parents and kids occasionally gathering in a clearing, and getting treated to what folklorists would happily index as a typical magic tale. This walk concluded with each child receiving a magic story stone from the animator's magic story stone box—material evidence for the experience, as well as for the generic magic gift of a folktale; they were dispensed with the promise that each stone would bring more stories if carefully placed under one's pillow.

An early evening walk with Del Vede, a storyteller who occasionally appears on German-language TV, set a very different tone. He began by reversing authority between children and their parents. Face paint given to each child and wild play marked a "reality" of childhood, within which parents were labeled as extraterrestrial or otherwise disturbing creatures. This narrator completely ignored the icons of familiar tales and books sprinkled through the forest. Instead he told fragments of nature myths, animating the trees and stones among which everyone sat. Into this fiction entered an elderly woman, seemingly just walking her dog. Del Vede greeted her as the forest witch, a role she clearly had enacted for him before, and from here the evening segued into a lesson on environmental protection and witchcraft's connection to it. Another reality was placed atop the fragile fictional one, when the forest witch reminded Del Vede that he had not made good on his promise to feature her on one of his story tapes.[11]

The most elaborate site to be discussed is, literally, arranged as a road through fiction: the "Diaper Hiking Mile" (*Windelwandermeile*) located above the village of Trebesing. Its entrance is flanked by dwarves in guardhouses, and dwarves appear throughout this walk, nestled between roots, sitting on tree branches, or as part of tale statuary. From a brochure about a different site we learn that dwarves are the ideal means to bridge between work/reality and leisure/fantasy.[12] Given the kinds of things dwarves tend to do in folk narrative—working hard in mines and accumulating riches—and given that the most common garden dwarves tend to be toiling away with wheelbarrows, shovels, and axes, this interpretation already points toward what is arguably true of touristic endeavor in general: being a tourist is exhausting work, and (like dwarves) most people look funny, or aberrant from their habitual existence while they are engaged in it. Other symbols of this nature are ladybugs made of painted flat stones; but dwarves are more potent and numerous in this and many other sites. Trebesing claims to be the first village in the world to be exclusively devoted to baby tourism. Its choice of marketing strategy grew from serendipitous circumstance.[13] According to one Carinthian tourism administrator interviewed in summer 1996, "Carinthia was a place where even in 1980 you couldn't get a high chair in a restaurant." The baby hotel, and, building on it, the baby village, was at least for this area an ingenious innovation. Fifteen years later, there are many imitations in other regions of Austria, and the Diaper Hiking Mile was developed in the early 1990s, precisely to keep up with the growing competition.[14] Though perhaps inspired by large-scale theming enterprises, such as Germany's *Die Deutsche Märchenstrasse* (Hemme 2009; Richter 1994), the Diaper Hiking Mile is pedestrian not just in practice but also in artistic execution. The dominant element in this site is nature. The path is broad in places, and sufficiently so even to push a baby cart, but walking amidst huge pine trees, or along a slippery wooden bridge passage next to a cliff, one cannot forget for a moment that one is outdoors in a high-altitude environment. Along the path, stories turned into painted cardboard, wood, and plastic are placed atop the natural landscape. *Lucky Hans* is recognizable by the goose under his arm; a little wooden structure can be identified as Hansel and Gretel's gingerbread house, and Snow White and the Seven Dwarves looking distinctly Disneyesque are here as well.

For those interested in the traditional narrative experience of the literate West, story texts are provided on metal plates made to look vaguely like storybooks, and chained to a metal storage receptacle. Families are meant to sit on the bench, then the narrator can pull the storybook out of its niche and read, for example, the tale of "The Magic Table" (*Tischlein Deck-Dich*). After the reading, the book is to be put back into its storage space on the bench. Thus, while figurines are nestled into the landscape, signaling the unruly forest and mountain as the space where such fiction resides, their association with books to be read out loud is scripted into this setup as well. The folkloristic endeavor of tale-collecting and publication, as well as the romantic spirit that located European legendry and tales in the wilds of nature, are then all part of what shaped this particular touristic endeavor.

To further control the way a family might take in this mile, a pencil is given to each child at the beginning of the hike, along with a checklist asking questions about all the tale and legend characters to be spotted, as well as about various plants and tree species that are flagged along the way. A field of learning and knowing is thus created, mixing real/natural and materialized/fictional elements. Filling out the form correctly results in further material benefit—a lollipop to be picked up at an inn at the end of the trail. Suddenly we realize that the experience of hiking through fiction, and the sense of vacation as play and time "away from it all" have acquired an undercurrent of school-like test-and-reward structures. To follow on Horkheimer and Adorno (quoted in Featherstone 1995, 18): "Amusement under late capitalism is the prolongation of work."

Along the path are various diaper-changing stations indicating that families are meant to spend hours along this rather short trail. The first such station is called a "diapering oasis."[15] Here we also find an open-air restaurant, each bench adorned with the pacifier designation. Right next to it is a Wild West playground and, at some distance, an Indian tepee circle.[16] The context here immediately explains what might otherwise require a lengthy account: in this European setting the American frontier experience and the Native American encounter with whites has been mediated by fiction. Playing Cowboy and Indian often enacts very specific fictional texts typically drawing from Karl May's popular trilogy about Winnetou and Old Shatterhand (see Plaul 1989). These fictions certainly saturate the popular imagination, further enriched by a neighboring valley's annual Karl May open-air plays, geared toward adult and youth consumption alike. The film industry has provided far more concrete templates for materialized imagination than the Grimm tales and similar folktale collections, and hence it should not surprise that among all the elements of this particular site, the Wild West playground is by far the most elaborate structure.[17]

The Diaper Hiking Mile thus assimilates and synchronizes diachronic layers of narration and fiction which took shape at particular historical junctures and which, through writing, printing, film, and enactment took on concrete contours at various moments in time. Unlike a theme park environment that seeks to fully control the visitor's experience, the Trebesing setup does no more than dot the landscape. Any major rain- or snowstorm affects the structures; potentially it could eliminate the entire site.

CONCLUDING QUESTIONS

What is to be gleaned from examples such as these, and what kinds of questions arise from them? For one, the Carinthian narrative theming of landscapes and built environments demonstrates the *surface dominance* of particular styles and corresponding ideologies in narrative materialization, as well as the localized interpretations and alterations of a globalizing strategy (see Robertson 1994). Disney aims to deliver an authoritative, globally adaptable system of narrative materialization, enforced with a reach into the international market that is quite unparalleled. Disney's narrative adaptations, whether in film or in theme park, are cordoned off and aim for perfection in terms of style, content, and control (Project on Disney 1995).

The quality of materialized narrative in Carinthia—heterogeneous and perhaps amateurish to those who have experienced a closed-off theme park site of the Disneyland variety—is evidence for a quite different and fragmented ideology. It attests to the layered, sometimes competing constituencies in Austrian tourism development and consumption. The Coca-Colonization of Austria (Wagnleitner 1991) has not necessarily transformed native aesthetic and economic patterns. Behind the borrowed products and images reside older preferences of display, and very different scales of conceiving of profit to be gained from materialized fiction. The Diaper Hiking Mile—free of charge for those who held the Carinthia Card, and almost free for everyone else—was meant as an attraction enhancing the location, and the real profit was to be made through nights and meals sold. By comparison, the *Märchenwald* (tale forest) in Styria's St. Georgen, founded in 1993, is slightly more costly, but here, too, it is the profit made from selling meals and trinkets that carries the enterprise.[18] Run by the *Schnitzelwirt* (also known as "Gasthof Sonnenhof"), whose menu predictably consists of schnitzel, this site consists of a mixture of largely animated sites (with hedgehog and bear figures familiar from German picture book illustrations), play equipment, and quite elaborate tale scenes nestled into the forest. Though an attempt is made to pipe children's music into the space, it is ultimately the tall trees and the loud voices of children at play that dominate the environment.[19]

The idea of a *Märchenpark* already enjoyed popularity in the early twentieth century (see Stein 1997), and in the margins of present-day high tech amusement parks one sometimes finds remnants of such earlier, milder pleasures. They were generally located near urban centers, unlike the kinds of sites discussed here, which thematize fractions of the natural environment for vacationers far from cities. The folktale as utopia remains consistent, but its place of materialized residence is shifting.

As sites of narrative materialization and consumption, each of these sites is fascinating in its own right. The placement and nature of statuary reveals cultural assumptions about where narrative resides. The popularity of the forest setting (a quite Germanic idea, cf., Lehmann 2000), emblazoned on the collective imagination in framed story collections (e.g., the German *Das Wirtshaus im Spessart*) lives on in name, even if some touristic tale forests are more tamed and peopled. Yet, the bourgeois sentiment of a tale properly belonging in a book is also preserved here, as an "abbreviated" book appearing on a metal tablet chained to a bench might be. Each site practices a wild coexistence of narrative genres and allusions to narrative media. Is it only the themed environment that wildly mixes illustrated children's books, folktales, young adult fiction, histories of conquest, and mythologies of so called "primitive peoples," thereby flying in the face of scholarly efforts at generic differentiation between the oral and the literate, and between countless genres amongst them? Or are fields of experience such as those in Carinthia testimony to the ways in which layers of narrative media and genres, as well as layers of history and colonial appropriation all coalesce into a tentative, transcultural, transgeneric, and transmedial space—a space where not genres and media, but experiences of fictional possibilities, past and present, are consumed?

The narrative theme sites offered in Carinthia could, precisely because of their heterogeneous and amateurish execution, contain a greater potential for constructing such a utopian space than the homogeneously styled worlds of Disney. But utopias—and the potential upheaval associated with them—is hardly the goal of a tourist enterprise. The tourist industry, rather, appeals to the touristic desire for utopian difference, and profits from the desire. And here, the heterogeneity of Carinthia's sites is less of an asset, for how can one predict how and through which kinds of artifacts visitors will relate or generate narrative memory? How predictable is a common denominator for such artifacts? Themed environments like Trebesing's count on the broad appeal of a very narrow aesthetic selection from the vast store of art historical evidence of narrative reification. Lacking the unifying gloss of the successfully themed environment, the bricolage of images invokes (but does not spell out) a common denominator where there may not be one. Radomir Runzelschuh's folktale automat discussed at the beginning epitomize the serialized artifact "folktale" (Lau 2000). The narrative reifications in themed environments seek to serialize tale, or more broadly, narrative experiences into a profitable branch of tourism. Yet, the jump between a folktale dispenser and a fiction-based experience dispenser is vast, and possibly negotiated far more effectively in virtual space than atop very real natural landscapes.

Though initiated in an attempt to shore up unstable tourism revenue, the frailty of some of these sites parallels the frailty of Austrian tourism. Although Austria looks back at two hundred years of touristic practice, the competition from destinations spanning the globe is strong and rising.[20] Perhaps, for a touristically exhausted region such as Austria, constructing a fictional overlay is not just an effort to copy American practices. Perhaps it rather seems like a natural course of action, not least because the wonder and magic of Austria's real landscape are believed to be too familiar for potential consumers.

The tourist trade builds on global economic presumptions and connections. It is the biggest, and perhaps most unpredictable trade to pursue, precisely because the market highs shift from the Alps to Tibet, and from luxury to adventure with little warning. For a country with a long history and dependency on touristic development, the global reach of tourism is devastating. It forces family businesses enmeshed in local tourism rivalries to acquaint themselves with marketing strategies and national, or even European Union policies spelling out which kind of tourism will receive state support. Better than the analyses of distraught Austrian industry experts could ever explain it, the Carinthian narrative materializations embody their producers' wavering between global strategies, European horizons, and local sensibilities.[21]

NOTES

This article appeared originally in *Ethnologia Europaea* 29 (1999): 29–40.
The fieldwork was supported by summer research grants from the University of Pennsylvania Research Foundation 1995 and 1996; the phenomena documented and analyzed were observed during those summers and have almost certainly been adjusted to new touristic interest. Thanks go to the tourist industry representatives who were interviewed and who provided me with a great deal of print materials on aspects of Carinthian tourism. The writing was supported by a National Endowment for the Humanities Fellowship for university teachers. Versions of this article were presented at the American Folklore Society Meetings in Austin, Texas, October 1997, and at the International Society for Narrative Research Congress in Göttingen, Germany, July 1998. Thanks go to Barbara Kirshenblatt-Gimblett for her stimulating comments, to Lee Haring and Kim Lau for their suggestions for revision, to Cristina Bacchilega and Konrad Köstlin for pointing me to further sites, and to my family for fieldwork assistance.

1. Since this article first appeared, numerous researchers have taken up the materialization of narrative as well as narrating through materials. Two recent examples are Fanfani (2016) and Salamon (2016).

2. Thanks to Sabine Wienker Piepho and Ingo Schneider for this information.

3. I saw the sedan chair in operation only once in August 1998, and doubt that it will break into the market easily, as the horse-drawn carriages are very firmly established in Vienna's Center City. The chair operators do, however, fit quite seamlessly into the spectrum of costumed appeals to tourists along Vienna's Kärntnerring. The whole area stretching from the Sacher Hotel and the Opera to the Stefansdom generally teems with young men and women in Baroque dress, trying to sell tickets for the popular Mozart and Strauss concerts, performed in period dress as well. They constitute their own materialization, not of fictional but rather historical imaginations in everyday life. On the fascination with historic reenactment for personal as well as commercial purposes, see Fenske (2007, 2013).

4. For discussions on theming landscapes, see Gottdiener (1997), Janowski and Ingold (2012), Schama (1995); Salazar (2010) considers the role of tour guides in assisting the creation of imaginaries.

5. The Valtice and Lednice area in today's Czech Republic is a splendid example of such aristocratic landscape theming. Here, the Liechtenstein family dotted their vast lands with follies such as Greek temples, Scottish ruins, and Islamic minarets. I am indebted to Veronica Aplenc for pointing me to this site; she has researched issues of historic preservation in this region (Aplenc 1997).

6. Regarding the efforts to market to the demand for experience, compare, Kirshenblatt-Gimblett (1998, 139–40).

7. There is a certain helplessness on the part of tourism managers to rationalize this procedure, evident from the following quote: "The 'tourist experience' is the culmination of a given experience which can be influenced by individual, environmental, situational, and personality related factors, as well as the degree of communication between people. It is the outcome ... which researchers and the tourism industry constantly evaluate to establish if the actual experience met the tourist's expectations. In other words, the 'tourist experience' is a complex amalgam of factors which shape the tourist's feelings and attitude towards his or her visit. Yet as tourism motivation and consumer research suggests, it is almost impossible to predict tourist responses to individual situations but a series of interrelated impacts may affect the tourist's experience" (Page 1995, 24).

8. This is of course in accordance with the tourist market in general which is driven by supply differentiation. The growth of a family-oriented tourism supply will also bring with it the growth of establishments or services for adults only in addition to services such as child care or children's camps to free parents for the adult only offering.

9. During summer 1996, there were small posters all over the Carinthian region between Klagenfurt and Villach advertising locally produced Little Red Riding Hood dolls. During Villach's big summer fair in August, the annual *Kirchtag*, we even encountered someone impersonating Little Red Riding Hood hawking her own image, this very doll.

10. One of the animators I observed in several settings, and subsequently interviewed, indicated that creative artists like himself had been practicing in the area for more than two decades, and the formalization of their tie-in to the Carinthian tourist offerings was a more recent development, associated with the increasing but not necessarily successful efforts to coordinate the tourist industry on the state and federal level.

11. The local tourist offices adjust to Del Vede's independent spirit, as he is a big draw for many children and thus also their parents. One day when I was there, Del Vede failed to make the show, and a substitute had to be found quickly. "He'll say that he's an artist, and artists cannot always be bothered," lamented the exasperated innkeeper at the facility where the show was to take place. "But good artists honor their commitments!" More than fifty families with children were milling about the premises, and the innkeeper naturally feared for his reputation, for Del Vede's was well established.

12. According to nanologist (dwarf researcher) Gerolf Urban: "Garden dwarves represent humankind's eternal longing for enlivening nature. Childhood is a time of unlimited fantasy which we never completely conquer. The dwarves offer us a return into this beautiful, and—compared to our total life span—much-too-short time" (Dwarf Park 1996 brochure).

13. According to one field consultant, the genesis was as follows: a young man inherited a family inn close to bankruptcy; he had small children himself, and the idea to target families with very small children germinated over many rounds of drink with friends also in the tourist business.

14. The summer 1998 advertising for Swiss tourism was also very heavily geared toward families, but in interesting ways it was trying to steer away from the "tasteless" and "touristic" by advertising itself as "non-touristic." Is this the ultimate in post-tourism? or just a spruced-up version of the old dichotomy between the tourists and the (positively valued) others who merely travel or vacation? See Buzard (1993) on the tourist/traveler dichotomy.

15. With a stretch of the imagination, one might see here a latent reference to *One Thousand and One Nights*, esp. since oasis is not a word usually associated with diapering.

16. For non-German audiences, the association of Wild West and Indian playacting devoid of any guilt is perhaps startling, but in the German-speaking area it is at least as widespread as the dwarves.

17. The history of travel-, exploration-, and conquest-turned-fiction, turned-play, turned-tourist destination is in itself an intriguing narrative that should be further explored.

18. While Disney Environments or parks, such as SeaWorld in Southern California (Davis 1997), also make considerable profit off concessions, toys, and trinkets, the entrance fee alone is already exorbitant, because the destination itself is conceptualized as the draw, not an added benefit to a vacation setting chosen for its landscape, rural architecture, or hotel facility.

19. Although I do not have access to any statistics, any observant traveler in the alpine regions of Austria, Switzerland, and Germany will notice that the number of these kinds of sites is growing, alongside the effort to expand and diversify "family tourism" offerings. A more complex event, supported by scholars from Innsbruck University, is the *Tiroler Bergsagen Festival*, held for the second time in July and August 1998, in Matrei, Tyrol, Austria. Here nature tourism is coupled with a revisiting of "magic" in landscape, art exhibitions, enactments and readings of legends, a book publication, and participatory activities for old and young. The festival won first prize in the category "event tourism," sponsored by a national tourism trade magazine in 1997.

20. In 1998, for the first time in more than a decade, Austria made gains in some sectors of tourism revenue; however, most of these gains were in urban centers, esp. Vienna, where in 1998, the one hundredth anniversary of Empress Sisi's death brought forth a flurry of special exhibits.

21. Throughout the 1990s, articles in the Austrian magazine *Profil*, as well as materials from the Austrian federal- and state-level tourism bureaus (not to speak of the local press) voiced their distress about the Austrian inability to hop onto the new waves, to get with it, to play in the big tourism stakes, to streamline housing offers, to collectively advertise, and to eliminate outdated inns and hotels.

## REFERENCES

Aplenc, Veronica E. 1997. "Conservation of Cultural Identity Through the Care of Monuments: Guidelines for the Lednice-Valtice Monument Zone." Master's thesis, University of Pennsylvania.

Baycroft, Timothy, and David Hopkin, eds. 2012. *Folklore and Nationalims in Europe During the Long Nineteenth Century*. Leiden: Brill.

Buzard, James. 1993. *The Beaten Track: European Tourism, Literature, and the Ways to "Culture" 1800–1918*. Oxford: Oxford University Press.

Dann, Graham M. S. 1996. *The Language of Tourism: A Sociolinguistic Perspective*. Wallingford: CAB International.

Davis, Susan G. 1997. *Spectacular Nature: Corporate Culture and the Sea World Experience*. Berkeley: University of California Press.

Dundes, Alan. 1985. "Nationalistic Inferiority Complexes and the Fabrication of Folklore: A Reconsideration of Ossian, the *Kinder- und Hausmärchen*, the *Kalevala*, and Paul Bunyan." *Journal of Folklore Research* 22 (1): 5–18.

Eco, Umberto. 1986. *Travels in Hyperreality*. San Francisco: Harvest.

Fanfani, Giovanni. 2016. *Spinning Fates and the Song of the Loom: The Uses of Textiles, Clothing, and Cloth Production as Metaphors, Symbol and Narrative Device in Greek and Latin Literature*. Oxford: Oxbow.

Featherstone, Mike. 1995. *Undoing Culture. Globalization, Postmodernism and Identity*. London: Sage.

Feifer, Maxine. 1985. *Going Places: The Ways of the Tourist from Imperial Rome to the Present Day*. London: Macmillan.

Fenske, Michaela. 2007. "Geschichte, wie sie Euch gefällt—Historische Doku-Soaps als spätmoderne Handlungs-, Diskussions- und Erlebnisräume." *Historizität* 13: 87–105.

———. 2013. "Vom Hobbyhandwerker zur feinen Dame: Doing Gender in spätmodernen Zeitreisen." In *Geschichte und Geschlecht in populären Medien*, 283–98. Bielefeld: transcript.

Gottdiener, Mark. 1997. *The Theming of America. Dreams, Visions, and Commercial Spaces*. Boulder, CO: Westview.

Greenhill, Pauline, and Sidney Eve Matrix, eds. 2010. *Fairy Tale Films: Visions of Ambiguity*. Logan: Utah State University Press.

Greenhill, Pauline, and Jill Terry Rudy. 2014. *Channeling Wonder: Fairy Tales on Television*. Detroit, MI: Wayne State University Press.

Haas, Hanns, Robert Hoffmann, and Kurt Luger, eds. 1994. *Weltbühne und Naturkulisse. Zwei Jahrhunderte Salzburg Tourismus*. Salzburg: Pustet.

Hemme, Dorothee. 2009. *Märchenstraße—Lebenswelten. Zur kulturellen Konstruktion einer touristischen Themenstraße*. Berlin: LIT.

Herzfeld, Michael. 1982. *Ours Once More. Folklore, Ideology and the Making of Modern Greece*. Austin: University of Texas Press.

Hopkin, David. 2012. *Voices of the People in Nineteenth-Century France*. Cambridge: Cambridge University Press.

Jafari, Jafar, and Richard M. Gardner. 1991. *Tourism and Fiction. Travel as Fiction, Fiction as a Journey*. Aix-en-Provence: Centre des hautes études touristiques.

Jeggle, Utz, and Gottfried Korff. 1974. "Zur Entwicklung des Zillertaler Regionalcharakters." *Zeitschrift für Volkskunde* 70: 39–57.

Janowski, Monica, and Tim Ingold, eds. 2012. *Imagining Landscapes: Past, Present, and Future*. Farnham: Ashgate.

Kirshenblatt-Gimblett, Barbara. 1998. *Destination Culture. Tourism, Museums and Heritage*. Berkeley: University of California Press.

Köstlin, Konrad. 1991. "Zu Intention und Praxis religiöser Erinnerung." In *Erinnern und Vergessen. Vorträge des 27. Deutschen Volkskundekongresses*, edited by Brigitte Bönisch-Brednich and Rolf W. Brednich, 427–40. Göttingen: Schmerse.

Lagerlöf, Selma. (1907) 1991. *The Wonderful Adventures of Nils Holgersson*. Translated by Velma Swanston Howard. Minneapolis, MN: Skandisk.

Lau, Kimberly. 2000. "Serial Logic: Folklore and Difference in the Age of Feel-Good Multiculturalism." *Journal of American Folklore* 113 (447): 70–82.

Leersen, Joep. Forthcoming. Gods, Heroes, and Mythologists: Romantic Scholars and the Pagan Roots of Europe's Nations. *History of Humanities*. (available on academia.edu)

Lehmann, Albrecht. 2000. *Der Wald—ein deutscher Mythos? Perspektiven eines Kulturthemas*. Berlin: Reimer.

MacCannell, Dean. 1976. *The Tourist. A New Theory of the Leisure Class*. New York: Schocken.

Oinas, Felix, ed. 1978. *Folklore, Nationalism, and Politics*. Columbus, OH: Slavica.

Page, Stephen. 1995. *Urban Tourism*. London: Routledge.

Plaul, Heiner. 1989. "May, Karl Friedrich." In *Enzyklopädie des Märchens* 9, edited by Rolf W. Brednich and Hermann Bausinger, 450–54. Berlin: De Gruyter.

Plochij, Serhij M. 2012. *The Cossack Myth: History and Nationhood in the Age of Empires*. Cambridge: Cambridge University Press.

Richter, Dieter. 1994. "Reisen ins Märchenland. Volkskulturelle Elemente im Tourismus und die Konstitution neuer Traditionen." In *Tourismus und Regionalkultur*, edited by Burkhard Pöttler and Ulrike Kammerhofer Aggermann, 95–105. Vienna: Selbstverlag des Vereins für Volkskunde.

Robertson, Roland. 1994. "Globalisation or Glocalisation?" *Journal of International Communication* 1 (1): 33–52.

Salamon, Hagar. 2016. "Embroidered Palestine. A Stitched Narrative." *Narrative Culture* 3 (1): 1–31.

Salazar, Noel. 2010. *Envisioning Eden: Mobilizing Imaginaries in Tourism and Beyond*. New York: Berghahn.

Schama, Simon. 1995. *Landscape and Memory*. London: Harper and Collins.

Spyri, Johanna. (1879) 1994. *Heidi*. New York: Grosset and Dunlap.

Stein, Helga. 1997. "Märchenpark." In *Enzyklopädie des Märchens* 9, edited by Rolf W. Brednich and Hermann Bausinger, 284–86. Berlin: De Gruyter.

The Project on Disney. 1995. *Inside the Mouse: Work and Play at Disney World*. Durham, NC: Duke University Press.

Urban, Greg. 1991. *A Discourse Centered Approach to Culture: Native South American Myths and Rituals*. Austin: University of Texas Press.

Urry, John. 1990. *The Tourist Gaze. Leisure and Travel in Contemporary Societies*. London: Sage.

Wagnleitner, Reinhold. 1991. *Coca-Colonisation und Kalter Krieg*. Vienna: Gesellschaftskritik.

Wilson, William A. 1976. *Folklore, Nationalism and Politics in Modern Finland*. Bloomington: Indiana University Press.

Zipes, Jack, Pauline Greenhill, and Kendra Magnus-Johnston. 2016. *Fairy-tale Films Beyond Disney*. International Perspectives. New York: Routledge.

# 3

⚜

# Fairy-Tale Activists: Narrative Imaginaries along a German Tourist Route (with Dorothee Hemme)

In 2005, the German Fairy Tale Street—or *Märchenstrasse*—will celebrate its thirtieth anniversary. Themed auto routes began to take shape in the 1950s and at the time when this particular initiative took shape, there were already around sixty registered themed auto routes in Germany (Deutsche Märchenstraße e.V.). One might consider such routes a special instance of what the Austrian ethnologist Bernhard Tschofen (2003) terms "hyphenated landscapes"—that is, regions that take on a label which stresses an economic as much as a cultural resource. Cars had become more affordable and allowed individuals to plot their leisure and vacation trips in more individualistic ways. Instead of hiking tours, people undertook motorized journeys—and travel guides with titles like *The Automobile Driver as Hiker* (Ess 1958) or *Hiking by Car* (Springorum 1963) attest to the transformation of locomotion if not terminology. The experience of built and natural environment was mediated in considerably faster speed than on foot or bicycle, and points to elements beyond John Urry's "gaze" that are of relevance in understanding tourist experience (1990).[1] Travelling by car enlarged the sense of how much could be taken in during a single journey and privileged a stop-and-go mode: stretches of high-speed travel could be followed by intensive interaction with selected places. The themed route developed, then, in tandem with faster means of locomotion. Simultaneously, such routes reached topically and symbolically back to the idea of historical routes: foot paths, river routes, Roman routes, even the Silk Route, with their connection to imagined and real pasts (Scharfe 1991). The "Romantic Street," the "Half-Timbered Housing Street," the "Street of Mills," or even the "Asparagus Street" employ what is considered a culturally attractive resource to assist automobile tourists in plotting their travel routes thematically. For the route running from the Grimm Brothers' birthplace—Hanau—to the city of Bremen, the cultural capital in question is narrative. So it was decided by an enterprising politician and a few entrepreneurs in and around Kassel a city where the Brothers Grimm worked as librarians for a number of years, and where a museum is devoted to their work and life. Had it not been for the division of Germany up to 1989, the route would undoubtedly have run to Berlin—the last place of work and residence of Wilhelm and Jacob. Instead, in 1975, the city prominently associated with one of the tales—"The Bremen Town Musicians," number twenty-seven in the Grimms' Children-and-Household Tales—was chosen to terminate the route.

In the course of nearly thirty years, more than sixty towns and villages have joined this loose touristic collaborative.[2] Some places, such as Hamelin, of Pied Piper fame, are extremely active with a play, statuary, legend-related foods (do not bite into the baked rats, they are meant to be ornamental!), and a musical.[3] Others use the folktale theme only as one among a number of options to market themselves. In addition, the generic term "folktale" is employed very liberally: legends, historical materials, and literary biography (such as those of the author, illustrator, and satirist Wilhelm Busch, or the poet Annette Droste-Hülshoff) all mingle into one "fairy tale imaginary," at least as far as the central coordinators' plan is concerned.[4]

Despite all idiosyncrasies, the Fairy Tale Street as a whole, works on the principle that this central German landscape is deeply interwoven with the folktales and legends collected and published by the Brothers Grimm and others of their time. While natives will naturally associate familiar narrative plots, especially legends. with their region, the idea behind the endeavor was to invite tourists into this imaginary, and to help them envision it through festivities, plays, representational figures, and readings. Much as tourism theorists Coleman and Crang (2002) have argued, performances are being utilized to activate and associate the imaginary with a given place. How successful reifications of narratives are in providing visitors with a feel for their magic is not the focus of this presentation[5]—though we have heard even gentle elderly ladies quite cynically talk of just how fairy-tale-like even the soap in their hotel seemed to be.[6] Despite all efforts to craft travel in terms of a narratable journey, the meeting of enacted folk narrative and automotive traveler is—in terms of media, speed, and temperament—hardly harmonious.

Our project seeks to rather explore the extent to which narrative imaginaries appropriate the minds and hearts of individuals who work to promote them. Drawing on fourteen months of ethnographic and archival research from eight such communities, this paper focuses on what we term "fairy tale activists," that is, individuals who have engaged with particular vigor in the potent combination of landscape, built environment, and narrative imaginary. The paper offers brief glimpses into the differential biographical investment of actors involved in productions of highly diverse caliber. The activism of the figure of Dietrich the Knight is explored in more detail. It must be stated that while these biographical investments are in some cases phenomenally strong, the Fairy Tale Street is economically extremely frail. The fast pace of tourism promotion demands constant innovation to draw visitors back to places they have already seen—or so at least tourism professionals feel. For the individuals working along this route, however, narrative imaginaries with their often outdated or mixed and homemade aesthetics are lifelong commitments and hence traditions in their own right, which have long grown beyond the economic impetus that produced them.

## A SAMPLE OF FAIRY-TALE ACTIVISTS

The longest running narrative imaginary in our sample is Hamelin's Pied Piper. Festivities around this legend are documented as far back as 1884. In 1955, Friedrich Flügge, a high school teacher, took on the task of organizing a Pied Piper play with lay actors and many school children.[7] For half a century, Mr. Flügge invested himself into this activity and, in the process, won over a number of individuals to embrace the legend and its performance. For the Hannover Expo of 2000, a "Rats Musical" was added to the Pied Piper program. Up until 1994, the lead role of the Pied Piper was personified and thus owned by one actor alone, which required a time investment far beyond summer Sundays. The figure of the Pied

Piper—like all Fairy Tale personifications—must be ready for countless representational activities at city functions, tourism fairs, and events deemed relevant for Hamelin's profile. Pied Piper tourism works, there is no doubt about it; but there is a social investment behind it that has little to do with the success of tourism.[8]

Kalle Schmidt has been with the Hamelin play since 1974 and has personified the Pied Piper since 1986. He was handpicked by teacher Flügge and embraces the role with a complex mix of fascination with the character, responsibility toward the city, and veneration for his old teacher. For decades he shifted his vacations to fall or Easter, and accepted the fact that summer weekends were Pied Piper times. "The play is a tradition," he feels, and while it may not compare to glitzy Broadway entertainment, he regards the community-building aspect as phenomenally important. However, he would never give his time to guide tourists through town. Correspondingly, he views Hamelin's latest efforts to raise sufficient funds for building a giant rat as a rather misguided tourist venture.

A contrast in scope and orientation, but an activist in her own right, is Gudrun Grünberg. She quit teaching school twenty years ago and trained to become a professional storyteller, attended seminars of the European Märchen Society, and was booked for telling stories all over Lower Saxony and Hessia. She has learned about twenty Grimm tales by heart—a process which requires approximately four to six months, as she remains true to the text as edited by the Brothers Grimm. Her hometown, Neukirchen, has been part of the Fairy Tale Street for a long time but did not really get its act together to pick a focus. Mrs. Grünberg did not see herself in a tourist setting; in her opinion, the tourism promoters know next to nothing about the power of Märchen. "They are asleep," she says. "They sleep Sleeping Beauty's sleep." Otherwise they would not dream up such blatantly commercial tale worlds, but instead would recognize the depth of narration and fairy-tale plots.

When a house became vacant, Mrs. Grünberg seized the moment—she called the mayor and said, "this house has to become Neukirchen's Märchenhouse." The house was officially dedicated in 2003 and it is open year-round for storytelling and for a limited number of other dramatic and visual stagings. Mrs. Grünberg is committed to communicating what she perceives as the depth of folktales. She believes deeply in their being rooted in the landscape in which the Grimms collected them, and she will undoubtedly continue her efforts on behalf of Märchen, whether the Fairy Tale Street officials honor her services or not. Thus, while Neukirchen is financially in a disastrous position and has had to cut its tourism budget, Mrs. Grünberg keeps going, and buses, particularly of Japanese tourists, apparently keep coming.

There are many other individuals who have taken hold of particular stories and made it their task to give them life and live through them. Adolf Hahn has portrayed the historic figure of Baron Münchhausen.[9] Until the German aviation bureau forbade it in 1992, he flew on a cannonball suspended from a helicopter to the annual Festival of Lights in Bodenwerder; he performed the play countless times in this little town, and he learned the *Münchhausensong* in Russian and Japanese to perform it on tourism fairs in faraway places. His paying jobs have been far less spectacular, and his primary identification is undoubtedly with his fictional character.

The disciplinary genres of folk narrative research are of little interest to activists along this route—legend, history, biography, and fairy tales belong together in one larger imaginary. Most importantly, through narrative performance and enactment these fairy-tale activists achieve levels of self-realization that their regular lives do not permit. Recognizing the power or charm or nostalgia—or all of the above—that these activities yield for their individual lives, leading enactors are (for the most part) also quite at ease with the touristic dimensions of their doings. Most fairy-tale activists receive nothing, or next to nothing, for their efforts—but most of them regard their volunteering as a means to bring tourism revenue to their home towns.

## DIETRICH THE KNIGHT

Living a personal fantasy while contributing to the revenue of one's region is perhaps best exemplified in the most stunning activist we have encountered, Dietrich the Knight, who is also the most thoroughly involved in experiencing and interpreting the landscape as both home of and foil for narrative fragments.[10] Dietrich Uffelmann is an employee of the tourist information bureau in Hofgeismar, another community along the Fairy Tale Street, located in the Reinhard's Forest. This nearly primeval forest can be termed the richest landscape along this themed auto route. Within and around it are Sleeping Beauty's castle, as well as Rapunzel's tower.

For a good part of his work time, and for some of his free time as well, Mr. Uffelmann turns into Ritter Dietrich. A product of Mr. Uffelmann's lively imagination, Dietrich is a seven hundred-year-old knight who strides through the forest as he pleases. He inhabits the forest with a certitude and pleasure that few other fairy-tale activists along the route can claim for themselves. People who book his tours are given a meeting place, and at the appointed time, he magically appears as a knight in chain mail. The tourists amble under the guidance of this guardian of the woods through the forest and listen to excerpts of his vast store of knowledge and fantasy. Guiding his guests to a deep pond, he will tell the etiological legend about the evil giantess, Trendula, who was killed by lightning, giving the pond its name: "The watery green grave of Trendula the Giantess." Dietrich then goes on to tell of the legendary gambling Count Reinhard, to whom the forest owes its existence. He has no problem weaving in narratives from other cultures: pointing to ancient, gnarly trees he will describe them as turtles, mammoths, or the three-headed hellhound Cerberus. With these mindscapes, which Orvar Löfgren (1999) considers typical for touristic experience, Dietrich renders the forest into a symbolic space. He points to a circle of oaks and beeches and thinks out loud what a Germanic assembly space might have looked like. With younger participants, he tests and deepens their botanical knowledge of trees. He also makes maximum use of his knightly stature to propound moral lessons: "Only the weak pull the sword, the mighty fight to keep their composure," is his guiding principle. Foolhardy medieval knights who fought too often and too hard could easily die of gangrene. The visitor emerges from a walk with Dietrich imbued with the forest's magical nature and beauty; a receptive mind will be filled with a mixture of legendary mystery and botanical diversity.

Mr. Uffelmann was born in Trendelburg—where today Rapunzel lowers her hair, as she is the tale-figure the city adopted as its focus for the Fairy Tale Street. He is a native of the forest, so to speak. In his youth he not only explored the woods and the ruins; he was also a passionate reader of chivalrous romances.[11] He invented Dietrich in the mid-1990s, after having heard complaints from visitors that there was not enough of the fairy-talesque to experience. Representational figures like Sleeping Beauty, or Cinderella, the Carrot King of Heiligenstadt, or the Rose Queen of Hann Münden are, for Dietrich's own taste, too static, in particular for performing the regional treasure trove of legends. Thus, he worked out this alter ego, which creatively draws on his reading preferences and travel experiences, his own explorations of the region and conversations with other connoisseurs, stints within the reenactment scene and many years of working with tourists. He embodies the knight with ease, as the performances are genuinely part of him. "I do not have to think about this anymore, it is just fun to do."[12]

Successful touristic advertising offers a mixture of tradition and trend, and Mr. Uffelmann analogously ties traditional collective fantasies connected to the German forest to a late modern reality, thus creating a tension between expectation and surprise: appearing suddenly, seemingly out of nowhere, is an important element of his performance.[13] Seeing a living and breathing knight at the edge of a forest is not part of the everyday experience of the modern visitor, and the moment one begins one's tour with this apparition, one also leaves a piece of everyday reality behind. On the other hand, the knight belongs, as Simon Schama has observed in his *Landscape and Memory*, to the collective imaginary geography of the German forest (1996, 113–17). Thus the mere appearance of the knight rekindles recognition and imagination and potentially allows for an experience under a mythic fairy-talesque premise.

Knight Dietrich's personal reading of the forest at once enriches and subverts traditional interpretations of landscape: facing a tree that resembles a turtle, he narrates a creation myth from the South Sea. For his intention is also to clarify for his guests that "their own world ... is but a puzzle piece in a very large world, even if they and I do not know it well. [Stories of this sort] can be found everywhere; instead of the South Sea story with the turtle I could take another one [to explain this]."

Choosing material from international folk literature, Uffelmann brings, analogously to general social trends, new elements into this forest thus far connoted—and marketed—with national and regional narrative traditions. The familiar medium of folktale and legend transports what he considers timeless and supra-individual values and structures

of understanding with ease. As Knight Dietrich, he thus contributes
to making an unfamiliar, globalizing modernity more understandable.
He is the narrator of traditional forest mythologies and simultaneously
their transmitter into the present. The descriptive title Knight Dietrich
has chosen for himself is "preserver of old legends and bridge between
past and present." Working for many years with vacationers, journal-
ists, and tourism professionals, the persona of Dietrich the Knight has
gained clear contours and has become a figure that can be deployed
in many contexts: he performs on marketing fairs from Hamburg to
Shanghai, representing more than one tourism association. He serves as
Master of Ceremonies for Sleeping Beauty or Rapunzel at small village
festivities and at New Year's receptions for international business associations. Tourists as well as regional inhabitants favor his tours through
the woods and the castles. He guides through the primeval forest as well
as through an animal park located near the Saba Castle and through all
the castles and ruins of the region. The downtown areas he leaves for
other tourist guides to do—his armor is, in his opinion, not suited to
represent bourgeois urban history. When disappointed guests ask for
Dietrich the Knight, his guiding colleagues are instructed to say that
he is on a Crusade.

CONCLUSION

From the point of view of creating an intimate connection between narrative and landscape, Dietrich the Knight is at present the most successful character along the Fairy Tale Street. His versatility in deploying the
legendary as part of local tradition, environmental consciousness-raising,
and touristic promotion within one landscape is unique. Yet other fairy-
tale activists pursue other linkages—to narrative wisdom, to their community, and (undeniably) to the market.

The success of any site along this themed auto route depends almost
entirely on the voluntary and energetic involvement of one or two individuals. The question is, however, what is the measure of success? Looking
at the front stage once more, that is, the one the visitors are supposed
to take in, we can turn to the available promotional material. In 2004,

The German Tourism Association's site entitled its entry on our research subject "Back to Childhood on the German Fairy Tale Street." The text began with "Welcome to the world of brave princes, graceful fairies, modest peasant lads and puss-in-boots." (Deutschland Tourismus 2004; our translation).[14] On a wintry day, the writer surmised, one might see Frau Holle shake out her pillows. The cities were described as beautiful, as if set in fairy tales, and the traveler would thus be reminded of imaginaries carried with her since childhood.

We would suggest that such imaginaries present themselves to the tourist best while driving—in the fleeting moment of passing forests and hills, foggy riverbeds, and snowy landscapes. Listening to a narrator in the Märchenhouse, watching a marionette performance, or shadow play may succeed in drawing a visitor into the promised never-never land. But the confrontation with plastic statuary, lay actors' plays, and fellow humans in fairy-tale costumery may create a break in this imaginary born of memory and passing landscape.

Indeed, the quotidian breaks through the frame of performance as a matter of course. In MacCannell's (1976) by now classic suggestion concerning the tourist's search for everyday authenticity, the glimpse behind the touristic front stage appeared as a quintessential mark of touristic success. Along the Fairy Tale Street, with its open-air stages, exhibits, signs, and spaces of encounter, staged, imaginary, and everyday instantiations mix, often without the clear-cut framing devices expected of "performance".[15] A number of the Cinderellas and Sleeping Beauties encountered speak a hefty dialect and converse in the vocabulary of a twenty-first-century teen who rides a motorcycle when she is not in her princess costume. Hence a good portion of goodwill and versatile pleasure-taking is necessary on the part of the tourist: biting into a slice of Pied Piper cake, a Cinderella cookie, or a Münchhausen cannonball, purchasing fragments of narratives as postcards, puppets, or key chains, and witnessing fairy-tale plays that bespeak the talent and budget of enthusiastic volunteers open one's eyes perhaps not so much to the fairy-tale imaginary, but to the intensely personal and communal endeavor to build and maintain the real world rather than tale worlds in the middle of Germany.

Recent theorizing in tourism studies accords a crucial space to the conjunction of place and performance in creating effective touristic

imaginaries (Coleman and Crang 2002). The focus may have rested too
strongly on sites that intend to project complete worlds, that is, hermetically sealed entertainment worlds where the everyday remains invisible.
Thus Kirshenblatt-Gimblett has argued that performances get routinized
and in the process trivialize that which is performed (1996, 64). But in
our case, with stages open to all sides and reaching into landscapes as
far as the eye wants to see, the experience of tourists and especially of
independent producers, such as the actors and activists along the Fairy
Tale Street, differs considerably. While a decade or more of staging a
narrative creates a certain level of routine, this does not trivialize experience; rather, there is a deepening of the identification with the narrative
material. Many of the activists are very successful in what the literature
of the turn of this century calls "locality production," enhancing home
for themselves.

Most of them are, however, only marginally successful in the eyes
of tourism entrepreneurs. The Fairy Tale Street teetered toward its
thirty-year jubilee in 2006 amidst considerable economic woes, caused,
according to some of its internal critics, by too many different and not
sufficiently glossy local contributions—in short, a lack of coherent and
convincing design and implementation.[16] Meanwhile, the "Legend Path
along the Rhein" was nearing conceptual completion, coordinated by a
single tourism promotion agency in Cologne. The official inauguration of
this new themed tourism route was to be in fall 2004; forty-eight towns
from Düsseldorf to Mainz planned to show one legend each, and its internet portal promised "the Legendary, the Historic, the Recommended"
(Rheinromantik 2012). In the meantime, this path has been integrated
in the larger framework of the Rhein Romance (Rheinromantik 2017).
And in the East, the adjoining state of Thuringia in the former GDR is
considering a "Legend and Ghost Street"; if it comes to pass, the name of
this imaginary is semantically all too fitting for a depopulating landscape
filled with splendid castle ruins of distant times and the ruins of social-
ism. For tourism, much like mining or steel refineries, which have turned
into sites of labor tourism, is also accumulating its own histories of labor,
leisure, and imagination, whose new and old ruins become part of the
toured landscape.

This chapter appeared originally in *Tautosakos Darbai* 21 (Folklore Studies, Lithuanian Institute of Literature and Folklore, XXI, 2004):187–97.

The research for this paper was supported by a grant from the Ministry of Science and Culture of Lower Saxony, Germany (2003–06), and resulted in the dissertation of this chapter's coauthor (Hemme 2009b). Interviews cited in this paper were carried out in 2003–04.

1. Schivelbusch (1989) develops an understanding of travel with increasing speed in his study on railways and how they altered notions of time and space.

2. The membership fluctuates. At present, around sixty cities and towns are listed, but members join or drop out, depending on budgets, changing emphases in local marketing strategies, and local interest. For a full listing of the members, see Deutsche Märchenstraße e.V. (2017).

3. Since the initial publication of this paper, the German UNESCO commission accepted Hamelin's identification with the Pied Piper on the German register for immaterial heritage; after the state of Lower Saxony recommended it, it was accepted by the federal state in 2014. Cf. Deutsche UNESCO Kommission (2017).

4. The linkage between narrative, literary imagination, literary biographies, and touristic development has been the focus of a considerable amount of research; see the introductory summary in Robinson and Andersen (2002).

5. For a treatment of this aspect, see "On the Road to Fiction" in this volume.

6. Visit Fieldnotes, Sababurg, September 2, 2004, overheard in the restrooms of the restaurant: "Jaja, es ist ja einfach alles märchenhaft hier" ("yes, yes, everything is just like in a fairy tale here")—spoken by an elderly lady to another who seemed to find the soap dispenser rather too modern and the efforts of the hotel with its Sleeping Beauty theme a bit overblown.

7. According to archival records, the Pied Piper Play started in 1949, and Mr. Flügge is generally named as the person behind it, but he himself provides 1955 as the time when he began participating in earnest.

8. In the early twenty-first century, for instance, many of the children participating in the play are Turkish-German, in part for the free ice cream after each performance, in part because unlike their German peers they likely have less opportunity for summer holidays and are thus available.

9. For a very early rendering of Baron von Münchhausen's "lying stories," see Raspe [1820].

10. Interviews with Mr. Uffelmann have taken place throughout the duration of this project; he has been accompanied on several of his tours and has been interviewed in his workplace and during tourism fairs as well.

11. He came to the tourist business on a circuitous route, having worked in city administration earlier.

12. His concept of nature with which he fashions a touristic experience for others, is based on mental engagement and personal experience in many forests:

> The primeval forest around Sababurg presents constantly changing pictures for me, each guided tour is totally different ... If I tell once that in this group of trees there are giants who have fought, the scene looks different the next

time, it is a new image because a couple branches have fallen. Sure, you find this
in every forest, mushrooms might sprout or there might be new and strange
looking growths. I spend a lot of time in other forests, so I am not blinded by my
local work space, there (are plenty of forests) from North to South and East to
West..., and you find stories (to go with them) everywhere, too.

13. In order not to spoil this effect, Uffelmann parks his car a ways away.

14. This was the description at the time of the original writing of this article; in the meantime, the website has been completely altered—not surprisingly, since the branding activities on national tourism sites tends to have a short half-life.

15. Coleman and Crang's point that tourists tend to take in more than they are meant
to might require revision for these sites where the separation of front and back stage is not
upheld very firmly by performers themselves, and where the "power of framing" is handled
quite differently, depending on the age and experience of the performers (2002, 13–15).

16. Since the initial publication of this article, the *Märchenstraße* has weathered various
storms but has managed to remain an association of participating communities rather than
transforming into a corporation. The various jubilee activities surrounding the two hundredth anniversary since the first publication of the Children- and-Household-Tales in 1812
has given new energy to some participating communities, and additional scholarship on the
intertwining of the Brothers Grimm, their narrative collections, and their joint impact on
culture and tourism has been undertaken (e.g., Zimmermann 2009; Hemme 2009b).

## REFERENCES

Coleman, Simon, and Mike Crang. 2002. *Tourism: Between Place and Performance.*
    New York: Berghahn.
Deutsche Märchenstraße e.V. N.d. "Einige (nützliche) Informationen zur Deutschen
    Märchenstraße." Information brochure. Kassel, Germany: Deutsche Märchenstraße e.V.
Deutsche Märchenstraße e.V. 2017. "Mitgliedsorte." Accessed May 4. http://www
    .deutsche-maerchenstrasse.com/de/reisen/reiseziele/mitgliedsorte/.
Deutschland Tourismus. 2004. "Deutsche Märchenstraße." Accessed Sep 30. http://www
    .deutschland-tourismus.de/d/2940.html (page deleted).
Deutsche UNESCO Kommission 2017. "Auseinandersetzung mit dem Rattenfänger von
    Hameln." Accessed May 4. https://www.unesco.de/kultur/immaterielles-kulturerbe
    /bundesweites-verzeichnis/eintrag/auseinandersetzung-mit-dem-rattenfaenger-von
    -hameln.html.
Ess, Jakob. 1958. *Der Automobilist als Wanderer.* Zurich: Buchverlag der Neuen Zürcher
    Zeitung.
Hemme, Dorothee. 2009a. "Die Deutsche Märchenstraße. Eine touristische
    Themenstraße auf den Spuren der Brüder Grimm." In *Zwischen Identität und Image—
    die Popularität der Brüder Grimm in Hessen,* edited by Harm-Peer Zimmermann,
    204–35. Marburg: Jonas.
———. 2009b. *Märchenstraßen—Lebenswelten. Zur kulturellen Konstruktion einer
    touristischen Themenstraße.* Münster: LIT.

Kirshenblatt-Gimblett, Barbara. 1998. *Destination Culture. Tourism, Museums and Heritage.* Berkeley: University of California Press.

Löfgren, Orvar. 1999. *On Holiday. A History of Vacationing.* Berkeley: University of California Press.

MacCannell, Dean. 1976. *The Tourist. A New Theory of the Leisure Class.* New York: Schocken.

Raspe, Rudolf Erich. 1820. *Die wahre Kunst, dergestalt zu lügen, daß es der Mühe lohnt, gedruckt zu werden; oder: Wunderbare Reisegeschichten des Freiherrn v. Münchhausen.*

Rheinromantik. 2012. "Der rheinische Sagenweg." Accessed Oct 23. http://www.rheinromantik.de/der-rheinische-sagenweg-am-romantischen-rhein/ (site discontinued).

Rheinromantik 2017. "Route der Rheinromantik." Accessed July 15. https://www.ferienstrassen.info/route-der-rheinromantik/.

Robinson, Mike, and Andersen, Hans Christian, eds. 2002. *Literature and Tourism.* London: Thomson.

Schama, Simon. 1996. *Der Traum von der Wildnis. Natur als Imagination.* Munich: Kindler.

Scharfe, Martin. 1991. "Die alte Straße. Fragmente." In *Reisekultur. Von der Pilgerfahrt zum modernen Tourismus,* edited by Hermann Bausinger, Klaus Beyrer, and Gottfried Korff, 11–22. Munich: Beck.

Schivelbusch, Wolfgang. 1989. *Geschichte der Eisenbahnreise: Zur Industrialisierung von Raum und Zeit im 19. Jahrhundert.* Frankfurt: Fischer.

Springorum, Friedrich. 1963. *Mit dem Auto wandern.* Munich: Süddeutscher.

Tschofen, Bernhard. 2003. "Bindestrichlandschaften. Die erzählte Region als Identitätsressource." In *Montanlandschaft Erzgebirge. Kultur—Symbolik—Identität,* edited by Sönke Löden, 13–26. Leipzig: Leipziger Universitätsverlag.

Urry, John. 1990. *The Tourist Gaze. Leisure and Travel in Contemporary Societies.* London: Sage.

Zimmermann, Harm-Peer. 2009. *Zwischen Identität und Image: Die Popularität der Brüder Grimm in Hessen.* Marburg: Jonas.

# 4

⚯

## Capitalizing on Memories Past, Present, and Future: Observations on the Intertwining of Tourism and Narration

On a spring day in 2000, I found myself in New York City's Central Park. Exiting the subway station at Central Park West and heading across the street into the park, I found a bench near a meadow called Strawberry Fields. Having grown up in Europe in the 1960s and 1970s, my memory instantly called up the Beatles song: "Strawberry Fields Forever," a voice sang in my head. After sitting for a while on that bench, I noticed groups of people, as well as individuals, who kept stopping at a black and white, circular mosaic at the park entrance. I heard Canadian French, German, British English, and languages I could not understand. Group pictures were taken. Someone left a bunch of carnations. Someone else knelt down on the circle. Another rearranged the flowers before taking a picture. After a while, a CD player with two speakers was set down on the circle. A young man with long, well-groomed hair, round sunglasses, and tattoos all over his bare arms instructed his girlfriend on the use of his video camera and then posed next to the mosaic. Another visitor to the park, sharing the bench I sat on, illuminated me in my ignorance. "That apartment building is the Dakota," he said, pointing to an apartment building. Seeing this meant nothing to me, he added, "John Lennon was shot in front of the Dakota." Suddenly, the circular mosaic made sense. In its center was the word "Imagine," evoking John Lennon's famous song for peace. What I was witnessing was the touristic pilgrimage to the memorial of a popular music idol of the twentieth century.[1]

Central Park is emblematic for the joint origins and blurred boundaries between urban leisure and tourist sites. Tourism is an outgrowth of both industrialization and democratization. The differentiation between work and non-work, and the accumulation of spending capital has facilitated leisure for social classes beyond Veblen's ([1899] 1967) "Leisure Class." The land for Central Park was set aside in 1853 and its appearance designed by Fredrick Law Olmsted (who won the design contest of 1857) with the intent to create a space for regeneration and relaxation in the rapidly growing immigrant port city. The park's construction displaced "roughly 1,600 poor residents, including Irish pig farmers and German gardeners, who lived in shanties on the site," as well as Seneca Village which "had been one of the city's most stable African-American settlements, with three churches and a school" (Central Park 2017). Their traces are visible only in historical documents, including the park's web page, but the stories of the displaced are not part of the park's extensive repertoire of tourist narrations.[2]

Other memories have, however, been scripted into the landscape. Among the thirty-two named "Sculptures, Memorials, Fountains," the forty-five "Features/Areas," and the twenty-two "Buildings" located in Central Park, one can discern the influence of different constituencies in naming and claiming portions of this space. Different periods in New York's history are registered in the statuary, though for the visitor, distinct phases of the city and park's history are all amalgamated or jumbled together into one momentary appearance. "Iphigene's Walk," "The Tempest," and statues of Beethoven and Shakespeare point to cultured lovers of everything from Greek mythology to theater and classical music. Mother Goose and Alice in Wonderland sculptures render material and concrete what were mental sites of whimsy and fantasy. The sculpture of the Indian Hunter and the memorial to the 107th Civil War Regiment evoke, albeit in ideologically vastly different ways, memories of conflict. Some statues, such as those of Albert Thorvaldsen, King Wladyslav Jagiello, and Giuseppe Manzini, require, at least for the young twenty-first-century visitor, a tour guide's explanation. These stories no longer resonate, and the ethnic groups that once felt a need to erect such symbols have entered another phase of assimilation.[3] "Strawberry Fields" and the "Imagine" memorial may very well have supplanted earlier, no longer broadly shared associations with the spaces they occupy. Likewise, the Dakota, long part of the New York City tour as "the oldest apartment building in New York," has now become, in German, Italian, and French tours, the "John Lennon House."

Short glimpses from sites such as Central Park are unique in their location and resonance, yet completely typical for any touristic site in terms of the kinds of practices tourists and tourism providers are likely to engage in. What I undertake in this chapter is a sketch of the deep interrelationship of narration with the endeavor of tourism, using a number of specific examples to characterize the typical. The tourist is, Dean MacCannell has argued, the quintessential representative of the modern condition (1976). The narratives that create and surround tourism are then evidence for understanding this condition—which may be neither modern nor postmodern but perhaps enduringly human.[4] After years of scorning the subject intellectually, the critical, intelligent writing that has been devoted to the tourism complex in recent years indicates the growing recognition of the centrality of tourism to the project of being human.[5] My major question, which may not necessarily find an answer in this essay, is the following: are the patterns of narration and memorialization we can observe finite, or is our narrative potential capable of helping us dream or think our way out of the patterns which invariably seem to lead to commoditization?

## TOURISM: MATERIAL NEEDS, MENTAL GOALS

During the last quarter of the twentieth century, tourism grew exponentially and globally. Today, it is the biggest employer worldwide. What is tourism? If we look at the academic journal production in the realm of tourism, leisure, and hospitality and recreation studies, tourism is a business preoccupied with facilitating transportation, lodging, nourishment, guidance, and various bodily and cultural leisure pursuits. It is a business, in short, that provides work for people serving other people who have taken leave from their work. The first studies of tourism were carried out in the field of economics, and economic issues—employment, development, and profit—remain what governments stress in analyzing tourism as part of their nation's assets.

Regular industries build on the consumer satisfaction gained from a material product: a well-functioning automobile or refrigerator, well-made paper, and tasty, affordable food are likely to bring the consumers back when they need more. Yet while tourism needs to supply a great deal of material satisfaction, what ultimately carries the business is the *intangible experience* of the customer.[6] As we can glean from Orvar Löfgren's (1999) history of vacationing, *being on holiday is largely a state of mind*. While it is the body that is physically set in motion and that needs to be taken care of as it travels away from the familiar safety of home, it is the mind that craves the experience and that will process the peregrination into strips to be remembered and communicated.[7]

As in all human endeavors, the material conditions we create through labor facilitate the thoughts, dreams, experiences, and memories that distinguish humans as a species. Examining the breadth of narration surrounding tourism production and experience demonstrates the versatile potency of narrating in, at once, creating, commoditizing, and critiquing an enormous, transcultural phenomenon and the joys, foibles, and pains humans have brought on themselves through this phenomenon. My observations build on Western practice and sensibility, which arguably has instigated the global spread of the tourism complex. But I want to make clear that I do not wish to make claims for a universal kind of applicability of what I outline here. If anything, I would hope that from other regions, alternate histories, practices and sensibilities could be brought into the discussion.[8]

## THE AURA OF THE TOURIST EXPERIENCE

Touristic memory and its narration are fueled by both actual and desired experience.[9]

Touristic experience is far less predictable than regular product satisfaction, and, what is worse, touristic experience has an inbuilt drive for something new. Tourism revenue is inherently unpredictable, because changes in tourists' desires (and anxieties) occur frequently.[10] While the idea of the vacation (as opposed to the journey) invites return visits to safe, welcoming places for rest and regeneration and thus would seem to avoid this drive for the new, the longing for the extraordinary, surprising, and memorable permeates all touristic endeavors, including the annual holiday. Returning to the same lake every year holds the promise that the gigantic fish might be caught the next time; skiing on the same slopes every year, one might have the golden opportunity to share a lift-ride with the Prince of Wales; and revisiting the same Turkish sea resort year after year might result in an unexpected, life-altering romantic adventure. The narrative scholar will recognize that each of these hopes holds the promise of narrative—tall tales masking as personal stories, rumor and legend, and personal anecdote or fairy tale come true.[11]

Other tourist offerings are billed to begin with as "once in a lifetime experiences": the journey to the Galapagos Islands, the visit to the Egyptian Pyramids, or the Great Wall of China, are all meant to yield unique memories. Hence, the touristic entrepreneur needs a constant supply of people who have not yet seen what he has to offer. Even worse from the businessperson's point of view is that "uniqueness" constantly shifts. If the Taj Mahal was a pinnacle of unique and desirable experience for a few generations of visitors, riding through the Arabian Desert with real nomads, or facing the threat of death from exposure while climbing Mt. Everest can quickly capture another generation's imagination. The vagaries of politics and wars also leave their devastating mark on tourist economies, with the tourist-deserted coast of the former Yugoslavia during the break-up wars as one poignant example. In all these, however, it is the narratives about a visited site or travel experience which are the key, bursting into private networks as well as the public sphere and influencing the rise, persistence, or decline of a particular touristic opportunity—a topic to which I will return momentarily.

How can we explain this craving for the new? Longing is an extraordinarily powerful force in human existence, as Susan Stewart has shown in her work on the interrelationship of longing and consumption. Longing is encoded in objects that contain within themselves narratives or memories of experiences had or wished for (Stewart 1993, 132–54). Within longing, though, there are aspects that are inexpressible, either in narrative or objects, and in early travel documents one may find traces of this essentially sensual-somatic component of longing. Naturalists and explorers as well as philosophers of the sublime in the eighteenth century assisted their contemporaries in uncovering the affective possibilities of sights hitherto unseen. In so doing, they offered a new language of the experiential

(Löfgren 1999, 13–28). From the eighteenth century onward, publishing the journals of one's travel was a popular means of sharing one's impressions and memories (Stagl 1983). This impulse arguably contributed to the shaping of a wealth of printed travel narrative genres, from the colonial report to the personal travelogue to the directive or predictive genre of the guidebook.

The German author Johann Wolfgang von Goethe was among the many to undertake what was called an educational journey (*Bildungsreise*), a type of journey that had become customary for the European nobility and bourgeoisie. In 1779, Goethe tried to grasp what impact viewing new landscapes had on him: "When we see an object for the first time, the soul—unaccustomed [to this view]—at first enlarges. This makes for a painful pleasure, a sense of overflowing, which moves the soul and draws a voluptuous tear from us. Through this operation, our soul enlarges and is, without knowing it, no longer capable of this first sensation. Man believes to have lost something, but actually he has won something. What he loses in sensuality, he gains in inner growth" (Goethe [1779] 1962, 10, my translation).[12] Goethe was sufficiently wise to emphasize the gain in inner growth. Touristic longing, however, tries not to acquiesce to inner growth (and the attendant acknowledgement of the shrinking likelihood of further soul expansions), and instead seeks ever-new experiences. The pleasure inherent to what some people term an authentic— that is, never-before-had-and-never-to-be-had-again—experience, couched in terms of an overflowing soul and the visceral impact it has on our body, haunts modernity. Travel and tourism may contain the quintessential and oh-so-rare manifestation of authenticity.

Walter Benjamin (1963) associated the term "aura" with the originality inherent to the work of art. The—often religious—placement and veneration bestowed on a work of art endowed it, according to Benjamin, with an irresistible attraction: it brought into material proximity what was felt to be inaccessibly remote (cf., Bendix 1997, 6). In successive periods of secularization, art lost its cultish aura (in Benjamin's argument this was of course facilitated through technological reproduction). People began to satisfy their craving for authenticity—that is, for a however-brief experience of the inaccessibly remote—less and less through a culturally offered, collective religious framework, and more and more through material possessions and individual experiences.[13]

Travel conveniently inserts itself here, as it offers both of these options at once: the experience of what has never been experienced before and making available token representations of that experience in the form of souvenirs and photographs.[14] The most powerful evidence of the search for the singular, unique, and authentic within tourist experience, however, is narration. Goethe's enlarging of the soul—the physical thrill experienced in anything from a first sighting of an ancient tomb to rappelling into the depths during a first cave exploration—lasts but a moment. The process of narrating the experience *recovers* the moment, if not its experiential singularity, and allows for its communicative restaging and its ever-new mental savoring. What is more, narrative license can transform the moment with evermore extravagant vocabulary and additional detail and seduce audience and narrator into believing touristic memories that never were.

In addition, the well-crafted story can transform the most humiliating, abhorrent, or terrifying experience into one of narrative success: how many travelers sustain themselves during a grueling journey with the thought, "this is going to make a great story"? Journalist Jody Weverka, after describing in graphic detail a ferryboat ride in Indonesia filled with the stench of vomit, cites her brother's dictum: "Any negative experience traveling in the Third World automatically becomes a positive one if it yields a good story" (*Wewerka* 1992).[15] By inserting the term "Third World," Weverka naturally also steers us toward the power imbalance in travel experiences, whether they entail inaccurate oppositions such as First and Third World, or simply acknowledge that by leaving the home and the habitual, the traveler enters an inherently liminal and vulnerable state.[16] Nelson Graburn (1989), building on Victor Turner's work, once connected the tourist's journey with the ritual liminality and license of pilgrimage.[17] The sense of endangerment the tourist feels, in whatever overt or repressed form, is real, no matter how domineering and competent his gestures, clothing, and spending habits, no matter how thoroughly subservient the host society behaves toward him.[18] Fear is part of the thrill of the touristic longing. We can recognize in Graburn's terminology, too, evidence for the longing for suspense: shedding the safety of the familiar also may make one more susceptible to the marvelous.[19] In after-the-fact narration, the vulnerability suffered in travel illness and deprivation or natural or human danger can be overcome, and the aura of the touristic experience can be attached to the narrating self who miraculously survived to tell his tale. Telling the stories back home restores competence and power, and offers psychic compensation for the powerlessness suffered during the actual tourist experience.

## NARRATIVE POTENTIAL AND ITS
## COMMODITIZATION

Against the backdrop of what I have termed the "aura of touristic experience," we can revisit the pilgrims to John Lennon's memorial in New York's Central Park. Plenty of men and women have been shot dead in or near Central Park, but their life histories have affected only a few. The life and death of a celebrity like Lennon or Princess Diana, however, touches the core of millions. The quasi-religious space such individuals come to inhabit in their admirers' imagination feeds a longing to connect, to touch, to have a shred of evidence that links one's own life to that of the icon. For the one-time visitor to New York who also happens to have been a Beatles fan, the Lennon Memorial and the Lennon House are sites of pilgrimage that hold tremendous narrative potential: they allow the tourist to link his life history with that of the celebrity. The video of "me next to the Imagine mosaic" or "me on Strawberry Fields" opens the floodgates of narrating memories that suddenly achieve uniqueness or suggest authenticity through the narrator's intersection with the place where John Lennon was shot to death.

The tourist is, however, not alone in his or her reliance on narration to make the experience endure. The individualized photograph or video, the scrapbook and the diary are all efforts to maintain the idiosyncrasy of one's experience in the face of commoditization's ability to render the most intimate moment into a commercial one. Narration and narrative potential was, from the inception of bourgeois travel, a powerful means to create tourist attractions, and tourists have struggled for almost as long to wrest a personal experience and an individual memory from the thick offering of prefabricated or suggested memories for sale.[20] While I have acknowledged the tremendous material underpinnings of the tourist industry, ranging from simple hotel beds to the quasi-medical equipment of the beauty farm, convincing tourists to come and spend their money requires narration. Any advertisement is ultimately a quick story, offering just enough imagery and text for the viewer or reader to insert themselves as potential buyers.[21] The hotel bed holds the promise of recovering sleep of a quality not had since one was a baby, sleep as luxurious as that of a royal personage, or nights as exciting as those of a long-gone honeymoon. The beauty farm holds out the hope for a body surpassing in shapeliness what one might have had in youth, and narrates a future full of erotic appeal and love that is well worth the pain of fasting, exercise, and even surgery. They will lead to experiences and narratable memories one hopes to have once had. Given travel and tourism's long narrative history, and given that tourism ultimately sells narratable experience, the thicket of intersecting and intermeshing stories offered to the potential traveler is mind-boggling.[22]

In addition to the straightforward sales pitch for "the experience of a lifetime" and "the trip that you will talk about for the rest of your life," there are offers for journeys that recapitulate both real and fictional travel, promising travelers a fulfillment of their longing through mimesis.[23] The Karen Blixen Museum, fifteen kilometers south of Nairobi in what has become a suburb, is a case in point. What are the stories that are meant to draw the tourist to this exhibit of an author's life and work, and what memories, past and future, are to resonate through the visitor's experience? There is Blixen's 1938 memoir, *Out of Africa*, which moved many readers, and even more viewers of the filmed version, into accepting and craving Blixen's narrative of what is Kenya. There is also the narrative of Blixen herself, a biography of the woman, and her male pseudonym Isak Dinesen, and the craving to know more about a woman who may or may not have been like her portrait of herself. A tourist attraction such as this very consciously employs, multiplies, and commoditizes the narrative potential inherent to Blixen and her work.

Other sites are far more extreme in the commoditization of narration to further tourist appreciation. The small Canadian Prince Edward Island (PEI) has completely embraced the assumption that the girlhood book series *Anne of Green Gables*, written by L. M. Montgomery starting in 1936 and set in PEI, will bring tourists. Visitors are folded into the Anne-experience from the moment they enter the first visitor center. Vacation cottages are named for Anne and other protagonists in the novel, amusement parks employ Anne characters, an entire district of the island is called

"Anne's Land," and an artificial village makes real the stores, church, and school of this fictional character's life. Sites like these reify narratives and make them available for touristic experience, offering not just a fictional reality, but also clearly scripted patterns along which to experience this dream-come-true world.[24]

What is it that happens here, and is it exclusive to tourism? When we craft stories out of the experiences in daily life that seem extraordinary, overwhelming, upsetting, or entertaining to us, rendering the events into a narrative pattern gives sequential gestalt and generic contours to what was perhaps a bewildering, not even sequenced event. Through narration, the potentially chaotic takes on a cultural shape and thus becomes manageable and aesthetically pleasing (cf., Bendix 1990, 1996). A tourist, by contrast, juggles his or her actual experience against the promised experiences that have been purchased, and depending on his or her disposition, can end up with a memory pragmatically following the pattern outlined in the brochure—a satisfied, obedient consumer—or a memory beset with disappointment or a sense of failure where the longed-for and promised experience of a lifetime (Goethe's enlarging of the soul) is sensually undercut through the mental presaging.

A third alternative is also almost as old as the tourist industry: it is the tourist who familiarizes him- or herself with the touristic offering and who then avoids at all costs the sights and experiences suggested by the guidebook or the advertisement. The tourist's narrated memories are characterized by contrasting his or her individual transcendent travel moments with mocking portraits of all the tourists, seen as trapped in the prescribed or typical and thus ordinary rather than longed-for and mind- or soul-altering experience.[25] Capitalism, however, is always at our heels. Sometimes it is the very people who have crafted journeys for themselves that avoided the available, commoditized tourist narratives, who then write guidebooks that advocate the "alternative experience" and render it, through mass printings, part of the commoditized and repeatable.

A tourist destination receives customers through the narrative morsels it plants itself or that are put in circulation by others, whether it be glossy tourist advertising, the mildly patronizing narrative voice of publications such as *Geo* or *National Geographic*, or the glowing and rapidly disseminating private stories of happy tourists. It should not surprise, then, that the greatest threat to a successfully launched tourist destination also resides in narration. Austria's extensive tourist businesses have not decreased in quality since February 2000, but the worldwide talk about the inclusion of the rightwing Freedom Party into Austria's new government immediately alters the narrative gloss and hence the appeal of this small nation as a tourist destination. Similarly, Switzerland's tourism took a rapid dive when the shady dealings of Swiss banks during the Second World War were revealed in the mid-1990s. The hotels, the ski slopes, the mountain paths, and the restaurants are as impeccably maintained as ever. But the tourist contemplates what impact an overtly xenophobic mentality or memories of Swiss collaboration with the Nazis will have on his or her own travel memories. The narrative potential of these tourist destinations is for the moment decidedly tarnished.

Stories of potential wars will keep travelers away—a narrative thread and threat that has repeatedly affected Turkey's tourism revenues, be this due to internal ethnic tensions or proximity to Iran and Iraq, and the Arab-Israeli sites of conflict. Actual hostilities against tourists—such as the Egyptian massacre of tourists in Luxor (November 1997), the killing of nature tourists in a border area of Kenya (in 1999), and in the 2010s, repeated occurrences of tourists taken hostage in North Africa and Indonesia—breed hosts of additional and unfounded rumors, feed the fear inherent to travel, and bolster assumptions of touristic decline. But to a great extent, it is the narratives resulting from actual as well as fictitious danger that contribute to tourism's eroding vitality. The power of travel storytellers in magazines and newspapers, on radio, TV, and the internet, is enormous. On occasion, one wonders just how aware they are of the impact their narration has on the future of a travel destination.[26] Gary Alan Fine has observed the dynamics of legends and hostile rumors in the world of manufacturing (1992, 141–204). In the world of tourism, negative stories and their ramifications are still more complex, precisely because tourism is not an "industry" in the same sense as manufacturing.

Commoditization is, however, a process that does not stop where socially sanctioned beauty and behavior end. There will always be tourism providers that take willing thrill-seekers to the boundaries of a war. Our journalistic practice is such that the CNN journalist reporting from the killing fields models the extremes of danger attractive to some intrepid travelers. There are, furthermore, those who travel to partake of experiences that are neither peaceful breaks from work nor even individualistic. The followers of soccer teams, for instance, travel with the awareness that their passion can lead to experiences of excess and violence. Both their anticipation and memory are so intensely physical and so much carried by crowd-action that they defy narration. But they are sufficiently recognizable as longed-for experiences that tourism will provide the infrastructure. Bill Buford, traveling among "the thugs" but living to tell about it as an individual, reports how a travel agency, charter planes, and even a British consul can be found to facilitate the journey of hundreds of violence-prone British soccer fans to Turin, Italy (Buford 1990, 32–43). Verbalizing the actual experiences proves difficult for the participants. Indeed, Buford, in part, undertook his participant observation to give voice and narration to what to the predominant number of participants remains in the domain of the felt and not narratable. Sex tourism is equally blocked from the public realm of travel narration and thus the social capital narration inherently holds in the home context. The illegality of many practices within sex tourism have, however, not hindered tourism providers from facilitating it. The dark underside of the voluptuousness we have encountered in Goethe's enlarging of the soul, too, has been commoditized to the hilt.

If narration offers us opportunities to express our experience and thus our individuality in ever-new shape, commoditization stands ready to harness not only the dreams we are willing to communicate to fellow human beings, but also the longings and experiences we were socialized to condemn.[27]

## REFLEXIVE CORRECTIVES

The tourist experience, more often than not, consists of the recognition that the epiphany, the fulfillment of our longing, has eluded us again.[28] Our repertoire of travel stories may contain an example or two of Goethe's soul-enlarging moments, though more likely than not those are the stories that we jealously guard within ourselves, narrating them internally to find strength in the memory of transcendence and personal growth. The stories we more likely share, at times when we are encouraged to show off the cultural capital accrued through travel, are tales of fortune and misfortune (the incredible treasure bought for a ridiculously low price; the lousy souvenir bought for far too high a price), anecdotes about tourists encountered (for "travelers," despite all efforts to cure them of the false dichotomy, insist on seeing others engaged in the same travails as "tourists," see Buzard [1993, 18–79]), and sketches of cultural contrast and linguistic confusion.

These stories are full of familiar narrative motifs and there are surely even corresponding tale types we could find in the standard classificatory tools for folk narrative.[29] Indeed, media travel programs build on and try to contribute to the narrative typification of travel experience. In the United States, the weekly radio program "The Savvy Traveler" contains several segments that point toward the mental preoccupation with organizing travel experience into narratable segments. During a program on June 3, 2000, the program host asked callers to report on "roadside diner adventures." Other topics in the year 2000 included asking callers to "tell us your travel resolutions and how they came about" (January 1), "friends made on the road" (January 22), and "embarrassing travel moments" (April 1).[30] Other features of the show, such as the occasional "Bad Taste Tour," or the "Guided Home Town Tour," allow contributors to mobilize their most compelling narrative skill to render outrageous or meaningful what to someone unfamiliar with the site would be devoid of resonance.

An outgrowth of America's National Public Radio program "Marketplace," the "Savvy Traveler," like its parent show, is a mixture of advice, analysis, and commentary. The separation between commercial offering and consumer commentary is blurred; yet out of this blurring also grows opportunity for reflection. In the case of the "Savvy Traveler," the reflection occasionally (though very rarely) grows to take in the conditions of those who are working for the tourists' benefit. When, on February 29, 2000, host Rudy Maxa recounts his one day of experiences as a housekeeper in Washington, DC's Four Seasons Hotel, the listener emerges with a glimpse of the labor that goes into providing his or her vacation comfort. It opens the listener to the possibility of the narrative repertoire of those who are laboring for those who are vacationing, while evoking the response, "I'm glad it is them and not me," by the double-framing of narration and radio. On the hosts' side, there is indeed no dearth of narration, though the salient motifs in stories of cross-cultural and cross-class encounter, mishaps and good fortunes, busloads of tourists, and idiosyncratic travelers point to different kinds of triumphs, insights, and critiques, and to different clusters of meaning.

While the Senegalese performer, Youssou N'Dour (1994), in his song, "Tourista," still admonishes his countrymen to welcome visitors and share their country with them so that good memories will bring them back, host countries have also brought forth critical narrations of life with the tourists. In Austria, a country with more than a century of touristic history, couplets about tourists and newspaper letters by offended hosts can be found throughout the twentieth century. In 1988, novelist Norbert Gstrein (1988) wrote a piece called *Einer* ("One") which chronicles the life of a boy who grows up loathing the pathologies of touristic interaction between Austrian villagers and their predominantly German guests. As an adult, he becomes a ski teacher and submits to evenings in bars where he is supposed to embody the typical native, supplying everything from indigenous conviviality to sexual gratification. The pretense and the split between backstage personhood and touristic identity lead to the protagonist's ultimate decay and despondency.

More cynical is Austrian playwright Felix Mitterer's TV-production *Die Piefke-Saga*. Described by its author as a combination of satire, comedy, tragedy, and "horror vision to laugh oneself to death," the play depicts the successive commoditization of all aspects of native life, all in an attempt to secure the continued presence and revenue of tourists. By the end of the saga, a team of Japanese doctors is hired to surgically alter real and "wannabe" residents into 100 percent Tyroleans, with language and behaviors fully befitting the homeland. All the annoying doubts and anxieties over role-play, authenticity, and selfhood are removed, as one's identity is medically and permanently fixed (Mitterer 1991).

In these turns toward reflection, a restorative, or at the very least a therapeutic, potential of narration reveals itself. Parodistic, acerbic, as well as tragic accounts of life within a tourist economy provoke critical reflection and ultimately new thinking to redress the social and economic infrastructure within which the intertwined experience of tourists and "tourees" unfolds. Tourism is carried, I have tried to demonstrate, through narratives of multiple order. The reflexive narratives that assess tourism's most frightening spoils and the individual's greatest failures are simultaneously critiques and sources for resistance and change. The late-twentieth century has seen the growth of ecotourism and efforts to understand sustainability. There has been development toward a variety of alternative vacation settings designed to bring about a valuing of local life, occupations, and ecosystems: each of these movements to redress material conditions is occasioned and accompanied by narration. Each of these efforts has its own, new aspirations, longings, and problems. Humans will continue to narrate them and hopefully achieve a sense of living and traveling appropriate for their time—much as did Elizabeth Bishop in her 1952 poem, "Arrival at Santos," in which she at once addressed the motivation and emptiness entailed in touristic endeavor: "and your immodest demands for a different world, and a better life, and complete comprehension," she chided herself and any traveler, disembarking after an eighteen-day boat trip overloaded with expectation (Bishop 1983, 89).[31]

While the tourist business is an outgrowth and a major component of a capitalist economy, a type of economy currently driving the globe, tourism is a great deal more than a product to purchase or make financial gain from. When I entitled this essay, "Capitalizing on Memories Past, Present, and Future," I wanted to capture the multivalence of the verb—to capitalize on something means to make the most of it. Human beings are unlikely to stop traveling, but they are capable of balancing more sanely what is gained and what is suffered during their journeys.

NOTES

This chapter originally appeared in *Anthropological Theory* 2002 (2): 469–86.

A version of this article was presented as a plenary address at the Congress of the International Society of Folk Narrative Research in Nairobi, Kenya, July 17–22, 2000. I am grateful for the generous comments by Roger D. Abrahams, John Bendix, Johannes Fabian, and Lee Haring.

1. The subway stop is West Seventy-Second Street and Central Park West, New York. Strawberry Fields was described on another web page as "Name of a triangular shaped area in honor of John Lennon. Peaceful and nicely landscaped. Ironically a favorite with old neighborhood residents." Given that the Beatles were at the peak of their fame in the 1960s, the preference of elderly people to sit near this spot may not be at all ironic (see Digital City 2002). On the twentieth anniversary of Lennon's death, hundreds of people gathered on the site (see *New York Times*, December 9, 2000).

2. Choosing memories of pain and injustice for touristic commoditization constitutes still but a small share of the market, though the urge to render leisure a realm of somber learning has been present since the aristocratic *Bildungsreise*. But it tends to be a script for new sites, not one added on to existing ones. The extremely popular United States Holocaust Museum would be a case in point; built as a new venture and not a part of the Smithsonian Mall in Washington, DC, its separateness and somberness of purpose contribute to its place in the leisure and tourism market. Consider, furthermore, Goree Island off the coast of Guinea, the embarkation point for slaves. This island has become a pilgrimage site particularly for African-Americans, and marketing is largely confined to this potential interest group. Sharon Macdonald (1997) recounts the difficulty of financing, building, and maintaining interest in a Scottish tourist site that remembers struggle and pain, a distinctly different effort from marketing *Scotland—the Brand* (McCrone 1995).

3. In her study of ethnic memorials in Lowell, Massachusetts, Martha Norkunas (2002) discovered the ways in which different ethnic groups who arrived in this (now defunct) industrial hub used to claim spaces in parks and along streets to erect monuments to their ethnic past. After decades, the memorial would lose in relevance; it might even get moved to a different place to make space for a newer monument relevant for another group.

4. The debates over whether our age is postmodern, poststructuralist, post-Fordist, modern, or reflexively modern are, perhaps, futile in their insistence on a periodization of human experience measured by technological and political change. While there is constant change, the assumption of some kind of linear movement forward owes too much to the Western narrative of progress, and not enough to the repetitive nature of daily existence, the recurrence of day and night, of seasons, and the circular motions of the earth within the equally circular solar system. "The more it changes, the more it is the same," says the proverb. Individual experience seeks to contradict this, and indeed the individual life is unique, not replicable in its movement from birth to death, down to the genetic level (and even genetic cloning cannot alter the difference in experience of genetically identical entities). Yet, the focus on the idiosyncrasies of a given age or period, the Middle Ages as opposed to the Renaissance, is but an effort to accentuate the exceptional, the things that "happened" and that brought about changes in thought, knowledge, and habit, as opposed to the things that remain steady. This being said, the phase or stage of existence that was brought about through the intertwined movements of democratization, industrialization, and colonization since roughly the sixteenth century is distinct, though whether "modern" is the word for it might be an appropriate question to ask. Marx used the label "All that is solid melts into air" (see Berman 1988). From the present vantage point, using spatial rather than temporal metaphor might yield a more poignant terminology. Caren Kaplan in her examination of theorists of modernism and postmodernism seems to think similarly when she states: "'Post-' will always privilege a temporal language and agenda over a spatial one" (1996, 21). The term "global age" could appropriately denote the age that brought about an economic dependency on global networks and, associated with these economic needs, the penetration of the capitalist imagination and practice around the globe. Narratives and the process of narration, one might argue, allow for an understanding of both the enduring, recurring qualities of human existence as well as of the surface changes in technique, aesthetics, and vision.

5. Among the works to be mentioned are, for example, Clifford 1997; Kaplan 1996; Kirshenblatt-Gimblett 1998; Krippendorf 1984; Löfgren 1999; and Pratt 1992. *Annals of*

*Tourism Research*, still the flagship journal of tourism study, started publication in 1972, which is very late indeed for a social phenomenon with a history reaching back deeply into the nineteenth century. Since the original publication of this article, the number of journals devoted to special aspects of tourism has grown, and initiatives such as the "tourism-contact-culture" network, is carried by a number of more localized research initiatives (Tourism 2016).

    6. Davidson argues very clearly against the designation "industry" for tourism; the term industry, in fact, leads to misjudgments of what tourism can or cannot do. "Tourism is a social/economic phenomenon that acts both as an engine of economic progress and as a social force" (1998, 28). Yet ironically, or sadly, Davidson's short article appears in an edited volume and is surrounded by many tourism and hospitality theory papers speaking adamantly of the tourist industry.

    7. I am aware that the emphasis on the cerebral aspects of tourism put forth here may be exaggerated or apply only to some tourists. Erik Cohen (1988) once suggested a fourfold categorization of tourists in which only the fourth and most extreme type was obsessed with the mental cohesiveness and authenticity of the tourist experience, and he likened this type to the ethnographer. The parallels between that which motivates travelers and that which motivates ethnographers have been noted repeatedly. James Clifford describes twentieth-century ethnography as "an evolving practice of modern travel" (1997, 19), and Barbara Kirshenblatt-Gimblett comments on the plight of the ethnographer who "cannot take away the intangible, ephemeral, immovable, and animate" and who instead "inscribes" what he cannot carry away in "field notes, recordings, photographs, films, or drawings" (1998, 10). In the spirit of the Writing Culture movement in anthropology (Clifford and Marcus, 1986), it is perfectly appropriate to see the parallels as well as the intermeshing of tourists and ethnographers not just in the effort to recover the intangible in the form of souvenirs/documents, but also, to reemphasize the topic of this article, in the effort to narrate the experience in the form of stories or ethnographies.

    8. Edensor's (1998) examination of tourism at the Taj Mahal is one of the few works that seeks to include non-Western travel sensibilities in his consideration of Western, Hindu, and Muslim ways of approaching this particular site.

    9. On the term "experience," its place within pragmatist philosophy, and its potential (and pitfalls) in anthropological research, see Abrahams (1986).

    10. The popularity of the so-called last minute holiday arrangement (especially practiced in Europe) is indicative of both the travelers' desire to surprise themselves with a destination not previously considered, and of the tourism facilitators' efforts to somehow harness this unpredictability for profit.

    11. If we were to peruse the collections of contemporary legends that have been put together by Jan Harold Brunvand (USA), Rolf Wilhelm Brednich (Germany), or Bengt af Klintberg (Sweden), we would be able to provide a good number of already collected vacation narratives—though generally focusing on the holiday mishap (such as the unexpectedly dying grandmother, or mishaps involving recreational vehicles), or damage wreaked on unsuspecting citizens (such as airplane wastes falling out of the sky).

    12. Goethe's use of the German term *Wollust* (sensuality, voluptuousness) and its associated adjective *wollüstig*, are not carelessly chosen terms; they are associated primarily with sexual pleasure, and in the early Romantic period, when Goethe wrote this statement about the effort to explore feelings and senses exuberantly, later bourgeois taboos were

not yet affecting his association of a visual experience with sensations resembling sexual pleasures. When Kirshenblatt-Gimblett (1998), in her groundbreaking work *Destination Culture*, devotes considerable attention to the "confusing pleasures" in tourist spectacles as well as the ways in which cultural exhibitions employ secrecy or humility to avoid making the sources of pleasure inherent to the exhibited objects fully known, we recognize both the presence of pleasurable (including physical) stimulation and two centuries' worth of practices designed to disguise it.

13. Many excellent works have been devoted to analyzing these intertwined changes in Western societies, seeking to understand a movement driven by industrial capitalism and the fragmentation of collective senses has brought about. Trilling (1971) and Taylor (1989) are perhaps the most comprehensive; Berman (1972, 1988) is most compelling. For a discussion of the intertwining of authenticity searches with the study of folklore, see Bendix (1997), which also offers brief summaries of some of the most relevant works.

14. Tim Edensor analyses such interplay of narration and experience with the case of the Taj Mahal (1998, 69–104).

15. Social movement of any sort naturally generates potentially sharable story material (cf., the considerable scholarship on personal narratives: Abrahams 1977; Bauman 1986; Rosaldo 1986; Stahl 1989). Travel intensifies and enhances this potential precisely because extraordinary experiences which authenticate the narrator's individuality are seen as more likely.

16. Ian Buruma, in a review essay, similarly goes for the imagery of bodily excretions, for they appear spontaneous, far from the civilized affectations the writers come from, and thus authenticating the experience: "Traveling recently by bus from Shigatse to Lhasa, squeezed in between a heavily made-up bar hostess from Sichua who was vomiting her breakfast out the window and a minor Tibetan official who asked me about Manchester United football club before noisily clearing his throat to deposit a green gob of spit beside my left shoe, I wondered what it was about Tibet that has made so many intelligent people go wobbly" (Buruma 2000, 12).

17. This is researched on a terminological and philosophical level in Kaplan (1996). Among more recent works on the pilgrimage dimension, see Swatos (2006), Cohen-Hattah and Shoval (2015), and Di Giovine and Picard (2015).

18. That there are no guidebooks which do not, in one form or another, address the tourists' concern for safety, speaks volumes about our tacit acknowledgment of this basic fear. The question of the wrangling for power in the host-guest relationship bears further examination, given the often long histories of colonial or at the very least economic interdependence. The first edition of Valene Smith's *Hosts and Guests* (1977) still contained the voices of anthropologists fundamentally offended by tourism's exploitation of cultures perceived as pristine; the revised edition from 1989 inserted some much needed corrections, although the acknowledgment that host cultures are neither clearly bounded (though they often choose to present themselves as such to appeal to the tourist's desire for the pristine) nor completely helpless in the face of tourism's economic intrusion has been slow in coming. Bouissevain (1996) also assembles a number of European case studies that seek to complicate the perception of power relations in tourism. Gisela Welz (2000) offers a case study on this topic, examining the symbolic ramifications of a traditional guest meal adopted into tourist practice in Cyprus. It must be emphasized, though, that these successful host-reassertions have been documented more extensively in areas with one hundred or more years of tourism histories.

Many host societies in developing economies are indeed more vulnerable, as the infra-structural know-how for tourist economies is still largely Western-developed, including the well-meaning but ultimately also patronizing efforts to foster sustainable tourism (see the critique by Mowforth and Munt [1997]).

19. Seeking and finding the "marvelous" is a trope inherent to Western travel since the time of the explorers (cf., Greenblatt 1991).

20. Löfgren notes that standardization of attractions had already created boredom in the late eighteenth century (1999, 27), and boredom is naturally anathema to the longed-for experiential surprise.

21. Advertisers have heightened this effect by drawing culturally already available stories and motifs into advertising scripts (Dégh and Vazsony 1979).

22. Graham Dann (1996) directs tourism researches toward examining tourism lan-guage both in terms of agency and its propensity to draw from a fixed set of cliches. His rich examples substantiate what is here only touched on briefly, though his wavering between systematically analyzing, critiquing, and promoting tourism's languages is a little unsettling.

23. While narration is a conscious engagement with and processing of experience, mime-sis resides between consciously willed and habitual, unreflected actions. For an elabora-tion on the interrelationship of (ethno-)mimesis and Bourdieu's concept of *habitus*, see Cantwell (1999).

24. Cf. "On the Road to Fiction," this volume.

25. Buzard (1993) offers some choice examples from late-nineteenth- to early-twentieth-century literature of this jaded "traveler" who seeks to distinguish himself from the "tourist," unable to see that the two labels denote ultimately the same endeavor.

26. In early summer of 2000, the *New York Times Magazine* carried a devastating report by Blaine Harden, on the decline of Kenya's tourism, putting the blame squarely on the nation's president. Yet there is no acknowledgement in this acerbic piece of travel journalism how the piece will contribute to further losses in Kenyan tourism revenue.

27. Rosemary Coombe's (1998) foray into the ways in which legal copyright processes facilitate the commoditization of ideas, looks, styles and similarly individual, if often imma-terial, "goods" usefully complements what I sketch here.

28. Abrahams writes about "the experience of the experience"—moments when we rec-ognize an unfolding pattern, where it is not that which we see, hear, or do that resonate but the underlying pattern that is familiar, even if on the surface there are new particulars (1986, 60–1). For tourist experience, this might be any number of motifs: the unfamiliar means of locomotion, the show of folkloric dances, the final banquet. After experiencing such ele-ments in Egypt, they become recognizable in Bali or New Guinea, no matter how different the faces, costumes, and tastes.

29. The two major tools are Aarne's Index of Tale Types (1911), revised twice during the hundred years since initial publication, and Thompson's Index of Motifs (1955–58). Numerous regional tale type catalogues have been produced in the interim.

30. The program has an extensive archive including audio files and is thus ready for anyone eager to carry out the full narrative analysis of content, structure, style, and performance of these tales generally narrated over the phone (Savvy Traveler 2016).

31. Bishop repeatedly addressed "Questions of Travel" in her poetry, even entitling a col-lection with this phrase, reprinted also in Bishop (1983, 93–4).

REFERENCES

Aarne, Antti. 1911. *Verzeichnis der Märchentypen.* FFC 3. Helsinki: Suomalainen
    Tiedeakatemian Toimituksia.
Abrahams, Roger D. 1977. "The Most Embarrassing Thing That Ever Happened:
    Conversational Stories in a Theory of Enactment." *Folklore Forum* 10 (3): 45–72.
———. 1986. "Ordinary and Extraordinary Experience." In *The Anthropology of
    Experience*, edited by Edward M. Bruner and Victor W. Turner. Urbana: University of
    Illinois Press.
Bauman, Richard. 1986. *Story, Performance, Event. Contextual Studies of Oral Narrative.*
    Cambridge: Cambridge University Press.
Bendix, Regina. 1990. "Reflections on Earthquake Narratives." *Western Folklore* 49: 331–48.
———. 1996. "Zwischen Chaos und Kultur: Anmerkungen zur Ethnographie des
    Erzählens im ausgehenden 20. Jahrhundert." *Zeitschrift für Volkskunde* 92 (2): 169–84.
———. 1997. *In Search of Authenticity: The Formation of Folklore Studies.* Madison:
    University of Wisconsin Press.
Benjamin, Walter. 1963. *Das Kunstwerk im Zeitalter seiner technischen Reproduzierbarkeit.*
    Frankfurt: Suhrkamp.
Berman, Marshall. 1972. *The Politics of Authenticity.* New York: Atheneum.
———. 1988. *All that is Solid Melts into Air: The Experience of Modernity.* New York: Penguin.
Bishop, Elizabeth. 1983. *The Complete Poems 1927–1979.* New York: Farrar, Straus, Giroux.
Bouissevain, Jeremy, ed. 1996. *Coping with Tourists: European Reactions to Mass Tourism.*
    Providence, RI: Berghahn.
Buford, Bill. 1990. *Among the Thugs.* New York: Vintage.
Buruma, Ian. 2000. "Found Horizon." *New York Review of Books* (June 29): 12–7.
Buzard, James. 1993. *The Beaten Track: European Tourism, Literature, and the Ways to
    "Culture" 1800–1918.* Oxford: Oxford University Press.
Cantwell, Robert. 1999. "Habitus, Ethnomimesis: A Note on the Logic of Practice."
    *Journal of Folklore Research* 36 (2/3): 214–34.
Central Park. 2017. Accessed May 4. http://www.centralpark.com/guide/history.html.
Clifford, James. 1997. *Routes. Travel and Translation in the Late Twentieth Century.*
    Cambridge, MA: Harvard University Press.
Clifford, James and George E. Marcus, eds. 1986. *Writing Culture: The Poetics and Politics of
    Ethnography.* Berkeley: University of California Press.
Cohen, Erik. 1988. "Authenticity and Commoditization in Tourism." *Annals of Tourism
    Research* 15: 371–86.
Cohen-Hattab, Kobi and Noam Shoval. 2015. *Tourism, Religion and Pilgrimage in
    Jerusalem.* London: Routledge.
Coombe, Rosemary J. 1998. *The Cultural Life of Intellectual Property. Authorship,
    Appropriation, and the Law.* Durham, NC: Duke University Press.
Dann, Graham M.S. 1996. *The Language of Tourism: A Sociolinguistic Perspective.*
    Wallingford: CAB International.
Davidson, Thomas L. 1998. "What are Travel and Tourism: Are They Really an Industry?"
    In *Global Tourism*, edited by William F. Theobald. Oxford: Butterworth-Heinemann.
Dégh, Linda and Andrew Vazsonyi. 1979. "Magic for Sale: *Märchen* and Legend in TV
    Advertising." *Fabula* 20: 47–68.

Di Giovine, Michael and David Picard. 2016. *The Seduction of Pilgrimage. Sacred Journeys Afar and Astray in the Western Religious Tradition*. London: Routledge.

Digital City. 2002. Accessed January 15. http://netscape.digitalcity.com/newyork /recreation/venue.dci?vid=22206 (site discontinued).

Edensor, Tim. 1998. *Tourists at the Taj*. London: Routledge.

Fine, Gary A. 1992. *Manufacturing Tales. Sex and Money in Contemporary Legends*. Knoxville: University Press of Tennessee.

Goethe, Johann Wolfgang von. (1779) 1962. *Reisen*. Goethes Werke 9, selected by Peter Boerner. Zurich: Artemis.

Graburn, Nelson H. 1989. "Tourism: The Sacred Journey." In *Hosts and Guests*, edited by Valene L. Smith. Philadelphia: University of Pennsylvania Press.

Greenblatt, Stephen. 1991. *Marvelous Possessions: The Wonder of the New World*. Chicago: University of Chicago Press.

Gstrein, Norbert. 1988. *Einer*. Frankfurt: Suhrkamp.

Harden, Blaine. 2000. The Last Safari. *The New York Times Magazine*. June 4, 2000.

Kaplan, Caren. 1996. *Questions of Travel: Postmodern Discourses of Displacement*. Durham, NC: Duke University Press.

Kirshenblatt-Gimblett, Barbara. 1998. *Destination Culture. Tourism, Museums and Heritage*. Berkeley: University of California Press.

Krippendorf, Jost. 1984. *Die Ferienmenschen. Für ein neues Verständnis von Freizeit und Reisen*. Zurich: Orell Füssli.

Löfgren, Orvar. 1999. *On Holiday. A History of Vacationing*. Berkeley: University of California Press.

MacCannell, Dean. 1976. *The Tourist. A New Theory of the Leisure Class*. New York: Schocken.

Macdonald, Sharon. 1997. "A People's Story: Heritage, Identity and Authenticity." In *Touring Culture*, edited by Chris Rojek and John Urry. London: Routledge.

McCrone, David. 1995. *Scotland—The Brand: The Making of Scottish Heritage*. Edinburgh: Edinburgh University Press.

Mitterer, Felix. 1991. *Die Piefke-Saga*. Innsbruck: Haymon.

Mowforth, Martin, and Ian Munt. 1997. *Tourism and Sustainability: Critical Perspectives on the Developing World*. London: Routledge.

N'Dour, Youssou. 1994. *The Guide (Wommat)*. Columbia Records.

Norkunas, Martha K. 2002. *Monuments and Memory: History and Representation in Lowell, Massachusetts*. Washington, DC: Smithsonian Institution Press.

Pratt, Mary Louise. 1992. *Imperial Eyes. Travel Writing and Transculturation*. New York: Routledge.

Rosaldo, Renato. 1986. "Ilongot Hunting as Story and Experience." In *The Anthropology of Experience*, edited by Victor W. Turner and Edward M. Bruner. Urbana: University of Illinois Press.

Savvy Traveler. 2016. "Shows." Accessed Sep 20. http://savvytraveler.publicradio.org /show/features/index.shtml.

Smith, Valene L., ed. (1977) 1989. *Hosts and Guests: The Anthropology of Tourism*. Philadelphia: University of Pennsylvania Press.

Stagl, Justin. 1983. *Apodemiken: eine räsonnierte Bibliographie der reisetheoretischen Literatur des 16., 17. und 18. Jahrhunderts*. With the assistance of Klaus Orda and Christel Kämpfer. Paderborn: Ferdinand Schöningh.

Stahl, Sandra D. 1989. *Literary Folkloristics and the Personal Narrative*. Bloomington: Indiana University Press.

Stewart, Susan. 1993. *On Longing. Narratives of the Miniature, the Gigantic, the Souvenir, the Collection*. Durham, NC: Duke University Press.

Swatos, William H. 2006. *On the Road to Being There: Studies in Pilgrimage and Tourism in Late Modernity*. Leiden: Brill.

Taylor, Charles. 1989. *Sources of the Self. The Making of the Modern Identity*. Cambridge, MA: Harvard University Press.

Thompson, Stith. 1955–58. *Motif-Index of Folk Literature*. Bloomington: Indiana University Press.

Tourism—Contact—Culture. 2016. "Research Network." Accessed Sep 20. https://sites.google.com/site/tourismcontactculture/.

Trilling, Lionel. 1971. *Sincerity and Authenticity*. Cambridge, MA: Harvard University Press.

Veblen, Thorstein. (1899) 1967. *The Theory of the Leisure Class*. London: Penguin.

Welz, Gisela. 2000. "'Wo sich neun sattessen, werden auch zehn besiegt.' Das Mesedes-Syndrom: Mutationen einer nahrungskulturellen Praxis." In *Volkskultur und Moderne: Europäische Ethnologie zur Jahrtausendwende*, edited by Institut für Europäische Ethnologie. Vienna: Selbstverlag des Instituts für Europäische Ethnologie.

Weverka, Jody. 1992. "Wish You Weren't Here," *Express (The East Bay's Free Weekly)*. 14 (28).

# Section II

---⌇⌇---

## *Introduction: Heritage Semantics, Heritage Regimes*

The United Nations Educational, Scientific and Cultural Organization—UNESCO—approved the world heritage convention in 1972. Critical scholarship on heritage began to take shape in the 1990s—an understandable lapse of time, as the impact of a new, globally initiated heritage regime took some time to manifest itself. Twenty years later, however, one can easily adapt David Lowenthal's phrase on heritage (1996, ix) to the scholarship about it: all at once, heritage research is everywhere, bringing into its fold research on tourism, museums and memory, sustainability, and cultural diversity. Barbara Kirshenblatt-Gimblett (1995, 1997) conceptualized this convergence early on and offered theoretical concepts for approaching the heritage complex. Her notion of heritage-making as a "mode of cultural production that has recourse to the past" (1995, 370) remains suggestive, and her later formulation that includes tangible as much as intangible heritage production warrants being cited in full:

> Heritage is created through metacultural operations that extend
> museological values and methods (collection, documentation,
> preservation, presentation, evaluation, and interpretation) to living
> persons, their knowledge, practices, artifacts, social worlds, and life
> spaces. While heritage professionals use concepts, standards, and
> regulations to bring cultural phenomena and practitioners into the
> heritage sphere, where they become metacultural artifacts, whether
> "Living National Treasures" or "Masterpieces of Oral and Intangible

Heritage of Humanity," the performers, ritual specialists, and artisans whose "cultural assets" become heritage through this process experience a new relationship to those assets, a metacultural relationship to what was once just habitus. Once habitus becomes heritage, to whom does it belong? How does heritage come to belong to all of humanity? (2006, 161–62)

Kirshenblatt-Gimblett's formulations entail a research program that continues to be pursued. The focus on metalevels has particularly motivated anthropologists, ethnologists, and folklorists to engage with the heritage complex.[1] They are themselves often called on to serve as experts in the creation or evaluation of UNESCO-heritage nomination dossiers and occasionally assist in developing governmental guidelines to implement heritage policies (cf., Bendix, Eggert, and Peselmann 2012; Bortolotto 2011). Working with such instruments and their inherently normative character poses a challenge for practitioners in fields of research that generally privilege hermeneutic over normative engagement. Reflexive engagement with the contribution of cultural scholarship to nation-building and nationalism, colonialism, communism, and fascism has made many scholars wary of any kind of applied research. Simultaneously, scholars from these fields have built up and worked in museums and related institutions since the late nineteenth century, and in their work as transmitters of scholarly knowledge to the public sphere, they have implicitly participated in shaping societal perspectives on culture past and present (Gorgus 1999; Karp and Lavine 1991; Smith and Cubitt 2011). The critical examination of both institutional practice and political complicity arguably assists in making reflection an inexorable component and companion of ongoing cultural research, so that one perhaps need not worry too much over the sprouting of heritage chairs and departments spanning the world from Australia to Abu Dhabi, and New York to Helsinki. UNESCO contributes to this boom, as the institution seeks expert advice, sponsors workshops and conferences, cooperates with new training programs and in the process also seeks to refine the ongoing work within the committees occupied with managing and enlarging the different heritage conventions. Caution remains advisable, as within the complex interplay of international organizations, states and their political, legal, and bureaucratic actors, students of culture are hardly participating from an empowered position. And while there are guardians of heritage and even (for instance in Cambodia) a heritage police (Hauser-Schäublin 2011, 17), beyond disciplinary self-reflection there are no police watching the involvement of cultural scholars in heritage practices.

Within scarcely three decades, heritage scholarship has diversified and quickly moved beyond anxieties of heritage endangerment and loss, to an exploration of heritage linkages in all kinds of cultural realms, such as childhood (Darian-Smith and Pascoe 2012) or foodways (Brulotte and Di Giovine 2013), to include critical and troubling components within cultural history, such as *Places of Pain and Shame* (Logan, Stewart, and Reeves 2009), human rights (Langfield, Logan, and Nic Craith 2010), and war (Gegner and Ziino 2011). Its lens has broadened to consider conflict in cultural diversity (Turnbridge and Ashworth 1996; Ashworth, Graham, and Turnbridge 2007), working-class heritage (Smith, Shackel, and Campbell 2011), and slavery (Smith and Cubitt 2011). Simultaneously there is a call—at present still more marginal—to deepen historical perspectives on heritage-making as a cultural practice (Harvey 2001) and to set the UNESCO heritage regime in relation to earlier and parallel national and local protection and preservation institutions and practices (Tauschek 2012). Finally, there are suggestions to theorize heritage within philosophical parameters (Zimmermann 2009a, 2009b) and to critically consider the resource nature of heritage (Berger 2009; Köstlin 2003). Both the historical dimensions and their entwining with philosophical perspectives deepen and to some extent challenge whether heritage-making truly is a new mode of cultural production or whether the turn to metacultural operations is ultimately an ever-present option when humans are faced with outdated practices or practices witnessed in other cultures.

The main journal of the heritage field, the *International Journal of Heritage Studies* published its first issue in 1994. Since then, it has become the journal of the *Association for Critical Heritage Studies*, which held its inaugural meeting in Gothenburg, Sweden, in 2012. Before this meeting, a manifesto was posted on the new association's home page, expressing its plan to launch new and interdisciplinary perspectives for the field of heritage research: "We want to challenge you to respond to this document, and question the received wisdom of what heritage is, energize heritage studies by drawing on wider intellectual sources, vigorously question the conservative cultural and economic power relations that outdated understandings of heritage seem to underpin and invite the active participation of people and communities who to date have been marginalized in the creation and management of 'heritage.'"[2] Acknowledging the long-term dominance of Western paradigms of heritage research and preservation—shored up particularly by fields such as archeology and architecture, history and art history—the association made it its urgent goal to include non-Western views and practices of heritage-making and heritage-preserving, to open the disciplinary angles to include fields without a set canon of heritage values and preservation measures, and to involve communities interested in and affected by heritage measures.

For a number of reasons, my own approach to heritage has always been critical; but arguably, that may also be what allows for productive engagement (Fabian 2007). Growing up in Switzerland, institutions such as *Heimatschutz* (homeland protection) and, perhaps to a lesser degree, *Denkmalschutz* (monument protection), stood not simply for conservation but for conservatism. When I began to study *Volkskunde* in 1978 (now renamed Cultural Anthropology, European Ethnology, and a variety of other names, see Bendix 2012), the discipline was in a process of transformation, focusing on everyday life across social classes, shedding the mantle of a field devoted to past (national) peasant ways of life, and firmly based in ethnographic and archival methods. Since heritage ventures draw fuel from those earlier scholarly interests, having to grapple with heritage-making as a cultural practice in its own right requires stamina: time and again one faces vestiges of one's disciplinary past successfully embedded in society as "fact." My own work on heritage thus began from irritation. The more heritage as a label encroached on everyday life, the more it aroused my suspicion. This may be most evident in the first chapter in this section, initially presented at a conference organized by Barbro Klein in the summer of 1998 in Sweden. I had worked for nearly a decade on the role of authenticity—one of the key terms in heritage proclamations and instruments—within the history of folklore studies (Bendix 1997). Observing the growth of a culture sector proclaiming authenticity as a seemingly evident, essential characteristic of heritage sites incited my polemic "Heredity, Hybridity, and

Heritage from One Fin de Siècle to the Next." Linking these terms offered an opportunity to examine the suggestively vague and hence imprecise semantics of the heritage concept and to bring into question what kind of value it bestowed on sites and monuments. The international mantel of a global movement seemingly depoliticized heritage. Drawing on Austrian examples from the Habsburg era, I argue that many of the sites deemed worthy of protection and heritage status are vestiges of the political power of monarchs overthrown or disempowered due to the rise of democracy. Yet, oddly, the call for heritage-making asks democratic citizens to protect and invest in these very sites.

The next chapter further pursues the placement of heritage between economic and political considerations. It was written initially for a German conference volume on the process of heritage-making (Hemme, Tauschek, and Bendix 2007) and was later revised for an English, interdisciplinary volume on intangible heritage (Smith and Akagawa 2009). Building on several, mostly German examples, I encourage a focus on actors and contexts of heritage-making on the ground and suggest, furthermore, that rather than only emphasizing issues of maintaining and bolstering identity, such matters had to be considered in tandem with the marginalized question of potential economic benefit and thus the resource quality of heritage. Aesthetic identification and historical memory are not only generated by the politics and economics of culture; ultimately, they also are maintained only due to political and economic investment.

Heritage implies an inheritance, and the next chapter, continuing the scrutiny of terminology embarked on in the first chapter in this section, endeavors to clarify the relationship between an inheritance in the personal or familial realm and heritage as carried from the past into the future, purportedly by humanity. To understand how culture deemed particularly valuable through the heritage label comes to be situated in the web of social life, it is worthwhile to examine the process with long-established practices of passing on things deemed valuable, such as inheritances. Such an approach also removes heritage somewhat from its status as different and new. The comparison assists in recognizing the features of heritage-making as a culture practice, and points to areas that have thus far been but poorly solved and require scholarly as much as political attention. As with an inheritance, heritage comes with rights and responsibilities. The considerable, economically taxing burdens of responsibility that are part of heritage nominations and implementations tend to be forgotten in the arduous competition to achieve a heritage nomination. And while a will, or if there is none, the law, regulates questions of ownership in the case of an inheritance, heritage ownership and the ensuing burdens attached to a successful heritage nomination can result in complex processes of negotiation, in dependencies of outside donors, and in the establishment of institutions overseeing the implementation of heritage status.

The final chapter in this section moves further into the area of acknowledging the resource nature of culture. Linked to the initial chapter of section one, and reaching back to three Swiss ethnographic examples I researched in the 1980s, I make a case for the power of actors and their capacity to negotiate the diverse kinds of "profit" they seek from cultural expressions. Rather than observing uniform developments leading to the demise of cultural integrity once components of marketing enter the picture, each case shows a different dynamic over the course of time, with some groups disinterested in heritage status and but moderate engagement in market possibilities, and others making use of the heritage regime as one among many options to reify facets of their culture, from museum building to CD-productions, while nonetheless continuing a deep emotional investment in their cultural performances.

Specialization is the hobgoblin of disciplines, and while the enormous attention to heritage processes has brought forth rich results (see Logan, Nic Craith, and Kockel 2015), it is important to embed seemingly new cultural phenomena into larger social and political configurations. Markus Tauschek, for instance, saw how heritage phenomena link with and partake of competitive impulses and thus contributed to integrating heritage alongside research on other late modern phenomena (2013). Similarly, heritage warrants examination from the perspective of governance so as to grasp how particularly bureaucratic cultures and business practices take hold of actors and phenomena in the heritage field, including the stranglehold of audits (see Shore and Wright 2015).

NOTES

1. The "res patrimony" network (http://respatrimoni.wordpress.com/. Accessed May 24, 2017), assembling particularly scholars from the Romance language areas of Europe, accompanies heritage developments vigorously and was one of the first groups to challenge complicit scholarly participation with a 2010 workshop entitled "Au-delà du consensus patrimonial: Anthropologie des résistances aux patrimonialisations." See Bondaz, Cysnart, and Leblon (2012).
2. Drawn from http://archanth.anu.edu.au/heritage-museum-studies/association-critical-heritage-studies. Accessed October 12, 2012.

REFERENCES

Ashworth, Gregory J., Brian J. Graham, and J. E. Turnbridge. 2007. *Pluralising Pasts: Heritage, Identity and Place in Multicultural Societies*. London: Pluto.

Bendix, Regina. 1997. *In Search of Authenticity. The Formation of Folklore Studies*. Madison: University of Wisconsin Press.

Bendix, Regina F. 2012. "From Volkskunde to the Field with Many Names: Folklore Studies in German Speaking Europe." In *A Companion to Folklore*, 364–90. Oxford: Wiley-Blackwell.

Bendix, Regina F., Aditya Eggert, and Arnika Peselmann, eds. 2012. *Heritage Regimes and the State*. Göttingen: University of Göttingen Press.

Berger, Karl C., ed. 2009. *Erb.gut? Kulturelles Erbe in Wissenschaft und Gesellschaft*. Vienna: Selbstverlag des Vereins für Volkskunde.

Bondaz, Julien, Cyril Isnart, and Anais Leblon. 2012. "Au-delà du Consensus Patrimonial. Résistances et Usages Contestataires du Patrimoine." *Civilisations. Revue international d'anthropologie et de Sciences Humaines* 61 (1): 9–22.

Bortolotto, Chiara, ed. 2011. *Le Patriomoine Culturel Immaterériel. Enjeux d'une Nouvelle Catégorie*. Paris: Éditions de la Maison des sciences de l'homme.

Brulotte, Ronda L. and Michael A. Di Giovine, eds. 2013. *Edible Identities: Food and Foodways as Cultural Heritage*. London: Ashgate.

Darian-Smith, Kate and Carla Pascoe, eds. 2012. *Children, Childhood and Cultural Heritage*. London: Routledge.

Fabian, Johannes. 2007. *Memory against Culture: Arguments and Reminders*. Durham, NC: Duke University Press.

Gorgus, Nina. 1999. *Der Zauberer der Vitrinen. Zur Museologie Henri Rivières*. Münster: Waxmann.

Harvey, David C. 2001. "Heritage Pasts and Heritage Presents: Temporality, Meaning and the Scope of Heritage Studies." *International Journal of Heritage Studies* 7 (4): 319–38.

Hauser-Schäublin, Brigitta, ed. 2011. *World Heritage Angkor and Beyond: Circumstances and Implications of UNESCO Listings in Cambodia*. Göttingen: Göttingen University Press.

Hemme, Dorothee, Markus Tauschek, and Regina Bendix, eds. 2007. *Prädikat Heritage*. Berlin: Lit-Verlag.

Karp, Ivan and Steven D. Lavine, eds. 1991. *Exhibiting Cultures. The Poetics and Politics of Museum Display.* Washington, DC: Smithsonian Institution Press.

Kirshenblatt-Gimblett, Barbara. 1995. "Theorizing Heritage." *Ethnomusicology* 39 (3): 367–80.

———. 1997. *Destination Culture: Tourism, Museums, and Heritage.* Berkeley: University of California Press.

———. 2006. "World Heritage and Cultural Economics." In *Museum Frictions. Public Cultures/Global Transformations,* edited by Ivan Karp and Lavine, 161–202. Durham, NC: Duke University Press.

Logan, William, William Stewart, and Keir Reeves. 2009. *Places of Pain and Shame: Dealing with "Difficult Heritage."* London: Routledge.

Logan, William, Máiréad Nic Craith, and Ullrich Kockel, eds. 2015. *A Companion to Heritage Studies.* London: Routledge.

Lowenthal, David. 1996. *Possessed by the Past: The Heritage Crusade and the Spoils of History.* New York: Free Press.

Shore, Cris, and Susan Wright. 2015. "Governing by Numbers: Audit Culture, Rankings and the New World Order." *Social Anthropology* 23 (1): 22–8.

Smith, Laurajane, Paul Shackel, and Gary Campbell, eds. 2011. *Heritage, Labor and the Working Classes.* London: Routledge.

Smith, Laurajane and Geoffrey Cubitt, eds. 2011. *Representing Enslavement and Abolition in Museums: Ambiguous Engagements.* London: Routledge.

Tauschek, Markus. 2012. "The Bureaucratic Texture of National Patrimonial Policies." In *Heritage Regimes and the State,* edited by Regina F. Bendix, Aditya Eggert, and Arnika Peselmann, 195–212. Göttingen: University of Göttingen Press.

———., ed. 2013. *Kulturen des Wettbewerbs: Formationen kompetitiver Logiken.* Münster: Waxmann.

Turnbridge, J.E., and G.J. Ashworth. 1996. *Dissonant Heritage: The Management of the Past as a Resource in Conflict.* New York: Wiley.

Zimmermann, Harm-Peer. 2009a. "Second Hand World? Zur Kritik der Heritage-Kritik in Hinblick auf das Kasseler Weltdokumenteerbe." In *Zwischen Identität und Image,* edited by H.-P. Zimmermann, 572–91. Hessische Blätter für Volks- und Kulturforschung, vol. 44/45. Marburg: Jonas.

———. 2009b. "Memory, Markt und Medien: Analyse des UNESCO-Programms 'Memory of the World' im Hinblick auf Fragen der Kommerzialisierung und Popularisierung." In *Zwischen Identität und Image,* edited by H.-P. Zimmermann. Hessische Blätter für Volks- und Kulturforschung, 542–71, vol. 44/45. Marburg: Jonas.

# 5

*Heredity, Hybridity, and Heritage from*
*One* Fin de Siècle *to the Next*

Reporting on a visit through several floors of storage space in a Belgian colonial museum, Johannes Fabian described the experience as surreal: "Here we were below ground, in spaces closed to the public. You look at endless rows of shelves laden with fetishes, objects that go for hundred[s of] thousands of dollars in the art market because they are so rare, and here there were so many of them, the visual impression of plenitude can only be described as surreal. And above ground there are the Congolese, clamoring for the return of these pieces, 'this is our heritage! give it back to us!'"[1] The visual experience may be surreal, the contrasts invoked perhaps rather more absurd. Below ground there is the abundance and order of the collection, above ground the idea of collection is almost negated, as the artifacts and cultural practices inscribed in them (both of using them and of collecting them) are gathered together in the notion of heritage. For the Congolese, as for so many ethnic and national groups around the world, heritage is a useful trope for demanding redress for past atrocities without holding an international tribunal, and without accounting for certain abuses of one's own.

The example is instructive. It assists us in understanding the arbitrary or even serendipitous ways in which something—an object, a cultural practice, an idea—enters the transcultural polities of ownership, monetary value, and representation. Reifying or "artifactualizing" (Stewart 1991) cultural practices and ideas and putting them on display is an old technique, whether it is put to use for sacred or secular politics. The currently so-popular term, "heritage," is unstable and ambiguous like others that have been used in the realm of public culture-preservation, authenticity, restoration, and so forth. What distinguishes heritage is its capacity to hide the complexities of history and politics. The term's popularity is symbolic of the dearth of political engagement we confront in the face of global capitalism.

"All at once heritage is everywhere," starts geographer David Lowenthal's (1996, 9) book, and the title already indicates that Lowenthal regards heritage not as only a trendy phenomenon, but also a further stage in the imprinting of market forces on the countryside.[2] Among all the terms associated with "culture" in the last decade of the twentieth century, heritage has incurred ever-greater employment in public discourse. Heritage is freely drawn upon by those in public life, as they associate it with efforts to preserve and celebrate ethnicity, locality, and history. We find it used as a concept and practice that local or indigenous groups can rally behind with pride. Simultaneously, heritage allows one to attract outsiders to come visit and admire it for a suitable price. We also find heritage in academic discourse, as a term that appears to link ethnicity, tourism, and nationalism, postcolonial existence, and diasporas. Examining heritage, as idea and practice, allows then for a critical understanding of the intersection of politics, markets, and social networks characteristic of the present *fin de siècle*, while simultaneously containing a history of cultural representation reaching back into the nineteenth century.

Heritage is one part of an intertwined triad of terms. At least in English they all conveniently begin with *H*: Heritage, Heredity, and Hybridity. History, a fourth *H*-word in English, lingers behind all of them, and it is the relative neutrality of historical introspection that I will use to examine the linkages of the terms. The term heritage acts like a beautifying gloss, rendering the specificity of past political, economic, and social experiences into a far less complex whole than what sociohistorical scrutiny would reveal. Heritage can be reveled in and consumed without contending with the specific features of power relations. Power relations, however, are profoundly inscribed in the meaning and usage of the terms heredity and hybridity—terms from which heritage arguably evolved. The mantle of heritage has the power to disempower. For heritage, as much as it promises a valuable past to all, is a concept and practice that encourages expenditure rather than conservation. Heritage demands specialists to restore and preserve it materially, or to render material what are mentifacts. Heritage requires facilities for its display, and guards for its protection.

The apparatus, which constructs and maintains things in the name of heritage, is derived from Western, enlightened science; the ideology of heritage is derived from Western romantic nationalism and its more recent avatars (including its ethno-nationalist descendants); the marketing of heritage is fueled by Western capitalism. One could argue that heritage is reflexive modernity's successor to Western colonial hegemony, potentially blocking alternate global strategies to arrive at liberty, fraternity, and equality.[3]

Heredity and hybridity are far more precise terms than heritage. They are historical antecedents and remain current, if latent, ingredients of present-day heritage politics. "Heredity" and "hybridity" crucially informed the idea of "culture" as it took shape in the nineteenth century. Both, I argue, were key ideas that warranted reflection when European feudal systems transformed into more or less democratic nation-states based on cultural homogeneity. The late twentieth century finds us in the midst of economic globalization, with the question of political globalization uncomfortably hovering in the background. Benjamin Barber's title *Jihad vs. McWorld*—ethno-nationalism versus global commoditization—encapsulates this poignantly, and I align myself here with his deep concern over the future of citizenship within the tensions of culture wars and cultural commoditization. Barber asks: "Can it be that what Jihad and McWorld have in common is anarchy: The absence of common will and that conscious and collective human control under the guidance of law we call democracy?" (1996, 5).[4]

Like all key terms in the discourse on culture, heredity, hybridity, and heritage are abstractions; what they signify is subject to interpretation, and their positive, negative, or ambivalent valuation fluctuate over time, depending on the politics for which they are put to use. For example, hybridity when applied to human beings has been a negative term far into the twentieth century. For many, hybridity continues to designate the impurity of racially mixed heritage. But it is also unmistakable that in the late twentieth century the idea of "hybrid culture" has been reevaluated and can connote vitality, innovation, and promise for the future.[5] Hybridity currently can travel within the semantic domain of such terms as creolization, transculturation, and globalization, and the sampling of world musics may be one of its most popular manifestations.[6] To foster awareness of the historical transformation of these central terms as they are applied to the notion of "culture" is then part of what I would like to use this chapter for.

I will provide three Austrian examples—a castle, a set of horses, and a wedding gift of songs and costume drawings—where the problematic interplay of the three terms heredity, hybridity, and heritage comes to the fore. Austria's geographic and political situation within Europe provides particularly poignant evidence for the changing meaning of the terms under investigation. Austria was once one of the most powerful empires on the continent, securing the sovereignty of the ruling Habsburg house through a politics of hereditary succession since the thirteenth century. The Revolution of 1848 brought a first, brief transformation, granting greater self-determination and a concept of citizenship to the individual.[7] The last gasp of this empire under Franz Josef's nearly seventy-year-long reign was Austria-Hungary, the *Vielvölkerstaat* (multiple peoples' state). It contained even within its name a reference to cultural diversity. The term heredity connoting noble bloodlines slowly expanded to refer to peoples and their cultures, as was typical of the nationalist project sweeping across Europe. One might argue that transferring the idea of heredity from genetic (or what was then thought to be bloodlines) to cultural "bodies" remains one of the most problematic legacies of the national project.

The end of empire and the formation of the Republic of Austria in 1918 brought an enormous loss of territory and power. The national segments within the former empire now achieved, however briefly, independent statehood. For Austria, this meant the beginning of a search for a national/cultural past that could fulfill the kinds of functions I have outlined already for "heritage," a rallying point for natives and an attractive destination for outsiders. Heritage is hardly a term one would want to associate with "loss," or if so, then perhaps nostalgia—the beautiful loss, not the pains of concrete political losses. Hence what we find in Austria is a selective mixture of imperial and folk, national, and more broadly cultural traits that form their own unique kind of "hybridity" within the umbrella of heritage celebrated today. The realities of social inequality, political struggle, and cultural—or at least linguistic—difference were removed to the realm of commoditizable "words and images" characteristic of the heritage industry.[8]

## THE SCHÖNBRUNN EXAMPLE

Since 1996, Schönbrunn castle has been designated a world heritage site by the United Nations Educational, Scientific and Cultural Organization (UNESCO). According to a small plaque, this grand castle of the Habsburgs at the outskirts of Vienna earned this designation because it is a "unique work of baroque art." Reading this plaque during a visit in March 1998 gave me pause. Here was, on the one hand, a beautiful palace, visited (it appears from the signage in many languages) by droves of people eager to see the splendor of chambers and furnishings inhabited by the tragic empress and emperor of the Austro-Hungarian monarchy, Sisi and Franz Josef. And here was, on the other hand, the world cultural organization UNESCO, a branch of the United Nations which came about, as its name already implies, due to the rise of nations and the downfall of monarchies.[9] Heredity: why does a vestige of nobility, an example of architectural size, not just art-historical style, that so clearly encoded wealth and power of the few over the many, enter the category "heritage"? The easy answer would be that more than two hundred years after it was built, this castle now belongs to all of us, its majesty now the majesty of all democratic politics. Alas, such an answer is not borne out by the ways in which visitors tour this and countless other remnants of monarchal heritage in Austria and elsewhere in Europe. In addition to the bourgeois preoccupation of learning about art history firsthand, many visitors display a cult-like reverence toward the public and private lives of dead and overthrown royals—a reverence that is suffused with nostalgia for a bygone time.[10] What democratic citizens appear to long for is (of course) not the lowly posts we would likely have occupied in this bygone era—footmen, soldiers, servants, or peasants. Rather, our nostalgia is fueled by the sobriety that responsible citizenship in a democratic arrangement brings with it. Doing away with kings did not make any of us royalty.

The distinction of royal heredity remains elusive, available only to the few who can trace their bloodlines to the Habsburgs, Bourbons, Windsors, or Bernadottes. Our heredity remains that of footmen, soldiers, servants, and peasants. But what we can claim is heritage. That final syllable "-age" in "heritage" does away with the particulars of history and heredity, who governed and who was governed. Heritage puts everything into a collective pot of "culture" and "past," possibly adding the adjective "important" to it. And because it holds importance and is valued as such, we pay for the privilege to see it. We pay to see the beauty and splendor of what "they" owned. We pay doubly, because we financially endow organizations to preserve vestiges of the past (paying for the idea of heritage), and we pay yet more to go see the actual artifacts (material that we designate to be heritage, but which we as a rule only permit ourselves to gaze at, not to sensorialy recognize in its materiality).[11]

Democratic heritage preservation is a costly endeavor. And while we have also undertaken to preserve heritage of different social classes and different ethnicities, the cost involved in preserving vestiges of former hereditary power is a great deal higher. Are our past rules getting the better of us, making us maintain what they once exacted from our forebears? Or is the claim of collective ownership that the term "heritage" seems to promise truly transformative, allowing us to own not simply the burdens of the past but also the sociopolitical gains we have made since? The answer to the latter can be made visible only in interpretations: plaques, texts available for purchase, scripts used by tour guides, and, in turn, embodied in the patterns of consuming heritage displayed by natives and tourists alike. Such interpretations are subject to their present-day context. Based on my observations in Vienna, the visitors to castles, royal graves, and imperial silver chambers are not behaving like liberated subjects reveling in joint ownership of spoils once reserved for the few. The tourist behavior is reverent, admiring, adhering to gazing rather than touching, staying within cordoned-off passages, and keeping off the lawns and gardens. The protection of the past, the (monetary) value that preserved history and preserved artifacts enjoy in our societies has the power to confine us mentally and bodily, much as the holiness of a church dictates restricted, restrained, or reverential behaviors. An invention of modernity, of the spirit of Enlightenment and political revolution, impossible without the enterprise of liberal capitalism, heritage, nonetheless, has the power to discipline and restrict us and to make us pay for the privilege. Capital is heritage's quintessential ingredient.

Heritage, then, has the potential of bodily and ideologically keeping us subject to the ghosts of past rulers and past ways of life. Efforts to construct heritage sites that memorialize struggle, subjugation, and violent victory against such rulers are far less common, far more fragile, and fraught with financial and staffing problems.[12] Memory of struggles, furthermore, tends to be recalled and celebrated as history, not heritage: the storming of the Bastille or the Winter Palace turn into holidays memorializing liberation. Similarly, many people find it problematic to treat sites of enslavement, concentration camps, and other traces of Holocausts as heritage sites.[13] However, the heritage phenomenon and the associated process of "musealization" (the German *Musealisierung*, cf., Zacharias [1990]; Lübbe [1982]) or "Museomania" (the French equivalent), have the unsettling ability to contribute to the emergence of what one might term "Holocaust tourism." The same cultural techniques of exhibition and experience are employed and thus could normalize what for the sake of global memory ought to remain out of the ordinary.

Still, there appears to remain a differentiation between heritage and history in popular practice. The failure of the Disney corporation to realize a historical heritage site in Manassas outside Washington, DC, is instructive here: societal resistance to turn America's war of independence and the Civil War into heritage points to a key characteristic of the heritage concept—it is timeless, static, and not punctual and transformative in the way we treat historical facts.[14] Civil War reenactments are—though perhaps absurdly—an acceptable heritage practice alongside chivalrous reenactments seen in Europe, or living history experiences in countless open air museums (Bendix 2000). But rendering the whole of history into one Disney site was too blatant a symbol of the commoditizing process.

A castle such as Schönbrunn, and the issues I have just enumerated, may strike one as an atypical case for examining issues of heritage. The term is so closely associated with issues of ethnic and minority cultures in heterogeneous societies, as well as with efforts of world organizations to bring into the global purview the cultural wealth and diversity that a colonizing West had marginalized and subdued in the name of unilinear progress. However, castles, those who inhabited them, and the kinds of cultural practices they modeled, are exemplary for examining the relationship in the meaning and politics of the terms heritage, heredity, and hybridity. Hereditary monarchies were ruled by nobility able to trace their physical bodies through bloodlines to ancestors who had already been in power and whose power in turn was ultimately legitimated through their serving the Christian God and his Holy Roman Empire. Noble heredity was thus mysteriously close to sacredness, ruling in God's place on this earth. We may need to ask the question, then, is "heritage" an effort to claim some of the sacredness lost with the advent of democracy and the political downfall of heredity?

Or alternately, is heritage a democratic achievement, amalgamating cultural remnants across class and making them the property of all? Or is it a pocket or an air bubble within which the inequalities of heredity are regarded as a playground within which we can replay the kinds of behaviors of status and gender—wearing costumes for instance—which democratic citizenship would permit (if not urge) us to leave behind? What exactly is the path from heredity to heritage? What role does hybridity play within it? Another example from Vienna may assist us here.

## THE LIPPIZANER EXAMPLE

The Spanish Riding School in Vienna's Hofburg is an institution of world renown. The white Lippizaner stallions perform their horse ballet in a manner that has undergone relatively little change in the almost four hundred years they have been raised and trained under the strictest rules of breeding and style. Their history is a casebook example of how heredity fuels heritage and scorns hybridity.

As a tour guide in March 1998 narrates the story, the arrival of the Lippizaner in Vienna was connected to the politics of heredity of the Habsburgs. Maximilian, the raucous son of Karl I, was already a heavy drinker by the age of thirteen; by fifteen he had fathered an illegitimate child. (Are not bastards the epitome of loathed hybridity?) What were his parents to do with this wayward adolescent? He was married off to a Spanish princess and, miracle upon miracle, he truly fell in love with her, as well as with her carriage drawn by white horses. Royal heredity was thus saved; Maximilian brought the princess, her carriage and horses to Vienna, and they begat sixteen children. Maximilian's younger brother, Karl II, liked the horses, too. He sent for stallions and breeding mares from Spain, and thus the Spanish Riding School began. While printed versions of this narrative offer more precise details, the tour guide's version reaches the poignancy appropriate for a critical discourse on heritage.

Why did the Habsburgs like those horses—which from an equestrian point of view are, again in the words of my outspoken guide, short and fat like empress Maria Theresia? For one, it was the Baroque taste, she says. For another, the white horses were impressive and capable of doing fancy footwork, which in turn made the royals sitting atop them appear all the more elevated and grand. There are records of young royals being trained to guide a Lippizaner through those Spanish steps, and their appearance in public parades atop purebred horses would correspondingly endow them with grace and nobility—even sacredness—thus legitimating their power. This tour guide, the first I have heard in Vienna who spoke with scorn of royals, saw right through the politics of splendor and representation, branding them an easy means to keep the masses quiet. The guide was only conflicted about the horses, which she truly loved and whose presence (and maintenance as a court appendage in a country that no longer has a royal court) she labeled a living museum.[15]

Lippizaner are horses bred white, and they were initially bred to carry noble-bred humans. Horses with carefully monitored genetic heritage for people with carefully monitored genetic heritage. How does one achieve a white horse? How does one achieve horses that are gifted to dance? One must be selective. Aiming for a gifted Lippizaner stallion, one breeds stallions with mares likely or certain to carry the dominant white gene. Inbreeding, inasmuch as it can be done without jeopardizing healthy offspring, is thus desirable. Therefore, all present-day Lippizaner descend from the same five stallions that arrived from Spain during Maria Theresia's time. New mares had to be added in again and again, due to various disasters, such as, for instance, a horse virus in 1983 that killed twenty of the Spanish Riding School's stallions. The danger of inbreeding, the danger of ascertaining heredity, is a lack of resistance and weakness. As a breeding experiment, the Lippizaner are similarly prone to the dangers of breeding within the Coburg/Windsor line with its hereditary hemophilia. All the same, the royal stallions' names and bloodlines remain constant, and are branded onto those horses in three places as signs of pure heredity and pure descent.[16]

If the Spanish Riding School as a whole is a living museum—from the type of riding to the type of socialization for the men who train and perform with the horses—so is maintaining the form of breeding selectively for purity. Democratization has sought to remove public discourse on breeding pure human beings—be it pure hereditary nobility or, (equally customary during feudal and colonial times) breeding races capable of withstanding hard labor. That the idea has not vanished is evident in the ways in which marriage for maintaining or improving social status through biological heredity is often practiced, if not spelled out as such.[17] Unions of whites and blacks remain suspect or endangered in their visibly hybrid offspring; unions across nationality and ethnicity, while increasing in numbers, remain subject to societal scrutiny and concern: how can the transcultural mix sustain the conjugal (biological and social) union?

The notion of human racial or ethnic purity has, since the Nazi era, become an extremely suspect idea, garnering world scorn in the 1990s during the Yugoslav crisis and its associated campaigns of ethnic cleansing. Within the propagation of animal species, however, purity of type remains a viable practice. Dogs, cats, sheep, and cows, aside from Lippizaner stallions, are subject to human endeavors to maintain hereditary purity and avoid the mongrel products of hybridity.[18] Scientifically, genetic engineering appears like a return of pure heredity, celebrated as scientific achievement and circumventing the messy acts of procreation which, in the joining of male and female, always imply hybridity.[19] The timelessness made possible by genetic cloning and invoked in heritage vocabulary and practices have evolved alongside each other. They are parallel preoccupations and products of our age, and they point to what seem to me efforts to simplify and render pure or mono-vocal that which is the complexity and messiness of human pasts and human existence.

The Spanish Riding School, then, is one example where over the past century specific notions of heredity and hybridity have been folded into the category of heritage. The enterprise is still located in what was once a royal palace, but the palace is now owned by the state. It is part of that conglomerate of cultural practices that were selected to be maintained, or in some other cases, carefully researched and rediscovered, even (re)invented to stand for the nation's heritage.

In the case of the Lippizaner, this transfer from heredity to heritage, from a feudal power structure to a democratic one is fully transparent. In 1918, when the First Republic of Austria was declared, all or most of the royal carriages and horses were auctioned off to raise funds for the new democratic state. What chaos it was! How much was auctioned off, how much was squirreled away? The Lippizaner were maintained not least because their caretakers fed them and ran from one ministry to another asking that the noble horses be maintained. The minister of agriculture finally declared that if no one else wanted them, he would take them into his portfolio. The other aspects are distributed between the ministries, so the building, the employees, the performance, and the touring arrangements each lie in the hands of different servants of the state. The royal heritage is democratically distributed over the entire executive.[20]

## THE WEDDING ALBUM EXAMPLE

The royal fairy-tale wedding of the nineteenth century joined Austria's emperor Franz Josef with Bavarian princess Elizabeth of Wittelsbach in 1854. Among the many gifts the new empress received was an ornate folder presented by a well-known publisher of music, Carl Anton Spina. The folder contained twenty-seven songs and melodies from Austria's crown-lands (*Österreichs National Melodien*), as well as twenty-three watercolor paintings by the-then-famous portrait painter Albert Decker. The paintings showed couples in folk costume, intended to represent a selection of the peoples in the empress's new realm. The purpose of the gift is clear: the empress was to gain a sense of the human beauty and variety within Austro-Hungary. What is of interest is the way in which traditional costume as well as traditional song entered the public sphere, and how they became modes of discourse between democratizing and monarchal interests.

Folklorists will easily acknowledge the deep connection between the collection of folk song and Romantic Nationalism—one need only mention Herder's *Voices of Peoples in Song* and its rich aftermath. In the Herderian vein, indigenous song was one means to demonstrate the uniqueness of cultural heritage, and based on such reified heritage (for example, song, narrative, or epic collections), claims for national cohesion and independence could be made. Alongside many other expressive cultural traits, traditional costume has been similarly invoked as a means to demonstrate cultural longevity and uniqueness. We know from our own discipline's history how such cultural resources were and are used as bases of national and democratic states. Folk heritage was one avenue to depart from the cultural, class-based heritage of feudalism. Romanticism bestowed a valuation on hitherto lowly expressive forms, pointed to their beauty and their antiquity, and afforded them a political relevance they had not previously held to the same extent.

Costume's history is, however, far more complex. For one, sumptuary laws had greatly contributed to the creation of dress codes (cf., Köstlin 1988; Noyes 1998; Stallybrass 1996). Their archaism or origin within peasant culture is thus vague at best. More importantly, the symbolic discourse on folk heritage did not go unobserved by conservative forces loyal to monarchs. Sisi's royal Bavarian family is exemplary in this regard. The House of Wittelsbach had appropriated the nationalistic folk costume discourse for its own purposes starting in 1810 when a royal wedding processional was augmented by couples of children wearing the costumes of the Bavarian regions. During the nineteenth century, royal costume initiatives and another wedding staffed by marrying folk couples from all over Bavaria demonstrated the rulers' interest in custom and tradition (Bendix 1998). In the process, the hereditary rulers attempted to subsume the claims for political legitimacy of folk heritage under their own mantle. The revolutionary potential entailed in attending to cultural rather than biological heredity was thus curtailed. Ideologically, the revolutionary, liberating potential inherent in romantic, nationalist cultural politics was hybridized: the idea of the strength of cultural pasts was wedded to the ideological need of conservative restoration.

This discursive complexity is evident, perhaps even more vigorously, in Austria. Through her administrative reorganization, Maria Theresia transformed earlier regions of the realm into countries with national consciousness. One part of this administrative transformation was the admission of regional costume as representative, appropriate clothing even in visits to the court (Kugler 1997, 23–24). Thus, costume was simultaneously an acknowledgment of regional or ethnic background but also a means of signaling place and status within the empire. A more heritage- and liberation-based discourse of costume was embodied by Maria Theresia's grandson, Archduke Johann, who wore a simple hunter's costume himself and who remains a figure idolized in Austria. However, the very fact that it was a royal who modeled this heritage—rather than empire-based discourse—undermined the revolutionary potential within the posture.

Emperor Franz Josef and Sisi themselves were frequently depicted in costume—with Sisi wearing a dirndl and Franz Josef in knee-length leather pants and the typical *Loden* jacket (Kugler 1997, 25). The sociopolitical complexity inscribed—but hidden—in the label "heritage" is very much in evidence in how Austrians, at the end of the twentieth century, view and value costume. In Vienna and other regional capitals, members of high society can be seen shopping for dressy costumes, ranging from classic folk cuts to expensive *Lederhosen*, even for women. Thus, in effect the *haute bourgeoisie* mimics or continues the royal or imperial efforts to inhabit the national while continuing to dominate economically and often politically over those from whom these items of heritage purportedly stem. Left-leaning politicians can be seen wearing jackets in costume style, and the notorious leader of Austria's right-wing party (*Freiheitliche*), Jörg Haider, proclaimed Erzherzog Johann as one of his heroes, and often dressed accordingly.[21]

## CONCLUSION

The symbolic discourse of costume, from Sisi's wedding album gift to the present, demonstrates the diffuse politics of heritage poignantly. Under the mantle of heritage, the same cultural artifacts can speak for socialist innovation and right-wing restoration. Heredity and hybridity both have a biological rather than a spiritual semantic basis: it is the purported biological purity of heredity that claims political domination and superiority over those of lesser heredity, or even of hybrid descent. Heredity unabashedly claims legitimacy, not least by controlling for hybridity. Heritage obfuscates such biologistic leanings, and obscures the political legacies and futures inherent in its practices. Within the discourse on ethnicity, the problematic of descent and consent was crucial (see Sollors 1986). The language and practice of heritage amalgamates the two into an avenue of ascent (see Michael 1998).

Ascending into the realm of a particular heritage requires reverence, learning, and investment. Evolving from the crumbling politics of late nineteenth-century heredity, heritage is a self-absorbing or self-realizing project, typical of late twentieth-century concerns with individuality and selfhood, projected onto problematic constructs of group or ethnic pasts. Heritage's fascination with maintaining the past within the present—such as the castle or the Lippizaner example—steers attention away from the politics of preservation to the mechanics of preservation: how to restore a seventeenth-century site, rather than why. The question *how* costs money; the question *why* requires thought.

Seemingly depoliticized, heritage, like any capitalist invention, wants to appeal to anyone who might want to purchase it. Heritage emerged in the late nineteenth century as the cultural treasury for modern, national states. In the late twentieth century, as I tried to demonstrate, heritage is first and foremost an investment; it requires capital. Its current trendiness among local, national, international, private, and governmental interests is both indicative of our age and suspect. The popularity of heritage symbolizes the lack of popularity of political thought and participation, as well as the erosion of citizenship and the responsibilities entailed within it.

### NOTES

This chapter originally appeared in *Folklore, Heritage Politics and Ethnic Diversity. A Festschrift for Barbro Klein* (2000). Edited by Pertti J. Anttonen, 37–54. Botkyrka: Multicultural Center.

Many thanks for insightful and helpful readings and comments to Roger Abrahams, John Bendix, Johannes Fabian, and Kim Lau. Research on tourism in Austria for summer 1995 and 1996, as well as March 1998 was supported by the University of Pennsylvania Research Foundation; the National Endowment for the Humanities granted a semester research in 1998 to research the *Kronprinzenwerk*.

1. This is a paraphrase from Fabian's orally delivered presentation "The 'Ethnic Artefact' and the 'Ethnographic Object': On Recognizing Things," at the May 26, 1998, Kolloquium at the Institute of Volkskunde and European Ethnology, Vienna.

2. Lowenthal's concern is ultimately with what he sees as the insincere premise of heritage vis-à-vis history: "History and heritage both refashion the past in present garb. But the former does so to make the past comprehensible, the latter to make it congenial.... For historians, presentist reshaping is unavoidable, a translation needed to convey things past to modern audiences. For heritage,... updating is not just a necessity but a virtue that fructifies links with the past" (1996, 148). Making the charge that heritage is contrived, Lowenthal thus creates a not very fruitful dichotomy, one which is all too familiar to folklorists and which precludes us from seeing the complexities of the interrelationship of historical and heritage work. Historians cannot deny their complicity in heritage work, just as folklorists and anthropologists cannot withdraw from this noose either.

3. In the English discourse, Ulrich Beck, Anthony Giddens, and Scott Lash (1994) work with the term "reflexive modernization," a term which I prefer over the notion of "Zweite Moderne" (second modernity) more customarily associated with Beck's German-language sociology. I use the term here, because unlike "postmodernity," "reflexive modernization" does justice to the continual recasting of modern thought.

4. What is perhaps problematic about Barber's position, though, is that he regards the nation-state as a needed, valuable means to protect citizen rights. In other words, citizenship protection comes at the price of upholding nationalism as well. The globalists counter with arguments about global citizenship, yet here one would have to acknowledge that global rights thus far have no or only weak institutions to guarantee them (UN, international courts, and so on.).

5. For an interesting consideration of hybridity with regard to "culture," consider Canclini's work based on the Mexican experience (1995). Among American anthropologists and folklorists, Deborah Kapchan's work has been particularly concerned with the notion of hybridity and marketplaces (e.g., Kapchan 1996).

6. The best-selling CDs of the group *Deep Forest*, which really consists of two Frenchmen mixing ethnographic recordings from all over the world into an appealing soundscape, is a good example. Concerning issues of world music, music industries, and globalization, consider for example Keil and Feld (1994) and Erlman (1996).

7. By 1851, the young emperor Franz Joseph I reversed the 1848 concessions toward reform and introduced a system of neo-absolutist centralism.

8. "Word and image" is, interestingly, also the core of the title of one of the first ethnographic endeavors undertaken in the crumbling empire: *Die Österreichisch Ungarische Monarchie in Wort und Bild* (1885–1902). Ignored for a long time by historians of ethnology as a popular effort, this work received attention at the end of the twentieth century; a conference entitled "Zwischen Vaterland und Nationalkultur" assembled scholars from all over central Europe in Slovenia in November 1998. Short considerations of the work can be found in Schmid 1995 and Johler 1998; compare the chapter, "Expressive Resources" in this volume.

9. Politically it is not quite as simple, but it is the surface paradox that interests me.

10. In 1998, Austria's major touristic theme was the hundredth anniversary of Empress Sisi's death. In Vienna alone, a tripartite exhibit in three different castles unfurled the beauty, tragedy, and inner life of Sisi. A free, monthly publication regularly available in Vienna's public transportation reported in August 1998, that this focus had already been a huge success, bringing one-third more visitors to the Austrian capital in the first trimester of 1998, alone, according to hotel statistics. Sisi died a violent death (she was assassinated in Geneva); she was also an unusual, if not aberrant royal, keeping away from her husband as much as possible, suffering what one would diagnose today as anorexia, and it should not surprise that the Sisi retrospective links up powerfully (both in the popular book market and in the museum visitor's searching) with the fate of the late Lady Diana Spencer, divorced from Prince Charles after fifteen years of unhappy marriage, and killed in a car accident in the summer of 1997.

11. Our museum practices, evolving from the Enlightenment's ideas of collection and display, for a long time denied the sensory taking in of the valuable objects we display. We are generally only permitted to use sight, and the materiality of objects is thus lost on us. Interestingly, touring Goethe's home in Weimar during summer 1998, one learned that Goethe purchased antique sculpture not only for display, but also to give an opportunity to literally *begreifen* (to touch all over, by hand and mind) these artifacts for those who were unable to undertake journeys. Museum practice has been alienated from this more holistic idea of understanding—or rather grasping—heritage.

12. Compare Macdonald (1997) who reports on the effort to create a heritage site on the Isle of Skye in Scotland. The site was to focus on class conflict and economic struggle; it has been plagued by difficulties in staffing and sponsorship, not least because the creators' ideology diverges from the economics of a "regular" heritage site.

13. Since this essay was first published, scholars (and the market) have made use of the category "dark heritage" or "difficult heritage" (Logan and Reeves 2009; Macdonald 2009). UNESCO had already inscribed the Island of Gorée onto the World Heritage List in 1978, and Auschwitz Birkenau in 1979, but discussions remain vibrant within the selection committee, as well as within the world of heritage scholarship, whether places where atrocities were committed fit within heritage (a term more celebratory in nature).

14. A more cynical interpretation would point to Manassas being so close to Washington, DC, (with its many "real" heritage sites) that a Disney park would have threatened the proceeds gained from tourists in the capital.

15. "Sisi," she says, "had a gift for horses. That she had, little or nothing else. People overestimate her role regarding Hungary. But she knew horses." All comments were collected during a tour I took on March 13, 1998, with Ddr Anna Ehrlich, the most knowledgeable (and yet bitter) guide I have had among the very well-trained individuals who constituted the Vienna Walking Tours.

16. One on the hindquarter, one under the saddle, and one on the lower left jaw.

17. A March of Dimes Foundation Study cited in *Harper's* (3/1993) found that about 30 percent would consider genetic engineering for their children if it "would improve their chances in life." Since this article was initially published, the possibilities in this realm have grown exponentially, with attendant ethical issues to consider—such as parents creating a healthy, genetically matched child to save the life of one born with problems (e.g., the *ABC NEWS* online story "Rare Bone Marrow Disease With Only One Cure,"

by Javid Farnaz [December 21, 2007]) http://abcnews.go.com/Health/story?id=4038908. Accessed December 20, 2017.

18. In alpine regions of Europe, for instance, one often encounters reports on efforts to save or else restore goat and sheep subspecies that appear to have lost their purity in breeding, as there are generally efforts (especially within ecologically informed farming) to keep rare species of chickens, rabbits, and goats, and to note this effort in the promotional literature about their products. Zoos have long become places to salvage endangered species, and with a zoo, in German often called a *Tiergarten*, or animal garden, the connection to God's Garden of Eden may resonate for many a visitor. Thus, the most advanced of genetic knowledge and forecasting, gained not least from the revolution of evolutionary biology, paradoxically fosters for some the hope of restoring a planetary zoological diversity as God had created it.

19. Dolly, the first cloned sheep, then, is a great solution: rather than mixing, we just make photocopies of ourselves. Without the mixing, however, even pure lines (Lippizaner) are not viable.

20. There are other aspects of Habsburg royal inheritance that took longer to be entered into the aegis of "heritage." Why, for instance, was the royal silver chamber renovated and reopened in fresh and up-to-date glory only in 1997? While part of the tableware had been used for dinners with heads of state, much of the silver, gold, and porcelain was previously displayed only in parts. How were such royal goods dealt with during a time of revolutionary change? And why were they entered into the realm of heritage in the late twentieth century? Why are the Austrians ready for such opulent nostalgia now? Nostalgia for riches inscribed onto porcelain services used only for conspicuousness, not consumption? The then head of the Royal Library Archives, Dr. Gerda Mraz, told me, "Well, we have nothing else! The 1. Republic was so thoroughly chastened, critiqued, there is nothing to be proud of, there are not very many years of history outside the empire, only 80!" Seeing the schizophrenia in it, she laughed at how her own archive had just become complicit in the imperial cult with a special exhibit on photos of the empress Sisi and the cosponsoring of the Sisi wedding gift exhibit and enactment (cf., Mraz 1997).

21. Jörg Haider was killed in a self-inflicted car accident in Carinthia in 2008. His role in (re)awakening a nativist discourse has been analyzed from an anthropological perspective by Andre Gingrich (2002).

REFERENCES

Barber, Benjamin. *1996. Jihad vs. McWorld*. New York: Ballantine.
Beck, Ulrich, Anthony Giddens, and Scott Lash. 1994. *Reflexive Modernization: Politics, Tradition and Aesthetics in the Modern Social Order*. Cambridge: Polity.
Bendix, Regina. 1998. "Of Names, Professional Identities, and Disciplinary Futures." *Journal of American Folklore* 111 (441): 235–46.
———. 2000. "Der gespielte Krieg: Zur Leidenschaft des Historic Reenactments." In *Volkskultur und Moderne: Europäische Ethnologie zur Jahrtausendwende*, edited by Olaf Bockhorn, Bernhard Fuchs, Reinhard Johler, Gertraud Liesenfeld, Klara Löffler, Herbert Nikitsch, and Bernhard Tschofen, 253–68. Vienna: Institut für Europäische Ethnologie.

———. 2003. "Ethnology, Cultural Reification, and the Dynamics of Difference in the Kronprinzenwerk." In *Creating the Other: Ethnic Conflict and Nationalism in the Habsburg Central Europe*, edited by Nancy M. Wingfield, 149–65. London: Berghahn.

Canclini, Nestor Garcia. 1995. *Hybrid Cultures: Strategies for Entering and Leaving Postmodernity*. Minneapolis: University of Minnesota Press.

Erlman, Veit. 1996. *Nightsong: Performance, Power and Practice in South Africa*. Chicago: University of Chicago Press.

Gingrich, Andre. 2002. "A Man for All Seasons: An Anthropological Perspective on Public Representation and Cultural Politics of the Austrian Freedom Party." In *The Haider Phenomenon in Austria*, edited by Ruth Wodak and Anton Pelinka, 67–91. New Brunswick, NJ: Transaction.

Johler, Reinhard. 1998. "'… die Lesewelt auffordernd zu einer Wanderung durch weite, weite Lande.' Zur Geschichte des Monumentalwerkes 'Die österreichisch-ungarische Monarchie in Wort und Bild,' dargestellt am Beispiel des 1898 erschienenen Bandes 'Galizien'." In *Galizien: Ethnographische Erkundung bei den Bojken und Huzulen in den Karpaten*, edited by Klaus Beitl. Kittsee: Ethnographisches Museum.

Kapchan, Deborah. 1996. *Gender on the Market*. Philadelphia: University of Pennsylvania Press.

Keil, Charles, and Steven Feld. 1994. *Music Grooves: Essays and Dialogues*. Chicago: University of Chicago Press.

Kugler, Georg J. 1997. "Tracht und Hofkleid." In *Österreich-Ungarn in Lied und Bild*, edited by Gerda Mraz. Vienna: Christian Brandstätter.

Köstlin, Konrad. 1988. "Zur frühen Geschichte staatlicher Trachtenpflege." In *Sichtweisen der Volkskunde*, edited by Albrecht Lehmann and Andreas Kuntz. Berlin: Reimer.

Logan, William, and Keir Reeves. 2009. *Places of Pain and Shame: Dealing with "Difficult Heritage."* London: Routledge.

Lowenthal, David. 1996. *Possessed by the Past: The Heritage Crusade and the Spoils of History*. New York: The Free Press.

Lübbe, Hermann. 1982. *Der Fortschritt und das Museum. Über den Grund unseres Vergnügens an historischen Gegenständen*. London: Institute of Germanic Studies, University of London.

Macdonald, Sharon. 1997. "A People's Story: Heritage, Identity and Authenticity." In *Touring Culture*, edited by Chris Rojek and John Urry. London: Routledge.

———. 2009. *Difficult Heritage: Negotiating the Nazi Past in Nuremberg and Beyond*. Oxford: Routledge.

Michael, Jennifer. 1998. "(Ad-)Dressing Shibboleths: Costume and Community in the South of France." *Journal of American Folklore* 111: 146–72.

Mraz, Gerda, ed. 1997. *Österreich-Ungarn in Lied und Bild*. Vienna: Christian Brandstätter.

Noyes, Dorothy. 1998. "La Maja Vestida: Dress as Resistance to Enlightenment in Late 18th-Century Madrid." *Journal of American Folklore* 111: 197–217.

Schmid, Georg. 1995. "Die Reise auf dem Papier." In *Kulturwissenschaft im Vielvölkerstaat. Zur Geschichte der Ethnologie und verwandter Gebiete in Österreich, ca. 1780 bis 1918*, edited by Britta Rupp-Eisenreich and Justin Stagl. Vienna: Böhlau.

Sollors, Werner. 1986. *Beyond Ethnicity: Consent and Descent in American Culture*. New York: Oxford University Press.

Stallybrass, Peter. 1996. "Worn Worlds: Clothes and Identity on the Renaissance Stage."
    In *Subject and Object in Renaissance Culture*, edited by Margreta de Grazia, Maureen
    Quilligan, and Peter Stallybrass. Cambridge: Cambridge University Press.
Stewart, Susan. 1991. *Crimes of Writing: Problems in the Containment of Representation.*
    New York: Oxford University Press.
Zacharias, Wolfgang, ed. 1990. *Zeitphänomen Musealisierung. Das Verschwinden der
    Gegenwart und die Konstruktion der Erinnerung.* Essen: Klartext-Verlagsgesellschaft.

# 6

⟶ ❧ ⟵

# Heritage between Economy and Politics:
## An Assessment from the Perspective
## of Cultural Anthropology

Heritage scholarship is difficult to categorize, which is an indicator of the mercurial nature of the phenomenon itself: constitution, use, evaluation, and critique of cultural heritage intertwine in scholarly discourse as much as they do within heritage itself. Thus the volume *Rethinking Heritage*, edited by Robert Shaman Peckham (2003), assembles contributions from geography, history and art history, landscape planning and philology. This hybrid composition signals that heritage concerns everyone, from the tourism expert to the philosopher of late modernity. Each grouping of practitioners and experts harbors its own conception of heritage; their expectations seldom harmonize with one another. In his introduction, Peckham tries to simplify the range of meanings as follows:

> For most people today "heritage" carries two related sets of meanings.
> On the one hand, it is associated with tourism and with sites of historical
> interest that have been preserved for the nation. Heritage designates those
> institutions involved in the celebration, management, and maintenance
> of material objects, landscapes, monuments and buildings that reflect
> the nation's past. On the other hand, it is used to describe a set of shared
> values and collective memories; it betokens inherited customs and a
> sense of accumulated communal experiences that are construed as a
> "birthright" and are expressed in distinct languages and through other
> cultural performances. (2003, 1)

The two poles of material and intangible goods entail obligations of preservation, on the one hand, and on the other hand a spectrum of emotions from sentimental affection all the way to aggressively political, collective (mis-)appropriation—which are both consequence and cause of cultural heritage. The consequences are evident in new institutions, expertise, and professional profiles; the causes bear witness to seemingly insurmountable problems of group-specific problems and anxieties. The fear of loss, Peckham argues, is what gives rise to instruments of honoring and preserving (Peckham 2003, 4–5). Yet preservation always also entails selection. Not everything is honored; some aspects must be forgotten, so as to increase the potential for identification of what is selected. Thus, within the potential for identification carried by cultural heritage, conflict also resides: certain marginalized remains of cultural historical memory will have been excluded from the process now being named *heritagization* or *patrimonialization, heritage-building process,* or simply *heritage-making.*

Within this jungle of multivalences, the ethnographic approach of cultural anthropology provides a chance to avoid vague and premature appraisals, and focus instead on the documentation of the processes that foster as well as hinder heritage-making. When doing research in this area, scholars in disciplines such as cultural anthropology or folklore encounter arguments, often outdated, from their own disciplinary history. These have been taken up as tools to legitimate the need for one or another practice to be reclassified as intangible heritage. The very familiarity of these tools or arguments prepares cultural anthropologists to approach heritage-making processes in a reflexive manner. Ethnographic and archival methods in folklore studies and cultural anthropology lead them to understand heritage-making as a cultural practice that has emerged over a long time. Heritagization itself has tradition. Organizations and institutions have been created to legitimate this practice and to contribute to turning evermore diversified notions of heritage into a self-understood, habitual aspect of culture. Encountering outdated disciplinary knowledge as part and parcel of heritage practices has been—and for some scholars continues to be—an irritant. Alas, the time has come to move beyond ivory-towered outrage at beholding economic and political actors who know how to turn cultural segments into symbolic as well as economic capital. Heritagization is an ingredient of late modern life. Understanding knowledge transfers from scholarship—as illogical as they sometimes appear—into this, as well as many other cultural practices, is a task for reflexively grounded fields of cultural research.

Over more than forty years, cultural anthropologists have built a solid scholarly foundation regarding the "discovery" of economic and political value-added practices of cultural good (Hann 2002, 293; Kasten 2004). The German debate on *Folklorismus*, which began in 1960, continued unabated for several decades (Bausinger 1988; Bendix 1988). Tradition was unmasked as a phenomenon of invention requiring actors and interests (Hobsbawm and Ranger 1983; Johler 2000). The concept of authenticity, so central to nomination processes in the heritage realm, has been thoroughly deconstructed (Bendix 1997; Seidenspinner 2006).[1] Finally, ethnographically working disciplines have acquired a deep awareness of the interdependence of cultural scholarship, nation-building, and the processes of cultivating symbolic and cultural capital. Thereby, ethnographic work has acquired a reflexivity, disciplinary modesty, and diplomacy which will be almost indispensable in taking on heritage-making as a cultural practice—even more so with intangible manifestations, given their naturally more vague contours, requiring of actors far more determination in making their case. At the same time, interdisciplinary cooperation remains equally vital, for declaring one bit of culture to be heritage opens economic and legal dimensions, and hence necessitates the willingness to grasp and interact with the discourses of fields such as cultural economics or international law, which pursue generally far more normative lines of inquiry than do ethnographers (Huber 2005, 59n42). Here I present questions and potential lines of inquiry to address these dimensions, based on empirical research with heritage practices in late modern contexts.[2]

Cultural heritage does not exist; it is made. From the warp and weft of habitual practices and everyday experience—the changeable fabric of action and meaning that anthropologists call "culture"—actors choose privileged excerpts and imbue them with status and value. Motivations and goals may differ, but the effort to ennoble remains the same. Cultural heritage thus represents the opposite of what Michael Herzfeld (2005) terms cultural intimacy, those cultural peculiarities that actors seek to hide from outsiders. The most familiar aspects of cultural workings may be considered problematic or morally compromising, but in their negative aesthetics, not mentioned in tourism brochures, they nonetheless contribute to everyday life. To understand processes of heritagization, cultural anthropology pursues two directions of empirical inquiry. The ethnographic gaze will focus first on the actors who generate these processes, exploring their intentions; second, it will examine the specific shape of the value-added mechanism: how the processes are linked to existing forms of everyday life and how new cultural practices are introduced so as to integrate successful cultural-heritage nominations in everyday life. This kind of ethnographic knowledge production is particularly challenging, because there is a demand for such knowledge transfer from institutions like the United Nations Educational, Scientific and Cultural Organization (UNESCO) to many international NGOs (non-governmental organizations), down to regional and local cultural decision-making institutions. These agencies seek information about the potential "heritage" itself as much as about the political, legal, and economic consequences that heritagitization might have. Ethnographic and cultural historical case studies are particularly pertinent as answers: only such micro approaches, in fact, can properly reveal the local specificity of a global heritage regime.

## THE SHAPING OF HERITAGE GOODS

The term *heritage* is both broader and more porous than the older terms used to designate cultural inheritance. In English, the phonemic difference between "heredity" and "heritage" steps audibly away from the precise biological notion of succession; it opens up the breadth of all that might potentially be included in cultural heritage, as well as all those who might potentially sun themselves in heritage's rays. On the global stage of heritage processes, the term broadened further with UNESCO's decision to add Intangible Cultural Heritage to its concern for natural and material heritages.

The spectrum of things with heritage potential in the realm of culture has unfolded over the past three to four centuries on two axes—a social and a temporal one. Initially, value and need for protection was largely bestowed on built monuments of high-cultural or upper-class provenience. The material culture of a nation's dominant ethnic groups could vie for status. Then, testimonies of industrial- and working-class culture also came to earn the title heritage. While the social axis broadened, the span of passed time that would qualify something to enter the realm of heritage decreased. Even as far back as the periods when the arguments permeating the discourse on cultural heritage were taking shape, this temporal compression is noticeable. The Renaissance and the Enlightenment developed an enthusiasm for classical antiquity; to this, the romantics added the cultural treasures of the Middle Ages. They did not forget classical antiquity, of course, but rather they thickened the stock of cultural patrimony, while awarding a higher value to cultural history. New institutions assisted in making this valuation a self-evident element of social life. Museums as well as preservationist associations on the one hand, innovations in the realm of legal measures on the other, contributed to the slow growth of what Barbara Kirshenblatt-Gimblett has called "metacultural operations" (Kirshenblatt-Gimblett 2004). In her view, the honoring, ennobling, preserving, and ultimately, branding into heritage are processes located on a metalevel, sufficiently removed from self-understood habitus to gaze reflexively upon it, cull segments from it, and bestow special value to it.

Kirshenblatt-Gimblett also notes the temporal thickening in heritage processes. In coining her definition of heritage as "a new form of cultural production of the present that takes recourse to the past" (Kirshenblatt-Gimblett 1995, 269), and in arguing that time is central to metacultural operations (Kirshenblatt-Gimblett 2004, 59), she points to the key role of the temporal axis.[3] The temporal tensions in cultural heritage matters can manifest in several layers: the noncontemporaneity of the matters and materials under discussion; the presence of things datable to different pasts in a present- and future-oriented lifeworld; a highly differentiated awareness of history, which has become part and parcel of education and daily life. Juggling such awareness of multiple pasts is in many ways an essential ingredient of being and feeling modern. In our concern to honor cultural pasts, we are reaching for phenomena that are younger and younger. One might even argue that in the case of some cultural innovations, their transformation into heritage is contemporaneous with their unfolding in daily life.

A case in point is digital cultural heritage. Proponents of this initiative claim, with justification, that the first digital cultural and knowledge achievements are threatened by rapid technological change unless measures are taken to protect and preserve the technologies necessary to access them (Lohmeier 2006). The success of such initiatives proves that societies today carry a strong sense that heritage preservation is relevant. Without such a nearly habitual commitment, firmly anchored in what is—through UNESCO's efforts—a worldwide mentality, a digital heritage initiative would hardly come to pass. In this case, the educational level and sophistication of digital developers must be kept in mind. Within this interest group, there is naturally also a very high awareness of the cultural ramifications of the digital revolution, coupled with a great deal of discussion, not to mention dispute, over the threat posed by commercial interests in robbing the digital realm of its cultural-commons status (Grassmuck 2004; Lessig 1999, 2004).

Thus, one task we face is research on how the social and temporal axes of heritagization move ever closer together, choosing present-day cases as well as selected cases from the past. We work and write in a present where the valuing, protection, preservation, and competitive evaluation of heritages, from regional to global scales, are natural or obvious; UNESCO's lists of chosen sites and practices dangle before us, an ever-tempting option for actors in the realm of cultural and economic policy-making. From such a present, we might take a look at places and moments in time where there were different, or perhaps no, regimes of comparative cultural (e-)valuation. Personal experience might serve as an example. In the small town in northern Switzerland where I was born, one of the sites considered important was an amphitheater from Roman times; associated with it was a museum exclusively devoted to the archaeological finds from the Roman settlement. Hence I grew up within a mentality that considered any kind of find from classical antiquity to be worthy of preservation and proper historical contextualization. Then in my early thirties, I visited a coastal town in southern Turkey, where I was astounded at the ease with which people handled the remnants of antiquity. There was an abundance of them, dating from different eras, the beach seemed positively littered with them. Houses had been constructed out of both new and antique material; the street crews refurbishing the sewage system seemed to be negotiating their way between antique foundations and more recent canal ducts requiring replacement. The sight provided a liberating feeling. There was so much potential cultural heritage here that its impact on the local mentality was—not nil—but somehow more reasonable than what I had grown up with. In my home town, the Roman finds were one of only a very few historical and possibly touristic resources; people in this Turkish town, by contrast, considered their beach location and climate as their most important economic ticket, not the abundance of antique remains. Turkey certainly features on the UNESCO world heritage lists—with Troy, the old town of Istanbul, or the cultural landscape of Pamukkale the most prominent examples—and the country imposes very rigorous conditions on archaeological finds. Yet, the richness of its antiquities has created a quite different attitude toward heritage than what I knew from my little Swiss hometown. There, the Roman finds are rarities and are handled accordingly, though their quality will probably never suffice for world heritage status. Still, the power of rhetoric deployed in heritage applications should never be underestimated.

## VALENCE/VALUATION AND THE ACTORS
## WHO BRING IT FORTH

Segments of culture acquire cultural heritage status once particular value is assigned to them. The predicate "heritage" is generated from experiential contexts and knowledges, which in turn take shape in discussions and application dossiers, employing indicators of valence.[4] How specific actors approach this task of such upgrading or revaluation is a further process requiring closer study. The checklist provided by UNESCO sets certain parameters, but in a number of points, it remains sufficiently vague for applicants to insert arguments for their specific locality or cultural practice. In a number of nations, the process is further aided by the fact that expert consultants stand ready to assist in carrying an application through evaluation and selection committees (UNESCO 2003).

Particularly relevant in heritage-making discussions appears to be the importance accorded to the difference between image and economic value. In practice, the two types of value overlap or even converge, yet discursively, much is made of the difference. Thus, cultural heritage is considered to have high social value and to be endowed with the capacity to foster positive identification within groups or entire polities. On the global stage, this value is further heightened. Here, cultural heritage is presented as emanating from one particular cultural context; actors within this context are claiming custodial care for it in the process of heritagization. Yet simultaneously, they assert that all of humanity can share the value of the ennobled piece of culture or cultural practice. Drawing on Werner Sollors's work on the tensions between descent and consent positions in ethnic politics (Sollors 1986), Kirshenblatt-Gimblett describes the process as follows: "World heritage lists arise from operations that convert selected aspects of localized descent heritage into a translocal consent heritage—the heritage of humanity" (Kirshenblatt-Gimblett 2006, 170). Achieving and maintaining world heritage status requires economic investments—renovations, protective measures, and so on—which are discussed only marginally. Discourse labels such costs as moral responsibilities, naturally important to the custodianship of a world heritage site or practice. Similarly, selection and award discussions marginalize the potential economic gains that achieving heritage status might bring about—as if economic considerations might besmirch or spoil the purity of heritage. In other contexts, however, such as regional or national decision-making bodies, the possibility of making economic use of heritage status, particularly in touristic development, is discussed openly and positively. For example, the central German Tourism Office (*Deutsche Zentrale für Tourismus*) is a member in the Association of German Heritage Sites and acts within it in a consulting capacity.

The prevalent dichotomization of image and economic value in public discourse arises from the long-standing modern differentiation between "genuine" and "fake" heritage. The fake or inauthentic garnered its bad reputation by lacking uniqueness. The very term *inauthentic* implies a deviation from the originality and hence uniqueness of the genuine.[5] "Uniqueness" is one of the criteria UNESCO requires for a cultural practice to be welcomed onto the list of world heritages. Quite logically, after something has achieved world heritage status, the danger of losing this very uniqueness preoccupies discussions between responsible actors and their opponents in many local and regional discussions. During the process of heritagitization, actors tend to weave authenticity/inauthenticity arguments into their presentations and documents. Once heritage status has been achieved, however, the intertwining of idealistic and economic components is unavoidable. George Yúdice has convincingly argued that the "expediency of culture" is ultimately neither harmful nor indictable—rather, it is an unavoidable occurrence, in particular in heterogeneous societies (Yúdice 2003). From the perspective of cultural anthropology, it is interesting to witness the constant attempts to cleanly separate idealistic from economic uses of heritage—not least because fields of cultural research collude in this tendency; at various times, and for various purposes they themselves have reintroduced the dichotomy. There is plenty of exploratory as well as reflexive scholarship contemplating the ambiguity of cultural heritage (Csáky and Zeyringer 2000; Csáky and Sommer 2005), but efforts to document specific cases, so as to understand how individuals and communities have turned heritage-making into a cultural practice—or have, alternately, been forced to be part of a heritage-making endeavor, continue to be an important task for heritage scholars. Case-by-case ethnographic documentation is very useful to identify specific actors, to follow how they initiate and fight for (or against) particular value-additions, and denote how they deploy knowledge transfers from cultural scholarship that is usually outdated. By screening actors' motivations and intentions, one can recognize what types of uses for potential heritage are foreseen, or—after a successful nomination—how the results are absorbed and worked with.[6]

The model behind the suggested approach can be seen in the diagram below. Culture, and the cultural heritage "extracted" from it, is lodged in a field of tension generated by the agency and interests of actors in society, politics, and economics. From a cultural-anthropological perspective, these three pillars are themselves components of culture at large and, like all of culture, are in a constant, dynamic process of change. In a democratic state, the three pillars cannot be clearly separated. From all three, actors have access to "culture" and the practices constituting it. From all three, actors may—in divergent ways and with variable levels of urgency—attempt to attribute heightened aesthetic potency to a given segment or excerpt of culture so as to bring forth cultural heritage.

Society

CULTURE
CULTURAL HERITAGE

Politics                                                          Economy

This schematic differentiation of potential loci of agency allows for clearer recognition on two counts:

1. the provenience of a given value-adding initiative will be made visible and put in relation to potential other loci of agency;
2. in comparing cases from different historical moments, shifts over time in the source of value-adding initiatives will become evident.

At a different historical moment, the pillar "society" or "politics" might be replaced by the pillar "belief" or the "sacred." While heritage-making invariably will bring all three areas of activity into contact with one another, different cases will nonetheless show different emphases.

If ennobling a cultural practice to the status of heritage is a process of canonization, any such process is also ultimately accompanied by an interest in utilization. What is interesting to cultural research is the question of what type of use is made of the new value and what kind of criticism of such use is voiced, by whom, and in what specific context. A further important research direction thus concerns the dynamics between social groups—from the smallest interest groups to global networks—generated by the needs and practices surrounding cultural heritage.

## INTERPERSONAL AND SOCIETAL CONSEQUENCES

Heritage allows close observation of the dynamic between economy and politics, with a focus on "culture" as an economic good. The process of heritage nomination openly declares this good independent of both spheres; hence, it contributes to intensive discussions between opponents, users, and mediators active in the discourses before, during, and after the nomination. However, heritagization also represents cultural practices that point to other research topics. I look at two examples: mechanisms of social control on the local, regional, or even global level, and competition as a regime permeating all spheres of life.

To small-town burghers who are annoyed by urban problems—such as trash in a public park—world heritage status affords a new variable in the game of social control. A voluntary culture caretaker in Goslar, Germany, threatened to call the UNESCO branch office in Bonn to inquire whether excessive trash might not be threatening the town's heritage status (Matt 2006). It is unlikely that these little public nuisances would move UNESCO to put a tangible or intangible heritage on the red list of threatened world heritage or heritage in urgent need of safeguarding. However, actors on local and regional levels utilize the existence of this international red list to exert social and political control. A case in point is the heated discussion surrounding new architectural projects in Cologne. Had they been built, say their opponents, the urban landscape into which the Cologne cathedral is embedded would have been permanently altered, thus transforming the vista included in the world heritage nomination of the cathedral. One of the planned buildings had already been erected when the storm broke loose. Ultimately, the city decided not to build the rest of the projected structures. The Cologne cathedral, having landed on the red list of endangered heritage sites in 2004, was removed from it in 2006 (Zacharias 2006, 279; cf., Zaika 2014). Here as elsewhere, the successful nomination curtailed architectural development: new structures must take into account the image that is to be preserved, or they must be placed elsewhere. Given the importance of innovative architecture in urban development and design, heritage regimes put a major constraint on the system. Alternately, the architectural establishment coupled with other forces in civil society may harness the heritage regime; by placing historic conservation above housing interests and needs of underprivileged groups, heritage endeavors may lead to gentrification (Herzfeld 2010). Heritage opportunities may also have some impact on the recruitment of patrons; individuals eager to support innovation or aesthetic transformation in urban spaces are not necessarily equally interested in supporting the aesthetic stagnation or privileging of historical memory encoded in heritage award policies. All through history, patronage has crucially contributed to the shaping of architectural change. Hence it would be interesting, from an anthropological perspective, to follow up on how the introduction of heritage interests and policies affects patrons as well as urban planners and architects.

More complex still is the situation surrounding the Wartburg, a castle on the UNESCO world heritage list located near Eisenach in Thuringia, Germany. The site was famous long before it reached world heritage status in 1999. It was known as an interesting building with architectural traces of different epochs. It was also a pilgrimage site of sorts, as it had served as the refuge in which Martin Luther hid from Catholic persecution and where he translated the Bible into German. Election into the UNESCO list, however, called into question other plans in the region. In 1993, an alternative energy developer had gotten permission from the regional council to put up a chain of windmills on a stretch of land near the Wartburg; construction was to begin in 2005. At that point, defenders of the heritage site voiced objection, arguing that windmills would dramatically alter the landscape around the Wartburg and thus might lead to a loss of its heritage status. They pointed to the economic losses that would be incurred should UNESCO withdraw its seal of approval; they also argued that for many inhabitants, there would be an emotional loss if the landscape around the Wartburg were suddenly altered through the addition of windmills. The investor, as well as local and regional politicians, argued that the region would get increased employment with the windmills and, in the post–Fukushima nuclear accident era, would also make an important contribution to the generation of alternative energy.

At this point, a third set of actors entered the fray. As it turned out, the piece of land in question was a habitat for a series of rare bird species, including an endangered type of owl. Environmental activists began to argue that windmills might alter the conditions so drastically that this owl would be further threatened. No studies verifying the viability of this claim had been done up to that point, but raising the specter of threat was sufficient grounds for the Wartburg versus windmill case to enter the courts. Although UNESCO has made no threat to shift the Wartburg on to its red list of endangered sites, the turmoil in Eisenach remains palpable. Signatures have been collected locally in favor of blocking all actions that might threaten the heritage status. The local press also takes sides with the Wartburg custodians; thus here, too, social control makes use of heritage policies. Economic and ecological arguments are available to all contestants in the dispute; hence, the question turns on who can make the biggest moral claim (Sander 2006). And while the court in 2010 made a step in favor of the windmill builder, a further chain of arguments has arisen with the approach of the five hundredth anniversary of the Reformation in 2017.[7] The German evangelical church decided to include the Wartburg as one of the commemorative sites and the state of Thuringia in turn will provide nearly half a million Euros for restoration work. Although restored, reimagined, and built up in the early nineteenth century, the Wartburg was included on UNESCO's world heritage list as a testimony of the feudal period, and such is the tone of an article praising the view from the Wartburg in a Christian weekly: "Looking southward over the Thuringian forest along with the curatorship, one feels oneself in a timeless world, forests and hills, hills and forests, a few slopes and fields. Nothing else. No sign of modern civilization. No chimney, no street, no windmill, not even a house. Such was the view south from the Wartburg already in Luther's time" (Sternberg 2011, my translation). Invoking the gaze of the most famous of the reformers, the potential intrusion of the windmills appears all the more offensive—against God's eternal plan. Archeological research elsewhere on planet Earth has, however, questioned a number of cherished myths of romanticism and modernity alike, such as the eternal existence of rainforests in Latin America (Erickson 2010). Correspondingly the rhetoric of a blissful, stable eternity associated with the rolling forests of Thuringia can be easily punctured, not least with Luther himself, whose work, if anything, constituted a resounding break and a massive transformation in the ideology and practice of Christianity.

For local and regional politicians, heritage thus turns into a tricky arena indeed. It is hard to clearly separate cultural, historical, economic, ecological, religious, and aesthetic arguments. Four decades ago, castle, windmills, and owls might have cohabited happily: indeed, they could have been placed together on a political platform. If the castle had been elevated to heritage status just as a monument, without making the surrounding forested landscape part of the site, the windmills might have met with less (or no) resistance. In the meantime, windmills have given rise to momentous arguments, not just about their impact on an ecosystem, but also about their very aesthetics. Thus, in the postnomination situation, different mechanisms of support and punishment have to be weighed carefully.

UNESCO nominations of humanly built landscapes and of intangible practices pose considerable problems of implementation. It is a great deal easier to set in motion the restoration, maintenance, and protection of, say, a half-timbered façade than to develop a protection policy favorable to an endangered species living in a decaying ruin. The latter requires different measures from the former. The Norwegian town of Røros illustrates further facets of such implementation issues. Nominated already in 1980, Røros as an old mining town constitutes an example of industrial heritage. Here, too, (but differently from Eisenach) the natural surroundings give rise to discussion. When there was still active mining in Røros, the surrounding woods had been cut down: timber was required for the mining process. The barren hillsides were part of the surrounding landscape that was nominated, along with the wooden housing structures of the town itself. Alas, Røros is now a former mining town; now the regrowth of underbrush and trees are considered problematic by some custodians of Røros' heritage status—whereas, of course, environmental activists are relieved to see the recovery of tree growth in the area, judging it a good sign for the health of the ground after long years of industrial work in the area (Bittlinger 2006). Similarly, heritage conservation purists oppose the securing of the town's exclusively wooden houses with fireproofing materials. Heritage regimes and the safety precautions that ought to be available to citizens clearly are at odds.

Intangible heritage also carries new concerns, which evolve into new social practices, though they may be different in timbre. The intangibility of that which has been ennobled requires(logically) mechanisms of making it tangible, so as to fully profit from the new status. This opens the question, however, of who is permitted to do so. Markus Tauschek documented and analyzed this development by following the carnival of Binche in Belgium (Tauschek 2007). Unlike a monument or a cultural landscape, an intangible good at first glance appears evanescent. A carnival performance thrives in performance, which in turn is carried by the (mental) competence of those who have traditionalized the practice. Yet naturally, a carnival also lives in photographs, as well as in the material culture of costumes and masks, all of which have been made amply available as highly tangible souvenirs in Binche. The carnival is celebrated not only in Binche but also in neighboring communities; hence, the people of Binche now struggle to disapprove the sale of the likeness of their major masked carnival figure in neighboring towns. Even the nomination document is an item of material culture, which embodies the valence bestowed upon the tradition. Markus Tauschek has documented the efforts of the principal actors to load this paper document with further potency and turn it into a tangible icon of their intangible possession. As the paper document did not quite capture the enthusiasm for this ascent to world recognition, the town also produced a neon sign announcing the award— certainly not an extension intended by UNESCO, but evidence of the need to somehow rally the local population with recognizable evidence of success.

Heritage-making seeks to ennoble a given intangible practice or a tangible excerpt of culture. Actors faced with "owning" heritage, or at least being considered the custodians of a site or an intangible practice, will, however, invariably seek to make the new status part of their everyday life, to integrate it into spheres of activity and social interaction. On the "inside," the nobility thus wears off quite quickly. The symbolic capital inherent in heritage invites social, economic and political contestants to vie for it; heritage becomes another tool or variable in the struggles for power on local and supralocal levels of governance. It is used to add additional contours to a given milieu, but also to control other people. Much depends on the ways in which different interest groups take hold of the power potentially inherent to this new toy.

However, as a relatively new practice, heritagization can also open possibilities and have an impact on extant development plans, such as in the realm of urban design, energy, or tourism. Therefore, one cannot simply classify this practice as new wine in old wineskins, nor is it possible, at this point, simply to reverse the cliché and call it old wine in new wineskins. Careful research is necessary to understand the gradations of social control that emerge when a cultural product is transformed into a good of morally and economically enhanced valence. Kirshenblatt-Gimblett (2006) has tried to follow this process for the local-global value-exchange in heritage matters. The examples sketched here seek to demonstrate the differentially lodged processes set in motion as cultural heritage gets integrated into everyday lifeworlds and contexts of action.

Heritagization is, finally, an ideal topic to research the omnipresence of two complementary mechanisms in late modern everyday life: competition and quality control. Competition fosters innovation, production, and marketing, and is thus an integral component of modern industrial development. Laws governing patenting rights, for instance, are intended to stimulate producers. If they manage to innovate, they have the opportunity to patent their invention: thus, for a limited time, they have sole rights to make a profit from it. The competing variables of quality and price guide producers and consumers and contribute to the dynamic nature of the value scales within a given economy. As the world inches farther and farther into a postindustrial era, the interest in broadening the dynamism of economic competition has expanded into work contexts other than (industrial) production. In a service-sector area such as sales or hotel room rental, it is not just the quality of a piece of furniture or the nature of the room that contribute to the price; it is also the quality and nature of service rendered by the salesclerks and staff. Service behavior is now part of market competition and has broadened the notion of quality management to include interpersonal behaviors and communicative forms. Arlie Hochschild speaks of the "managed heart" and emotional labor (Hochschild 1983). Increasingly, everyday life is filled with competitive and evaluative processes, which in turn are coupled with quality control and scales of commendation. While there is today a lot of justified talk about "knowledge society" (Nowotny, Scott, and Gibbons 2001) and how knowledge is continuously transferred and used in new social contexts, there is equal need to pay attention to "evaluation society." Regimes of quality control and evaluation bear witness to the existence of "audit culture." The success of such regimes demonstrates how one practice-oriented branch of scholarship, business administration, has permeated social life. Strathern (2000) and Shore (1999) have examined the effects of this in higher education; but its presence in heritagization is unmistakable. Indeed, these processes are an excellent arena for documenting and fostering a critical understanding of the nature of late modern competitive practices.

In selecting cultural sites or cultural practices as particularly valuable, actors on the heritage stage submit to the rules of competition and their consequences. The selection of cultural heritage is a relatively transparent process, the actors involved in the process are quite visible, and thus it is possible to observe the mechanisms they set in motion to make the intangible tangible on the world stage, and to turn what is value-free and obvious into something of special value. This kind of transparency permits a researcher in turn to make visible the components involved in constructing a competitive piece of heritage, and to thereby understand how cultural heritage is canonized. From the vantage point of an "evaluation society," one could see in proper proportion both small-scale powerplays around world heritage nominations and large-scale moralizing and ennobling, as well as their parallel critique. These processes and acts are ultimately just extremes of an economic cultivation, here applied to the fragile resource "culture." Although from a scholarly standpoint, the nomination and thus circumscribing of *intangible heritage* and *memory of the world* are close to absurd, they give evidence of a late modern existential order (or, perhaps a sense of helplessness?) in the face of the capitalist drive to husband all potential resources.

Heritagization is communicated at a hyper-intensive level—which makes the researcher's study easier and more accessible, with ethnography of communication as a useful methodological approach. Cases, both respectable or simple and explosive, are generally talked about in print, online, and in face-to-face settings on- and off-screen, as well as in growing stacks of memoranda. These media allow for an examination of which regimes are being deployed; one can follow the whole spectrum of other issues, far from heritage itself, that are confirmed and achieved— or in some cases foiled or undermined—on the platform of heritage-making. In the case of intangible heritage, one may discern issues of inclusion and privileged access, custodianship and profit from scarce resources—issues, in other words, that are harder to be raised on their own. For instance, an annual festivity elevated to world heritage status can give rise to discussions whether nonnatives of the town should be permitted to participate in the festivity. The discussion can go both ways, depending on the strength of relevant interest groups. Some may argue that logically, someone born far away could not be part of this local inheritance, while others might argue that world heritage implies an opening up to the world, sharing the knowledge of competent festive, "intangible" performance. Likewise, intangible knowledges have always been transported easily, certainly within the immediate environs of a purported place of origin. It is thus not surprising that tradition bearers in towns and villages located near the site of an intangible heritage manifestation seek to showcase festivities of their own that are similar. This in turn can lead to harsh efforts to delimit the freedom of regional competitors to partake of the economic boon of intangible heritage performances; or alternatively, to devise friendly schemes of variable festive dates, so as to allow competitors to profit from migrating seasonal tourists within a single region (e.g., Fournier 2004, 2012).

Anthropological attention to heritage matters entails looking at the handling of culture not only as an ideological but also as an economic resource. The role of culture in bolstering identity, thematized since the early nineteenth century, has been carried forward—or, perhaps more to the point, traditionalized—all the way into the UNESCO debates that brought forth the world heritage programs. Yet as important as the identity factor is, especially emphasized in the moral dimensions of heritage discourses, it is the economic potential of heritage that has long since grown to be the primary incentive. The procedures surrounding selection and their competitive nature foster a sense that one is dealing with a finite or at least a very limited resource. It is crucial to try to understand the power that resides in this image of a limited reservoir of valuable excerpts of culture, as invoked in the UNESCO Convention of 2003. While many cultural anthropologists have grave reservations about the economic value-adding processes they observe, paying close heed to them is nonetheless essential, not least because economic utilization will have repercussions on heritage's role in identity discourses.

Privileged access to a particular cultural identity resource has been defended with weapons, not mere words, in both nationalistic and religious contexts. One can postulate, as does Yúdice (2003), that a group might also be filled with pride to land on the world heritage list. Such pride might loosen rather than tighten possessive feelings, and allow for a shared ideological ownership, as long as the economic benefits flow primarily to the privileged circle.

The UNESCO Cultural Heritage Convention is fueled by the goodwill that was already inherent in the primary tasks UNESCO took on at its founding in 1945: "Education, Social and Natural Science, Culture and Communication are the means to a far more ambitious goal: to build peace in the minds of man [*sic*]" (UNESCO 2008). Anthropology's most famous twentieth-century representative, Claude Lévi-Strauss, often a UNESCO consultant, embraced this goal also. When UNESCO celebrated its sixtieth anniversary in Paris on November 16, 2005, a frail Lévi-Strauss, addressing the assembled crowd, renewed his hope that mutual understanding of cultural difference might contribute to world peace. All the more important is it, then, for cultural anthropologists to study the UNESCO regimes; to follow their impact on local, regional, and global actors and their interrelationships; and to uncover new webs of meaning as they arise. One need not be a heritage expert to recognize that peace is not yet forthcoming. Studying deeply the role of the economic utilization of heritage, and the competitive and evaluative regimes associated with it, is a worthy professional goal.

NOTES

This chapter appeared in *Intangible Cultural Heritage*, edited by L. Smith and N. Akagawa (London: Routledge, 2009), 253–69.

Parts of this chapter appeared in German as "Kulturelles Erbe zwischen Wirtschaft und Politik." (Hemme, Tauschek, and Bendix 2007, 337–56). Thanks go to the coeditors of that volume, to Lee Haring for his helpful comments on an earlier English version of this paper, and to Laurajane Smith and Natsuko Akagawa for including it in their 2009 volume *Intangible Heritage*. For the present volume, further revisions were undertaken.

1. Since this chapter was originally published, further relevant work has appeared exploring authenticity, and, adjoining it, nostalgia as factors motivating heritage-making; see, for example, Angé and Berliner (2015).

2. Some of the case material was compiled in a seminar I taught on "cultural heritage between economics and politics" at the University of Göttingen in 2006. Thanks are due to the participants who have given permission to cite from their research papers.

3. One might debate, however, whether it really is a "new" form. As indicated above, the mechanisms of cultural production evident in heritagization build on a genealogy of practices valorizing culture. See Hemme (2007, 2009) and Tauschek (2007, 2010).

4. In her first theses on heritage, Kirshenblatt-Gimblett spoke of heritage as a "value added industry" (Kirshenblatt-Gimblett 1995, 370).

5. Lionel Trilling's essay *Sincerity and Authenticity* (1971) is a useful rediscovery for anyone working with heritage, as is Benjamin's (1968) well known "Work of Art in the Age of Mechanical Reproduction." For a consideration of the key place of authenticity discourses in cultural research, see Bendix (1997).

6. Many such case studies have been published since this chapter was originally published, for example, Adell, Bendix, Bortolotto, and Tauschek (2015);
Bendix, Eggert, and Peselmann (2012); Brumann and Berliner (2016); Foster and
Gilman (2015). Yet, what remains lacking is a more systematic and comparative analysis of the many case studies that have appeared—possibly because such a system-
atization would likely be a solid springboard for more normative assessments and
suggestions regarding heritage-making's future, a direction that cultural researchers
generally prefer not to take.

7. In 2013, the windmill builder withdrew his claim, and the state of Thuringia in turn
withdrew its charge against him; the regional land use policy has been redrawn so as
to prevent all future windmill initiatives. See "Investor verzichtet auf Windmühlen".
Accessed May 25, 2017. https://web.archive.org/web/20140201204421/http://www
.mdr.de/thueringen/mitte-west-thueringen/windkraftanlagen_milmesberg
_wartburg100.html.

## REFERENCES

Adell, Nicolas, Regina F. Bendix, Chiara Bortolotto, and Markus Tauschek, eds. 2015.
    *Between Imagined Communities and Communities of Practice. Göttingen Studies in
    Cultural Property Vol. 8.* Göttingen: Göttingen University Press.
Angé, Olivia and David Berliner, eds. 2015. *Anthropology and Nostalgia.* New York:
    Berghahn.
Bausinger, Hermann. 1988. "Da Capo: Folklorismus." In *Sichtweisen der Volkskunde.
    Zur Geschichte und Forschungspraxis einer Disziplin,* edited by Albrecht Lehmann and
    Andreas Kuntz, 321–29. Berlin: Reimer.
Bendix, Regina. 1988. "Folklorismus: The Challenge of a Concept." *International Folklore
    Review* 6: 5–15.
———. 1997. *In Search of Authenticity: The Formation of Folklore Studies.* Madison:
    University of Wisconsin Press.
Bendix, Regina, and Gisela Welz. 2002. *Kulturwissenschaft und Öffentlichkeit.* Frankfurt:
    Institut für Kulturanthropologie und Europäische Ethnologie.
Bendix, Regina F., Aditya Eggert, and Arnika Peselmann, eds. 2012. *Heritage Regimes
    and the State.* Göttingen Studies in Cultural Property, vol 5. Göttingen: Göttingen
    University Press.
Benjamin, Walter. 1968. "The Work of Art in the Age of Mechanical Reproduction." In
    *Illuminations,* edited by Hannah Arendt, translated by Harry Zohn, 217–51. New York:
    Schocken.
Bittlinger, Levke. 2006. "UNESCO Weltkulturerbe in Norwegen: das Beispiel Roros."
    Unpublished seminar paper. Institute for Cultural Anthropology/European
    Ethnology, University of Göttingen.
Brumann, Christoph, and David Berliner, eds. 2016. *Heritage on the Ground.* New York:
    Berghahn.
Csáky, Moritz, and Sommer, Monika, eds. 2005. *Kulturerbe als soziokulturelle Praxis.*
    Gedächtnis—Erinnerung—Identität 6. Innsbruck: Studien.

Csáky, Moritz, and Zeyringer, Klaus, eds. 2000. *Ambivalenz des kulturellen Erbes: Vielfachcodierung des historischen Gedächtnisses.* Innsbruck: Studien.

Erickson, Clark L. 2010. "The Transformation of Environment into Landscape: The Historical Ecology of Monumental Earthwork Construction in the Bolivian Amazon." *Diversity* 2 (4): 618–52.

Foster, Michael Dylan, and Lisa Gilman, eds. 2015. *UNESCO on the Ground. Local Perspectives on Intangible Cultural Heritage.* Bloomington: Indiana University Press.

Fournier, Laurent Sébastian. 2004. "Kulturerbe: Ein Indikator der Modernität. Über einige Feste in der Provence." *Ethnologie Francaise* 34: 717–24.

———. 2012. "Intangible Cultural Heritage in France: From State Culture to Local Development." In *Heritage Regimes and the State*, edited by Regina Bendix, Aditya Eggert, and Arnika Peselmann, 329–42. Göttingen: Universitätsverlag Göttingen.

Grassmuck, Volker. 2004. *Freie Software zwischen Privat- und Gemeineigentum.* Bonn: Bundeszentrale für politische Bildung.

Hann, Chris M. 2004. "Epilogue: The Cartography of Copyright Cultures Versus the Proliferation of Public Properties," In *People and the Land: Pathways to Reform in Post-Soviet Siberia*, edited by Erich Kasten, 289–304. Berlin: Reimer.

Hemme, Dorothee. 2007. "'Weltmarke Grimm'—Anmerkungen zum Umgang mit der Ernenung der Grimmschen Kinder- und Hausmärchen zum 'Memory of the World'." In *Prädikat "Heritage". Wertschöpfungen aus kulturellen Ressourcen*, edited by Dorothee Hemme, Markus Tauschek, and Regina Bendix, 225–52. Münster: LIT.

———. 2009. "Die Deutsche Märchenstraße. Eine touristische Themenstraße auf den Spuren der Brüder Grimm." In *Zwischen Identität und Image—die Popularität der Brüder Grimm in Hessen*, edited by Harm-Peer Zimmermann, 204–35. Marburg: Jonas.

Hemme, Dorothee, Markus Tauschek, and Regina Bendix, eds. 2007. *Prädikat "Heritage". Wertschöpfung aus kulturellen Ressourcen.* Münster: LIT.

Herzfeld, Michael. 2005. *Cultural Intimacy: Social Poetics in the Nation-State.* New York: Routledge.

———. 2010. "Engagement, Gentrification, and the Neoliberal Hijacking of History." *Current Anthropology* 51 (52): 259–67.

Hobsbawm, Eric, and Terence Ranger, eds. 1983. *The Invention of Tradition.* Cambridge: Cambridge University Press.

Hochschild, Arlie R. 1983. *The Managed Heart: Commercialization of Human Feeling.* Berkeley: University of California Press.

Huber, Birgit. 2005. "Open-source Software und 'kulturelles Erbe' indigener Bevölkerung zwischen Markt und alternativer Rationalität—Von der Anthropologie des Rechtes zu einer Anthropologie als Basis des Rechtes." In *Recht und Religion im Alltagsleben: Perspektiven der Kulturforschung*, edited by Manfred Seifert and Winfried Helm, 41–59. Passau: Dietmar Klinger.

Johler, Reinhard. 2000. *Die Formierung eines Brauches: der Funken- und Holepfannsonntag: Studien aus Vorarlberg, Liechtenstein, Tirol, Südtirol und dem Trentino.* Vienna: Selbstverlag des Instituts für Europäische Ethnologie.

Kasten, Erich. ed. 2004. *Properties of Culture—Culture as Property. Pathways to Reform in Post-Soviet Siberia.* Berlin: Reimer.

Kirshenblatt-Gimblett, Barbara. 1995. "Theorizing Heritage." *Ethnomusicology* 39: 367–80.

———. 2004. "Intangible Heritage as Metacultural Production." *Museum International* 56: 53–65.

———. 2006. "World Heritage and Cultural Economics." In *Museum Frictions. Public Cultures/Global Transformations,* edited by Ivan Karp, Corinne A. Kratz, Lynn Szwaja, and Tomas Ybarra-Frausto, 161–202. Durham, NC: Duke University Press.

Lessig, Lawrence. 1999. *Code and Other Laws of Cyberspace.* New York: Basic.

———. 2004. *Free Culture: How Big Media Uses Technology and the Law to Lock Down Culture and Control Creativity.* New York: Penguin.

Lohmeier, Felix. 2006. "Kulturelles Erbe in der Informationsgesellschaft: Aktivitäten zum Schutz von digitalem Kulturerbe und ihre Folgen für den Alltag." Unpublished seminar paper. Institute for Cultural Anthropology/European Ethnology, University of Göttingen.

Matt, Kristina. 2006. "Ehrenamt im Bereich Welterbe am Beispiel der Stadt Goslar." Unpublished seminar paper. Institute for Cultural Anthropology/European Ethnology, University of Göttingen.

Nowotny, Helga, Peter B. Scott, and Michael T. Gibbons. 2001. *Rethinking Science: Knowledge and the Public.* Oxford: Blackwell.

Peckham, Robert S. 2003. Introduction to *Rethinking Heritage. Cultures and Politics in Europe,* edited by Robert S. Peckham, 1–16. London: I. B. Tauris.

Sander, Susan. 2006. "Weltkulturerbe Wartburg Kontra Windradbau. Über die Unvereinbarkeit von Wirtschaft und Kultur am Beispiel der Wartburg bei Eisenach." Seminar paper. Institute for Cultural Anthropology/European Ethnology, University of Göttingen.

Seidenspinner, Wolfgang. 2006. "Authentizität: Kulturanthropologisch-erinnerungskundliche Annäherungen an ein zentrales Wissenschaftskonzept im Blick auf das Weltkulturerbe." *Volkskunde in Rheinland-Pfalz* 20: 5–39.

Shore, Cris, and Susan Wright. 1999. "Audit Cultures and Anthropology: Neoliberalism in British Higher Education." *Journal of the Royal Anthropological Institute* 5: 557–76.

Sollors, Werner. 1986. *Beyond Ethnicity: Consent and Descent in American Culture.* New York: Oxford University Press.

Sternberg, Jan Philipp. 2011. "Was würde Luther dazu sagen?" *Christ & Welt. Wochenzeitung für Glaube, Geist, Gesellschaft,* no. 24.

Strathern, Marilyn. 2000. *Audit Cultures: Anthropological Studies in Accountability, Ethics, and the Academy.* London: Routledge.

Tauschek, Markus. 2007. "'Plus Oultre'—Welterbe und kein Ende? Zum Beispiel Binche." In *Prädikat "Heritage." Wertschöpfungen aus kulturellen Ressourcen,* edited by Dorothee Hemme, Markus Tauschek, and Regina Bendix, 197–224. Münster: LIT.

———. 2010. *Wertschöpfung aus Tradition: der Karneval von Binche und die Konstituierung kulturellen Erbes.* Berlin: LIT.

Trilling, Lionel. 1971. *Sincerity and Authenticity.* Cambridge, MA: Harvard University Press.

UNESCO. 2003. "Third Session of the Intergovernmental Meeting of Experts on the Preliminary Draft Convention for the Safeguarding of the Intangible Cultural Heritage." July 31. http://unesdoc.unesco.org/images/0013/001312/131274e.pdf.

UNESCO. 2008. "About UNESCO." Accessed May 9. http://portal.unesco.org/en /ev.php-URL_ID=3328&URL_DO=DO_TOPIC&URL_SECTION=201.html. This page has been modified: there is now simply a title phrase reading "UNESCO. Building

Peace in the minds of men and women." Accessed December 20, 2017. http://www
.unesco.org/new/en/unesco/about-us/.

Yúdice, George. 2003. *The Expediency of Culture*. Durham, NC: Duke University Press.

Zacharias, Diana. 2006. "Cologne Cathedral versus Skyscrapers." *Max Planck Yearbook of
United Nations Law* 10: 273–366.

Zaicha, Natalie. 2014. Den Dom im Blick. Hochhäuser im Diskurs um das kulturelle Erbe
in Europa am Beispiel der Stadt Köln. CP101 Concepts and Institutions in Cultural
Property. Working Paper 7 (Available at: http://cultural-property.uni-goettingen.de
/de/publications/. Accessed May 24, 2017).

# 7

*Inheritances: Possession, Ownership,*
*and Responsibility*

How can one—an individual, a group, a nation, the world population—inherit cultural expressions, from material monuments and cultural landscapes to intangible culture? What does "to inherit" entail in the formulation "intangible cultural heritage"? A first—though perhaps too easy—answer is to note the semantic difference between "inheritance" and "heritage." A more complicated train of thought leads to an outline of the entanglement between inheriting—a gerund which always points to future ownership—and heritage, a noun which does not have a related verb to accompany it. The 2003 United Nations Educational, Scientific and Cultural Organization (UNESCO) convention to safeguard the intangible cultural heritage, as Laurajane Smith and Natsuko Akagawa have noted, constitutes "a significant intervention in international debate about the nature and value of cultural heritage" (2009, 1).[1] Enlarging the scope from material culture and landscape to cultural practices, the concept of intangible cultural heritage also adds further dimensions to the question of what it is that is being inherited and who it is that inherits. While the 1972 convention is entitled "Convention Concerning the Protection of World Cultural and Natural Heritage," the 2003 convention does not carry the word "world" in its title, pointing already to the increased complexity of the question of ownership in the realm of immaterial knowledges and practices (UNESCO 1972, 2003).

Participants debating the need and contours of safeguarding culture have, over the past four to five decades, continually absorbed fragments of scholarly input concerning the nature of "culture." One can argue that the enlarged repertoire of UNESCO world heritage categories from monuments to memory and intangible culture reflect the slow und subtle growth of awareness that material culture is ultimately but an expression of mental human capacities. While Article 1 of the convention concerning cultural and natural heritage from 1972 focuses on the materiality of works, sites, or buildings (World Heritage Centre 1992–2009), Article 2 of the convention for intangible heritage acknowledges actors and their agency, and with them the fluidity and dynamic inherent to cultural expressions: "This intangible culture heritage, transmitted from generation to generation, is constantly recreated by communities and groups in response to their environment, their interaction with nature and their history, and provides them with a sense of identity and continuity, thus promoting respect for cultural diversity and human creativity" (UNESCO 2003, art. 2.1).

Such insight would—if one were consistent—likely demand that earlier heritage conventions be adjusted based on the recognition that culture is forever flexible and its material expressions but fleeting evidence of human creativity. Accepting the dynamic of human creativity would ultimately require the acceptance that communities interact with their history, their ancestry, and their inheritance in culture- and context-specific manner. Indeed, communities might see fit to destroy or dismember extant monuments and sites to transform them into something new.

Internationally sanctioned heritage regimes, however, limit and channel creative agency, and states that have ratified conventions develop further mechanisms to institutionalize and manage heritage programs (Bendix, Eggert, and Peselmann 2012). The impulse to safeguard disciplines the culturally divergent ways of interacting with the past. In particular, heritage regimes are closely intertwined with processes of cultural commodification. Heritigization expresses not simply historical and moral values, it opens up an arena for questions of ownership and opportunities for sale.

Given the complexity and long duration of achieving an international convention and its subsequent ratification in member states, the successive heritage conventions remain in force next to one another. In the intangible heritage convention, this is even stipulated, for under Article 3 which is concerned with the convention's relationship to other international instruments, one reads: "Nothing in this Convention may be interpreted as: (a) altering the status or diminishing the level of protection under the 1972 Convention concerning the Protection of the World Cultural and Natural Heritage of World Heritage properties with which an item of the intangible cultural heritage is directly associated; or (b) affecting the rights and obligations of States Parties deriving from any international instrument relating to intellectual property rights or to the use of biological and ecological resources to which they are parties" (UNESCO 2003, art. 3).

One might regard this as an inheritance in and of itself, a result of the slow learning process within international consciousness raising, with the successive conventions for material and natural heritages, cultural landscape, memory of the world and, finally, intangible culture each maintaining their respective goals which in part conflict with one another.[2] One might equally well acknowledge that it is not (or not only) slow organizational learning processes that bring about a change in perspective and scope. The deficits or asymmetries in information are but one component; motivation to work toward change (or stagnation) as well as, on a macro level, the political and economic constellation of actors capable of bringing about change have an influence on the breadth of heritage options.[3]

Enlarging heritage recognition from material to enacted and ultimately mental categories complicates, in turn, notions of ownership. Territorially located, monuments pose seemingly less problems for determining who is responsible for their safeguarding, even if the cultural ownership may be more difficult to solve in nation-states comprising heterogeneous cultural groups. There certainly are conflicts on record here, too, with Preah Vihear, nominated in 2008, on the border between Cambodia and Thailand being a prominent example.[4] Expanding notions of heritage to include intangible culture constitutes a materialization of fluid tradition (Brown 2004, 50–51) and shifts questions of ownership into the realm of intellectual property. The category "cultural property" which predates UNESCO's heritage work takes on renewed potency. The World Intellectual Property Organization (WIPO) and UNESCO had, as a matter of fact, cooperated for a considerable amount of time on issues of culture, but parted ways in 1988, with UNESCO focused on safeguarding and preserving, and WIPO addressing "questions of ownership and exchange" and, attendant to such concerns, protection, with list-making as an emergent practice of such regimes evident in both organizations (Hafstein 2007, 86).[5]

The work of international organizations by necessity dwells on levels of abstraction on the one hand and terminological opaqueness on the other in order to move forward at the negotiation table. The following essay builds on some accounts concerning the generation and aftermath of this most recent heritage convention (e.g., Bortolotto 2011; Hemme, Tauschek, and Bendix 2007; Smith and Akagawa 2009), and reflects on the nature of this intervention from the perspective of cultural research. In particular, I would like to explore the semantic shifts in concepts such as inheritance and ownership. What impact do new components of world heritage regimes have on the meaning and daily practice of inheriting, owning and—potentially—selling culture? What kind of semantic connection, if not analogy, do such sequences share with the matter of inheriting the material and immaterial stuffs of family and kin and the questions of ownership that ensue? What occurs in the shift from privately regulated and experienced passing-on of material and immaterial inheritance to a global regime of heritage?[6]

Semantics are, of course, tied to particular languages and the present thoughts are penned with English vocabulary in mind. In a comparative study of heritage terminology, Astrid Swenson (2007) sought to delineate conceptual shifts that eventually led to "heritage," "patrimoine," and "Kulturerbe" in English, French, and German, respectively. These terms circumscribe in the respective languages what is to be safeguarded from the point of view of UNESCO as well as many national and regional institutions and initiatives concerned with honoring, protecting, and profiting from the cultural past.[7] Swenson reaches the conclusion that despite differences, the terms achieved, in the three language contexts investigated, a similar meaning: "It is never a neutral term, it always carries the moral implication that things must be preserved, and almost always the term is emotionally charged. At the same time the fluidity of the concept, its role as 'empty signifier,' permits one to perceive more distinctly opposing ideas and motives, the mechanisms of social control and the power play" entailed or hidden within the term (Swenson 2007, 72; my translation).

In this spirit, I would like to build on earlier reflections regarding the relationship and interplay of the heritage construct, with terms and practices in social life that are considerably less opaque and thus have more concrete consequences in everyday life.[8] As I am a European as well as a Europeanist cultural anthropologist and folklorist by training, my examples are likely Eurocentric. The emergent heritage regimes, too, are decidedly Western in their conceptualization and implementation, simply because they draw on the cultural patterns of Western evaluation regimes and—initially—build on the bureaucratic apparatus built to implement and maintain them.[9] Indeed, even the competitive selection procedure and the resulting lists reflect on Western practices of establishing scales and priorities.[10] Nonetheless, the reader is asked to think further and comparatively, as an understanding of notions of ownership, responsibility, and generation must work toward including culturally diverse ideologies of handling death, the past, and continuity (i.e., systems of time), as well as notions of inheritance and ownership (i.e., systems of property and attendant rights).[11] It is the latter that interest me here, but one cannot treat this without also touching on the former.

INHERITING WRIT SMALL—PRIVATE "HERITAGE"

On the heels of a death, aside from ritual leave-taking and grief, follows the necessity to deal with what the individual left behind, both in terms of debts and material and/or monetary possessions: inheritance is rarely solely a matter of welcome material gain for those left behind. A comparative survey of ethnographic studies done world-wide on funerary and post-funerary practices would reveal a good deal of difference on how possessions are handled, depending on whether a given culture permits or values personal possessions. Possessions might be placed in a funerary pyre to burn with the corpse; they might be distributed within the entire social group; they might go into the possession of the culturally determined heir or heirs. Heirs, in turn, are generally kin, that is individuals who are related to the deceased. In traditional language use that is "blood relatives." In the era of genetic testing, the relation can be established through DNA; heirs can also be individuals who married into a kin group. Depending on the kinship system and its legal interpretation, a hierarchy of heirs is established. While indigenous societies may adhere to customary laws of inheritance, the political success of the nation-state has ensured that there are codices of law, albeit divergent, regulating the ways in which inheritance is to be dealt with in the family context.[12]

"To inherit" implies, semantically, a great deal more than "to own," though this, too, will depend on the cultural context. Inheritance confirms or establishes a continuity of kin and perhaps validates additional social relationships. Heirs are likely to be guided (if not also observed and talked about) as they take on the responsibility encoded in an inheritance. The more closely knit and homogeneous a community, the more intensively the forces of social control will be at work. There is the moral expectation that the debts of a deceased are paid, just as there is a moral expectation that his or her possessions be tended properly and respectfully. Personal property such as land, real estate, or a business are to be handled wisely, ensuring that their value be maintained or increased. In distributing the personal effects, emotional wishes and/or obligations come into play. The children, grandchildren, further relations, or friends who receive the coat or the painting, the ring or the butterfly collection of the deceased receive not just an object but are also entrusted with the memory of this individual, his or her way of assembling a life including the predilections and obsessions. The inherited objects encode the inheritors' relationship with the deceased person. Some individuals seek to control the management of their inheritance by specifying in a last will who is to be gifted with what and who is to be in charge of what assets for the greater benefit of further descendants; some descendants in turn seek to contest such arrangements. The social relations between the dead and the living, hence, continue with regard to inherited property, much as property is, in adaptation of Chris Hann's definition, best viewed as social relations between people with regard to objects and assets (Hann 1998, 4).

Thus, within an inheritance both material value and mental valorization are passed on to the future and recipients face decisions of how to carry forward this individually and generationally marked boon and burden. In addition to the mesh of intangible memory encoded in inherited tokens, there are further memories—positive and perhaps also not so positive—which are woven into the fabric of family and kin folklore; stories that are passed on, components of ritual that the person might have created in a family, recipes, and other knowledge that may begin to form a temporary or long-term part of a given family's traditions. Barbara Kirshenblatt-Gimblett has reflected on the duality of valuation and valorization for public heritage practices (2006, 193). They appear to derive, in intent if not in morphology, from the rights and responsibilities, material and emotional of the familial, more private context of inheriting writ small.

The quite precise contours of a family inheritance—tangible and intangible—extend over time into a more inchoate bundle of memories and cultural practices one might term private heritage. Individual actors touched by a death take on ownership as well as responsibility of such an inheritance. While there may be customary, as well as local, and state laws on how such ownership and responsibility are to be enacted, the *emotional* investment can at best be subject to a sociocultural regime. The actual level of familial and individual feeling cannot be assessed, though the process of enculturation naturally does condition individuals to be aware of what is culturally expected of them. Nonetheless, there is for individuals and families the option to discard what is inherited. The house willed to the eldest daughter might be in ruins and she might opt to tear it down and build a new one. The family traditions upheld by the deceased *pater familias* might have been stifling and oppressive, and a widow or family may break with them with enormous relief. While the powerful hold of custom and social control mechanisms cannot be underestimated, individuals faced with familial inheritance have a measure of freedom of choice. The bigger and the more heterogeneous a group is, the weaker are the forces of social control and the greater the measure of such familial or individual freedom to uphold or to abandon an inheritance.

This is, of course, the nexus where the anxiety of cultural loss is lodged, as it is invariably also tied to feelings of alienation which, I would argue, contribute to the emergence of heritage practices—inheritance writ large. To grasp the leap into the inheritance analogy entailed in material and intangible cultural heritage regimes, and to understand where the bridge between inheritance and heritage is located, it is worth summing up the relevant factors involved: social actors, dead and alive, are kept in a relationship over a generation or more through values of material and immaterial dimensions. There are customary and legal, economic and moral obligations, rights, and responsibilities.


## INHERITING WRIT LARGE—PUBLIC HERITAGE


Inheriting within the family context materializes continuity and generation—connections which perhaps facilitate and which are certainly deeply implicated also in the ideology that has generated world heritage regimes. The "loosened ties" connected with industrialization, urbanization, and migration provide individuals with greater freedom in fashioning their lives. As much as "good" can only be evaluated on the basis of its opposite, freedom is felt only vis-à-vis experiences of bondage; the social and cultural ties of tightly knit custom can, in retrospect, turn into havens of communal support, common tradition, and individual safety within a collective. This very contrast between lasting tradition and unrelenting modernization is, ultimately, where the romantic vision of culture finds its origin. A desire to salvage and with it the foundations for the study and preservation of culture took their beginning from such longing.[13] There are reams of studies on migration and ethnicity, as well as on the effects (more broadly speaking) of modernization, documenting the impact of changing everyday contexts on the individual. The sense of individual empowerment goes hand in hand with a growing realization of individual responsibility for managing the risks of such a liberated life (Beck 1992). Richard Sennett accounts in the manner of historical, comparative case studies how such processes of individualization transform public life. Individuals searching for empowerment within their own lives undermine their attention to social competence; they gain individual freedom yet pay the price of social isolation.[14] The disembedding brought about by a second or reflexive modernization observed by Beck and attributed to the dual pressures of a globalized and individualized lifeworld (1996, 2004), is, in Sennett's earlier study, more closely tied to the relevance of "tradition"—a term with semantic powers much like heritage but in current social discourse subservient to the latter. Sennett portrays the emergence of the individual who seeks new relations and opportunities, and who is in a quandary of how to manage such unfolding while tending to the emotional space offered by tradition or folklore and hence "group" or cultural context. An increasing reliance on the self and an assured self-determination reshapes the connection to the reservoir of cultural expressions within one's group. The norms of interpretation loosen in terms of what exactly constitutes a proper execution of such tradition—a phenomenon highly visible for instance in the realm of "new folk music" in Europe. To what extent such developments and associated trains of thought apply to non-Western and less privileged lives remains to be examined.

Individualization has also loosened the immediacy of responsibility for aging kin—without necessarily reducing the interest in the property held by such kin. Industrial and postindustrial societies show increased mobility, largely due to occupational opportunities. Both by necessity and will, this has increased the distance between the living and death. The once customary proximity between the aged and ailing and their next of kin has made way for institutions for the aged and correspondingly less social contact and kin responsibility. There are more and more services stepping in where family used to be in charge of eldercare as well as, eventually, funerary preparations. I doubt that the separation of dead individuals from inheritable property and associated memory is ever complete. But I would argue that inheriting as a "complex cultural technique of preservation" (Langbein 2003, 335, my translation) has gained in shades of emotional-moral impact through the increased alienation from processes of dying and death itself. The ensuing gap opens emotional space for reflecting on the past—not just personal but also cultural—tied to material and immaterial inheritance. Here I see the convergence with inheritance writ large.

The leap from familial to (world) cultural heritage requires further transformations not only on the emotional but also on the legal plane. Stefan Willer locates a crucial step toward such regimes in the aftermath of the French Revolution and the practice of making large cultural treasures the property of the state:

> The World Heritage program is—in its own turn—inheriting cultural economies of a national orientation. This is particularly the case in

European national cultures of the late-nineteenth and early-twentieth century. And even those concepts of inheritance are transmissions: there were nationalizations of the transfer of legally privately owned goods which thus far had occurred between individuals. Within this ancestral site of inheritance each case of succession also implies a death which occasions the inheritance-succession in the first place. The collectivist vision of a cultural inheritance thus came about in the aftermath of the *dis*inheritance practices of the French Revolution. (Willer 2007, 125, my translation)

Moving sites deemed of national significance into the property of the state prepared the way for building institutions in charge of the restoration and maintenance of monuments. Such organizations on local, regional, and national levels, however, also planted and traditionalized the seeds of a preservationist rhetoric, which would eventually form the backbone of heritage regimes (cf., Tschofen 2007). One might argue that the second half of the twentieth century proved to be an era where the mourning of the loss of traditions transformed itself into institutions which in turn enforced a maintenance of the material as well as increasingly also the immaterial facets of such traditions. The maintenance of cultural expressions appeared no longer guaranteed in continually modernizing, individualizing societies. Individuals, institutions, scholarly disciplines and eventually—to put it in this grossly abbreviated sequence—international organizations, such as UNESCO, took it upon themselves to ensure the maintenance of at least the "best" of such cultural artifacts and expressions. The construction or "naturalization" of an international responsibility for preserving the past and the emergence of supralocal and supranational norms associated with this development still awaits further documentation and analysis.

If we were to sum up the relevant factors involved in bringing forth an inheritance writ large, that is, practices of public heritage, we note first and foremost the change involved from the private level with regard to social relationships. On the familial level of inheriting, it is the relationship between known social actors—one side dead, the other alive—that is marked through processes of inheriting. On the global stage of heritage, specific individuals recede. Rather, it is the moral obligation of "all" to generate programs ensuring the preservation and protection of chosen aspects of cultural pasts.[15] For this imagined global community, cultural heritage is conceived as a commons of humanity.[16] To forestall the decay of material heritage, UNESCO as the United Nations organization entrusted with culture (linked to peace!) generated a series of conventions to save and preserve such physically manifest sites, starting with the World Heritage Convention of 1972. The switch in the international vocabulary is worth noting. Earlier international deliberations spoke of cultural property and not heritage; by relegating the property dimension (at least linguistically) to the background, the safeguarding component gained in importance and visibility.[17] Such a move de-emphasizes ownership rights and moves to the foreground collective responsibilities vis-à-vis monuments, landscapes, historical memories, and so forth. UNESCO's intangible cultural heritage convention contributed not only to the valorization of the intangible aspects of a cultural inheritance. It also contributed to the recognition of the resource-quality of certain aspects of culture. To forestall a "tragedy of the commons" of intangible cultural heritage—which Garrett Hardin (1968) deplored for natural resources already in 1968—measures to protect it against excessive use and abuse have been seriously debated at the World Intellectual Property Organization since 2001. Philosophical, scholarly, and scientific expertise legitimizes the installation of such regimes to restore and protect cultural values encoded in monuments and artifacts, landscapes, and intangible practices. Rather than specific social ties, it is generalized relations between "the world" and the diversity of its cultural ancestors that is to be kept alive.

The commons idea suffuses the conventions. It is, however, immediately undermined by the fact that international conventions can only be acted on at the level of states, as all UNESCO conventions must be ratified by the individual states. Thus, while the "world community" is insisting on everyone's moral obligation to uphold cultural inheritances for the future, it is actors and institutions on the local and national level who have the social, political, and, most of all, economic responsibility to nominate cultural expressions for heritage status and—if successful—to see to their proper protection.

Inheriting writ large unfolds on a magnitude of scale that cannot be upheld simply with the forces of social control—as is, at least to an extent, still possible with familial inheritances. Within the familial setting, the material inheritance is obvious; the intangible aspects establish themselves in the course of time. For world heritage, however, there is nothing obvious about what is to be inherited and how the inheritance is to be carried forward into the future. Choices of worthiness and urgency are not immediately clear to cultural communities, experts, and politicians, despite the voices who consider value, beauty, and importance self-evident. Depending on historical experience and station, power, or lack of power within the world community, actors on the world stage will have different notions of what is to be part of world heritage. The repercussions of colonialism and postcolonial awakenings are in this regard a latent but powerful component of heritage decision-making.

Complicated mechanisms have to be set into place in order to bring forth applications, evaluations, and nominations, followed by guidelines and processes to ensure the proper maintenance of an item that has achieved world heritage status (Bendix, Eggert, and Peselmann 2012). If the legal accompaniment of a familial case of inheritance might seem to some cumbersome and alienating, the apparatus required to identify and ensure that the world's cultural heritage is passed on is of truly bewildering proportions. Barbara Kirshenblatt-Gimblett has spoken of the work of heritagization as "meta-cultural production" (1995). Yet as some recent research on "heritage work" has begun to point out, heritage practices appear to be moving out of the shadows of a meta-existence and taking on the shape of traditions themselves. As one interviewee in Markus Tauschek's study on the carnival in Binche noted, soon, the people of Binche might celebrate the anniversary of their nomination to intangible heritage of the world, and the carnival might become of secondary importance in their year cycle (Tauschek 2010). Here, the analogy to the private sphere may ring truer again—for families who have engaged in extensive legal battles over inheritances may celebrate a legal victory more than whatever material goods remain to be inherited after the struggle.

Heritage practices are, despite their tendency toward bureaucratization, not devoid of emotion.[18] The moral high ground of preserving a cultural commons brings forth competitive energies, pathos, jubilation (or disappointment). Perhaps this was not foreseen by those who crafted, in a long, drawn-out process, the convention for intangible cultural heritage. In his participant observation in the halls of UNESCO, Valdimar Hafstein registered a great deal of concern for how to contain the potentially boundless volume of applications from communities wishing to see their cultural expressions added to a list of intangible cultural heritage (Hafstein 2009, 105–7). In reining in that possibility and establishing criteria of selection, however problematic, distinction was introduced into the intangible cultural commons, much as it is present in other, earlier UNESCO heritage categories. The capacity to achieve distinction vis-à-vis competitors brings forth winners and losers, good players and neglectful rogues. Albeit achieved through a very different route than private inheritance, heritage practices appear to generate just as much if not more agency in the present and for the future. The primary mission of preserving evidence of cultural pasts pales by comparison.

Archaeologist Denis Byrne's hope for introducing a notion of "feeling heritage" signals a discomfort among international, cross-cultural heritage workers, and a desire to (re-)capture culturally divergent ways of honoring cultural pasts. Yet is that not a revisiting of the same nostalgic longings that suffuse heritage-generating practices in the first place, albeit spurred on by encounters in new fields and saturated with the experience of the effects of one's own work? The moral mission embraced by the conventions will only achieve sustainability, says Byrne, if conservation solutions mesh "with local beliefs and practices," in particular with regard to how the social ties to the dead, to ancestors, are culturally marked and felt. UNESCO, to him, is mired in its "own fantasies of universal value." Byrne argues that the world does not need more archaeologists and heritage professionals recording and conserving intangible heritage. Rather, "we would be better employed, first, in examining the politics of visibility in the production of heritage and second, in reconnecting emotionally to the past via the traces we already have recorded" (2009, 249–50). Notwithstanding such sobering calls for reevaluating the state of cultural inheritance in the world, the matter of ownership and attendant responsibility so patently inscribed into familial inheritances plays a considerable role also in public heritage.

## CULTURE AS A RESOURCE, BATTLES FOR OWNERSHIP

Once heritage conventions have been ratified by states, and once actors from the national to the local level get ready to implement them, the responsibility of the world at large to ennoble particular sites and practices and elevate them into heritage status has, for the most part, concluded. UNESCO cannot, other than through the list of endangered sites and practices, serve as an agency that puts into practice the ideology encoded in its heritage program. The moral ownership of the world does, for the most part, not include the financial responsibilities necessary to fulfill the safeguarding measures, not least because UNESCO is completely underfunded by comparison to other UN organizations. UNESCO's task is to focus attention on cultural value; the task of investing and protecting such value rests in the hands of actors within nation states.

Yet, if the production of heritage is strongly couched in moral responsibilities on the global stage, one cannot deny or overlook the fact that in local and national practice, heritage presents an economic opportunity. Much as a familial inheritance can entail economic gain, cultural heritage presents possibilities for economic growth. Profiting from such opportunities depends on ownership. Hence the question of "who owns native culture" (Brown 2003) turns crucial: heritage practices heighten consciousness for culture as a resource. While UNESCO, as well as a number of other actors, prefer to emphasize heritage's role as an identity resource, its caliber and growing importance as a renewable economic resource cannot be denied.[19] More than a century of cultural tourism constitute ample evidence for this transformation, as does the more recent merchandizing activity in museums, in the environs of traditional performances, and ritual. The political and economic resource qualities are thus closely paired.

The terms "cultural property" and "cultural heritage" are closely interlinked not just in the history of international conventions. There are efforts to mark their distinction and to further differentiate their semantics, depending on which language is examined. Nonetheless, proximity in usage can be observed time and again, and this proximity is indicative of the fluid transition from valorization to valuation raised by Kirshenblatt-Gimblett (2006). Scholars of international law, in particular, have pointed to the problematic, conceptual vagueness in the definition of both concepts, with Lyndel Prott and Patrick O'Keefe (1992) observing the slow supplanting of "property" by "heritage" and arguing for the latter's inclusion of the former. Manlio Frigo has pointed to the problematic of both terms even on the small–scale, international level of the European Community, as any international legal instrument requires translation into member states' languages. Additional shades of meaning sneak into the language—such as "treasure" being used as an equivalent to "heritage"—which necessitates the implementation of legal interpretations within the courts, from the local to the international (Frigo 2004, 371–73). The vagueness of the conceptual differentiation is thus occasioned by different interpretations of earlier safeguarding conventions, different semantic connotations depending on which language is spoken, and divergent national interests that express themselves more or less openly through such language use.

Following Frank Weigelt's chronicling of the use of the terms, one is tempted to see a kind of circularity, depending on whether global and moral or political and economic issues are traced. From a first mention of material and immaterial cultural property in the context of The Hague Convention in 1954, efforts of dealing with "mobile cultural property," including body parts, were added in 1968 (Weigelt 2007). The UNESCO cultural and natural heritage convention of 1972 shifted away from the connotations of property, so as to circumvent the economic component and to make a claim for culture to be a commons of humanity—that is the property and responsibility of all of humankind. Then, as UNESCO debated the intangible heritage convention, WIPO chose to concentrate on the discussion of cultural property. After extensive consultation with different stakeholders in the late 1990s, WIPO constituted an international committee devoted to traditional knowledge, genetic resources, and traditional cultural expressions/expressions of folklore in 2001, and has met in more or less half-yearly sessions to provide "for international policy debate and development of legal mechanisms and practical tools concerning the protection of traditional knowledge (TK) and traditional cultural expressions (folklore) against misappropriation and misuse, and the intellectual property (IP) aspects of access to and benefit-sharing in genetic resources" (WIPO, 2009).[20]

As is characteristic for international policy activity, issues that cannot be properly addressed within one organization are taken to another forum. In this case one can observe how political and economic concerns emerging with the interest to safeguard intangible heritage could not be handled within UNESCO. Actors engaged in the WIPO committee naturally seek concrete outcomes, and so the moral obligations entailed in heritage transform into questions of determining ownership and property rights more typical of an inheritance. And as an internationally accept-able policy solution will be a long time in the making, the battle over the resource aspects of culture will be taken to organizations such as the World Trade Organization, or will be handled by small-scale bilateral agreements where legally secured economic gain generally has priority over moral obligation.

## CONCLUDING THOUGHTS

Responsibility and ownership are two intertwined and deeply ingrained aspects of the international heritage regime that has emerged in the course of the second half of the twentieth century. By declaring first tangible and later intangible selections or excerpts of culture as world heritage, UNESCO claims moral ownership for the world's nations of selected cultural sites and practices, rendering these into a cultural commons on a moral level but leaving the political and financial care necessary to tend to this commons in the hands of the nation states. UNESCO also imposes a string of responsibilities that go with heritage ownership. Thus, in the UNESCO convention on intangible cultural heritage, this world insti-tution defines safeguarding as follows: "'Safeguarding' means measures aimed at ensuring the viability of the intangible cultural heritage, includ-ing the identification, documentation, research, preservation, protection, promotion, enhancement, transmission, particularly through formal and non-formal education, as well as the revitalization of the various aspects of such heritage" (UNESCO 2003, art. 2.3).

All of these tasks are costly, all of them require sets of expertise. Yet given that every member state is likely to differ in its organization of cul-tural policy and support, this document does not specify which actors are entrusted with which aspects of this list of tasks. It is precisely this impre-cision that can cause confusion and indeterminacy on the ground. The application procedures are highly regulated; although the initial actors moving forward with such an application are, in democratic settings, often self-selected, the subsequent path of what needs to be assembled, what form it needs to be presented in, and what kind of expertise needs to be consulted are spelled out.[21] For the postnomination phase, suddenly new processes and responsible people and institutions have to be determined. After the initial joy of having garnered a world heritage title for an "item" of intangible heritage, particularly local actors are somewhat bewildered as to who holds what rights and responsibilities for a communally generated intangible practice which now is to be maintained according to the specifications outlined in the dossier that led to heritage victory. Unlike the clearly defined inheritance relationships on the familial level, world heritage leaves in its wake a lack of clarity concerning particularly the moral responsibilities and rights of heritage ownership.

Heritage designation fosters a view of cultural expressions as a resource. As it is not the global community that tends these resources as a commons, it does not surprise that many actors seek to stake a claim for themselves; much as in other resource domains such as coal, oil, diamonds, and gold, prospectors sought to stake claims to build an economic future for themselves. Culture has the potential of being renewable—ultimately cultural creativity is what keeps transforming environments and milieus. But in contrast to the future orientation of inheritance practices, heritage regimes are strongly focused on valuing the past and point rather more toward culture as a finite, sustainable resource. This perspective of a limited good further supports interest in protecting cultural property rights, so as to give the power to open, limit, or close access to traditional knowledge and traditional cultural practices. Michael F. Brown (2003) as well as Dorothy Noyes (2006) add to this the enormous political role that cultural property has taken on in struggles to assert political identity and self-determination for communities marginalized within states governed by a cultural majority.

"The movement toward legal protection of intangible heritage offers rewarding vistas for connoisseurs of irony," writes Michael F. Brown: "To defend their cultures from commodification, indigenous leaders deploy Western idioms of property in their protests and communiques.... Most of these plans, however well intentioned, have a powerful tendency to flatten difference in the interests of procedural uniformity" (Brown 2004, 59–60).

Such flattening, I would argue, is also tied to the imprecise semantics of the term "heritage," which in contrast to the concept of inheritance leaves a great deal of room for interpretation regarding responsibility and ownership. Recent scholarship in international law on cultural property rights and its linkages to human rights legislation (Lewinski 2003) demonstrates the importance of examining the translation of heritage ideologies and property regimes into specific juridical systems. As vague as a heritage designation may be in its denotation of "heirs," it always has the power to disinherit individuals—or entire groups (cf., Ashworth and Turnbridge 1995). A combination of anthropological, legal, and economic expertise may be the most cogent avenue toward clarifying terms and the social agency made possible or inhibited by them.

NOTES

This chapter appeared originally in *Traditiones* (Ljublijana) 38, no. 2 (2009): 181–99.

A somewhat different version of this paper appeared also in French (Bendix 2011). Thanks go to Johannes Fabian and Stefan Groth for their respective comments to the originally published version of this paper.

1. The Budapest Declaration on World Heritage of 2002 uses both heritage and inheritance; in the 1972 document, inheritance does not appear.

2. Some interpreters of the convention for intangible cultural heritage focus less on its expanded definition of culture, but rather emphasize the geopolitical balance it sought to achieve. As the earlier conventions privileged states in possession of a rich monumental heritage, the new convention permitted largely "developing" nations or "the global south" to participate in the global competition of heritigization (cf., Meyer-Rath 2007, 173–4).

3. Research of the Göttingen research group on cultural property at the World Intellectual Property Organization in Geneva supports the latter view, though the component of "organizational learning" cannot be discounted. For a close analysis of international negotiation practices, see Groth (2012); for anthropological research more broadly on policy making and institutionalizing, see Shore and Wright (2011), as well as the ongoing work led by Birgit Müller at the *Laboratoire d'anthropologie des institutions et des organisations sociales* in Paris, and the EASA Network on the Anthropology of Law, Rights and Governance or Law-Net. Accessed May 9, 2017. http://www.easaonline.org/networks/lawnet/index.shtml.

4. Research on the issues surrounding the nomination and implementation of the Preah Vihear site are discussed in Hauser-Schäublin (2011) and Mißling (2011).

5. Wend Wendland, secretary for the Intergovernmental Committee concerned with matters of cultural property at WIPO, stressed this distinction between preservation and protection in an interview conducted by Stefan Groth (October 24, 2008).

6. Of course, there are state and federal laws regulating the inheritance of private property; nonetheless, there remain private, "customary" sensibilities and individual experiences that are free of a more comprehensive public regime.

7. With regard to assessing the need for follow-up on the *longue durée* of political efforts to preserve and protect aspects of cultural practice deemed valuable, see Tschofen (2007).

8. Nelson Graburn has provided a farther-reaching comparative exploration of the linked terminologies of kinship and heritage—whereby the title of his essay does not really do justice to its content (2001).

9. As an example for how culturally patterned implementation measures impact on the lives of those living within a heritage site, see Miura's study on Angkor, Cambodia (Miura 2004, 2005). Her ethnographic study painfully illustrated what complex, contradictory, and often unproductive bureaucratic hoops are introduced, and how extant political structures lead to developments not at all likely to embody the spirit of UNESCO's heritage conventions.

10. The generating of lists as instruments of heritage regimes is superbly discussed by Hafstein (2009). While I am aware that the impetus to introduce intangible heritage into UNESCO's work was a result of Japanese lobbying for safeguarding models ("living national treasures") that had a long history in Japan, the bureaucratic paths chosen to bring about the competitive application and certification programs appears to be built on Western cultural certification patterns.

11. On the conceptual connections of inheritance and world heritage from a literary, legal, and economic perspective, Stefan Willer and others at the Berlin *Zentrum für Literatur- und Kulturwissenschaft* carried out the project "Generationen in der Erbengemeinschaft" (see Willer, Weigel, and Jussen 2013). Though more strongly guided by research questions from the field of literature (albeit assisted with expertise from law), a number of relevant projects on the notions of generation, tradition, and heredity are emerging there; compare, for instance Weigel (2006) or Müller-Wille and Rheinberger (2007).

12. David Sabean (2007) provides a brief assessment of the emergence of restricted inheritance practices in Europe, with some emphasis on the gender disparity that was introduced, and calls for a more comprehensive comparative study of nineteenth century legal codes that restructured inheritance law with relation to family.

13. Questions of the emergence of heritage practices are invariably closely tied to the emergence of ethnological disciplines. From the legion of works addressing the latter, the reader is referred to just a few examples: Bausinger (1971), Bendix (1997), Kaschuba (1999, 20–38), Köstlin and Nikitsch (1999), Stewart (1984, 1991), and touching on the linkage between the ethnological disciplines and heritage, compare the chapter "Expressive Resources" in this volume.

14. Ulrich Beck's work on reflexive modernization similarly points to the disembedding entailed in an at-once globalized and individualized lifeworld (1996, 2004).

15. Yet, how are such purportedly global morals legitimized? At this juncture, the debate regarding morals and norms in global governance needs to at least be pointed out. Scholarship on an emergent global polity has emphasized norms rather than morals as an avenue to avoid the imposition of universal moral values. The concept of morality can, in a Durkheimian social analysis, only be invoked within specific, socially circumscribed contexts where there exist shared assumptions governing social action and interaction and hence shared values and notions of "morality." On a global level, shared moral obligations are certainly invoked in speech-making and program-building, but as sociologist Helmut

Willke has argued, shared norms rather than morals are what is needed: "We took centuries to overcome the paternalism of morals and achieve the rationality characteristic of democratically shaped norms." Willke insists on the necessity of separating privately held moral frameworks from the politically achieved norms, particularly as a means to overcome the longing for universal norms: "The longing for universal norms appears to be fed from similar sources as the longing for eternal world peace. Both longings are understandable, and yet both remain fiction.... A universal moral order remains fictional because there are no mechanisms for solving opposing moral postulates" (Wilke 2008, 4, my translation). Even so, the question remains whose norms are deemed "good," as Amitav Archarya has pointed out. Acharya further showed how the adaptation of purportedly global norms into regional and local settings undergoes a process of assimilation with locally valid norms (2004). Groth (2013) works on establishing the ethical and moral dimensions within discourses on cultural heritage and property on an international level.

16. As Rosemarie Wilcken, then president of the German Endowment for World Heritage formulated in a public address 2004: "One basic tenet of the world heritage convention is that here is a joint responsibility of all for the protection and maintenance of cultural and natural heritage of the world for future generations" (Wilcken 2008).

17. Hafstein (2004) and Weigelt (2007) each render the history leading from earlier international concerns and conventions to the new heritage conventions; see discussion further on.

18. Naturally one cannot claim that bureaucratic culture is devoid of emotion. Indifference, as Herzfeld's work has demonstrated, is a culturally produced form of seeming nonemotion which in turn can generate a great deal of aggression and frustration (Herzfeld 1993).

19. Frank Weigelt goes so far as to state that the cultural property notion embraced by UNESCO is intended to prepare cultural excerpts "for the markets of culture on this planet as well as a concept to protect such goods and to facilitate a regulated 'movement of goods'" (Weigelt 2007, 143).

20. See also the essays in Part 3 of this volume.

21. Consider the case studies from Italy (Broccolini 2012) or France (Adell 2012; Bortolotto 2012; Tornatore 2012) for an impression of the complexity of the implementation on the ground.

### REFERENCES

Adell, Nicolas. 2012. "The French Journeymen Tradition: Convergence between French Heritage Traditions and UNESCO's 2003 Convention." In *Heritage Regimes and the State*, edited by Bendix, Eggert, and Peselmann, 177–94. Göttingen: University of Göttingen Press.

Acharya, Amitav. 2004. "How Ideas Spread: Whose Norms Matter? Norm Localization and Institutional Change in Asian Regionalism." *International Organization* 58: 239–75.

Ashworth, G. J., and Turnbridge, J. E. 1995. *Dissonant Heritage. The Management of the Past as a Resource in Conflict*. London: Wiley.

Bausinger, Hermann. 1971. *Volkskunde. Von der Altertumswissenschaft zur Kulturanalyse*. Berlin: Habel.

Beck, Ulrich. 1992. *Risk Society. Towards a New Modernity.* Translated by Mark Ritter. London: Sage.

———. 1996. *Reflexive Modernisierung. Eine Kontroverse.* Frankfurt: Suhrkamp.

———. 2004. *Entgrenzung und Entscheidung: Was ist neu an der Theorie der reflexiven Modernisierung?* Frankfurt: Suhrkamp.

Bendix, Regina. 1997. *In Search of Authenticity: The Formation of Folklore Studies.* Madison: University of Wisconsin Press.

———. 2011. Héritage et patrimoine: de leurs proximités sémantiques et de leurs implications. In *Le patriomoine culturel immaterériel. Enjeux d'une nouvelle catégorie,* edited by Chiara Bortolotto, 99–121. Paris: Éd. de la Maison des sciences de l'homme.

Bendix, Regina F., Aditya Eggert, and Arnika Peselmann, eds. 2012. *Heritage Regimes and the State.* Göttingen: Universitätsverlag Göttingen.

Bortolotto, Chiara, ed. 2011. *Le patrimoine culturel immatériel: Enjeux d'une nouvelle catégorie.* Paris: Éd. de la Maison des sciences de l'homme.

———. 2012. "The French Inventory of Intangible Cultural Heritage: Domesticating a Global Paradigm into French Heritage Regime." In *Heritage Regimes and the State,* edited by Bendix, Eggert, and Peselmann, 265–82.

Broccolini, Alessandra. 2012. "Intangible Cultural Heritage Scenarios within the Bureaucratic Italian State." In *Heritage Regimes and the State,* edited by Bendix, Eggert, and Peselmann, 283–302.

Brown, Michael F. 2003. *Who owns native culture?* Cambridge, MA: Harvard University Press.

———. 2004. "Heritage as Property." In *Property in Question. Value Transformation in the Global Economy,* edited by Katherine Verdery and Caroline Humphrey, 49–68. Oxford: Berg.

Byrne, Denis. 2009. "A Critique of Unfeeling Heritage." In *Intangible Heritage,* edited by Laurajane Smith and Natsuko Akagawa, 229–52. London: Routledge.

Frigo, Manlio. 2004. "Cultural Property vs. Cultural Heritage—A 'Battle of Concepts' in International Law?" *International Review of the Red Cross* 86 (854): 367–78.

Graburn, Nelson. 2001. "Learning to Consume: What is Heritage and When is it Traditional?" In *Consuming Tradition, Manufacturing Heritage. Global Norms and Urban Forms in the Age of Tourism,* edited by Nezar AlSayyad, 68–89. London: Routledge.

Groth, Stefan. 2012. *Negotiating Tradition: The Pragmatics of International Deliberations on Cultural Property.* Göttingen: University of Göttingen Press.

———. 2013. "Allmendgemeinschaften und Cultural Commons in der Diskussion um kulturelles Eigentum." In *Kultur_Kultur. Denken, Forschen, Darstellen,* edited by Reinhard Johler, Christian Marchetti, Bernhard Tschofen, Carmen Weith, 59–65. Münster: Waxmann.

Hafstein, Valdimar Tr. 2004. *The Making of Intangible Cultural Heritage: Tradition and Authenticity, Community and Humanity.* PhD diss., University of California. ProQuest (3052103449).

———. 2007. "Claiming Culture: Intangible Heritage Inc., Folklore©, Traditional Knowledge TM." In *Prädikat 'Heritage,'* edited by Hemme, Tauschek, and Bendix, 75–100. Münster: LIT.

———. 2009. "Intangible Heritage as a List. From Masterpiece to Representation." In *Intangible Heritage*, edited by Laurajane Smith and Natsuko Akagawa, 93–111. London: Routledge.

Hann, Chris M. 1998. "Introduction to Property Relations." *Renewing the Anthropological Tradition*, edited by Chris M. Hann, 1–47. Cambridge: Cambridge University Press.

Hardin, Garrett. 1968. "The Tragedy of the Commons." *Science* 162: 1243–8.

Hauser-Schäublin, Brigitta. 2011. "Preah VIhear. From Object of Colonial Desire to a Contested World Heritage Site." In *World Heritage Angkor and Beyond. Circumstances and Implications of UNESCO Listings in Cambodia*, Göttingen Studies in Cultural Property, vol. 2, edited by Brigitta Hauser-Schäublin. 33–56. Göttingen: University of Göttingen Press.

Hemme, Dorothee, Markus Tauschek, and Regina Bendix, eds. 2007. *Prädikat "Heritage." Wertschöpfung aus kulturellen Ressourcen.* Münster: LIT.

Herzfeld, Michael. 1993. *The Social Production of Indifference: Exploring the Symbolic Roots of Western Bureaucracy.* Chicago: University of Chicago Press.

Kaschuba, Wolfgang. 1999. *Einführung in die Europäische Ethnologie.* München: Beck.

Kirshenblatt-Gimblett, Barbara. 1995. "Theorizing Heritage." *Ethnomusicology* 39: 367–80.

———. 2006. "World Heritage and Cultural Economics." In *Museum Frictions. Public Cultures/Global Transformations*, edited by Ivan Karp, Corinne A. Kratz, Lynn Szwaja, and Tomas Ybarra-Frausto, 161–202. Durham, NC: Duke University Press.

Köstlin, Konrad, and Herbert Nikitsch, eds. 1999. *Ethnographisches Wissen. Zu einer Kulturtechnik der Moderne*. Vienna: Institut für Volkskunde.

Langbein, Ulrike. 2003. "Erbsachen: Erbprozess und kulturelle Ordnung. Kulturelle Ordungssysteme als Orientierung." In *Komplexe Welt*, edited by Silke Göttsch, and Christel Köhle-Hezinger, 333–41. Münster: Waxmann.

Lewinski, Silke von, ed. 2003. *Indigenous Heritage and Intellectual Property. Genetic Resources, Traditional Knowledge and Folklore.* The Hague: Kluwer Law International.

Meyer-Rath, Anne. 2007. "Zeit-nah, Welt-fern? Paradoxien in der Prädikatisierung von immateriellem Kulturerbe." In *Prädikat "Heritage,"* edited by Hemme, Tauschek, and Bendix, 147–76. Münster: LIT.

Mißling, Sven. 2011. "A Legal View of the Caose of the Temple Preah Vihear." In *World Heritage Angkor and Beyond. Circumstances and Implications of UNESCO Listings in Cambodia*, edited by Brigitta Hauser-Schäublin. Göttingen Studies in Cultural Property, vol. 2, 57–66. Göttingen: University of Göttingen Press.

Miura, Keiko. 2004. "Contested Heritage. People of Angkor." PhD diss., University of London.

———. 2005. "Conservation of a 'Living Heritage Site': A Contradiction in Terms? A Case Study of Angkor World Heritage Site." *Conservation and Management of Archaeological Sites* 7 (1): 3–18.

Müller-Wille, Staffan, and Hans-Jörg Rheinberger, eds. 2007. *Heredity Produced. At the Crossroads of Biology, Politics, and Culture, 1500–1870.* Cambridge, MA: MIT Press.

Noyes, Dorothy. 2006. "The Judgment of Solomon: Global Protections for Tradition and the Problem of Community Ownership." *Cultural Analysis* 5: 27–56.

Prott, Lyndel, and Patrick J. O'Keefe. 1992. "'Cultural Heritage' or 'Cultural Property'?" *International Journal of Cultural Property* 1: 307–20.

Sabean, David Warren. 2007. "From Clan to Kindred: Kinship and the Circulation of Property in Premodern and Modern Europe." In *Heredity Produced. At the Crossroads of Biology, Politics, and Culture, 1500–1870*, edited by Staffan Müller-Wille and Hans-Jörg Rheinberger, 37–59. Cambridge, MA: MIT Press.

Sennett, Richard. 1977. *The Fall of Public Man*. New York: Knopf.

Shore, C.N. and Susan Wright. 2011. "Conceptualising Policy: Technologies of Governance and the Politics of Visibility." In *Policy Worlds: Anthropology and the Analysis of Contemporary*, edited by C. N. Shore, Susan Wright, and Davide Pero, 1–26. Oxford: Berghahn.

Smith, Laurajane, and Natsuko Akagawa, eds. 2009. *Intangible Heritage*. With an Introduction by Laurajane Smith and Natsuko Akagawa. London: Routledge.

Stewart, Susan. 1984. *On Longing. Narratives of the Miniature, the Gigantic, the Souvenir, the Collection*. Baltimore, MD: Johns Hopkins University Press.

———. 1991. *Crimes of Writing: Problems in the Containment of Representation*. New York: Oxford University Press.

Swenson, Astrid. 2007. "'Heritage', 'Patrimoine,' und 'Kulturerbe': Eine vergleichende historische Semantik." In *Prädikat 'Heritage,'* edited by Hemme, Tauschek, and Bendix, 53–74. Münster: LIT.

Tauschek, Markus. 2010. *Wertschöpfung aus Tradition: der Karneval von Binche und die Konstituierung kulturellen Erbes*. Berlin: LIT.

Tornatore, Jean-Louis. 2012. "Anthropology's Pay Back: 'The Gastronomic Meal of the French.' The Ethnographic Elements of a Heritage Distinction," In *Heritage Regimes and the State*, edited by Bendix, Eggert, and Peselmann, 341–65.

Tschofen, Bernhard. 2007. "Antreten, ablehnen, verwalten? Was der Heritage Boom den Kulturwissenschaften aufträgt." In *Prädikat 'Heritage,'* edited by Hemme, Tauschek, and Bendix, 19–32. Münster: LIT.

UNESCO. 1972. "Convention Concerning the Protection of World Cultural and Natural Heritage." Accessed December 20, 2017. http://whc.UNESCO.org/archive /convention-en.pdf.

———. 2002. "Budapest Declaration on World Heritage." Accessed December 20, 2017. http://whc.UNESCO.org/en/decisions/1217/.

———. 2003. "Convention for the Safeguarding of the Intangible Cultural Heritage." Accessed December 20, 2017. http://unesdoc.UNESCO.org /images/0013/001325/132540e.pdf.

WIPO. 2009. "Traditional Knowledge." Accessed Jan 15. http://www.wipo.int/tk/en (page modified).

Weigel, Sigrid. 2006. *Genea-Logik. Generation, Tradition und Evolution zwischen Kultur- und Naturwissenschaft*. Munich: Wilhelm Fink.

Weigelt, Frank André. 2007. "Von 'Cultural Property' zu 'Cultural Heritage'. Die UNESCO-Konzeption im Wandel der Zeit." In *Prädikat 'Heritage,'* edited by Hemme, Tauschek, and Bendix, 129–46. Münster: LIT.

Wilcken, Rosemarie. 2008. Keynote at the Annual Meeting of the German Commission for UNESCO 2004. February 8. http://www.UNESCO-welterbe.de/de/uebersicht /jahrestagung/2004/vortrag_wilcken.pdf (page deleted).

Willke, Helmut. 2008."Gespräch mit dem Bielefelder Soziologen Helmut Willke."
    *Marburger Forum* 9 (4). Accessed July 20, 2009. http://www.uni-bielefeld.de/soz
    /globalgov/Lit/Willke_Moral_Marburger_Forum.pdf.
Willer, Stefan. 2007. "Welt-Erbe. Zum aktuellen Verhältnis von Globalität und kulturellem
    Kanon." In *Akten des XI. Internationalen Germanistenkongresses Paris 2005: Germanistik
    im Konflikt der Kulturen'. Vol. 8*, edited by Jean-Marie Valentin, 125–6. Bern: Lenz.
Willer, Stefan, Sigrid Weigel, and Bernhard Jussen. 2013. *Erbe: Übertragungskonzepte
    zwischen Natur und Kultur*. Berlin: Suhrkamp.
Yúdice, George. 2003. *The Expediency of Culture*. Durham, NC: Duke University Press.

# 8

*The Dynamics of Valorizing Culture:*
*Actors and Shifting Contexts in*
*the Course of a Century*

Examining cultural heritage in the larger context of (mass) tourism signifies, indirectly, more than a modicum of social critique focused on political and economic phenomena. This can hardly be avoided when the protection and preservation of culture have become so heavily steeped in ideology, in a tradition reflected in the United Nations Educational, Scientific, and Cultural Organization (UNESCO) World Heritage Conventions. It is especially unavoidable in tourism research in the fields of anthropology and folklore, which, in the Anglo-American world, struggled to break away from critique associated with indictment, exemplified by the title "Culture by the Pound" (Greenwood 1977; cf., MacCannell 2011, 36, 235–36), before it finally took the path of documenting and understanding touristic practices in the same manner as other cultural phenomena. In German-language research, too, pessimism and criticism of tourism long carried greater weight than attempts to understand tourist phenomena, though critique of criticism related to conventional mass tourism began quite early (Enzensberger 1958). Here, then, there is also an interface—not necessarily a productive one—between cultural heritage and tourism in cultural research: the protective and preservative impulse in the notion of "patrimonialization" meets the lingering salvage mentality to which scholars doing ethnographic work, despite their best intentions and knowledge of the history of their subject, are apt to fall prey.[1] Over years of fieldwork, researchers have explored the daily and ritual life of a region in the ethnographic present, and they experience the ravages of time, manifested in economic and political change, more as a radical upheaval than as an inevitable transformation, one helped along in most cases by the actors under study themselves.

Implied in both impulses—patrimonialization and the ethnological "rescue before it's ruined"—is the notion of loss.[2] In both, conflicting perspectives on restricting the cultural commons also play a role: The cultural heritage regime wants to grant worldwide access to a cultural form or practice that is regarded as valuable, yet at the same time, it arranges things so that the culture bearers more or less suddenly become aware of their ownership function, not least because they are confronted with the corresponding responsibility. So, it should not be surprising that these owners of cultural heritage also feel entitled to define more precisely the commons from which the corresponding cultural good stems and to use it for economic gain. Some of the ethnographically oriented academic protectors would like to be part of the commons whose "culture" they have documented and thus, in a way, would like to keep the form or practice in question confined within a scientific and timeless present. Or, as the economists say in contemporary language, they want to participate in culture as a club good. At the same time, they want to exclude the tourists, the television cameras, and the corruption of the global market. Economic growth would then be limited to an imaginary "locally grown" degree. Admittedly, this attitude on the part of ethnographic professionals has increasingly changed over a good forty years of productive research, but the historically deep-rooted reflex that seeks to catalog economic change as potential corruption is found again and again, whether in subtle or thoughtless statements.

Additionally, these two phenomena, the cultural heritage regime and tourism, can be described as quite aggressive dynamics. Everyone may strive for gentle and sustainable tourism, but the tourism industry, as the primary and most obvious economic sector with a global network, affects and opens up lifeworlds in a way that many other economic restructurings exhibit less tangibly. The movement to protect culture, showing the influence of UNESCO, entails governmental and bureaucratic tools of implementation, which, depending on the political culture, can also have severe effects (Bendix, Eggert, and Peselmann 2012). Both the heritage regime and tourism—to varying degrees—use culture as a resource, meaning that in both, cultural goods and practices are associated with values. That can, but need not, facilitate transfer to a market.

This chapter uses Swiss examples to examine how potential cultural patrimony is dealt with. The examples were chosen because the often-embedded processes of valorization can be tracked over a considerable period of time. What is essential here is the continuous intermeshing of nonmaterial, social, and economic evaluations and revaluations, which the actors involved rarely separate as neatly as do scholars. Before I turn to examples from Urnäsch, Schwyz, and Altdorf, there follow a few thoughts on what valorization actually means. I use that term deliberately to emphasize the conceptual possibilities, in contrast to commoditization. The latter refers to transformation of a resource into a product and thus implies the detachment and alienation of this resource from human or cultural values. A look at the actors' use of cultural resources over an extended period suggests that the separation of economic values from other values cannot be maintained, and it seems appropriate to replace the automatic negative rating of the economic dimension with a more sober and holistic perspective on valorization practices.

## THE VOCABULARY OF VALORIZATION

Both heritage and tourism are based on processes of valorization.[3] It is worth taking a closer look at the terms associated with this, because the conceptual level makes possible a cultural anthropological view that considers the two phenomena in a more integrated way, as part of cultural (system) development over time. Moving away from the specifics of patrimonialization and cultural tourism to the more general category of "bestowing value" also allows for a more neutral placing of these phenomena within a wider range of human activity having to do with real and symbolic resources. This seems all the more urgent as the booming field of heritage research threatens to become overspecialized. What is needed is broadly based theorizing of heritage in fields of social and cultural research on the one hand, and theory-guided, practice-related work on the other hand. This connects to another article in which I have grappled with what heritage is, and what nuances are added when we speak of cultural or even world heritage sites.[4] Here, I would now like to concentrate on "valorization" and "bestowing of value," because this cultural gesture shapes both tourism and world heritage practices.

Concerning oneself with the verbs—that is, the activities—that produce heritage and tourism also means overcoming the division into cultural and metacultural outputs. Barbara Kirshenblatt-Gimblett formulated this split into two parts in 1995 as a basis for her groundbreaking theories about heritage; it has been extremely productive from a research perspective. Her heritage concept encompassed phenomena ranging from museum exhibitions through tourism performances to cultural heritage (1995, 2004). She described cultural heritage as a form of metacultural production that refers to the past but that creates something new. Cultural tourism would then be analogously (and simplistically) formulated as metacultural production that makes use of cultural contexts and turns them into goods that can be purchased and experienced.

However, I would like to argue that valorization, the assigning of value, is an intrinsic part of cultural agency, and that setting aside the distinction between metapractices and actual practices proves useful precisely for capturing the intricacies of cultural heritage and tourism.[5] This will control or stop the lingering assumption that only players (in most cases, even outside players) operate on a metalevel that uses culture, while the "culture bearers" experience alienation from their cultural heritage due to such metacultural operations. What Foucault in his work on governmentality has referred to as "conduct of conduct" (1994, 237) is available to all stakeholders as a space of action—but they may articulate different preferences. Such governmentality can be discerned as a cultural gesture in "regular inheriting" as much as in "inheriting culture" or heritage, in bestowing "value," and in "bestowing value to culture." Kirshenblatt-Gimblett differentiated the phenomena into two levels, so that cultural change could be analytically addressed through the framework of an action level and a metalevel that directs the action. Ultimately, however, this dichotomy must be overcome: an awareness of (political, social, economic, symbolic) valuation accompanies each action; the transformation of culture into economic goods is one of many different possibilities of valorization. A political or religious valorization, too, has consequences for actors. Therefore, I see the valorization of culture as being within any and all practices developed by humans. Practices, in turn, always are more or less obviously directed or controlled by newly emerging norms.[6]

The following questions are the starting point for my considerations:

1.  What leads actors to (consciously) assign value to segments of their cultural activity? The continuation of rituals, performances, songs, and similar intangible cultural heritage, as well as the maintenance of constructed tangible heritage, is itself an implicit attribution of value: there is a passion and a desire to conserve tangible and intangible cultural elements so that they can be experienced in the lifeworld.[7] The aspect of patrimonialization, which is made dominant in the discourse, can change this dynamic, but need not do so.
2.  What latitude and scope of action do actors have for attributing value?

As culturally informed behavior is not hermetically self-contained, both questions must be considered in conjunction with the additional contexts. Local actors live in local, regional, national, and global political and economic relationships. This life is shaped by the past as well as by hopes and expectations for the future. Valorization develops accordingly within a field defined by a temporal axis and a spatial-political axis.

One must consider, then, the history and theoretical penetration of the cultural practice of attributing value. Not least because cultural anthropology has long studied the assigning of value in its symbolic embedding and sought to disregard the contact of cultural systems with (global) economic markets, this history and its terminology instead are more apt to have their place in political and economic theory and in philosophy.[8] It was Arjun Appadurai's groundbreaking volume *The Social Life of Things* (1986) and its introduction to the cultural and political dynamics of (economic) goods that first articulated an enlarged approach. However, the bulk of publications in the fields of cultural and social anthropology reveals a reticence to use terms from the economic lexicon. There seems to be an aversion to a perspective informed by economic thought, though work and economic activity are the most basic practices by which people secure the necessities of life. Through work, institutions that profoundly influence social coexistence have developed and continue to develop. They are interwoven with institutions, such as kinship or religion, which have been more favored in ethnological research. It was precisely because of this marginalization of the perspectives of economic anthropology that John and Jean Comaroff's *Ethnicity, Inc.* (2009) had such a massive impact—even though this excellent analysis of the ways culture is utilized by culture carriers themselves does not recognize and discuss a considerable part of the research that has been done.[9] The initial passages of the book indicate that the Comaroffs had to overcome an inner resistance to address this phenomenon, and they seemed to be almost a bit surprised by the level of skill that can be discerned in cultural self-marketing on the part of indigenous actors. However, economic terms are useful and well-suited for the question of the valorization of culture, with which the heritage and tourism discussion must deal: actors in the tourism industry and the heritage industry are working with this vocabulary and the associated mind-set. Cultural scholarship will do well to perceive cultural actors as economic actors, too, whose (global) economic activity is part of cultural development and dynamics.

Pivotal here is the concept of commons and the corresponding potential for inclusion in, and exclusion from, the group or association of those who benefit from a common good—for example, the knowledge encoded in a handicraft, an annual custom, a traditional recipe or method, or even an archaeological site located in their own rural area. These are all cultural assets that have been provided with economic mechanisms of inclusion and exclusion, both through tourist attention and through UNESCO certification. For if cultural practices are removed from their habitual context—perhaps the most fundamental and most unconsidered of all the commons—and assigned nonmaterial and/or market-based values, another question immediately arises: Who is allowed to continue sharing in aspects of the former commons that have been revalued, upgraded from cultural practices to cultural assets? Valorization is thus accompanied by propertization. Even if many actors do not experience this step toward property and ownership in the economic sense—and, ideally, in the legal sense as well—it nevertheless does take place. One problem of touristic and patrimonializing valorization is that legal positions on property rights and usage rights are not necessarily firmly established in the respective regimes: precisely because culture is experienced as a commons, actors often are not aware that it has solidified into a resource until individual actors have already registered exclusive rights for themselves.

It is these dimensions which are covered by the concept of transaction costs: What do actors accept when valorization is in process? What are the effects of the intertwined social and economic consequences of such decisions? And to what extent do stakeholders consciously let themselves in for such consequences? The notion of transaction costs covers everything that is incurred when buyers and/or sellers buy or sell a good. It includes efforts to find someone from whom one can buy something and negotiate an appropriate contract—in the context of the present topic the touristic use or the heritage nomination of a cultural asset—and extends all the way to monitoring the contract in the case of long-term deliverables, as well as taking any legal action needed to enforce it. Transaction costs can include monetary amounts as well as a range of nonmonetary factors, such as fear of exploitation through breach of contract or legal uncertainty. Certainly, cultural anthropologists have also focused on the social and political energies that people need to muster to accomplish an exchange or purchase. However, most of the research focuses on the (precapitalist) exchange of gifts and its interpersonal consequences, and a certain refusal to use the term "costs" for this can definitely be perceived.[10] By contrast, there are no similar barriers in economics, where economists such as Bruno Frey (e.g., 2010) or David Throsby (e.g., 1999) gave a significant boost to the subdiscipline of cultural economics, resulting in subject-specific insights that could be sharpened and tested in cooperation with cultural and social sciences.

Kirshenblatt-Gimblett used this approach when she dealt with the array of values proposed by Frey and Werner W. Pommerehne (1989):

[They] distinguish five types of value: option, existence, bequest, prestige, and education. *Option value* refers to the value of having the opportunity to benefit from an asset, whether or not one ever does. *Existence value* (also called non-use value) refers to the value one places on the mere existence of a cultural asset such as the Garifuna language, without reference to whether or not a global citizen will ever hear it or personally benefit from it in some way. *Bequest value*, as the term suggests, is the value that the asset may have for later generations. *Prestige value*—the primary value of being proclaimed a masterpiece of world heritage—refers to the benefits that follow from being endowed with elevated status. This is the logic of awards, designations, proclamations, registers, and lists. Moreover, a rise in prestige value, while it may have economic benefits in terms of tourism, for example, may have negative effects on property value by limiting what the owner can do with a building. *Education value* refers to the value of the asset as an educational resource, understood in the context of UNESCO as contributing to positive identity, pluralism, dialogue, culture of peace, and economic development. (2006, 193–94)

It is clear from this—as well as from the other authors referenced by Kirshenblatt-Gimblett—that economic analyses are not interested in financial markets alone. The epistemological interests of economics (which aim at predictability) require, however, that "parcels of value" be compartmentalized, so as to also create models with predictable utility for the different values. Kirshenblatt-Gimblett also emphasizes that only examination of this wide range of values can prepare the way for a reasonable debate in civil society: "The conversion of habitus into heritage and heritage into cultural assets, cultural capital, and cultural good, a process that is integral to concepts of public domain, public goods, fair use, and global cultural commons, can engender the kind of public debate associated with a public sphere" (2006, 195).

All these developments are not new; people have always bestowed value upon both things and ideas. Some they bring to a market to earn their living from them, and others they guard carefully to deny market access—precisely because the transaction costs are gauged as being too high. Tourism and heritage are two separate areas, tied somewhat differently to the market. Both force actors to decide on aspects of their lifeworld they would like to bring to market, and in what way. However, tourism and cultural heritage are not the only means for bringing added value (from a market economy perspective) to cultural excerpts. Other possibilities, such as the geographical indication (GI) system, common especially in the European Union, should also be mentioned. GIs make it possible to mark agricultural products and foodstuffs on the basis of their place of origin and the culturally influenced formulas and methods used in their production. This indication grants the producers exclusive rights to use the respective terms—such as Germany's version of Emmental cheese, *Allgäuer Emmentaler.*[11] Precisely because of their emphasis on cultural knowledge—an emphasis that is clearly economically motivated—indications of geographic and cultural origin have an advantage over heritage nominations;

valorization is associated also with nonmaterial factors, and offers actors a legally safeguarded and institutionalized instrument which openly declares that market advantages can be pursued through cultural and geographic exclusivity. Indisputably, this exclusivity is meant to convey to both producer and consumer the appreciation and valuation of traditional and regionally based knowledge and methods. However, the open commitment to economic benefit does justice to the motivation: culture is a resource that people bestow with value not only on grounds of ethnicity or of allegiance to a locality or region, but also because they can derive profit from it in the complex market of cultural attributions—if they so choose.[12]

In its history, however, tourism has often used "culture" as a production staged for vacationers, made available at virtually no charge. Only with the emergence of a specific "cultural tourism" recognized by the industry, have cultural actors partially come into view as beneficiaries of tourist curiosity who potentially must be remunerated. Heritage discourses, after all, emphasize the ideational necessity of identifying, documenting, restoring, and/or maintaining and certifying goods that are particularly valuable from a global perspective. The visitors to be expected as a result of a UNESCO listing may indeed bring about an economic boom—but the UNESCO conventions avoid this economic component, and they do not offer guidelines or legally binding institutions that successful heritage applicants could use to regulate the economic profit so that it flows to specific groups, such as those who have generated a specific cultural asset.[13] UNESCO nominations must include development plans, and the catalog of criteria to be met is steadily being defined more precisely. Yet the only way to combat World Heritage abuse commanded by UNESCO itself is the threat to withdraw the UNESCO heritage title. All legal measures are in the hands of the states ratifying a convention, and it is in the purview of the states whether they consider it necessary to introduce legal measures governing the economic use of heritage (Mißling 2010; cf., Bendix, Eggert, and Peselmann 2012). Of course, cultural assets should not be nominated as World Heritage because of tourist-related interests; yet it has been shown that the award, in most cases reinforces existing tourism, leads to increased tourism, and that it is an effect that many actors desire.

## CULTURE AS A RESOURCE:
### EXAMPLES FROM SWITZERLAND

How does the resource of culture differ from resources such as land, forests, water, coal, oil, and other natural resources? Debates on cultural property and heritage are not the first approach to this question: transforming something into property and assigning values to it—including the prices payable for it—is an activity that can be traced far back in time, as contributions to Appadurai's (1986) previously cited volume show. However, I would argue that people in reflexive, knowledge-based societies have learned to treat culture as a different kind of resource. To prove that, there is no need to review the complex history of the "discovery" of the "uniqueness" of cultures. It is more than familiar to folklorists and anthropologists, because the emergence of their respective disciplines was entangled with the concept of the nation-state and with colonial appropriation respectively. Rather, what is at issue here is to show that actors share an awareness of their cultural resources and know how to handle them, and that a constant interplay of different values (social, political, ideational, economic) is present, in which profitability manifests itself in different ways. I would like to illustrate this with examples from Switzerland.

Switzerland may be a surprising choice, not least because it was not until 2010 that the country decided to ratify the UNESCO Convention on Intangible Cultural Heritage and to identify cultural practices for potential nomination.[14] If you look at tiny Switzerland, it nonetheless offers a great many contextual factors that affect locally established actors or that are embraced by these actors. A large part of the heritage-related literature in the field of cultural research deals—with good reason, no doubt—with newly industrialized countries and, using titles such as *Reclaiming Heritage* (De Jong and Rowlands 2007), discusses the empowerment movements that are under way in the heritage field (also supported by ethnological research). You will notice little of that in the following examples, perhaps also because some of these facets developed in the past and can be considered with the benefit of hindsight. Accordingly, the examples can be kept in perspective as different arenas of cultural valorization.

Each of the following examples of cultural resources has the potential
to become World Heritage, though only one of them is actively seeking
to be nominated. Each of them has touristic potential, though it is very
differently used. All offer ways to address the questions posed at the
outset regarding actors' motivations and scope of action for valorizing
segments of their culture. The Silvesterklausen in Urnäsch (located in
the canton of Appenzell Ausserrhoden), the Japanesen play in Schwyz (in
the canton of Schwyz), and the Tell plays in Altdorf (in the canton of
Uri), are three different events. All three are performative, but the separation between active and passive participation escalates from the first to
the third. Each of these events contains ideational and economic potential, which has been used variously since the late nineteenth century.
Each example has experienced more or less intrusive levels of scientific
monitoring and thus has experienced a raising of awareness as well—
aspects that are expanded on below, in context-specific discussions.
Five points that enhance comparability are contextually important for
all the examples:

(a) The political context of the Swiss Confederation, which likes to call
    itself the oldest democracy (though Iceland has verifiable reasons
    to disagree): The federalist structure, successful at least since the
    post-Napoleonic era, influences the authority with which citizens
    autonomously make political and economic decisions.

(b) The tourist development of Switzerland stretches back to the early
    nineteenth century (Krippendorf 1975): The magnetic appeal of
    the Alps resulted in the development of tourism as a business in
    some impoverished mountain regions, starting in 1800. Since the
    late nineteenth century, the Alps have systematically ensured such
    development throughout Switzerland, and the local populations
    have had to come to grips with that (Bendix 1989b; Risi 2011).

(c) Switzerland did not become rich until the interwar period; in the
    early twentieth century, urban-rural differences were still very
    large, migration from poor regions to other countries overseas was
    significant, and the gross national product was low. Accordingly,
    the turn to cultural assets as potential ideational and economic
    resources was not unexpected.

(d) The phenomena to be examined have been documented for more
    than one hundred years, and this accumulation of information over
    time allows us to look at the development of the value dynamic.

(e)　The way aesthetically elevated cultural segments are handled
can be researched over long stretches of time, and perhaps also
productively compared with regions where the ideational and
economic options for transforming culture into cultural asset
accumulate more quickly and more densely.

In what follows, I am interested in which valorizations actors have made,
and to what extent this range of values survives over time. For this purpose, I will briefly describe the respective traditions, and then consider the
levels of practiced or perceived values—levels that cannot be completely
separated—as well as value awareness and valorization.[15]

## SILVESTERKLAUSEN IN URNÄSCH,
## APPENZELL AUSSERRHODEN

This New Year's Day tradition has been well documented since the mid-
nineteenth century (Bendix 1985). Groups of men walk from house to
house, wearing three different types of costumes with masks and head-
dresses; they also wear cowbells and jingling sleigh bells, with which
they announce their arrival in front of the houses. For the inhabitants,
they perform wordless yodeling (*Zauren*), which is highly regarded in the
region, and get wine and a gift of money in return for this New Year's greet-
ing. Urnäsch indulges itself in two performances of Silvesterklausen: on
December 31 and also on the old New Year's Day of the Julian calendar,
January 13. Until the beginning of the twentieth century, it was spoken of
as a "begging practice," because it allowed the poorer people—wearing
only a simple costume—to beg for New Year's food and drink. In the
interwar period, an aesthetic enhancement of the costumes began, and
after World War II, the characteristics of a custom of affluence emerged:
the single costume differentiated into three types, and the investment of
the male players in the design of these costumes, as well as the care taken
with the singing, increased. Adjustments can be identified correspondingly over the decades. The aesthetic dimensions of the experience were
emphasized and differentiated; the food and drink disappeared from the
direct offer of thanks by the people visited; in exchange, they increased
the monetary gift given to those carrying out the custom. These, then,

invested more in their costumes, and were able to afford larger shared meals with this payment during their periods of rest in the course of the traditional day's festivities.

The practice and appreciation of the visual and aural aesthetics have significantly increased in the course of the last century. The positive awareness of the (male) physical ritual experience has also increased— not least because physical activity too has been shifted, with the decline in farming as a way of life, more strongly to the positive connotations of pastimes. *Silvesterklausen* is perceived on the local level as an important and highly valued renewal of the village community—in the course of the two physically demanding days, the groups of men go through both the village center and around the far-flung farms and thus mark them as belonging to a recognized village entity.

In the postwar period, value awareness experienced a significant boost from the transfer of knowledge through cultural research. A teacher and amateur folklorist, relocated from the lowlands to Urnäsch, conveyed the information known at that time about pre-Christian winter customs (long since superseded in the scholarly world), and persuaded young people to undertake a "repatriation" of the custom, even in its aesthetic embodiment. He was so successful that the village community continues to support the idea that they are performing an ancient, and therefore particularly valuable, custom in *Silvesterklausen*. The aesthetic invest-ment and the augmentation can be directly related to this impulse. A gen-eration later, a second amateur folklorist, the village doctor, along with a teacher interested in history and other interested parties, promoted the establishment of a local museum.

Here, not only was *Silvesterklausen* now accepted, but so were other facets of what the international discourse refers to as traditional cultural expressions and traditional knowledge, and they were edited and refined for both local and tourist appreciation. Transhumance customs and the corresponding clothing and jewelry, naive painting from the region, embroidery work, cheesemaking, and the field of naturopathy were gradu-ally incorporated into the exhibition, and also scientifically examined in book publications. The custom of *Silvesterklausen* remains quite cen-tral, but the work that goes into this museum is delegated to just a few. The tradition bearers themselves have little to do with its operation; their main contribution is to make especially well-preserved, disused costumes available to the museum.[16] Appenzell Ausserrhoden does not have large numbers of tourists—people on day hikes, bus tourists in transit, and at the most school groups visit the museum. The museum's focus is accordingly more ideational: the exhibition is meant to create identity and preserve tradition. A film about the Silvesterklausen, made in 2011 by a non-Urnäscher, conveys the aesthetic depth of experiencing the ancient practice and may show why young men return to the region to take part in the custom and to stay involved (*Silvesterklausen* 2011). The conviction that residents are performing a rare and very beautiful tradition has now also led the canton of Appenzell Ausserrhoden to propose the *Silvesterklausen* for designation as intangible cultural heritage of Switzerland.[17]

The economic valorization of the custom can be demonstrated in parallel with the rise in its aesthetic valuation; however, it remains far less marked than the non-material and social awareness of its value. Tradition bearers initiate and practice this in different ways. There is the bus and railway tourism for the old and new New Year's Eve, which tradition bearers do not perceive as disturbing. The local hospitality industry benefits a little, while during the rest of the year the numbers of visitors are moderate—the seats in restaurants are filled more by locals than by strangers. There are individual initiatives such as the publication of calendars and, parallel to the museum initiative and also influenced by deeper awareness of participation in a special heritage, actors of the tradition have even recorded CDs with their *Zauren*, taken part in traditional performances outside the village, and backed photo publications. A naive painter who died a decade ago has perhaps dedicated a bit more canvas space to this traditional theme than to other painting motifs typical of the region. Overall, however, one can argue that local estimation and experience of value are not impacted by the valorization of the cultural asset of *Silvesterklausen*. Looking at the tradition bearers in Urnäsch, we see mostly men with considerable knowledge of the dynamics of the custom, but also with enormous pleasure in their New Year's Eve ritual. Museum development, publications, and annual newspaper reports do not leave the events unchanged, but they have further increased, rather than diminished, the array of value attributions, in which the aesthetic and physical experience is dominant.

## THE JAPANESEN IN SCHWYZ

This theatrical play, loosely connected with Shrove Tuesday traditions, in the town of Schwyz in Central Switzerland emerged from ironic commentary on a failed Swiss foreign mission in the nineteenth century: despite considerable investment, the delegation came back with no trade agreement.[18] A rich tradition of amateur theater is documented throughout all of Central Switzerland, and plays were, and still are, often integrated into Central Switzerland's Shrove Tuesday celebrations. But the *Japanesen* play, which is performed every five years in the first half of January, held fast to a pseudo-Japanese costume style and set of characters—such as the Emperor *Hesonusode*, who is addressed by the title *Taikun*. In terms of content, the piece always takes up contemporary aspects of politics and public life; it also looks back at antiquated contrasts between mountain farmers' traditions and the scholarly life in the nineteenth century, which are presented in a humorous way, in rhyme. The focus on the Far Eastern activities of the Confederation was a one-time occurrence, but the *Japanesen* costuming remained.

Which values are practiced and perceived here? The *Japanesen* play is supported by an association in which officeholders organize and take responsibility for, and thereby also ensure, the continuation of the tradition. The five year rhythm indicates that an annual repetition would be too much of a good thing, and would reduce the value of the event. Anyone who wishes to participate may do so, regardless of sex or age. The leading roles, however, are carefully assigned. The costumes, which differ in their exoticism from Shrove Tuesday masquerades, together with the names used for the characters, communicate physical and mental exuberance. The open-air site of the performance in front of the town hall enlivens public life during the cold season. Because the play is always dedicated to new topics, it requires the investment of talent and wit, generated from the interaction between local awareness and politics from the national to international level.

In Schwyz too, value awareness has increased as a result of the interests of local knowledge brokers versed in cultural research. A teacher, now retired, also acted as the archivist of the *Japanesen* society and in this capacity organized the existing sources and thus bolstered awareness of their relevance. He controlled and supervised the oral history of the play and published on this subject, so that local consciousness of having developed a special tradition was raised. The actors share a strong sense of worth, derived from the theater's position as one of the few in the region with a long tradition, but as a very different kind of theater as well. The performances of Calderon's "Great Theater of the World" in the nearby monastery town of Einsiedeln and the Tell play in Altdorf, which will be described below, are also pieces based on established texts of world literature, while the *Schwyzers* change the content of their production each performance year. Almost since the beginning of the *Japanesen* play, the interest of the Japanese Embassy in Switzerland and the "Japanese population" as a whole has increased the awareness of maintaining a special tradition. Although the Schwyzers have created a "bogus" mixture that employs comedy to achieve a distancing effect, with Oriental references serving as a frame for their play, they were honored at quite an early stage in the tradition with visits from the Japanese consul and gifts of real kimonos. The Schwyzers probably were caught slightly off guard by the first gift of the Japanese consulate in the nineteenth century, because what they had produced was just a pre-Shrove Tuesday play. Here, however, the public eye also triggered the setting of a course, namely, the development of precisely these figures, which now no longer change: the *Japanesen* are locked into place and thereby also traditionalized. The appreciation from outside led to a close connection, which, however, simultaneously implied an increase in value for the local community. The friendly relationship has continued to the present day; Japanese television is present at each performance, so that the initial reason for the play—poking fun at a Swiss failure in Japan—has resulted in a serious valuation and appreciation of the Schwyzer *Japanesen* plays. The Schwyzer actors perpetuate this very different value awareness along with the focus on seeing the comical aspect of their own politics and society. The *Japanesen* play actually scheduled for 2012 was postponed for a year, because it was seen as irreverent to indulge in this humorous tradition less than a year after the great earthquake and nuclear disaster in Japan.

There is little valorization for the purpose of commercial benefit. Resources are needed to continue the performance as it has developed over the last 150 years. Therefore, a great deal more fundraising is done to organize the event. After the turn of the millennium, a website was set up, and today it is possible to buy tickets online two months before the performance (Japanesengesellschaft 2011). In the meantime, the increased size of the audience now necessitates the construction of temporary seating. However, anyone who visits the town of Schwyz will look in vain for souvenirs, *Japanesen* cakes, or similar treatments of abstractions as commodities.

## THE TELL DRAMA IN ALTDORF

Altdorf is one of the scenes of Friedrich Schiller's drama *Wilhelm Tell*.[19] Uri is one of the founding cantons of the Swiss Confederation and bears the burden of having been the majestic site of the (partially authenticated) historical events at the turn of the fourteenth century, which brought forth the liberation from Habsburg rule and the beginning of democracy. Enthusiasm for Schiller, especially for his Tell, ran high in many parts of Europe in the nineteenth century, and aroused feelings of both duty and economic hope in Altdorf—after all, what freedom-lover would not like to see Schiller's *Tell* performed in its original location? A Tell Play Association was founded in 1898, and a temporary theater building was replaced by a grand Tell Playhouse inaugurated in 1925. The association has sought to maintain standards of high-caliber theater for more than a hundred years. It uses local amateur performers, whose life histories are interwoven with the roles they sometimes play over several decades, roles that were passed down in fragments in local oral history. Nonmaterial, formative values ensure the strength of the work, and this theatrical tradition can be kept financially afloat to some degree by the business skills of the association management.

Anyone who actively participates in the Tell drama identifies him- or herself—to varying degrees—with the play, with theater as a vehicle of individual self-awareness and communality, and with the Altdorfer Tellspiel-und Theatergesellschaft as an association and a social space. In contrast to the Tell play tradition on the outdoor stage in tourism-oriented Interlaken, where the drama is staged annually and more traditionally, the people of Altdorf endeavor to constantly reinterpret the national myth. The actors are also willing to pay a significant price to keep the content topical and therefore appealing and interesting for both fellow actors and spectators.

This arrangement generates a value awareness that lets the actors experience their theatrical tradition as exciting and as a source of energy; they also exhibit a competitive motivation (vis-à-vis professional theater), while the Tell Play Association also performs a community-building function. Though by no means all locals actively participate, a great many will nevertheless view the latest new production and talk about the theatrical accomplishments of their neighbors. Although the Tell material has often been historically, literarily, and socially deconstructed, its power in the Swiss consciousness remains enormous, all ironic alienation notwithstanding. In addition, the recurring discussion about the material and its firm position in the Swiss school curriculum accordingly conveys to the Altdorfers constant recognition of the values guiding their activity. The most reliable spectators are school children from about the sixth grade—and to this extent there also exists an awareness of transmitting patriotic and/or political values.

The founders of the Altdorfer Tell Plays in the late nineteenth century still had hopes for an economic boom in the village along the Gotthard Pass route. Extensive advertising campaigns, even in other German-speaking countries, were launched to generate income from tourism revenue by performing the play at an almost "sacred" place. The economic valorization, however, proved less successful than the nonmaterial and social values of the enterprise. Today, Altdorf engages in fundraising so that it can afford a professional director, and advertises each season in a superb manner—but often with talent from its own ranks. Constructing its own Tell Playhouse and managing it in the years between performances is a challenge for the association. The transaction costs for maintaining the building and keeping the Tell Play going are high; that they are provided is an indication of the noneconomic values that the play connotes. Of course, every visitor to Altdorf, whatever the season, can visit the Tell memorial and Tell chapel(s), and buy souvenirs—but these are not connected with the Tell Play.[20]

## THE USE OF CULTURAL RESOURCES:
## THOUGHTS ABOUT FUTURE PROSPECTS

These three examples have strong, albeit extremely different, local support structures. In each case, one can speak of a high to very high emotional gain for the active players, a gain associated with preserving and consciously representing the cultural asset. The profit in terms of "endowment with identity" is different in each case, and the ideational potential, as well as the economic potential, is handled in varying ways. All three enjoy differing measures of public affection and attention in the nonmaterial sense; both the Schwyzers and the Altdorfers additionally must regularly search for financial support.

The public perception and documentation also brings a measure of responsibility—we *must* keep it going—an element that is sensed in far greater degree in other case studies, however, as a result of the World Heritage regime and tourist attention. At the same time, it must be stated that nomination proposals for inclusion in the World Heritage List, which according to the UNESCO Convention should be produced by—or at least with—the communities, in many cases are essentially driven by outside individuals and organizations, or the state.[21] In the three examples outlined, responsibility for implementing and configuring the valorizing of the relevant cultural resource rests in the hands of the local actors, for whom World Heritage status is not necessarily desirable. This is partly due to the federalist structure of Switzerland: tradition, whether informal or transmitted through an association, is a club good in the economic sense and not a commons of the nation-state. In addition, there is an ever-intensifying perception of culture as a vital resource. This perception is also conveyed and shared by academic research, even though its tone often is critical (see Eggmann, Schürch, and Risi 2010; Eggmann and Oehme-Jüngling 2013). Cultural research in the early twentieth century, with its rescue and preserve impulse, helped create awareness of the value of tradition and thus promoted a form of valorization: appreciation of one's own traditions. The tenor of cultural research at the recent turn of the century, shaped by constructivism, postcolonial debates, and a Foucauldian search for an apparatus (*dispositif*) of discipline and of power, contributes mainly to the understanding of the role of one's own academic field in the externalization of the habitual and its path to the resource phase (which this paper also engages in, but simultaneously tries to overcome). How much of the knowledge paradigms from which era, in the form of knowledge transfer, again becomes an internalized and/or carefully considered aspect of cultural practice can be surmised at most on the basis of case studies. The interaction and collaboration between culture bearers and cultural scholars in making it clear that culture is a resource ought to be known to both sides by now, and this is also evident from the Swiss engagement with UNESCO opportunities. Since 2010, Switzerland has been engaged in ratifying the 2003 Convention on Intangible Cultural Heritage.[22] For this purpose, it has set up a federal and democratic procedure. This procedure respects the sovereign handling of local culture, as illustrated by the three examples, as a resource to be enjoyed, utilized, and changed by the local community itself, and it provides room for innovation at the same time. The body that was entrusted with the task (a body in which cultural scientists play a part) assigned the job of nomination to the cantons, which in turn are to promote nominations at the cantonal level themselves—again, with support from cultural scientists in some cases.

At the same time, a website—"Lebendige Traditionen" (Living Traditions)—was set up, so that citizens from all quarters could make suggestions as to what they regarded as intangible cultural heritage, and would like to see nominated.[23] The Swiss procedure, which has been taken up—with a faint irony by some citizens and with sporting ambition by others—shows what actually can be seen in every country as a result of UNESCO conventions: any country that decides to ratify the conventions must devise a procedure for selection, nomination, and, if successful, implementation. It definitely requires a framework that also has legal underpinning.[24] Bureaucracies will form around these processes, and the result, also in purely visual terms, will be lists of lifeworld phenomena that previously were lived in and experienced more or less consciously. But, over the course of more than two hundred years of tourism and federalist development, the Swiss have already gone through this process in their respective cantons and regions in so many ways that the request to generate a list of World Heritage of an intangible kind for the great world stage became instead an occasion for reviewing valorizations in the domestic scene. Supposedly outmoded cultural assets were compared and contrasted with cultural innovations resulting from technology, the influence of immigrant populations, and phenomena of the urban youth culture. The small number of final nomination dossiers still to be determined is likely to be far less influential than the federal process, which encouraged discussions of hundreds of potential "cultural assets" (see Graezer Bideau 2012).[25]

Processes involving valorization of culture and hence the perception of culture as a resource, in Switzerland and elsewhere, have a tradition, as does the culture to which they assign a rating or value: to call the former metacultural is, accordingly, as detailed at the beginning of this essay, most useful from a scientific point of view, but hardly makes practical sense. We will better understand the spectrum ranging from passion to economic calculation, one that people come to know and apply both from experiencing and valorizing their cultural resources, when we break through the barrier separating these two spheres

This article was translated for this volume. It previously appeared in German in Burkhard Schnepel, Felix Girke, and Eva-Maria Knoll, eds. *Kultur all inclusive. Identität, Tradition und Kulturerbe im Zeitalter des Massentourismus.* (Bielefeld, transcript, 2013), 45–73. Copyright of the German edition: Transcript Verlag (2013).

1. What terminology to select for cultural heritage to indicate its placement in the international discourse is an issue that remains undecided. The English term "heritage" is linguistically blurred, in contrast to the term "heredity," which refers to a clear relationship between originator and descendants (cf., the chapter "Heridity, Hibridity, and Heritage" in this volume). In a first attempt to point out the processual nature of *Kulturvererbung*, or turning culture into heritage, *heritagization* was tried as a working term during a conference in Göttingen (Bendix, Hemme, and Tauschek 2007). In the French academic and practice-related discourse on cultural heritage, a discourse that now is one of the liveliest, one finds *patrimonialisation* used for this process. The French term is derived from the French word for heritage, *patrimoine. Patrimonium*, meaning "patrimony," exists in German, at least as a Latin loanword, and, though the term patrimonialization is problematic, perhaps, from the perspective of gender-neutral language, it is used here to denote the valorizing of cultural heritage, not least because the conservatism inherent in the concept of patrimony also nicely conveys the linkage of preservation with economic advantage. On the histories of the various terms *heritage, patrimoine,* and *Kulturerbe,* compare, Swenson (2007).

2. Noyes (2014) considers the heritage complex as a whole within a dynamic that, through the (perceived) scarcity of cultural heritage as a good, generates its opposite: a scaled economy of valorization.

3. In the original German version of this paper, I use the term *In-Wertsetzung,* which more clearly describes the process I seek to trace here: the "assigning of value to something" in a given sphere, not necessarily the economic sphere.

4. See the chapter "Inheritances: Possession, Ownership, and Responsibilities" in this volume.

5. See also Tauschek (2010).

6. The shifting of cultural and socio-anthropological attention to the "conduct of conduct" level can certainly be noted as an important and profitable innovation. It was fostered by linguistic anthropology and pragmatics, under Anglo-American influence, and is seen very clearly in the "anthropology of expertise" (Carr 2010).

7. Laurajane Smith (2006, 54) has made it clear that material heritage is ultimately a product of immaterial movements of thought and of traditionalization. The UNESCO discussion, which unfolded over three decades (and led to the 2003 Intangible Heritage Convention) illustrates—in its protracted length—the hard-won global administrative realization that material culture is an expression of the inherently mental predisposition of cultural dynamics.

8. Of course, this is represented here in a simplified way, and there are significant exceptions, such as Mintz (1985) and Wolf (1982), among others; compare Wilk and Cliggett (1996); what I am trying to express is the strange lack of overlap between heritage studies and the entire subfield of economic anthropology.

9. The monograph is perhaps, but only at first, a bit irritating to European readers, precisely because it overlooks research on the commodification of culture in European ethnology, research that has, after all, been going on since the 1960s (cf., Bendix 2010).

10. The classic and influential work on this topic is Marcel Mauss's *Essay sur le don* from 1923–24 (1968). Appadurai also noted the tendency "to see these two modalities of exchange as fundamentally opposed" (1986, 11; cf., Liebersohn 2011). Appadurai's proposal that this duality be examined through Bourdieu's approach, viewing the gift exchange as a possible form of the circulation of "commodities," opens up, in a desirable way, the spectrum in which I would like to see economic practices contextualized and analyzed (Bourdieu 1977, 171; Appadurai 1986, 12).

11. The GI system undergoes steady policy changes to foster a simplification of the categories and a clearer emphasis on the cultural exclusivity of the product; see Bicskei et al. (2012), May (2017), May et al. (2017), and Schröder (2011).

12. In democratic societies, such as those working together in the EU, community participation in negotiation is reasonably assured. This is not the case in many member states of the United Nations. It should not be concealed that valorizations of culture take place without involving the culture bearers or community members (see, e.g., Hauser-Schäublin 2011). UNESCO has sought to address this by emphasizing community participation in the nominating process and documentation, yet this, too, cannot be solved easily, as community is a highly malleable and, as Hertz has pointed out, problematic category (Hertz 2015).

13. See Hauser-Schäublin (2011) for a multiperspective presentation of a case study in Cambodia, where the economic and sociopolitical conflicts that can arise from heritage nomination are powerfully depicted.

14. On this, see the Swiss National Science Foundation research project led by Ellen Hertz of Neuchatel, "The Midas Touch." Accessed May 31, 2017. https://libra.unine.ch /Projets/15191. Cf., also Graezer Bideau (2012).

15. The representations of the three events are greatly simplified here; the respective social situations present themselves in a considerably more complex way in their historical development as well.

16. Some actors, however, conserve their unused costumes themselves, sometimes at considerable expense, even creating a climate-controlled room. This personal

responsibility for the cultural asset of annual tradition is not unique to Urnäsch. It can also be seen in the Roitschäggätä in Switzerland's Lötschental valley, where traditional actors have begun to buy back masks, which have been sold on the worldwide market for a long time, and bring them home (thanks go to Thomas Antonietti for this information).

17. The Silvesterklausen was added to the national list of Intangible Cultural Heritage in winter 2012.

18. For a more detailed description, see Weibel (2006); for an analysis, see Bendix (1993).

19. A detailed study comparing the Altdorfer Tell Play with the even older Tell Play tradition in Interlaken can be found in Bendix (1989a). The Tell Play Association maintains a German-language website (Tellspiele 2016).

20. Certain similarities with the Oberammergau Passion Play, performed every ten years, can be indicated here, though the Altdorfers would argue that the "authenticity" of their venue sets it apart.

21. In turn, this led UNESCO, at a meeting on Intangible Cultural Heritage, November 22–29, 2011, to decide to check nominations more stringently in the future, to determine whether the communities bearing a cultural asset have themselves actively and noticeably helped put together the nomination dossier (personal communication from Chiara Bortolotto, who attended the meeting in Bali).

22. See the chapter "Expressive Resources" in this volume.

23. The page can be viewed as before, although active nomination ended in the summer of 2011. At http://www.lebendige-traditionen.ch/index.html?lang=en (accessed June 10, 2017) partial results can be seen, such as the merger of some cantons to generate a combined list (Lebendige Traditionen 2016). The mechanisms of coordination, too, are discernible.

24. During the operational life of the website just mentioned, one could also read the following:

"The Ministry of Culture reserves the right, without justification, to shorten or not publish entries, especially if they violate legal regulations, are off-topic, or are not written in German, French, Italian, Romansch, or English. The Federal Government is entitled to use the entries in any form, namely electronically and on the Internet, without restriction as to time and place, and free of charge. The Federal Government accepts no responsibility for the use of the entries by third parties. The person entering the data is responsible for the content of entries and releases the Federal Government in this respect from any claims by third parties. It is possible that the item may be picked up by search engines and appear on other websites" (Accessed January 15, 2011. The site has since been modified).

25. Also see the article "Eine Schweiz zwischen Kräutergarten und Töfftreff" by Mark Lettau published in the magazine *Schweizer Revue* (January 2012).

REFERENCES

Appadurai, Arjun, ed. 1986. *Introduction to The Social Life of Things*, 3–63. Cambridge: Cambridge University Press.
Bendix, Regina. 1985. *Progress and Nostalgia: Silvesterklausen in Urnäsch, Switzerland*. Berkeley: University of California Press.

————. 1989a. *Backstage Domains. Playing William Tell in Two Swiss Communities.* New York: Peter Lang.

————. 1989b. "Inventing Traditions for Whom?" *Journal of American Folklore* 102 (404): 131–46.

————. 1993. "Of Mohrenköpfe and Japanesen: Images of the Foreign in Swiss Expressive Culture." *Journal of Folklore Research* 30: 15–29.

Bendix, Regina F., John Comaroff, and Jean Comaroff. 2010. *Review of Ethnicity Inc.,* HSozKult. April 27. http://www.hsozkult.de/publicationreview/id/rezbuecher-13779.

Bendix, Regina F., Aditya Eggert, and Arnika Peselmann, eds. 2012. *Heritage Regimes and the State.* Göttingen: Universitätsverlag Göttingen.

Bendix, Regina, Dorothee Hemme, and Markus Tauschek. 2007. "Introduction." *Prädikat 'Heritage'. Wertschöpfungen aus kulturellen Ressourcen,* edited by Dorothee Hemme, Markus Tauschek, and Regina Bendix, 7–17. Münster: LIT.

Bicskei, Marianna, Kilian Bizer, Katia L. Sidali, and Achim Spiller. 2012. "Reform Proposals on the Geographical Indications of the European Union for the Protection of Traditional Knowledge." *The WIPO Journal* 3 (2): 222–36.

Bourdieu, Pierre. 1977. *Outline of a Theory of Practice.* Cambridge: Cambridge University Press.

Carr, Summerson. 2010. "Enactmens of Expertise." *Annual Review of Anthropology* 39: 17–32.

Comaroff, John, and Jean Comaroff. 2009. *Ethnicity Inc.* Chicago: University of Chicago Press.

De Jong, Ferdinand, and Michael Rowlands, eds. 2007. *Reclaiming Heritage. Alternative Imaginaries of Memory in West Africa.* Walnut Creek, CA: Left Coast Press.

Eggmann, Sabine, and Karoline Oehme-Jüngling, eds. 2013. *Doing Society. "Volkskultur" als gesellschaftliche Selbstverständigung.* Münster: Waxmann.

Eggmann, Sabine, Franziska Schürch, and Marius Risi, eds. 2010. *Vereintes Wissen: Die Volkskunde und ihre gesellschaftliche Verankerung.* Münster: Waxmann.

Enzensberger, Hans-Magnus. 1958. "Vergebliche Brandung in der Ferne. Eine Theorie des Tourismus." *Merkur* 12: 701–20.

Foucault, Michael. 1994. *Dits et écrits IV.* Paris: Gallimard.

Frey, Bruno. 2010. *World Heritage List: Does it Make Sense?* Munich: Center for Economic Studies.

Frey, Bruno, and Werner W. Pommerehne. 1989. *Muses and Markets. Explorations in the Economics of the Arts.* Oxford: Blackwell.

Graezer Bideau, Florence. 2012. "Identifying 'Living Traditions' in Switzerland: Re-enacting Federalism through the UNESCO Convention for the Safeguarding of Intangible Cultural Heritage." In *Heritage Regimes and the State,* edited by Regina F. Bendix, Aditya Eggert, and Arnika Peselmann, 303–26. Göttingen: Universitätsverlag Göttingen.

Greenwood, Davydd J. 1977. "Culture by the Pound: An Anthropological Perspective on Tourism as Cultural Commoditization." In *Hosts and Guests,* edited by Valene L. Smith, 129–38. Philadelphia: University of Pennsylvania Press.

Hauser-Schäublin, Brigitta, ed. 2011. *World Heritage Angkor and Beyond. Circumstances and Implications of UNESCO Listings in Cambodia.* Göttingen: Universitätsverlag Göttingen.

Hertz, Ellen. 2015. "Bottoms, Genuine and Spurious," In *Between Imagined Communities and Communities of Practice. Participation, Territory and the Making of Heritage,* edited by Nicolas Adell, Regina F. Bendix, Chiara Bortolotto, and Markus Tauschek. Göttingen Studies in Cultural Property, vol. 8, 25–57. Göttingen: Göttingen University Press.

Japanesengesellschaft Schwyz. 2011. Accessed December 20. http://www.japanesen.ch/.

Kirshenblatt-Gimblett, Barbara. 1995. "Theorizing Heritage." *Ethnomusicology* 39: 367–80.

———. 2004. "Intangible Heritage as Metacultural Production." *Museum International* 56: 53–65.

———. 2006. "World Heritage and Cultural Economics." In *Museum Frictions. Public Cultures/Global Transformations*, edited by Ivan Karp, Corinne A. Kratz, Lynn Szwaja, and Tomas Ybarra-Frausto, 161–202. Durham, NC: Duke University Press.

Krippendorf, Jost. 1975. "Die Landschaftsfresser: Tourismus und Erholungslandschaft, Verderben oder Segen?" Bern: Hallwag.

Lebendige Traditionen. 2016. Accessed Sep 21. http://www.lebendige-traditionen.ch.

Liebersohn, Harry. 2011. *The Return of the Gift*. Cambridge: Cambridge University Press.

MacCannell, Dean. 2011. *The Ethics of Sightseeing*. Berkeley: University of California Press.

Mauss, Marcel. 1968. *Die Gabe: Form und Funktion des Austauschs in archaischen Gesellschaften*. Frankfurt: Suhrkamp.

May, Sarah. 2016. *Ausgezeichnet! Zur Konstistuierung kulturellen Eigentums durch geografische Herkunftsangaben*. Göttingen Studies in Cultural Property, vol. 11. Göttingen: Göttingen University Press.

May, Sarah, Katia Laura Sidali, Achim Spiller and Bernhard Tschofen, eds. 2016. *Geographical Indications as Cultural Property*. Göttingen Studies in Cultural Property, vol. 10. Göttingen: Göttingen University Press.

Mintz, Sydney. 1985. *Sweetness and Power: The Place of Sugar in Modern History*. New York: Viking.

Mißling, Sven. 2010. "Die UNESCO-Konvention zum Schutz des immateriellen (Kultur-) Erbes der Menschheit von 2003: Öffnung des Welterbekonzepts oder Stärkung der kulturellen Hoheit des Staates?" In *Die Konstituierung von Cultural Property: Forschungsperspektiven*, edited by Regina Bendix, Kilian Bizer, and Stefan Groth, 91–114. Göttingen: Universitätsverlag Göttingen.

Noyes, Dorothy. 2014. "Heritage, Legacy, Zombie: How to Bury the Undead Past." In *Cultural Heritage in Transit: Intangible Rights as Human Rights*, edited by Deborah Kapchan, 58–86. Philadelphia: University of Pennsylvania Press.

Risi, Marius, ed. 2011. *Alpenland: Terrain der Moderne*. Münster: Waxmann.

Schröder, Simone. 2011. *Die neue EU-Qualitätspolitik für Agrarerzeugnisse*. Agribusiness-Forschung 26 Giessen: Institut für Agri-Business.

*Silvesterchlausen—im Appenzellerland*. 2011. Documentary, directed by Thomas Rickenmann. Wattwil: MovieBizFilms.

Smith, Laurajane. 2006. *Uses of Heritage*. London: Routledge.

Swenson, Astrid. 2007. "'Heritage,' 'Patrimoine,' und 'Kulturerbe': Eine vergleichende historische Semantik." In *Prädikat 'Heritage.' Wertschöpfungen aus kulturellen Ressourcen*, edited by Dorothee Hemme, Markus Tauschek, and Regina Bendix, 53–74. Münster: LIT.

Tauschek, Markus. 2010. "Kulturerbepolitik in Belgien. Zugleich theoretisch-kritische Bemerkungen zur aktuellen Heritage-Forschung." Keynote at the Annual Meeting of the Suiss Anthropological Association. Nov 12–13. Bern, Switzerland.

Tellspiele Altdorf. 2016. Accessed October 1. http://www.tellspiele-altdorf.ch.

Throsby, David. 1999. "Cultural Capital." *Journal of Cultural Economics* 23: 3–12.

Weibel, Viktor. 2006. *Hesonusode. Theater, Geschichte, und Fasnachtskultur.* Schwyz: Triner.

Wilk, Richard, and Lisa Cliggett. 1996. *Economies and Cultures: Foundations of Economic Anthropology.* New York: Westview.

Wolf, Eric. 1982. *Europe and the People Without History.* Berkeley: University of California Press.

# Section III

⎯⎯⎯ ✑ ⎯⎯⎯

## *Introduction: Culture as Resource, Culture as Property*

If early scholarly reactions to value-enhancement regimes surrounding culture were alarmist, decrying commoditization as a threat to cultural integrity or even authenticity, more recently there has been a shift toward acknowledging culture as a resource that is enjoyed, used, bargained over, and sold (Yúdice 2003). This shift is owed to a number of developments in cultural scholarship. Economic actors and processes have become the focus of ethnographic studies (e.g., Hertz 1998; Löfgren and Willim 2006). Some scholars have offered a vigorous refocusing on the interface of culture and economy (e.g., Appadurai 1986; Hann 1998; Hann and Hart 2011). Finally, the international debate on negotiating a viable regime for cultural property, based on the long-established intellectual property regime encompassing copyright and patent law has encouraged anthropologists and folklorists to contribute their perspectives to conversations previously held among economists and lawyers (Bendix, Bizer, and Groth 2010; Brown 2003; Comaroff and Comaroff 2009; Kasten 2004; Kirshenblatt-Gimblett 2006).

Both the challenges and the opportunities for researchers within cultural fields are great: there is the challenge to be acknowledged as meaningful interlocutors in the interdisciplinary work of law and economics—both normative fields bound to operationalize the complexities of cultural processes and to disregard the burden of global history and its contribution to rendering excerpts of culture into properties whose ownership requires not just legal but also social and political clarification. The field of law and economics has established itself as a strong new branch of both disciplines, examining the economic efficiency of laws; cultural economics, in turn, is a subdiscipline of economics that has since the late 1960s taken shape and concerns itself with cultural values ranging from "high" art to world heritage (Frey 2010; Ginsburgh and Throsby 2008). Neither field has as yet ventured far in consulting ethnographically based research and theory, nor have legal and economic anthropologists made great strides to go beyond disciplinary boundaries. Nevertheless, given that culture has been increasingly moved center stage as more and more players recognize its resource-quality, scholars of culture are challenged to contribute, as they are best prepared to give insight on questions such as, what are the "properties" of culture? How renewable a resource is it? Is there such a thing as ownership of culture and if so, how can it possibly be handled as it shifts from local economies to national and international markets?

It is in part thanks to leading actors within the World Intellectual Property Organization (WIPO), that there has been more disciplinary exchange and mutual participation of disciplinary representatives. When WIPO was tasked with tackling the notion of cultural property, the organization carried out fact-finding missions and commissioned an initial set of case studies on *Minding Culture* (Janke 2003) so as to prepare states' parties for engaging in the topic.[1] More than most other UN-organizations and committees, WIPO has invited the participation of indigenous groups and searched for effective ways to make their voices be heard. It is perhaps easiest to involve folklorists and anthropologists in the discussion on culture and value within organizations such as the WIPO intergovernmental committee on cultural property or UNESCO (United Nations Educational, Scientific and Cultural Organization) committee sessions deliberating on new nominations. A growing anthropology of policy (Shore and Wright 2011) and ethnography of international organizations (e.g., Muller 2013) opens the ethnographers' sensibility not just for the issues at hand but also for the disciplinary backgrounds within which most actors on the international negotiation stage are trained, that is, law and economics.

The chapters in this section seek to contribute to our understanding of culture framed as resource and the questions of use rights and ownership that arise from it. Ideational, emotional, and economic value are in many cases hard to pull apart—indeed, this is the burden or, rather, opportunity ethnographers have qua discipline: we tend to see the interwoven nature of differently motivated interests. It is a vantage point that perhaps allows one to better foresee the impact of decision-making in the realm of claiming or according rights of ownership to culture than is the case in more normatively oriented disciplines. Whether political or economic, questions of ownership can be both empowering and divisive agents for communities and individuals. Yet to what extent do we know the divergent (or comparable) force of emotional investment and economic interest in owning expressive forms vis-à-vis other resources if not through careful ethnographic and historical documentation and analysis?

Chapter 9 was originally presented as a presidential address at the Ulster Congress of the *Societé International d'Ethnologie et de Folklore* in 2008. Here, I look more closely at the role ethnological knowledge production has played in contributing or even solidifying the resource nature of culture. Drawing on examples from ethnic and popular music as well as folk art, I explore the multivalence of such aesthetic resources far beyond a once local context of production and point to scholarly techniques such as documentation and classification, which in turn facilitated the circulation in multiple contexts.

The papers in this section certainly owe a great deal to the opportunities I and other members of my research team on cultural property have had as observers at WIPO.[2] Chapter 10, a previously unpublished talk in German, introduces the WIPO negotiations as the most recent step in a long development that has transformed a taken-for-granted cultural commons. I hope to show that ownership has latently always been part of cultural practices, barely reflected in the habitual performance of selfhood and group membership; once the habitual is marked—perhaps because it is no longer practiced, passé, replaced with new behaviors and practices—it can (though it does not have to) enter into the realm of commodities. Problems arise when actors have different interests with regard to such reified facets of culture: some group members might perceive a profit potential, others see their group's cohesion endangered; actors from different contexts may encroach on a cultural commons and seek to gain possession with or without the knowledge of the present owners. It is at this juncture that WIPO's intergovernmental committee on cultural property came into being, and it is here, too, that researchers of culture can make a contribution.

Chapter 11, published previously in a volume on *Edible Identities*, works with the specific case of bread baking and protagonists highly interested in this craft, the German bakers guild. It is a small case study encouraged in part by work among colleagues on the cultural property instrument "geographic indications" (May, Sidali, Spiller and Tschofen 2016; cf., also Welz 2015), and by my surprise that bakers did not pursue this avenue for increasing the value of their product. Bakers are actors fully aware of the potential of different regimes of value for a culturally coded craft such as baking and I explore why these protagonists lobby for bread baking as a form of intangible cultural heritage. Working from the assumption that the heritage designation enhances the value not just of bread (the price of which cannot really be raised) but also of the bakers' profession, the guild seeks to halt the dwindling number of independent bakeries and enhance the prestige of the profession so as to attract more apprentices.

The twelfth and final chapter considers the long-term effect of different value regimes applied to excerpts of culture and how they have contributed to creating class- and market-based categories from "high" culture to "popular" and "vernacular" culture. Looking at ways individuals and society have supported or invested in culture over centuries, I seek to find the parallels between patronage and various preservationist or protectionist regimes. Along with shifts and innovations in the production of aesthetic forms, I consider the heritage endeavor—not least due to its global reach and impact—a vehicle that contributes to the transformation of cultural value scales.

NOTES

1. WIPO continually updates its online resources on the topic. Accessed May 28, 2017. www.wipo.int/tk/en/index.html#tacb.

2. Thanks are due here to Wend Wendland, head secretary of the Intergovernmenal Committe on Traditional Knowledge, Traditional Cultural Expressions, and Genetics who has gone out of his way to open up to our interest and has offered a lot of interesting insights from his perspective.

## REFERENCES

Appadurai, Arjun, ed. 1986. *The Social Life of Things. Commodities in Cultural Perspective.*
Philadelphia: University of Pennsylvania Press.

Bendix, Regina, Kilian Bizer, and Stefan Groth, eds. 2010. *Die Konstituierung von Cultural
Property. Forschungsperspektiven.* Göttingen Studies in Cultural Property, vol. 1.
Göttingen: Göttingen University Press.

Frey, Bruno S. 2010. *World Heritage Lists: Does it Make Sense?* Munich: Center for
Economic Studies.

Ginsburg, Victor and David Throsby, eds. 2006. *Handbook of the Economics of Art and
Culture,* vol. 1. Amsterdam: Elsevier.

Hann, Chris. 1998. *Property Relations: Renewing the Anthropological Tradition.* Cambridge:
Cambridge University Press.

Hann, Chris and Keith Hart. 2011. *Economic Anthropology. History, Ethnography, Critique.*
Cambridge: Polity Press.

Hertz, Ellen. 1998. *The Trading Crowd: An Ethnography of the Shanghai Stock Market.*
Cambridge: Cambridge University Press.

Janke, Terri. 2003. *Minding Culture. Case Studies on Intellectual Property and Traditional
Cultural Expressions.* Geneva: WIPO.

Kasten, Erich, ed. 2004. *Properties of Culture—Culture as Property: Pathways to Reform in
Post-Soviet Siberia.* Berlin: Reimer.

Kirshenblatt-Giimblett, Barbara. 2006. "World Heritage and Cultural Economics."
In *Museum Frictions: Public Cultures/ Global Transformations,* edited by Ivan Karp,
Martin Hall, Barbara Kirshenblatt-Giimblett, Corinne A. Kratz, and Christine Mullen
Kreamer, 161–202. Durham, NC: Duke University Press.

Löfgren, Orvar, and Robert Willim, eds. 2006. *Magic, Culture, and the New Economy.*
Oxford: Berg.

May, Sarah, Katia Laura Sidali, Achim Spiller, and Bernhard Tschofen, eds. 2016. *Taste,
Power, Tradition, Geographical Indications as Cultural Property, Göttingen Studies in
Cultural Property,* vol. 10. Göttingen: Göttingen University Press.

Muller, Birgit, ed. 2013. *The Gloss of Harmony: The Politics of Policy-Making in Multilateral
Organisations.* London: Pluto Press.

Shore, Cris, and Susan Wright, eds. 2011. *Policy Worlds. Anthropology and the Analysis of
Contemporary Power.* London: Berghahn.

Welz, Gisela. 2015. *European Products. Making and Unmaking Heritage in Cyprus.* Oxford:
Berghahn.

Yúdice, George. 2003. *The Expediency of Culture.* Durham, NC: Duke University Press.

# 9

*Expressive Resources: Knowledge,
Agency, and European Ethnology*

"What makes us unique and strong is our shared past in misery and poverty, and our joint struggle for liberation!" The calm, pathos-laden voice of one of the lead singers of the folk group *Canta u Populu Corsu* speaks over a background of eerily familiar, enveloping sounds—Celtic guitar and rhythm passages. The sound immediately absorbs the audience into and beyond the European audio-cultural commons. The sound system is set on "very loud." It is past ten o'clock at night, the August sky has darkened, stars appear, and an audience of perhaps four hundred people has gathered in front of this small, open-air stage in Ghisonaccia, just a little south of Corsica's capital, Aléria. Some thirty years ago, in the 1970s, the police forcefully broke up the Corsican independence movement's occupation of a farm owned by a nonnative nearby. Since then, the National Front for the Liberation of Corsica has taken responsibility for more than a thousand attacks. Numerous activist and separatist splinter groups give testimony that some Corsicans are far from what Michael Billig calls "banal Nationalism" (1995, 38), that is, the state of collective forgetting that nationhood was achieved with brutality. Yet, if one is to believe an assessment in *Le Monde*, already in 2004, "the very idea of nationalism seems to have run its course" (quoted in BBC News 2004) in Corsica. So, what is one to do with the ambience of the performance of *Canta u Populu Corsu*? Many of their songs invoke in hymn-like chords the struggle and will for liberty; some of their fans wear T-shirts and wave large flags with the Corsican emblem ('U Moru,' a Moor's head)—but just as many are bathing in the sound while concluding their outdoor picnic, and the infusion of the Celtic as much as the electronic fortification into the traditional cadences bespeaks more than a nationalist interest.

With its complex connections and power of aesthetic affect, the Corsican polyphonic male song tradition *Paghiella* on which this group was originally built, arguably exemplifies a local, European, even global aesthetic resource. Its territorial and ethno-national reach is but one among many possibilities of identification. This is facilitated through a number of intertwined developments that will be taken up in sequence:

1. The isolating and formatting of expressive forms supported by ethnological and folkloristic knowledge production which facilitates their circulation in multiple contexts;
2. The expansion from a primarily political identification with aesthetic resources to an economic appropriation of the production and consumption of such resources;

Israeli sociologist Motti Regev has offered a revised concept of "aesthetic cosmopolitanism" that may serve as a helpful, more general background for understanding our fields' place in transferring expressive culture into the realm of economic resources. Regev locates late modern cosmopolitanism not on the individual level, where it resided in early modernity, but rather on a structural, collective level, "as a cultural condition that is inextricable from current ethno-national uniqueness" (2007, 126). Regev further explains: the production of ethno-national cultural uniqueness in late modernity is inverted. Instead of looking exclusively back to their own group's history, or inside, to their own community's tradition, cultural producers and artists receive much of their techniques and expressive patterns from the "outside," from cultural products and art works that signify "otherness."' Drawing on Garcia Canclini, he asserts that "ethno-national uniqueness in late modernity is produced with the help of 'others,' it is a coproduction" (Regev 2007, 126). The other has, of course, participated in such processes continuously, as Johannes Fabian's (1983) work demonstrates, but the nature of the coproduction is shifting, as the level of reflexivity concerning the process intensifies.

I would like to explore and differentiate the work and debate around aesthetic resources primarily with examples from music and folk art.

The resource aspect can be traced more easily here as the mobility—and hence the "social life" (Appadurai 1986)—independent of a supposed home base can be realized more easily. The complex and composite ritual performances and sites undergoing heritagization are generally more tied to location; indeed, their transformation into world heritage is often connected, among other issues, to interests in enhancing locality (see Hemme, Tauschek, and Bendix 2007; Kockel and Nic Craith 2007; also Smith 2007; Smith and Akagawa 2008). The elaboration from cultural practice to resource can perhaps be illustrated more transparently with the examples chosen, not least as their economic relevance has been undisputed if embattled—to which a quite extensive literature in ethnomusicology gives testimony (e.g., Feld 1988, 1992; Greene 1999; Lessig 2008). The goal will be first to assess both the place of folkloristics and ethnology in the transformation of expressive culture into expressive resources and the stance one might take at a time when culture appears for some to be locked into a box of nonrenewable, identity-bound resources, while for others—such as George Yúdice (2003)—culture is a highly renewable market good as long as one is able to make peace between an economics and a politics of cultural recognition (see also Fraser 2000; Gutmann 1994). Next, I revisit the *canti corsu* and a narrow array of differently lodged examples from Switzerland that illustrate the interdependence of ethno-nationalist and cosmopolitan moves, from music to indigenous arts to folk-pop-high art fusions.

I

"Expressive culture" is a term used in some Anglo-American scholarship since the early 1970s so as to avoid the perennial problems inherent to a term like William Thoms's "folklore" (Bendix 1998; Feintuch 2003). What is to be included in this term has been a subject of debate to some, or simply a product of local scholarly practice to others. A canon of topics given disciplinary attention has emerged, as have genre definitions which in turn have assisted in recognizing relevant materials in the field. The scope of the discipline has ranged from a narrow conception of folklore as "verbal art" to a broad and wonderfully vague and inherently dynamic notion, such as "the frills of culture," suggested by Edmund Leach in a talk in October 1986 at the Department of Anthropology at Indiana University. Encoded in such terms is an emphasis on the aesthetic dimension of cultural practices and products. While aesthetics need not connote "beautiful," the term signals the deeply *affecting* potential inherent to the materials studied. Expressive culture is thus a powerful agent within homogeneous groups as much as within complex, heterogeneous societies.

A growing market of decontextualized aesthetic resources appeals to producers as much as consumers, for human beings are united—if in little else—in their openness for sensory, affective pleasure. The question is how the market dimension has crept up on us, because encounter, exchange, sampling, and curiosity as much as aesthetic pleasure have been there all along. As Eisendle and Miklautz argued in 1992, the market for goods that are not primarily "useful" or "necessary" has enlarged the consumer potential of things cultural and has added signifiers such as "identity" or "lifestyle" to product choices (1992, 11). An increased market interest in cultural commoditization has "hardly furthered the precision of the concept of culture" (1992, 13). However, goods "loaded" with cultural significance or cultural excerpts made ready for the market point the way for cultural research to tackle the intersection between culture and the economy. This is an area that fields such as folklore studies and ethnology have historically avoided, not least because it was assumed that culture that had entered the market was somehow no longer pristine. This scholarly resistance to venturing into the realm of commerce is deeply connected to assumptions about cultural authenticity and uniqueness and the market's spoiling of this connection (Bendix 1997; Lindholm 2008, 53–64).

Scholarship has social, political, and economic repercussions, as has been shown in numerous studies on the history and agency particularly of ethnological fields—which really should not have been as surprising as it seemed to be when the first critical studies of the history of the field were written. The literature on folklore and nationalism is, at this point, legion (for an interim assessment of this literature, see Bendix 1992). Wilson's (1976) work on Finland was one of the first, and the recognition of the instrumentalization of the epic *Kalevala* in Finnish nation-building was eye-opening for a great deal of works that would follow.

Research that has made the riches of everyday life the focus of a discipline will invariably result in the transfer of that knowledge back into and beyond the realms studied. In tandem with scholarly collecting and archiving of expressive culture, such materials began to kindle the aesthetic appreciation of individuals and groups among and beyond those from whom the material was collected. Thus, while scholarship increasingly criticized decontextualized bodies of "items" of folk culture, it was precisely such itemization and clearly delineated cultural attribution which allowed for their recontextualized deployment. Collecting was one of the first methods of accumulating ethnological and folkloristic data. Archiving and, more so, exhibiting such collections furthered reflection about self and other, stimulated comparison, and encouraged an interest in imitation, appropriation, and possession (Cantwell 1993; Stewart 1984, 1991).

The institutionalization of sites and formats of collection facilitated the transformation of embedded expressive culture into a free-floating expressive resource. And for the past four decades, scholars have shown signs of consternation or even remorse that their intellectual forebears would have contributed to the instrumentalizing of expressive culture for political and economic ends. Yet in the rapidly growing heritage field, be it on the global level of the United Nations Educational, Scientific and Cultural Organization (UNESCO) or smaller initiatives on the national and regional level, our fields have been actively called to task to either legitimize or evaluate various groups' claims for turning material or intangible cultural practices into heritage—which is the ultimate and universally sanctioned process for acknowledging culture's resource potential, in all of Pierre Bourdieu's forms of capital. Associated with the heritage complex is the rendering of cultural practices into "cultural property." This process has moved along rapidly on the international stage of the World Intellectual Property Organization (WIPO) and ethnologists and folklorists have variously lamented, observed, or actively participated in the negotiation of this complex legal undertaking (Groth 2012).

Both heritage and cultural property are considered identity resources. Identity is inherently political, while resources are inherently economic, as capital of this nature is inevitably both symbolic and monetary. The heritage complex thus leads actors from within our disciplines into the realm with which scholars have had the most problematic interface, the political and economic instrumentalization of expressive culture. Yet taking a step back, looking at the broader interface of society and research or knowledge production at large, I wonder sometimes about the caution, fear, and rejection on the part of humanistic scholarship to involve itself in societies beyond "educating" or "documenting" and "interpreting" or "understanding." Economists are never scared of the impact their knowledge has on the nation-state. Indeed, they regard it as their task to produce such knowledge, the more quickly the better—one applicable theory chases the next, modelled, tested, used, discarded—a process that deserves ethnographic attention, in and of itself! Economists, much like professors of law, moral philosophers, or medical researchers *intend* to affect a polity, a society, or ailing bodies. Hence, I would wish for more ethnologists to have the courage to think about their own agency as made possible through the knowledge they produce. Our field was one of the first to examine its disciplinary history in the postwar period and gained momentum precisely from this self-reflective move. It is arguably better equipped than many to practice engaged knowledge transfer in a circumspect fashion and to advise cautiously in the realm of heritage, cultural property, and the use of expressive resources.


II


I return now to the *canti corsu* and other instances of cultural fragments turned resources. As I tried to show thus far, the ethnological and folkloristic canon has assisted in this process. In addition to embracing the full spread of media and sites within which expressive resources are encountered, it is necessary to acknowledge the selective construction of ethnic and national aesthetic contours, on the one hand, and their interaction with countless other such constructions on the market of aesthetic ideas and ideals, on the other.

Corsican *Paghjella* contains links between local orientations and needs, knowledge about cultural forms and practices in multiple contexts, and supralocal opportunities and pressures. In addition, the agency facilitated by cultural scholarship played a rather larger role than we might think. This is evident for instance in the *Paghjella* group *I Compagnoli*, who won a polyphonic song competition held in the Pyrenees a few years ago—an international venue for competing national aesthetic traditions. Competition is a device to sort and thereby establish hierarchies. The complex relations between the vast array of competitions humans have dreamt up still requires ethnographic and theoretical attention (e.g., Tauschek 2013). The very notion of competition is, in any case, potentially a direct bridge to symbolic capital that can enhance opportunities on the financial market. *I Compagnoli* still sing a few of the more nationalistic and revolutionary songs, in which Che Guevara occasionally makes an appearance, but they have also begun to do research in isolated villages, uncovering so-called intact sacred polyphonic repertoires. They are not the only *Paghjella* group that ornaments its concerts with short educational sequences about folk instruments and social history—a feature that invariably reminds one of the kind of teaching activity ethnologists and folklorists undertake in museum settings and public speaking. It is one of many examples of how not just the knowledge produced by our field, but our entire disciplinary practice—from fieldwork to archiving to publication formats—has been transferred, albeit in fragmentary fashion, into the public sphere. This is of course a legacy that has been with our disciplines since their emergence. The large number of amateur or lay practitioners accompanying our discipline's history is a crucial yet poorly researched area for understanding the ways in which our knowledges have been interwoven into daily life (Noyes 1999).

A differently positioned musical example is the popular group *Marquess*. This is a male group which burst onto the central European music scene in 2006; they made it to the Top Ten in the three German-speaking nations Austria, Germany and Switzerland, as well as Finland, Poland, and the Czech Republic, with their song *Vayamos Companeros*. Many of the Corsican polyphonic singers, by contrast, compete almost exclusively for the attention of other Corsicans and regard their work with the expressive resource music as part of cultural restoration and ethno-nationalist consciousness raising—yet they do so with aesthetic allusions to numerous cultural others. *Marquess*, too, employs culturally patterned musical resources, including polyphonic male song; it just happens not to be of their own background—the four musicians making up *Marquess* are all German; their lead singer is German-Italian. Most of the songs on their album *Frenetica* are sung in Spanish, a significant marker not just of changes in the creative and economic shifts in the global music scene but of the possibilities of feeling and sounding out cultural pluralism or culture building *à l'Européenne*. *Marquess* had a first summer hit in 2006, *El Temperamento*, which reached cult status in various Mediterranean vacation sites of Europe—where of course the northern Europeans were spending their summer holiday. Their album was recorded in a *finca* on Mallorca. Both the reception and the genesis of the music points to life-styles and tastes grown from biographies shaped by movement in, and familiarity with, the European continent.

To avoid any easy differentiation between folk musicians with a political agenda and popular musicians having fun and making a profit by employ-ing musical resources of another ethnic and linguistic tradition, one only need look at a number of other Corsican groups. *Zamballarana* combines *Paghjella* with Balkan-syncopated rhythms and brass instrumentations familiar to aficionados of Balkan gypsy bands. Some of their pieces fea-ture a marimba—a Latin American instrument. Clearly, these musicians, too, have had mobile biographies, be that simply musical travel or also physical movement. *Cantu a Populo Corsu* made connection with world music—both ideologically and technologically by borrowing fashions appealing to the eye and ear: Celtic sound fragments magically open the ear toward notions of folk, marginality, mystery, power, human rights, and self-definition present in the collective consciousness of a broad European population segment. *I Muvrini*, another *canti corsu* group, features among its collaborators world musician Stefan Eicher and considers its music a "symbol for harmonious unity" of mankind and an "*ambassador* for cul-tural diversity" (I. Muvrini 2016, my translation). The "*A Filetta* magic" is described in a press release as having "its roots deep in the Corsican soil" and as mastering the art of polyphony with "unlimited talent, a piercing vocal sensitivity and overwhelming emotional fervor": "No one leaves their concerts unmoved" (Terracorsa 2016). In such descriptions, ethnolo-gists and folklorists will hear an almost direct continuity reaching back to Johann Gottfried Herder's praise of folk song and his call, from the late eighteenth century, to collect these goods. The rawness and beauty of the local against the backdrop of the globally connected remains the most potent illustration of the intertwining of aesthetics and politics. *Marquess*, by contrast, rides on a mass cultural sense of ownership of language and sound. While their initial success may have been furthered by a Mallorcan holiday feel and the sense of intermingling with cultural otherness during the licentious and liminal period a vacation can represent, they tour year-round now, playing at home and in winter as much as being heard in the summer months. They are not plagued by guilt for being linguistic impostors, robbers of culturally typified beats and sound cadences. They are just mixing and creating a feel of belonging, even contributing to and broadening the aesthetic playground that is open for participation and consumption to all who want to have part in it.

The employ of culturally recognizable aesthetic resources is abundant. As consumers of such musics, we might simply feel happy to hear these productions, have our souls enlarged as is the power of aesthetic work and as is one mission of musical arts. As cultural researchers we are, however, fully aware that all these examples sit right in the middle of simmering new sociopolitical and economic hotspots. Next to the ethno-nationalist potency of musical affect, traditional musics have come to the attention of agents interested in cultural property regimes. Legal cases from France, Sweden, and the US, surrounding the embattled Mbuti pygmy lullaby featured on *Deep Forest*'s sound-engineered album (Feld 1988, 1992) have gained scholarly attention. These are, along with legal altercations surrounding Native American jewelry starting in the 1980s (Evans-Pritchard 1987), just the beginnings of increasingly complex negotiations around what seems to be one of the last renewable resources available in the world market.

Yet, when we listen to purported folk musics such as *Paghiella* and declared pop music, such as *Marquess*, we find a great deal of similarity in technological production, cultural borrowing, and reliance on (albeit different) markets. As the vocabulary of authenticity is part of everyday discourse, both producers and consumers would likely draw differentiations between these styles and locations. But both types would get into trouble with cultural property regimes, should an initiative of this nature grab hold of European music the way it has in a number of African states, or as also occurred in the realm of European foods (Welz 2007).

I will turn now to a different example of expressive culture-turned-aesthetic resource. In 2006, the Swiss agency for culture, Pro Helvetia, initiated a program-*cum*-competition called "echoes." Pro Helvetia sponsors mostly what, in an older terminology (still used by some), was called "high culture"—fledgling literary authors, classical orchestras, theatre troupes, and so forth. With "echoes," such categorization was to be called into question, and the mutual influence of aesthetic traditions on one another was to be stimulated. I quote from the program's mission statement:

> The Swiss have mixed feelings about their cultural traditions. The roles seem clearly defined: tradition means customs, crafts and folklore, whereas innovation is the remit of contemporary art. But what is truly innovative and what is merely rehashed or repackaged? Is contemporary art really as free from past influences as it sometimes claims? And does traditional culture really only look to the past or does it in fact draw inspiration from all sides? With its thematic programme entitled "echoes," Pro Helvetia is opening a forum on folk culture of the 21st century. Questions are raised and discussed with all those concerned: cultural practitioners from the worlds of art and folk culture, organisations promoting culture, politicians and the arts public. The programme proves that folk culture is on the move, that tradition has a future. (Pro Helvetia 2008)

With its competition—for which more than one hundred submissions were entered—Pro Helvetia wanted officially to stimulate cross-fertilization between different creative sectors of society. Only projects seeking collaboration between "traditional" and other types of arts could compete. Parallel to the exhibition and performances of winning entries, public debates were staged with experts from politics, cultural management, scholarship, and performance practice to address a broad array of questions circling around folk culture's emergence and place in a polity. The questions for debate posed by Pro Helvetia were:

- How popular is folk culture?
- How does culture become folk culture?
- Will folk culture ever die out?
- How much tradition is good for innovation?
- When does folk culture play a role in identity?
- Does folk culture strengthen democracy?
- Does folk culture promote a national feeling of togetherness? Does folk culture contribute to the integration of non-Swiss sectors of the population?
- Is folk culture a product of globalization? What is authentic about folk culture?
- In what way is folk culture different from lay culture?

- For whom is folk culture worthwhile? To what does folk culture not give a voice?
- Why bother promoting folk culture?
- Is folk culture too successful to be promoted?
- Does public promotion of the arts have a particular obligation toward folk-cultural creation?
- What are the criteria for promoting folk culture? Does cultural promotion distort folk culture?

Among the ten winners was a traveling narrative troupe, two designers who wanted to work with traditional carpenters to produce fusion furniture, and the traditional pastoral benediction of alpine cowherds, called "Loba," which was taken to the biggest urban areas and projected via loudspeakers over cityscapes: "Inspired by ... cowherds who express their wishes and fears loudly every evening [by means of "Loba"], Loba Town has taken the unexpressed joys, annoyances and visions of city people ... and spoken them into a contemporary form with the assistance of [several traditional] cowherds and four representatives of Swiss rap culture" (Lobatown 2009; my translation).

The reasons for initiating "echoes" are complex and not entirely transparent. Switzerland, like many European countries, as the volume by Gingrich and Banks (2006) has illustrated, has had a strong upsurge of right-wing political interest. A particular type of folk music and assorted aesthetic allusions to "the folk" have been used for a political program that is conservative and antiforeigner. Funded with taxpayers' moneys, Pro Helvetia by contrast has time and again come under political scrutiny for programs considered too liberal, too off the beaten track. "Echoes" can be read as an effort to demonstrate—across all segments of the population—that expressive culture is a resource, and that conscious confrontation with the economic and political dimensions of handling this resource will also wrest folk culture free from one particular political corner.

The "echoes" program is an example of a bravely invasive initiative in cultural politics; running parallel and occasionally intersecting with it is a research project in European Ethnology at the University of Basel, entitled "Culture and Politics: Volkskultur between Scholarship, Cultural Practice and (Cultural) Political Sponsorship" (Culture and Politics 2006–2009)— the only scholarly effort from our field I know of that seeks to understand both empirically and theoretically how the concept of folk culture is used in daily practice from the grassroots levels up to political decision-making bodies. Those engaged in the "echoes" initiative accept the existence of a folk culture that was once a construct and that has been naturalized in discourse and practice. Emphasizing sponsorship and competition in aesthetic dimensions, it is, however, also a project that downplays the economic in favor of the political and aesthetic innovation. To some extent, "echoes" thus echoes the volume on Swedish Folk Arts coedited by folklorists Barbro Klein and Mats Widbom (1994).

## III

In scholarship on nontraditional or neo-pagan religions, the processes of reaching for an imagined past and fashioning new practices for the future is labeled "reclamation" (Hutton 2001; Magliocco 2004). The term's reach, in its political thrust, certainly differs from the notion of "retraditionalization," which, in the wake of discourses on invented traditions, is also used in our field. Both terms focus, however, on the comparability of the practice in past and present, and less on the heterogeneity of the practitioners or users and consumers. No one would downplay the relevance of the political in practices reaching for and working with culture's aesthetic resources. But the economic dimension has often remained marginalized in cultural analysis, and scholarly agency has long been such that it problematized the economic activities of cultural actors with what Kockel (2007) terms "reflexive traditions"—namely, the habitual that has been lifted from habitus and foregrounded in anything from Herder's booklet gathering "voices of people in song" to a cultural heritage park. The 1980s saw a strong focus in work on the aesthetics and politics of culture. However, it is an inseparable trio that is to be considered: expressive culture, politics, and the market. Politics and the market are differently weighted, depending on the case at hand. It is thus high time that our fields not only reflect but also act more confidently on that playful label of the "culture broker" that Richard Kurin (1997) put into the world. The Swiss colleagues accompanying Pro Helvetia's "echoes" program are one example of such engagement where critical scholarly documentation is combined with participation in public fora and publications. New scholarly findings and positions are thus transferred into public settings, productively countering a more passive and perhaps more typical stance among scholars bemoaning the outdated culture concepts evident in society and political practice. In the realm of cultural property rights, anthropologist Michael Brown (2003) has been most active in making his research on processes and conflicts visible and useful to those engaged in solving new cultural property regimes (see also Brown's website [2014]). For two hundred years, cultural scholarship has acted as a midwife to turning the flow of cultural experiences into reflexive traditions and, in effect, smoothed the path for aesthetic cosmopolitanism, and all the complicated (but also quite marvelous) practices emerging from it. While a great deal of these practices of production and consumption could be global, I would argue that there are European contours, both on the political and the economic level. SIEF and its membership would have the brain power and qualification to embark on comparative work with policy relevance in this field.

SIEF is a largely European scholarly society, albeit welcoming its supra-European ties and members. At the time of its founding, SIEF was concerned with academic politics—the congresses were to facilitate continued East-West contact and scholarly exchange, and to strengthen the disciplinary contours. During an era of Cold War and Iron Curtain, European ethnologists had (it would seem) no problem feeling the Europeanness of their work, and acting to overcome the new boundaries resulting from the Second World War. The fellowship of scholars across borders has continued more or less successfully, but contributing to a new understanding of an emergent Europe has proven more difficult. There is scholarship examining the pitfalls of various top-down efforts to construct Europe. What I tried to sketch here is evidence for the European aesthetic imagination and experimentation that has in the last decades brought forth alternate territorial spaces and alternatives to ethno-nationalist deployments of essentialized folk materials—alternatives that have been facilitated not least through the vocabularies and practices from our field that have been transferred into the public sphere.

This paper was first presented at a congress organized and held in Northern Ireland, one of the places in which experimentation with aesthetic resources has contributed to a boundary crossing Celticism—evident, as was demonstrated in the beginning of the paper—even in Corsican polyphonic song stagings. The organizers of this congress invited the participants to liberate the ethnological imagination. The deployment of aesthetic resources, in the intertwining of political and economic markets, is one place where I would suggest European ethnologists might find much that contributes to an emergent Europe and lead to scholarship that accompanies the process.

Once we acknowledge that one arm of heritagization in effect transcends the political and territorial identification of cultural fragments, we are also on the path of transcending boundaries we have readied for all those eager to establish property regimes running along such group identity lines.

NOTES

This chapter previously appeared in the *Anthropological Journal of European Cultures* 17 (2008): 114–29.

This is a revised version of the author's Presidential Address at the ninth SIEF (Societé Internationale d'Ethnologie et de Folklore). Congress, delivered at the University of Ulster on June 18, 2008. For their readings and comments of the draft, I would like to thank Dorothee Hemme and Andre Gingrich.

REFERENCES

Appadurai, Arjun, ed. 1986. *The Social Life of Things.* Cambridge: Cambridge University Press.

BBC News. 2004. "European Press Review." August 9. Accessed December 20, 2017. http://news.bbc.co.uk/go/pr/fr/-/2/hi/europe/3547480.stm.

Bendix, Regina. 1992. "National Sentiment in Enactment and Discourse of Swiss Political Ritual." *American Ethnologist* 19 (4): 768–90.

———. 1997. *In Search of Authenticity: The Formation of Folklore Studies.* Madison: University of Wisconsin Press.

———. 1998. "Of Names, Professional Identities, and Disciplinary Futures." *Journal of American Folklore* 111 (441): 235–46.

Billig, Michael. 1995. *Banal Nationalism.* London: Sage.

Brown, Michael F. 2003. *Who Owns Native Culture?* Cambridge, MA: Harvard University Press.

———. 2014. "Who Owns Native Culture?" Last modified April. Accessed December 20, 2017. http://web.williams.edu/AnthSoc/native/.

Cantwell, Robert. 1993. *Ethnomimesis. Folklore and the Representation of Culture.* Chapel Hill: University of North Carolina Press.

Culture and Politics: Volkskultur between Science, Cultural Practice and Politics. 2006–2009. Project 5713, research database, University of Basel, Switzerland. Accessed December 20, 2017. https://forschdb2.unibas.ch/inf2/rm_projects/object_view .php?r=5713.

Eisendle, Reinhard, and Elfie Miklautz. 1992. "Artefakt und Kultur. Dynamik und Bedeutungswandel des Konsums." In *Produktkulturen. Dynamik und Bedeutungswandel des Konsums,* edited by Reinhard Eisendle and Elfie Miklautz, 11–20. Frankfurt: Campus.

Evans-Pritchard, Deirdre. 1987. "The Portal Case: Authenticity, Tourism, Traditions, and the Law." *Journal of American Folklore* 100: 287–96.

Fabian, Johannes. 1983. *Time and the Other.* New York: Columbia University Press.

Feintuch, Burt, ed. 2003. *Eight Words for the Study of Expressive Culture.* Urbana: University of Illinois Press.

Feld, Steven. 1988. "Notes on World Beat." *Public Culture* 1 (1): 31–7.

———. 1992. "Voices of the Rainforest: Imperial Nostalgia and the Politics of Music." *Arena* 99/100: 164–77.

Fraser, Nancy. 2000. "Rethinking Recognition." *New Left Review* 3: 107–20.

Gingrich, Andre, and Marcus Banks. 2006. *Neo-nationalism in Europe and Beyond.* Oxford: Berghahn.

Greene, Paul. 1999. "Engineering Spaces in Nepal's Digital Stereo Remix Culture." Paper presented during the panel "Sound Engineering as Cultural Production," Meeting of the Society for Ethnomusicology, Austin, November.

Groth, Stefan. 2012. *Negotiating Tradition. The Pragmatics of International Deliberations of Cultural Property.* Göttingen Studies in Cultural Property, vol. 4. Göttingen: Göttingen University Press.

Gutmann, Amy, ed. 1994. *Multiculturalism: Examining the Politics of Recognition.* Princeton, NJ: Princeton University Press.

Hemme, Dorothee, Markus Tauschek, and Regina Bendix, eds. 2007. *Prädikat "Heritage." Wertschöpfung aus kulturellen Ressourcen.* Münster: LIT.

Hutton, Ronald. 2001. *The Stations of the Sun: A History of the Ritual Year in Britain.* Oxford: Oxford University Press.

I Muvrini Infoseite. 2016. Published by Brigitte Kühn. Accessed August 30. http://www .muvrini.info/.

Klein, Barbro and Mats Widbom, eds. 1994. *Swedish Folk Art: All Tradtion is Change.* New York: H. N. Abrams in association with Kulturhuset, Stockholm.

Kockel, Ullrich. 2007. "Reflexive Traditions and Heritage Production." In *Cultural Heritages as Reflexive Traditions,* edited by Ullrich Kockel and Máiréad Nic Craith, 19–33. New York: Palgrave.

Kockel, Ullrich, and Máiréad Nic Craith, eds. 2007. *Cultural Heritages as Reflexive Traditions.* New York: Palgrave.

Kurin, Richard. 1997. *Reflections of a Cultural Broker.* Washington, DC: Smithsonian Institution Press.

Lessig, Lawrence. 2008. *Remix: Making Art and Commerce Thrive in the Hybrid Economy.* New York: Penguin.

Lindholm, Charles. 2008. *Culture and Authenticity.* Oxford: Blackwell.

Lobatown. 2009. "Loba Town Was?" Accessed January 22. http://was.lobatown
.ch/?view=:de (site discontinued).

Magliocco, Sabina. 2004. *Witching Culture*. Philadelphia: University of Pennsylvania
Press.

Noyes, Dorothy. 1999. "Provinces of Knowledge. Or, Can You Get Out of the Only Game
in Town?" *Journal of Folklore Research* 30 (2/3): 253–8.

Pro Helvetia. 2008. *"Echoes—Folk Culture for Tomorrow."* Accessed June 5.
www.pro-helvetia.ch/index.cfm?id=4821 (page deleted).

Regev, Motti. 2007. "Cultural Uniqueness and Aesthetic Cosmopolitanism." *European
Journal of Social Theory* 10: 123–38.

Smith, Laurajane, ed. 2007. *Cultural Heritage*. London: Routledge.

Smith, Laurajane, and Natsuko Akagawa, eds. 2009. *Intangible Heritage*. With an
introduction by Laurajane Smith and Natsuko Akagawa. London: Routledge.

Stewart, Susan. 1984. *On Longing. Narratives of the Miniature, the Gigantic, the Souvenir, the
Collection*. Baltimore, MD: Johns Hopkins University Press.

———. 1991. *Crimes of Writing: Problems in the Containment of Representation*. New York:
Oxford University Press.

Tauschek, Markus, ed. 2013. *Kulturen des Wettbewerbs: Formationen kompetitiver Logiken*.
Münster: Waxmann.

Terracorsa. 2017. "Corsican Music, Groups, Concerts, Culture and Art." Accessed May 30.
www.terracorsa.info/music.html.

Welz, Gisela. 2007. "Europäische Produkte: Nahrungskulturelles Erbe und EU-Politik.
Am Beispiel der Republik Zypern." In *Prädikat "Heritage". Wertschöpfung aus kulturellen
Ressourcen*, edited by Dorothee Hemme, MarkusTauschek, and Regina Bendix, 323–35.
Münster: LIT.

Wilson, William A. 1976. *Folklore, Nationalism and Politics in Modern Finland*.
Bloomington: Indiana University Press.

Yúdice, George. 2003. *The Expediency of Culture*. Durham, NC: Duke University Press.

# 10

*Daily Bread, Global Distinction?*
*The German Bakers' Craft and Cultural*
*Value-Enhancement Regimes*

The Lord's Prayer includes the simple wish, "give us this day our daily bread." Indeed, bread made of grain flour, leavened or un-leavened, is one of the most widespread basic foods on earth, rivaled at best by rice.[1] So basic and widespread is bread that one might think its universal significance so self-evident that no mention need be made of it. Thus it was with some surprise that I took note of the following news item reported in the German media on May 22, 2011: "German Agriculture Minister Ilse Aigner (CSU) wants to have German bread protected as World [Intangible] Cultural Heritage. "In its variety and quality, German bread is unique," Aigner declared on Sunday in Berlin. With this, she supports suggestions made by the German bakery trade federation to create a 'Bread Registry'" (*rp-online*, May 22, 2011).

As I soon realized, this was not the first press report on the topic of German bread as cultural heritage. Already on March 21 of the same year, the *Zentralverband des deutschen Bäckerhandwerks* (German Federation of the Bakery Trade) had placed the following notice on its home page: "With its globally unique diversity, Germany is rightly regarded as "the land of bread." But how many varieties actually exist? The answer will come soon thanks to the Bread Registry the German *Zentralverband des Deutschen Bäckerhandwerks* is now compiling. For the first time, this abundance will be documented. And that is just the beginning, since by 2012 German bread is to become UNESCO World Cultural Heritage!" (Zentralverband 2011).

The bakers' trade federation is the late modern institution representing what in early modernity were the bakers' guilds. They put out four more press releases providing information about how far the registry had progressed. When I asked how the efforts to nominate varieties were being implemented, I received the following email answer from the office responsible for foodstuffs law at this federation:

> Dear Mrs. Bendix,
>    Together with the Academy of the German Bakers' Craft in Weinheim (ADB Weinheim) and the Institute for the Quality Assurance of Baked Goods (IQBack e.V.), the *Zentralverband des Deutschen Bäckerhandwerks* is creating the so-called Bread Registry (www.brotregister.de). On behalf of its members, the *Zentralverband* is applying to be taken onto the Intangible Cultural Heritage list. (Sep 30, 2011, email)

A visit to this registry site revealed that an impressive 2,509 types of bread had thus far been registered. Alas, any heritage nomination requires that a state ratify the corresponding international convention, which Germany, in 2011, had not yet done. I sent a query to the head of the Culture Bureau at the German UNESCO (United Nations Educational, Scientific, and Cultural Organization) Commission in Bonn in early October 2011 and received the response that there was no discussion at the German UNESCO Commission about a "German Bread Registry."[2] In the summer of 2012, the German parliament still had not ratified the 2003 UNESCO Convention on World Immaterial Cultural Heritage. Thus, while the number of breads registered on the German Bread Registry continued to rise, the biggest hurdle German bakers faced with regard to a UNESCO listing was within the political process in Germany itself.

From this cluster of press reports, inquiries, and facts on a potential bread nomination, a number of research questions arise about the contemporary processes surrounding the "valuation of culture," which I wish to address in turn. The goals pursued by the various actors involved are worthy of serious consideration, as they provide insight into what has been set loose by a now forty-year-old "World Cultural Heritage" regime and parallel value-added procedures. To shed light on the German bakers' actions, I will examine why these actors develop the ambition to render a basic foodstuff into world cultural heritage. I will also study the role the state has been allotted within UNESCO's heritage conventions, and follow with an examination of the role that ethnological and anthropological fields of inquiry have—or have not—played in this particular heritage-making endeavor. Finally, I will probe the motivation of the German bakers more deeply and lay open the rationale for pursuing a UNESCO nomination for intangible cultural heritage for German breads rather than pushing for any other extant value-added regime.

## A BASIC FOODSTUFF AS CULTURAL HERITAGE?

Thinking about bread, one would logically first think about its taste, texture, variety, and history. The German celebrity cook Wolfram Siebeck did so when addressing the potential heritage status of German bread in his column in a German weekly. Not interested in the political hurdles or the fine points of the UNESCO heritage regime, he immediately immersed himself in the history of German bread, and eventually argued that the only really tasty bread, though it does get rock-hard, is found in the Alps. His conclusion was that "if it is a matter of originality, then (only) pumpernickel and the related black bread [*Schwarzbrot*] have a chance at World Heritage status" (*Zeitmagazin*, April 14, 2011). Siebeck, the cook, naturally and rightfully is focusing on taste. However, in the context of cultural heritage, we can leave aside the question of which breads (for whatever taste-related reasons) really deserve the status of being called an intangible world heritage. The primary issue here is neither bread itself nor the cultural practices of sowing, reaping, grinding, mixing, kneading, and baking that surround it. It is not even about the pleasure derived from eating good bread. Rather, it is about the practices that lead to valuing this cultural product.

Barbara Kirshenblatt-Gimblett has called the heritage-labeling of bits of culture a "'value-added' industry" (1995, 370–72). She coined the term "metacultural production" for this process which includes attitudes, values about traditional cultural expressions, and their instrumentalization (2004).[3] It has been sixteen years since she published her five theses on heritage (1995), and her argument at the time certainly constituted a watershed in both tourism and heritage research. In light of the growing density of heritage designations and the space they take on the economic and political stage, I would, however, argue that these processes should no longer be called "meta." They are themselves cultural practices, and if one looks at some existing or planned world heritage sites and intangible cultural practices in creating officially acknowledged cultural heritage, these processes seem to have almost become more significant than the slices of intangible cultural heritage, the existing and designated cultural monuments, or the cultural heritage landscapes themselves.

It is not that surprising that foodstuffs, or dining complexes, are honored as immaterial cultural goods. Individual foods as well as cuisines have a long history as distinguishing (as well as derogatory!) markers of nation and ethnicity. UNESCO's Intangible Cultural Heritage (ICH) convention affords an opportunity to enhance the symbolic value of cookery on the world stage—with recipe knowledge and cooking crafts as intangible, passed-on traditions. After a first wave of nominations from the realm of customs, musical styles, and narrative forms to become ICH, nominating stakeholders from around the world have gradually widened the scope of traditional practices to be considered. At the fifth meeting in Nairobi in November of 2010, for example, UNESCO's Intergovernmental Commission for selecting immaterial cultural goods decided to include Mediterranean cuisine as world cultural heritage. Greece, Italy, Morocco, and Spain, working together, were successful in this—an unusual but increasingly common practice, as the Italian ethnologist Alessandra Broccolini, who was involved in this application, has documented (Broccolini 2012). In the same year, Croatia was successful in having its gingerbread placed on the list. Mexico, too, convinced the selection committee in the area of nutrition with a nomination that even met the precondition demanded by UNESCO, namely that a tradition must be endangered, and that a place on the world heritage list would help preserve the tradition or might even lead to its revival. France, with a certain amount of cockiness and clever packaging of its claim, was able to have the "French meal" be nominated (Tornatore 2012). So it is no surprise that stakeholders in nations like Korea and Japan were following suit, or at least pursued the worthiness of their respective meal cultures within the media, though no nominations have reached committee decision yet (Asahi 2011, Korea.net 2011). Peru has made several efforts to pull together a nomination, which thus far have not reached the world stage (Matta 2016).

In light of this competition as well as the linkages into the world nutritional discourse occasioned by food nominations of ICH, it might be understandable that German bakers, too, want to be on the heritage map, though, as will be shown, this is neither the only nor the main reason to pursue such a goal.[4]

## WHAT LEADS A GERMAN FEDERAL MINISTER TO SUPPORT A POTENTIAL HERITAGE NOMINATION FOR BREAD?

Bread is ultimately an agricultural product, and Ilse Aigner, as German minister of agriculture, is well advised to examine and support potential opportunities that might increase the value of a German product within and beyond the realm of German consumption. One may nonetheless wonder why Aigner—and the German bakers' association—turn to the heritage route. World heritage is a global label. Agreements under international law, as made by every suborganization of the UN including UNESCO, do not have the force of law. The UN is composed of member states that (still) have a territorial basis, and every agreement, convention, and declaration needs to be ratified by every member state. If a member state does not do so, it is not bound by the agreement.[5] In the case of the Conventions on World Heritage, it then also cannot take part in the nominations—and, hence, cannot take part in the international glory that results from successfully being placed on the heritage lists.

The ICH Convention does not only result in online lists and printed representations published by UNESCO (cf., Hafstein 2009). As soon as they are officially ratified, nominations also create a new bureaucracy (this, of course, is also true for international or European agreements on trade, labor policy, human rights, and so on). The heritage regime is reflected in measures that themselves can create further institutions and lead to evermore complex bureaucratic measures. Such institutions might be established with reference to older protection or preservation bureaucracies, for in the end, cultural valuation mechanisms are not new. One need only think of movements protecting architectural heritage or other types of monuments, such as *Heimatschutz* (homeland protection) and *Denkmalschutz* (monument protection) in the German-language areas

of Europe. Such preservation-oriented values result, once institutionalized, in precise demands, for instance, in the preservation of nominated
structures. Another example is the "musealization" of entire building
complexes as takes place in open-air museums since the late nineteenth
century.[6] Each of these valuation mechanisms has a "rescuing intent" and
each has brought forth a not small administering bureaucracy over time
(Tschofen 2007). Bread, however, hardly needs rescuing—and neither did
most of the other already successfully nominated foods. Again, one might
wonder what propels actors to seek a nomination.

The world heritage regime unavoidably brings arguments by global
actors into domestic discourses: drawing on his research in North Africa,
cultural geographer Thomas Schmitt discussed this under the appropriate
term and title, *Cultural Governance* (2011, cf., Schmitt 2014). The centrality of these practices and scholars' theoretical focus away from considering them as a "meta" level activity become clear here. A specific heritage
regime emerges, also taking its cues from the type of state within which
it unfolds.[7] This can be a very totalitarian and top-down process, as is the
case, for example, in China or Cambodia. At the other end of the spectrum,
there can be a federalist openness, as is currently evident in Switzerland.[8]
The German bread registry, growing digitally since the spring of 2011, was
also dealt with in a very open and participatory manner, but unlike in the
Swiss case, the state had not decided yet to ratify the convention and the
effort to convince politicians to do so was part of the rationale for the bread
registry on the part of the major stakeholders, the German bakers' guild.

Germany, like various other European countries such as Ireland or
Switzerland, held back on this ratification for good geopolitical reasons.
The ICH Convention came about not least because the list of monuments
accepted into UNESCO's world cultural heritage had been hopelessly over-
crowded by the global North, the (Western) industrial nations. Precisely
because countries like Germany, France, or Italy can look back on a considerable history of monument preservation, it was easy for them to prepare
monuments, building complexes, and the like for the nomination process.

With the introduction of the ICH convention, the global South was to be
given a chance to find international recognition for its cultural wealth. At
the same time, potentially endangered traditions were to receive more recognition and through it also develop new dynamics. One can also remark

in passing that behind this Convention stand decades of work to rethink and update the notions of culture and tradition used by UNESCO—as Valdimar Hafstein (2007) and Richard Kurin (2004) have documented and analyzed. Thus, UNESCO too has reached a less static, less closed definition of culture, though perhaps still not sufficiently so with respect to the idea of group cultures, whether in terms of nations or ethnic, indigenous, or autochthonous groups. Yet, it has also become clear to those responsible for world heritage that cultural practices change, and that nominations if not handled carefully, can lead to ossification. Not all actors in the heritage-making process work with a more flexible culture concept, however, and particularly at the local level, some stakeholders rely on antiquated theories of culture partly due to the lag inherent to knowledge transfer, and partly because some intellectually no-longer-tenable culture theories remain politically powerful and hence useful. Overall, matters have improved, but as any observer of international negotiations in the realm of cultural policy will witness, there are many definitions of culture and tradition, deployed depending on stakeholders' differential goals (Groth 2010, 2012).

The genteel restraint shown by European states with respect to the ICH came to end, not least with the spectacular nominations from the area of nutrition and meals as mentioned earlier. While Sarkozy's original announcement, in February 2008, that French cuisine deserved world heritage status was greeted with a mixture of amusement and outrage by the international press, the food nominations have created a certain degree of emulation and competition (Oneindia 2008). It is not only the bakers in Germany whom one can regard as stakeholders in the effort to move Germany to join this UNESCO Convention. There were also other food-related custom bearers in Germany, such as the manufacturers of dumplings from Thuringia, supported by the dumpling museum, who increased efforts to mobilize their parliamentary representatives (Vates 2011). Minister Aigner did not stand alone. The SPD (Sozialdemokratische Partei Deutschlands) parliamentary group, for example, published the following statement on June 30, 2011: "It is finally time that Germany ratifies the UNESCO Convention on Immaterial Cultural Heritage. [One hundred thirty-six] nations have already ratified the Convention, including many of Germany's neighbors. With implementation of the Convention, Germany will be able to give special recognition to living traditions, practices, rituals and customs, as well as to the knowledge of traditional craft techniques. Even knowledge and practices in dealing with nature and the universe belong to immaterial cultural heritage" (SPD 2011).

But the mills of ratification grind slowly. As of late June 2010, representatives of various parliamentary groups submitted motions to proceed more rapidly with the ratification.[9] Yet such motions need to be examined: What might the costs be? What institutional consequences could result? In other words, the discussion of ratification goes hand-in-hand with weighing and working out an appropriate regime for introducing this new procedure. Adopting the convention can, furthermore, not be done by the federal parliament alone: German law requires that the individual states consult and agree with any federal decision. Therefore, it is not just national competition that plays a role, though the pressure to keep up with other nations is evident at the grassroots level, and exerts pressure on individual parliamentarians in national politics. But in a time when crisis negotiations are being held to try to stave off the potential bankruptcy of Greece, Italy, or the EU as a whole, the ratification of a UNESCO Convention—and the potential honoring of German bread—does not exactly have priority.

Regardless of what is playing out on the political stage, the *Zentralverband des deutschen Bäckerhandwerks* continues to add further varieties of bread to its online registry. Amin Werner, president of this modern-day institution representing the once-powerful early modern guilds, emphasizes the positive effect of this endeavor: to him, it is important to raise popular consciousness for the quality and craft inherent to artisanal breads. More and more, industrial bread production is replacing neighborhood bakeries, and if a bread registry assists in raising the self-esteem of bakers, then perhaps a nomination as ICH might alert German bread consumers that the baking craft is a value worthy of artisanal rather than fast-food prices (Amin Werner, November 28, 2011, pers. comm.). Werner and the organization and profession he represents are ultimately concerned with the labor and food market—concerns that do not match the perhaps more regionalist or nationalist (not to say chauvinist) impulses of other ICH nominators. Before I turn to the truly burning issues for German bakers, I would like to take a brief detour to the scholarly antecedents of mapping cultural practices such as baking and the peculiar gap between scholarly effort and public use of such endeavors as evidenced in the bread registry.

FOLK ATLASES, HERITAGE LISTS, BREAD
REGISTRIES, OR: THE TRANSIENCE OF SPECIALIZED
KNOWLEDGE IN FOLKLORE STUDIES

Bread has been a topic of cultural research, though its omnipresence
has also chastened researchers into frugality when it came to the topic.
Camporesi's (1989) history of food's role in hungry people's actions
and imaginations is just one of many examples of scholarly works taking bread as a metaphor for food's place in sociocultural and political
processes in general. There are a number of German bread studies (e.g.,
Eiselen 1995), some of them associated with open-air museums, which
are the kinds of institutions that naturally instrumentalize the scent and
allure of bread as an inroad into regional pasts (Gentner 1991; Kaiser
and Ottenjann 1989). Bread museums—of which there are two major
ones in Germany, one in Ulm and one in Ebergötzen—provide historical
and cultural documentation as well, and there are the occasional dis-
sertations focusing on bakers and their place in changing times, such as
Koellreuter and Unternährer's (2006) study of bakers in the city of Basel
since medieval times.

But if one, as a cultural anthropologist or folklorist with European
training, examines the bread registry map, she or he is likely reminded of
the many large-scale atlases of folk culture produced in the inter- and postwar years, and will see certain similarities between the efforts of the bread
bakers' federation to create a bread registry and such scholarly inventory-
ing efforts. The opening paragraphs of the German Wikipedia entry to the
*Atlas der deutschen Volkskunde* reads as follows:

> Following the models of the surveys conducted by Wilhelm
> Mannhardt in 1865 and for compiling the *Deutscher Sprachatlas*
> [Atlas of German Speech], five-part questionnaires, sub-divided into
> 243 main questions, were sent out between 1930 and 1935 to 20,000
> informants. Through a close connection between the ideologically
> charged categories of *Volk* and *Raum*, the idea was to establish that
> "despite all variety and diversity ..., the German *Volk* was an indivis-
> ible unity" (Fritz Boehm).
> The results of the survey were published, until 1939 and in six
> installments, as 120 (uncommented) dispersion maps. Beginning in 1938,
> a further evaluation was conducted in the context of the *SS-Ahnenerbe*

[SS-Ancestral Heritage]. After 1958, the survey answers were re-evaluated, and the maps in the new series received extensive critical commentary. (Wikipedia 2011a)

The most expensive production in the realm of cultural research supported by the German Research Foundation in the interwar era, thus, was searching to create a systematic inventory of regional folk culture. One should add that it was by no means the case that the Germans were the only ones to do so. It was just that in the political context of the Third Reich, the intent of territorial mapping of course served as legitimation for political aggression (Schmoll 2009). That inventories of this kind were returned to after 1945, and were even used as a means for international scientific cooperation (see Schmoll 2011) indicates the empty potential of these information-gathering methods. Their theoretical paradigm, which was already worked out in the last decades of the nineteenth century, searched for evidence to prove hypotheses about origin and diffusion.

Using the approaches typical for the time, and wholly without digital techniques, Question 196 of this German atlas survey asked reliable local informants about bread-related topics. The goal was to systematically evaluate this information. But the collection resulted in far more information than there were researchers to evaluate it all. For it is not enough for a researcher to simply produce a geographical depiction: one needs commentaries for each map as well. In the case of bread, Günter Wiegelmann wrote the commentary to "daily bread," though he limited himself to bread spices and began with the sober assessment: "The maps NF 11a-d show bread spices. This is drawn from the highly differentiated complex of questions asked which were related to daily bread. To include all aspects of Question 196 would have called for a long series of maps. This would have heavily freighted the entire cartographic process, one which must take many viewpoints into account both thematically and methodologically. Given the rich material gathered by the ADV survey, the entire complex surrounding bread could likely only be adequately addressed in a broadly conceived monograph" (1965, 251).

Tough luck, therefore, for the bakers. The maps and studies necessary for submitting a cultural heritage nomination are simply not available from our discipline. Where the spices anise, caraway, fennel, and dill were used in bread in the 1930s, and how far back one can trace their use, does not generate much by way of prose for a heritage application.

Nevertheless, it is precisely with the nominations for world cultural heritage in the realm of food preparation and the culture of meals that one sees with particular clarity the connection between the documentation of culture that researchers carry out and the global valuation of culture itself. In its earliest incarnations, folkloristic research was involved in the statistical survey of folk culture (Rassem 1951). This supported the territorial confines of the discipline. At the same time, the research supported the interest of modernizing states to administer folk culture. A second, ideologically powerful pillar of folklore research, though, was the romantic-national glorification of agrarian and pastoral life. From this emerges a praising, and thus valorizing (if not upgrading), of cultural practices rooted in tradition. Territorial rootedness—as strange as it may sound—is also a basic principle of UNESCO. For while nominated monuments, landscapes, and cultural practices belong to the heritage of mankind, their use and administration "belong" to the respective nation-state, as well as to those who in this nation-state emerge as the beneficiaries.

While cultural research has replaced veneration, as well as "saving by collecting," with various approaches marked by an—often critical—understanding of culture, the knowledge transfer of basic folklore terms and canonical knowledge to the public sphere has been quite successful. Voluntary associations and local museums have in many places taken it upon themselves to preserve customs of all kinds, and thereby provide a basic group of actors who not infrequently become involved in putting together UNESCO World Heritage dossiers. In the case of the planned bread nomination in Germany, the bakers' guild has entrusted the Ulm bread museum with putting together the requisite information (Amin Werner, November 28, 2011, pers. comm.). In the arena of cultural governance, what remains of the complex research techniques used to document culture is at times little more than registration. That in turn promotes lists, which foster a not altogether productive competition, as Valdimar Hafstein (2009) has convincingly shown. However, the adoption of registering and mapping by the *Zentralverband des deutschen Bäckerhandwerkes*, and its convincing the German parliament to adopt the ICH convention, calls for a further explanation, which I will consider in the conclusion.

WHY THIS IS NOT ONLY ABOUT BAKING BUNS:
CRAFT AND IMMATERIAL CULTURAL HERITAGE

There are other systems available to add value to cultural products in the realm of food, particularly in Europe. One needs to therefore ask why the German bakers opt for the heritage route, and did not choose to use "Geographical Indication" (GI) as a means to help the many German types of bread receive greater recognition, and thereby appreciate economically (Bramley and Kirsten 2007). A GI can be applied for with the European Union, and does not need to take the detour through state or national legislatures. Regional actors can apply directly to the EU, though they must also reckon with being turned down. Varieties of sausage and cheese and even particular types of vegetables, including the lamb's lettuce [Feldsalat] grown on the island of Reichenau, the asparagus from Schrobenhausen, or even—a baked good, after all!—gingerbread [Lebkuchen] from Nüremberg, have all received such "indications" related to geographic origin. While France has long had such a system (appelation d'origine contrôlée), the "protected designation of origin" framework only came into effect in the EU in 1992. The justification for these instruments can be summarized as follows (cf., Bicskei et al. 2011):

- Agriculture can, in this manner, be diversified. For economically backwards, rural areas, this can be a tool to help in economic development.
- Agricultural products receive a boost, as imitations are blocked, or are at least marked as such.
- The measures are intended to protect consumers from fraud.

In addition to the advantage in the marketplace promised through the emphasis placed on traditional and locally anchored forms of production, the corresponding manufacturing processes as well as the diversity of types (such as in varieties of cheese) is emphasized.

At the moment, there are three types of such protection, whereby the territorial-cultural localization is the most exclusive variant:

- Protected Designation of Origin: Here the quality of the product "is significantly or exclusively determined by the geographical environment, including natural and human factors." Production, processing, and preparation take place in this specified geographical area and the product must be *entirely* manufactured in the designated region.

- Protected Geographical Indication: At least one level of the production must take place in the designated geographical area, so "the entire product must be traditionally and at least *partially* manufactured" there. There needs to be a connection between product and region, but that connection need not be exclusive.
- Protected Traditional Specialty: Here the product does not have to be produced in a particular or geographically limited region. However, it is important that its production "be manufactured using traditional ingredients or must be characteristic for its traditional composition, production process, or processing reflecting a traditional type of manufacturing or processing," and that it is "different from other similar products" (Wikipedia 2011b).

This may be enough to demonstrate that these three categories are defined in ways that can lead to confusion. While manufacturers can, in fact, engage in delicate competition here, these differences are not nearly so easy for consumers to follow. Considerable public relations or translation may be needed (cf., Hegnes 2010) to convince manufacturers that this instrument brings a competitive advantage with it, and that consumers will actually pay attention to these labels, and through their purchases contribute to keeping certain manufacturing practices alive. Generally, GI products seek to keep and develop niche markets, reaching customers willing to pay the higher price necessitated by the specific production process.[10]

Yet bread is too large a category, and its manufacture is easy to move around. After all, within one year, the German Bread Registry accumulated more than 2,500 varieties of bread. Bread is not an exclusive product the way a smoked meat or a sheep or goat cheese might be. For these, consumers are willing to pay a little more; for bread, however, the opposite is true. One only need be reminded that it was an increase in the price of bread in 1789 that contributed to setting off the French Revolution.

For the bakers' craft, a Geographical Indication thus brings little or no economic gains. What is lacking, in fact, are not bread buyers, but bakers themselves. Beyond the pleasing smell of freshly baked bread, apprenticeship and training to be a baker means hard physical labor and extremely early rising and working hours. There are, correspondingly, simply not enough apprentices who want to take up this craft, which furthermore cannot offer competitive wages.

The path to becoming a baker looks, ideally, like this: The baker (according to the Handicrafts Code, a "trade" with the obligation to become a "craftsmaster") begins a three-year apprenticeship in a bakery enterprise headed by a master-baker.[11] Nevertheless, he receives one to two days' instruction at a trade school to be taught all that one does not learn working within the enterprise itself. At the end of three years, he must pass a test to become a journeyman, which is organized by the Handicrafts Chamber. The entrepreneur with whom the apprentice is training must be a member of that Chamber and pay dues to it. The Handicrafts Chambers (of which there are fifty-three in Germany) go back to, or are based on, local guilds. These guilds, however, are voluntary associations, mostly organized at the district level. This is what creates the conflicts between guilds and chambers. The guilds do what can be done on a voluntary basis; the chambers do what is mandatory and exercise sovereignty. But since the chambers lack the necessary specialized knowledge, they must repeatedly rely on the guilds. The guilds, however, are losing members, as more and more bakeries are closing.

If the apprentice passes his test at the end of three years, he becomes a journeyman. After five years in a leading position, he may, as "senior journeyman," take over the running of an enterprise. Until now, the regular path required him to pass a test to become a master craftsman, one which included training in sales and personnel management. A journeyman should already have all the necessary specialized knowledge of his *métier* but the breakthrough in terms of business only comes with becoming a master craftsman. After that, he can train others and run his own firm. There are also special rules or exceptions for senior journeymen. Given the economic pressures, the practice at this point is to say "If the capacity is there, they should be allowed to run their own firm."

A 2011 study of craft and trades development found that "between 2000 and 2007 ... the number of those employed (and subject to social insurance provisions) in the bakery trades has fallen by around 25,000. The number of the marginally employed is increasing, the number of those with a training in the profession is decreasing" (Scholz 2011, 4). Add to this the closure of smaller bakeries and an increase of chain stores. The president of the *Zentralverbandes des Bäckerhandwerkes*, Werner, estimates that about three hundred bakeries go out of business annually. This, in turn, reduces the power and effectiveness of the traditional craft association. The erosion of guilds as well as guild associations, in turn, leads to a weaker position in wage negotiations—which means that their ability to convincingly argue for wage stability in the bakery trades has weakened (Scholz 2011, 1). The result is increased wage undercutting, precarious employment at low wages, and an absence of standardized wages.

From this perspective, it will hopefully have become clear that though people in many parts of the world presumably love oven-fresh bread of all kinds of varieties, there is a real danger of losing daily access to this pleasure, which has little to do with UNESCO, but a great deal to do with the socioeconomic valuation of craft and handiwork. Bakeries are not the only type of craft or trade that have an increasingly hard time finding apprentices. But there are few enterprises where the discrepancies between consumption and the conditions of production are so intrinsically obvious as in bakeries.

It should be evident why German bakers seek cultural valorization through a nomination as Intangible Cultural Heritage. In the meantime, the bakers' federation is using a well-established strategy of increasing appreciation and esteem in an effort to ensure the future of its craft—not just in how it is carried out, but how it is remunerated. UNESCO tries, using its Convention on ICH, to support endangered cultural practices. Compared to the cultural goods thus far acknowledged in the area of foodstuffs, the German bakers have every reason to draw attention to their craft and the manifold products it brings forth.

The German Mission in the United States featured the bakers' crusade in an online article in October 2011—surely a good indication that the German bakers had solid reasons to hope that the German parliament is well on the way to ratifying the ICH convention (Germany. info 2011). And, indeed, in 2012, the German cabinet decided to do so; the decision was submitted to UNESCO in 2013. Since 2014, "German Bread Culture" has at least garnered a place on the German ICH register (Deutsche UNESCO Kommission 2017). Whether it will ever reach the UNESCO list remains to be seen—and whether the acclaim won through the German listing is improving the number of apprentices in the baker's profession is a matter of further, long-term inquiry.

This chapter previously appeared in R. Brulotte and M.A. di Giovine, eds. *Edible Identities: Exploring Food and Foodways as Cultural Heritage.* (Burlington, VT: Ashgate, 2014), 185–200.

1. Thanks go to student assistant Nora Kühnert, who helped in the research for this paper, Dr. Sven Mißling, international law, who assisted with retrieving documents from German parliamentary discussions, as well as to other colleagues and junior researchers in the Göttingen research group on the constitution of cultural property, supported by the German Research Foundation since 2008 (DFG FOR772). In addition to thanking the DFG for supporting our research endeavors, I also thank the Göttingen Lichtenberg Kolleg, which granted me an association during 2011–12, during which the paper was written. An earlier version of this paper was published in German with the title, "Unsere verdiente Wertschätzung gib uns heute: Gedanken zu Brot, Handwerk und globaler Cultural Governance," *Vokus* 21, no. 1 (2011). All translations from the German are my own.

2. Thanks for this inquiry to my student Sina Wohlgemuth. who carried out a practicum with the culture division of the German UNESCO office, and communicated this information to me via email on September 28, 2011.

3. "Traditional cultural expressions" (TCEs) and "traditional knowledge" (TK) are the technical term used within the World Intellectual Property Organization (WIPO) to refer to practices and knowledges designated as folklore within an American context.

4. The World Public Health Nutrition Organization (2011) announced the 2010 ICH nominations and linked them into world discourses on ecologically sound agriculture and the nutritional value of traditional cuisine in comparison to fast food.

5. UNESCO's general conference admitted Palestine as a member on October 31, 2011. The vote was understandably highly controversial, as Palestine is not a recognized, territorial state. On June 12, 2012, UNESCO conferred world heritage statues to the Church of Nativity and the Pilgrimage Route to Bethlehem, leading the USA and Israel to withhold UNESCO funding in 2012; cf. e.g., "US pulls UNESCO funding" (2011); on the Palestinian activities in the heritage realm prior to the controversial decision, see de Cesari (2010).

6. "Musealization" is a term coined by the German historian Wolfgang Zacharias (1990), subsequently taken on by German museum theorists such as Gottfried Korff or Martin Roth.

7. The Göttingen conference, "The Heritage Regime and the State" (Bendix, Eggert, and Peselmann 2012) examined precisely this confluence.

8. For a look at the ongoing process of compiling a possible ICH inventory in Switzerland, visit "Lebendige Traditionen" (2017); the website is still active and the list is currently being revised and will be published in 2018.

9. For example, on June 29, 2011, there was a proposal from a representative of the bipartisan governing coalition of CDU/CSU (Christlich Demokratische Union Deutschlands, Christlich-Soziale Union in Bayern) and FDP (Freie Demokratische Partei) to ratify the convention, published as Drucksache 17/Vorlagennummer 2415, AK6.

10. Actors interested in participating in the G.I. regime naturally also need to learn new bureaucratic procedures—see May (2016) for an excellent comparative case study on large and small-scale cheese producers engaged in cheese production with G.I. approval. Welz (2015) has pointed to the restructuring of cheese-production enterprises that can result due to requirements entailed in producing under G.I. regimes: making "European"

foods, gathered on the approved lists of the European Union, contributes also to the unmaking of small-scale food production in various European locales where producers cannot uphold the production standards imposed by European food hygiene and safety measures. For further case studies and reflections on the GI regime, see May, Sidali, Spiller, and Tschofen (2016).

11. Thanks to Kilian Bizer and other colleagues at the Volkswirtschaftliches Institut für Mittelstand und Handwerk (ifh) at the University of Göttingen for this depiction.

## REFERENCES

Asahi Shimbun. 2011. "Panel Wants UNESCO Recognition for Japanese Food." November 11. http://ajw.asahi.com/article/cool_japan/culture/AJ201111117101 (page deleted).
Bendix, Regina F., Aditya Eggert, and Arnika Peselmann, eds. 2012. *Heritage Regimes and the State.* Göttingen: Universitätsverlag Göttingen.
Bicskei, Marianna, Kilian Bizer, Katia L. Sidali, and Achim Spiller. 2012. "Reform Proposals on the Geographical Indications of the European Union for the Protection of Traditional Knowledge." *The WIPO Journal* 3 (2): 222–36.
Bramley, Cerkia, and Johann F. Kirsten. 2007. "Exploring the Economic Rationale for Protecting Geographic Indications in Agriculture." *Agrekom* 46 (1): 69–93.
Broccolini, Alessandra. 2012. "Intangible Cultural Heritage Scenarios within the Bureaucratic Italian State." In *Heritage Regimes and the State,* edited by Regina F. Bendix, Aditya Eggert, and Arnika Peselmann, 283–302. Göttingen: Universitätsverlag Göttingen.
Camporesi, Piero. 1989. *Bread of Dreams: Food and Fantasy in Early Modern Europe.* Translated by David Gentilcore. Chicago: University of Chicago Press.
De Cesari, Chiara. 2010. Creative Heritage: Palestinian Heritage NGOs and Defiant Arts of Government. *American Anthropologist* 112 (4): 625–37.
Deutsche UNESCO Kommission. 2017. "Deutsche Brotkultur." Accessed May 28. https://www.unesco.de/kultur/immaterielles-kulturerbe/bundesweites-verzeichnis/eintrag/deutsche-brotkultur.html.
Eiselen, Hermann, ed. 1995. *Brotkultur.* Cologne: Dumont.
Gentner, Carin. 1991. *Pumpernickel—das schwarze Brot der Westfalen.* Detmold: Westfälisches Freilichtmuseum.
Germany.info. 2011. "German Missions in the United States—German Bread." Accessed September 21. http://www.germany.info/Vertretung/usa/en/04__W__t__G/04/03/02/Feature__2.html.
Groth, Stefan. 2010. "Perspektiven der Differenzierung: Multiple Ausdeutungen von traditionellem Wissen indigener Gemeinschaften in WIPO Verhandlungen." In *Die Konstituierung von Cultural Property: Forschungsperspektiven,* edited by Regina Bendix, Kilian Bizer, and Stefan Groth, 177–95. Göttingen: Universitätsverlag Göttingen.
———. 2012. *Negotiating Tradition: The Pragmatics of International Deliberations on Cultural Property.* Göttingen: Universitätsverlag Göttingen.
Hafstein, Valdimar Tr. 2007. "Claiming Culture: Intangible Heritage Inc., Folklore©, Traditional Knowledge TM." In *Prädikat "Heritage." Wertschöpfungen aus kulturellen*

*Ressourcen*, edited by Dorothee Hemme, Markus Tauschek, and Regina Bendix, 75–100. Münster: LIT.

———. 2009. "Intangible Heritage as a List. From Masterpiece to Representation," In *Intangible Heritage*, edited by Laurajane Smith and Natsuko Akagawa, 93–111. London: Routledge.

Hegnes, Atle W. 2010. "Der Schutz der geographischen Nahrungsmittelherkunft in Norwegen als Übersetzungs- und Transformationsprozess." In *Essen in Europa. Kulturelle "Rückstände" in Nahrung und Körper*, edited by Susanne Bauer, Christine Bischof, Stephan Gabriel Haufe, Stefan Beck, Leonore Scholze-Irrlitz, 43–64. Bielefeld: transcript.

Kaiser, Hermann, and Helmut Ottenjann. 1989. *Das alltägliche Brot: über Schwarzbrot, Pumpernickel, Backhäuser und Grobbäcker. Ein geschichtlicher Abriss*. Cloppenburg: Museumsdorf Cloppenburg.

Kirshenblatt-Gimblett, Barbara. 1995. "Theorizing Heritage." *Ethnomusicology* 39: 367–80.

———. 2004. "Intangible Heritage as Metacultural Production." *Museum International* 56: 53–65.

Koellreuter, Isabel, and Nathalie Unternährer. 2006. *Brot und Stadt: Bäckerhandwerk und Brotkonsum in Basel vom Mittelalter bis zur Gegenwart*. Basel: Schwabe.

Korea.net. 2011. "Korea seeks UNESCO Intangible Cultural Heritage status for its cuisine." Accessed July 7. http://www.korea.net/NewsFocus/Culture/view?articleId=87649.

Kurin, Richard. 2004. "Safeguarding Intangible Cultural Heritage in the 2003 UNESCO Convention: A Critical Appraisal." *Museum International* 56 (1–2): 66–77.

Lebendige Traditionen. 2017. Accessed May 26. http://www.lebendige-traditionen.ch.

Matta, Raúl. 2016. "Food Incursions into Global Heritage: Peruvian Cuisine's Slippery Road to UNESCO." *Social Anthropology* 24 (3): 338–52.

May, Sarah. 2016. *Ausgezeichnet! Zur Konstituierung kulturellen Eigentums durch Geographische Herkunftsangaben*. Göttingen Studies in Cultural Property, vol. 11. Göttingen: Göttingen University Press.

May, Sarah, Katia Laura Sidali, Achim Spiller, and Bernhard Tschofen, eds. 2016. *Taste, Power, Tradition: Geographical Indications as Cultural Property. Göttingen Studies in Cultural Property*, vol. 10. Göttingen: University of Göttingen Press.

Oneindia. 2008. "Sarkozy wants UNESCO to honor French cuisine." February 24. Accessed January 30, 2016. http://news.oneindia.in/2008/02/24/sarkozy-unesco-honour-french-cuisine-1203851100.html (page discontinued).

Rassem, Mohammed. 1951. *Die Volkstumswissenschaft und der Etatismus*. Graz: Akademische Druck- und Verlagsanstalt.

Rogan, Bjarne. 2008. "The Troubled Past of European Ethnology. SIEF and International Cooperation from Prague to Derry." *Ethnologia Europaea*, 38 (1): 66–78.

Schmitt, Thomas M. 2011. *Cultural Governance. Zur Kulturgeographie des UNESCO-Welterberegimes*. Heidelberg: Franz Steiner.

———. 2014. *The World Heritage Regime*. London: Routledge.

Schmoll, Friedemann. 2009. *Die Vermessung der Kultur: Der "Atlas der deutschen Volkskunde" und die Deutsche Forschungsgemeinschaft 1928–1980*. Stuttgart: Steiner.

———. 2011. "Das Europa der deutschen Volkskunde. Skizzen zu Internationalisierungsprozessen in der Europäischen Ethnologie des 20. Jahrhunderts." In *Mobilitäten. Europa in Bewegung als Herausforderung kulturanalytischer Forschung*,

37. *Kongress der Deutschen Gesellschaft für Volkskunde*, edited by Reinhard Johler, Max Matter, and Sabine Zinn-Thomas, 425–34. Münster: Waxmann.

Scholz, Jendrik. 2011. "Strukturveränderungen, Tarifsituation, Einkommensentwicklung und gewerkschaftliche Revitalisierungsansätze im Handwerk." Unpublished IHF Report, July 28.

Simon, Michael. 2003. *"Volksmedizin" im frühen 20. Jahrhundert. Zum Quellenwert des Atlas der deutschen Volkskunde.* Mainz: Gesellschaft für Volkskunde in Rheinland-Pfalz e.V.

SPD. 2011. "SPD fordert: UNESCO-Konvention unverzüglich umsetzen." Press release 794/2011. June 30. http://www.spdfraktion.de/node/31813/pdf.

Tauschek, Markus. 2009. "Cultural Property as Strategy. The Carnival of Binche, the Creation of Cultural Heritage and Cultural Property." *Ethnologia Europaea*, 39 (2): 67–80.

Tornatore, Jean-Louis. 2012. "Anthropology's Pay Back: 'The Gastronomic Meal of the French.' The Ethnographic Elements of a Heritage Distinction." In *Heritage Regimes and the State*, edited by Regina F. Bendix, Aditya Eggert, and Arnika Peselmann, 341–65. Göttingen: Universitätsverlag Göttingen.

Tschofen, Bernhard. 2007. "Antreten, ablehnen, verwalten? Was der Heritage Boom den Kulturwissenschaften aufträgt." In *Prädikat "Heritage." Wertschöpfungen aus kulturellen Ressourcen*, edited by Dorothee Hemme, Markus Tauschek, and Regina Bendix, 19–32. Münster: LIT.

US pulls UNESCO funding. 2011. Accessed May 26, 2017. https://www.theguardian.com /world/2011/oct/31/unesco-backs-palestinian-membership.

Vates, Daniela. 2011. "UNESCO—Klöße als Weltkulturerbe." *Frankfurter Rundschau*, November 10.

Welz, Gisela. 2015. *European Products: Making and Unmaking Heritage in Cyprus.* New York: Berghahn.

Wiegelmann, Günter. 1965. "Das tägliche Brot: Brotgewürze." In *Atlas der deutschen Volkskunde. Neue Folge. Karten NF 44a-44d. Erläuterungen Band II*, edited by Matthias Zender, 251–75. Marburg: Elwert.

———. 1995. "Täglich Brot." In *Brotkultur*, edited by H. Eiselen, 231–43. Cologne: Dumont.

Wikipedia. 2011a. "Atlas der deutschen Volkskunde." Accessed November 28, 2016. http:// de.wikipedia.org/wiki/Atlas_der_deutschen_Volkskunde (page modified).

———. 2011b. "Protected Geographical Status." Accessed December 23, 2016. http:// en.wikipedia.org/wiki/Protected_Geographical_Status (page modified).

World Public Health Nutrition Organization. 2011. "UNESCO Cultural Heritage. The Intangibles." HP1, March. Accessed December 23, 2016. http://www.wphna.org /htdocs/2011_mar_hp1_unesco.htm.

Zacharias, Wolfgang, ed. 1990. *Zeitphänomen Musealisierung. Das Verschwinden der Gegenwart und die Konstruktion der Erinnerung.* Essen: Klartext-Verlagsgesellschaft.

Zentralverband des Deutschen Bäckerhandwerks e.V. 2011. "Vielfältiges Kulturerbe: Das Brotregister als Archiv der Deutschen Brotsorten." Press release 009/2011. March 21. http://www.brotkultur.de/fileadmin/downloads/PM_009_Brotregister.pdf.

# 11

⚜

## TK, TCE, and Co.: The Path from Culture as a Commons to a Resource for International Negotiation

The sixteenth session of the Intergovernmental Committee of the World Intellectual Property Organization is coming to a close in Geneva today, as I am presenting here.[1] Four days ago, around three hundred delegates from nation-states, international organizations, nongovernmental organizations (NGOs), and other types of groupings entered the imposing glass building that houses the World Intellectual Property Organization (WIPO). The delegates will have needed to show identification near the entrance, and proven that they have a right to be present; after that they will have gone to the large meeting room where during this week the so-called IGC for TK, GR, and TCE/Folklore met. Old hands who have been a part of this committee since it was founded in 2001 have no trouble with these acronyms: Traditional Knowledge (TK) and Traditional Cultural Expressions (TCE) are the terms that ultimately found general agreement in this negotiation body where UNESCO (United Nations Educational, Scientific, and Cultural Organization) discussions and terminology were also referred. The more problematic term "folklore" was used during initial sessions instead of TCE; while folklore was shifted to the back, the word still features in documents and discussions.

Genetic Resources (GR), placed between the two other terms that are clearly referencing culture, makes one pause at best at first glance. There are good reasons for enumerating genetic resources alongside traditional, culturally shaped knowledge and esthetic traditional forms of expressions.

WIPO founded this committee among other reasons, because the pharmaceutical industry's interest in traditional plant knowledge of indigenous groups has long led to international confrontations.[2] Plants are a genetic resource, and indigenous groups as well as nation states have for years pushed for measures against biopiracy and bioprospecting (see Hayden 2003; Robinson 2010). The goal is to hinder biotechnical and pharmaceutical firms and corporations from harvesting and patenting traditional knowledge without paying adequately for them. Models such as patent and profit sharing have slowly but surely gained more currency, as have suggestions to leave patents entirely in indigenous hands, and partnerships which seek joint training and research.

The IGC–the deliberating body with which I begin my reflections–usually meets for five days. Sometimes the meeting is prolonged to achieve more graspable progress, which in turn is used to convince the WIPO general assembly to extend the mandate of this IGC. Accompanied by simultaneous translation in six languages (WIPO 2017)—considered insufficient by many participants—delegates read prepared statements that generally have been vetted by their government or organization. The chair makes every effort to speed up what is a presentational modus that drags on interminably, and the most relevant discussions resulting in suggestions—or vigorous opposition—occur during breaks and meetings of regional groupings within WIPO as well as the IGC.[3] Arriving at internationally acceptable suggestions regarding copyright and patenting parameters for excerpts of traditional knowledge, genetic resources, and traditional cultural expressions may be the central concern of the IGC; but the established manner of diplomatic speaking and processing insure minimal progress and minimal results.[4]

During one of the sessions I documented, one of the Japanese delegates admonished in a mixture of patience and desperation, saying, "Content and definition of terms are still not there. We lack common understanding—hence it is premature to talk about legally binding principles."[5] And reliable definitions are needed to decide whether something can be placed into the IP realm, that is, whether rights for intellectual property may be demanded. Thus, the concluding, sixteen-page protocol of the tenth session of the 2006 IGC meeting contained an appendix that listed future work to be accomplished. The following point was mentioned first regarding TCE:

1. *Definition of traditional cultural expressions (TCEs)/expressions of folklore (EoF) that should be protected.*

And regarding TK, the open question list began with:

1. *Definition of traditional knowledge that should be protected.*
2. *Who should benefit from any such protection or who holds the rights to protectable traditional knowledge?*[6]

In the following, I would like to show how such an international committee, one tasked with shaping internationally supported agreements regulating legal (and thus economically viable) uses of components of culture, could come to be in the first place. I am particularly interested in what kind of economic motivations, political hopes and experiences, and perceptions and realizations about culture converge to bring forth such specialized activity at WIPO. Foundational is the acknowledgment that "excerpts" of culture or elements of culture come to be seen as possession or property. The questions cultural researchers need to pursue then, both ethnographically and historically, are what kinds of actors make efforts to declare cultural excerpts as cultural property, what contextual conditions encourage such a move, and what aspirations carry the initiative forward. My presentation will sketch a few building blocks for how one might tackle the constitution of cultural property. The phenomenon is inherently transcultural and transnational, and so benefits from the interdisciplinary input from economics and law.

OWNERSHIP: COMMONS AND PRIVATE PROPERTY

What is property? Philosophers have grappled deeply with this question since antiquity, while everyday life is punctuated with small occurrences illustrating property concerns and quarrels. Even just observing children at play yields insights into the haggling over building blocks, a toy car, or a cookie. More often than not, an adult arbiter is required, unless—as is sadly another human constant—"might makes right." In a survey of philosophical statements on questions of property, Andreas Eckl and Ernst Ludwig formulated in their introduction what seemed to them a consensus on property, from Plato to Habermas: "An external something is my property in the face of other people, if I can exclude them—with their consent—from the use of this something; when I can use it or use it up at my own discretion, perhaps with some constraints, and when I can sell or bequeath it.... A possession turns property through a generally sanctioned regulation between persons about the thing—the rule may be attributed to god, nature or the people. But even within this formal designation reside a thousand problems" (2005: 8–9, my translation).

What defines a person as able to own property is subject to context: in times and places of slavery, individuals were themselves the property of others and not permitted to own property themselves. Is a person always an individual, or can a corporation, a village, or an ethnic group be a proprietor? The philosophical approach to property and the questions generated through it have a strongly Western imprint. Property has, however, culturally specific definitions. What might be, in a European context, clearly identified as "yours" or "mine," could—for instance in a Balinese context—be considered a loan, actually owned by an ancestor to whom it will always belong. The reasoning driving WIPO's IGC described at the beginning of these remarks also derives from Western thought and practice, particularly concerning commerce, with power relations shifting from colonial to postcolonial times questioning Western assumptions in more and less subtle ways.

To meaningfully study—or participate in—a committee such as the IGC and its efforts to draft regulations for cultural property rights, the question of community ownership is one of the central problems. Folklore studies and related fields long assumed the "folk" or a "folk community" to be the social base of its inquiries before more differentiated, individualized formulations were introduced (Noyes 2016). Hence this question is at once troubling and crucial, as a holistic community concept, much like the long-abandoned holistic culture concept in social anthropology, has been overcome in scholarship but is alive and well in the public sphere. Dorothy Noyes addressed the issue of communal ownership under the title "The Judgement of Solomon," and reached—as the title indicates—a conclusion pointing to emotional interests and questions of responsibility and sacrifice. It is difficult to fix the borders of groups or communities for all times. An internationally negotiated circumscription with regard to what classifies as "community ownership" would most certainly generate a great deal of bureaucracy. From the perspective of cultural research such a new legal institution would not be tenable, given the fluid boundaries of community and the interests and agency of individuals who bring forth that very fluidity (Noyes 2006). The question of what might be property has also expanded from the material to the immaterial, conceptual, and mental realm. Today, intellectual property is subject to a legal codification with economic consequences. But before I turn to the entanglements of intellectual property, copyright, and patent law, and their relevance for cultural property, the commons as a form of shared ownership—as opposed to private property—needs to be explored.

With the invention of the computer and associated possibilities for programming and communication, the concept of the commons awakened from its already quite dusty resting place in Western societies and resurfaced in new vocabularies. Programmers often work in networks and are highly attuned to each other's potentials: they recognize each individual's dependency on the shared pool of ideas, and hence they vehemently and cleverly seek to prevent individual group members from attempting to separate their inventions from the common pool. Microsoft's Bill Gates and Apple's Steven Jobs—to mention two early, but not singular examples—cordoned off their ideas and turned them into profitable private property. The concept of an "intellectual commons" was introduced by theorists critical of such privatization, such as Lawrence Lessig (2004) or Volker Grassmuck (2004), and has found a following beyond the world of computing. The concept and practice of the "creative commons" has found a growing following, and is engendered by an ideology that considers knowledge, including its creative tentacles, the most important resource of humanity that must be made available for free, albeit not devoid of conditions.[7]

This present-day meaning of commons is in many ways akin to the commons of an agrarian and pastoral economy during a medieval and early modern period. "The commons" (in German *Allmende*) referred to large tracks of land and forests; in some parts of England this is the case to this day. Commons means "that which is common to all" and concerned communally used property: a village or a group of livestock-owning peasants, for instance, constituted the community that shared in the profit and burden of the property implied. Alpine pastures, fish-holding bodies of water, forests, or the fountain on the village square all could be a commons. In England, agricultural land or forest might be the property of a wealthy individual or a corporation; but those who shared in the labor of tending it had usage rights.

However, the commons do not belong to everybody. Those who jointly cultivate a commons, be this in clearing a hillside of trees and brush, cultivating it for grazing, or cleaning out a pond so as to improve it for the shared stock of fish, do so for their group or for a village community. A commons is thus ruled not only through economic but also social mechanisms of exclusion: excluding the neighboring village from using a part of the forest also strengthens a social group. In shaping, tending, and defending means of production, a commons community concretizes its sense of belonging together.[8] Alas, the commons is as strong or as frail as the bonds between its members. A well-functioning commons community wields social control effectively, and the economic benefit within it carries further rewards of social cohesion. Commons arrangements persisted next to emerging private property regimes, and new kinds of commons have reemerged in late modernity, but historically, economic arrangements based on commons slowly gave way to private property arrangements.[9] How could this happen? Not all individuals within a group stayed within the commons' socioeconomic bind—some moved away or changed their line of work; others proved more effective in husbanding these resources and were charged with administering them by the collective. Eventually, the group might allow an individual to make seasonal use of, for instance, the common land, and eventually, such use rights might be accorded to just one individual and his heirs. Such easily traceable historical transformations smoothed the path toward private property.

On such a backdrop we can easily recognize how difficult it is to devise a "cultural commons" within a transnational trade setting: it is difficult to develop the informal mechanisms of social control and trust that make a commons feasible in the first place. At the same time we can easily foresee what kind of opposition and rancor will arise when individuals within a group try to claim exclusive rights for the economic use of a shared cultural commons.

Turning to the rise of private property, one can observe an increasing refinement of monetized economies in early modernity, assisting the logic of private ownership. Even in agricultural settings, where the labor-intensive maintenance of pastures would favor shared labor and use rights, private property began to take hold. Actors within economic sectors such as crafts tended toward private property with even greater ease; goods made could be bartered or bought, and their value was determined on the quality of their make and the rarity or omnipresence of the materials used for their production.

But how did private property enter into the realm of the immaterial? The decisive move originated within the printers' guild in late seventeenth-century England. The *stationers company* was able to acquire, in 1662 under Charles II, the exclusive rights to works they had printed. Until then, everything printed tended to be copied and reprinted by others without permission. With the 1662 decision, printers received the sole right to distribute a given manuscript in printed form and print further copies of it. The rights to printing and distributing, and the rights of the author were thus separated, and the craftsmen, transforming the work into a book as a tradable, material object had the upper hand. In 1710, with the Statute of Queen Anne, the author as a creative actor producing ideas for distribution began to be a legally acknowledged person holding ownership rights to the work.[10] Poets, narrators, or singers had been conceptualized as drawing from a common pool: creativity. While many authors were known by name, the evanescent art of performance, adding the new to the familiar, was perhaps more resistant to monetization than a work printed as a book and circulating in countless copies of identical content. The emergence of the author as an identifiable individual has been the object of research for literary theorists, comparativists, and narratologists as much as for folklorists. The Greek epics, *Iliad* and *Odyssey*, and the figure of Homer may be the most discussed example. Even Milman Parry and Albert Lord's insights on oral formulaic composition (Lord 1960) were not able to completely dispel the belief in Homer as a singular, creative genius, although they had found twentieth-century epic singers whose craft showed a communally known narrative to be told and retold, with identifiable individual performance markers also shared plot configurations. Folklorists, as Valdimar Hafstein (2004) has expertly shown, toyed with the issue of individual genius versus collective creative origins over more than a century. As the concept of individual authorship solidified, as intellectual property took hold as a concept, shared expressive forms became its "worthless" opposite: "Folklore, in fact, came to be defined as such only with reference to norms of originality and ownership intrinsic to authorship and the intellectual property regime" (Hafstein 2014, 15).

Folklore's formation as a concept can be considered an addition to Charles Taylor's tracing of the emergence of selfhood as a defining aspect of Western modernity (1989). As authorship crystallized into a category, bestowing rights and remuneration to a creative individual, folklore, as a shared category, appears as a residual concept which, as Hafstein argued, "is brought into being through the formation of authorship in much the same way as the public domain was brought into being through the formation of intellectual property.... The formation of folklore as a discursive category is thus to be sought in the rise of possessive individualism in the expressive sphere" (Hafstein 2014, 15–6).

Media and distribution cannot be overlooked in this process. Individual recognition is bestowed also on an artist in performance, but claiming rights and remuneration for authorship was intrinsically tied to writing, printing, and distribution. These new technologies and practices bestowed materiality to intellectual property and made it, literally, graspable; they furthered the "outsourcing" of mentifacts from the commons, analogously to artifacts or land.

In the course of time, there are more aspects of culture where intellectual property claims are formulated; the question regarding who the owners might be increases in complexity. If asked, most people would likely argue that culture is a commons, carried and continuously and dynamically renewed by those who feel themselves to be part of a specific group. But how can one draw boundaries around such a group? Michael F. Brown's question *Who Owns Native Culture?* (2003) is everything but rhetorical; one cannot answer with a simple "the natives, of course." There is no natural relationship between a group and a group-specific culture. Relying on a closed, holistic concept of culture, anthropologists and folklorists have, in the past, contributed to such a misconception. Alas, there are no groups living in splendid isolation, and in a globalized, heterogeneous present, most individuals live in more than one cultural configuration. To realize one's individuality within one particular group is—in a free sociopolitical context—a decision and not the result of geographic, political, and religious constraint.[11] It is predominantly groups that find themselves in such situations where there is a desire and need to extract aspects of their culture from the global cultural commons and to see exclusive ownership rights for themselves. Brown has analyzed a number of such cases and shown that it is not just economic interests that generate such processes. Erich Kasten (2004), working on a set of Siberian cases, came to the conclusion that culture, understood as property, is part of a complex process of identity construction. In other words, when global players show interest in native, indigenous, even "local" cultures, this awakens a sense of endangerment of one's way of life among those who see themselves as targets. When shamanic practices, local musical expressions, or culinary delights are produced beyond their "place of origin"— however problematic this term may be—and when patents are claimed by "outsiders" who attach price tags to such practices, anxieties arise and "cultural identity" takes on a new, reflexive firmness. This happens particularly in groups who have few "natural" resources. Communities who wield rights over oil, coal, or other sources of energy will have few concerns about the predatory exploitation of cultural property. Groups who have experienced decades or centuries of colonial suppression or who live in marginal alpine or subpolar existence find themselves far more alarmed when confronted with excerpts of their culture on the world market, copyrighted by Simon and Garfunkel or marked as "made in China."[12]

Much as the idea of the commons, this situation, too, needs to be taken apart so as to better grasp the evolving layers leading to a desire for TK and TCE.

## LIVING CULTURE—HONORING CULTURE—OWNING CULTURE

As I have shown, removing creative language arts from the cultural commons and turning them into a potential intellectual property was closely intertwined with the invention of print. Print endowed language arts with an expanded materiality beyond what had been possible with handwritten manuscripts. It is thus likely that the concept of cultural property with attendant rights also developed alongside technical innovations. Not every step in this development is recognizable as clearly as is the case with copyright. Nonetheless I would argue that we can identify steps or stations from a reflexive awareness of having or "living" culture to "honoring" the specificity of such culture which then leads toward the propertization of cultural excerpts. Tracing these steps in turn allows for a better understanding of why the rights to TK, GR, and TCE have become a focus of international negotiations. Ethnographically working disciplines played a major, if largely inadvertent role, in this process.[13] Colonial and postcolonial entanglements and ensuing positions surface here as well, with consequences in states that themselves were neither colonizers nor colonized. The role of tourism's continued economic promise is enormous, as is that of a growing number of other industries and, more recently, agriculture.

But allow me to proceed step by step.

Forever dynamic and hence changing, cultures offer order and organization. We are born into particular families, milieus, and social classes, and from birth we are enculturated so as to internalize the systemic nature of living and moving within a given living environment by learning practices and acquiring what Pierre Bourdieu called habitus (1977). Some of these practices are small and structure everyday life and social relationships—making and eating breakfast, dressing in appropriate clothing, bidding goodnight before going to bed. Other practices are symbolically loaded and unfold perhaps in yearly rhythm. To be properly staged, they required complex and specialized knowledge, distributed among actors of divergent status and expertise. As long as there is no exposure to other options and patterns, cultural practices generally remain unquestioned—although there is, of course, cultural innovation also in environments that are more or less closed off; human beings are, after all, characterized by a propensity toward innovation and imitation. The greatest potential for change, or, conversely, for the strengthening of one's own patterns is the encounter with other ways of life and other systems of organization. This can be witnessed on the smallest of scales: a child visits a playmate and discovers that this other family eats ready-made meals instead of cooking themselves. At home, the child may report this enthusiastically, and his own family might decisively reject this with expressions like "home-cooked tastes better," or, alternatively, a discussion might ensue where the

child's family begins to consider whether ready-made meals might add
to the efficiency of the household. Whatever the outcome, the child has
gained consciousness that his family's practice is just one option among
several, and reflection regarding persistence and change, hybridity and
syncretism commence—questions, in short, that cultural research has
worked on continuously in areas such as generational continuity and rift,
migration, technological innovations, and so forth.

Let us look at this dynamic in an area documented and analyzed by
folklorists and anthropologist: an alpine, Swiss community performs a
New Year's Eve custom every year. During a trip to a valley in the neighboring country, Austria, to purchase new bells for this custom, a peasant
discovers that in this Austrian valley another year cycle event is celebrated
where beautiful masks are used as part of the disguise. He brings home
pictures of this other custom as well as samples of these factory-made
wax masks. The better part of custom bearers in his village begin to use
these masks, and over time, the masks replace the rags of fabric with holes
for the eyes that one had used before. This is what happened in a small
community in Eastern Switzerland in the late nineteenth and early twentieth century. The custom bearers of that time perceived this neither as
treason of their own festive practice nor as theft of an element from elsewhere. The village was becoming slightly wealthier and some participants
could afford an improvement of the New Year's Eve outfits (Bendix 1985).
However, toward the end of the twentieth century, the reflexive awareness
regarding elements of their traditional culture had grown immensely. A
museum was built, and along with the need and desire to mark their difference from neighboring villages (not faraway valleys!), a reflexive discourse
regarding the specificity of their own traditions as perhaps older or even
better has grown as well. While intangible heritage aspirations present
themselves as an option for the Swiss only since 2008 (with the ratification
of the UNESCO convention of 2003), and actors within the community
have thus far not made noises in direction of cultural property, the reflexive awareness necessary for isolating elements of culture and endowing
them with ideational as well as economic value is present.

Several factors contributed to this growing consciousness of having
attractive or desirable cultural practices. One of them is cultural research
which categorized and documented culture in recognizable genres from

ballads to recipes to proverbs to traditional sports, and returned it suitably interpreted and packaged as knowledge transfer back to societies. Technical innovations ranging from early print and graphics to (especially) photography were essential; they increased mutual acquaintance of customs and other cultural practices, and suggested innovative directions as well as limitations of aesthetic expression. In short, this kind of packaging and visualizing assisted in a general raising of awareness of what the WIPO IGC has come to call TCE, traditional cultural expression.

The multiplication and circulation of such materials on storage and distribution media has been increasing steadily and contributes to the relativizing of self-understood, habitual cultural practice. In cultural scholarship, the ever increasing dynamic of "own" and "other" has grown to be part of the research canon, with social and political dimensions of this oppositional construct remaining a constant focus. In addition, there is the emotional as much as economic ownership claim to one's "own cultural expressions" and there is the desire to also possess those of the "other." Cultural conflict connects with xenophobia and its aggressive tentacles, culture contact with xenophilia and its practices of imitation and appropriation (Cantwell 1993). These two tendencies in handling the culturally foreign are not diametrically opposed. They may be carried out differently—in attempts at war and annihilation and in strategies geared toward a loving incorporation (literally so in the xenophilic approach to exotic foods). But the political and economic motivations to engage in one or the other are more closely related than cultural research has admitted. Scholarship has been more interested in understanding how geopolitical boundaries came to be drawn between "us" and "them" (building on Barth 1969). Folklorists and cultural anthropologists have contributed a great deal toward understanding the political instrumentalization of both culture and cultural scholarship. This reflexive move has to be broadened to include the economic component which has contributed just as much to actors' alienation from their cultural particularity, thus assisting in their ability to affix a price to it.

"Honoring culture" is the significant step between "living culture" and "owning culture." It is not a new phenomenon, as monuments and their protection (from local to national) initiatives prepared minds and policy paths toward heritage regimes (Tschofen 2007). Since the early 1990s, many of us have contributed toward the scholarly boom in exploring

this phenomenon, as international, national and local interests to generate heritage permit such a close look at the construction of a venerable
aura around cultural excerpts. To protect a piece of material culture or
an immaterial cultural practice is simultaneously also a step toward sev-
ering oneself from it. Lived culture turns into observed, evaluated, and
compared culture. In examining the nomination process for such a piece
of culture to world heritage status, we can return to the issue of the cultural commons. A local cultural good is brought into this global cultural
commons. Yet the collective that shares the responsibility for this commons is far too heterogeneous to rely on mechanisms of social control.
Instead, we find conventions with rules and a network of tiered organizations maintaining a kind of policing and auditing of listed monuments
and practices. Though devised as a means to honor the rare, beautiful,
perhaps endangered aspects of culture, the heritage regime smooths the
path toward using culture and thus toward questions of ownership. Here,
the circle closes, for this is what the WIPO IGC is concerned with: who
are the owners of culture and which parts of culture are even conducive
to be claimed as property.

*****

The constitution of cultural property is—I hope to have shown—a complex process. Local circumstances and their historical trajectories can be
researched to show how they place themselves—or fail to do so—within
a global matrix, from diverse points of view. From the perspective of
economic anthropology, one can recognize the agile agency of individuals and groups to declare cultural excerpts and wholes as new, transna-
tionally marketable resources in a time when other types of resources
are getting scarce (Comaroff and Comaroff 2009). This opens up new
questions for research such as whether and if trade with culture changes
continental and intercontinental power structures. Legal anthropology
may want to acknowledge cultural property as an example that generates
questions regarding national and international legal systems and—as
ethnographic observations in sites such as WIPO negotiations illustrate—begin to examine the generally unquestioned habits and habitus
of actors in the legal, diplomatic realm. Legal systems seek to structure

and regulate social, cultural, political, and economic relationship. The IGC described at the beginning of this talk contributes to the emergence of further transnational legal systems. From our research group's observations up to 2014, the WIPO IGC process is clearly dominated by a Western, juridical habitus (not least because legal training and lawyerly performance in the Global South were also introduced during colonial occupation). Naturally, native speech patterns have been woven into this legacy, yet it is hard not to see them as chastened by the entire nature of the UN-apparatus. Legal practices are subject to cultural shaping and dynamics as much as any other human practice on this planet, and hence they warrant research by cultural scholars interested in transnational developments and conflicts (cf., Dundes 2012). Before the turn toward an anthropology of policy since the mid-1990s (Shore and Wright 2011), and attendant ethnographic work on the formation and implementation of policy, accompanied by many branches of the bureaucratic apparatus, folklorists and cultural anthropologists (at least in German-speaking Europe) researched historical legal practices. Jacob Grimm documented "legal antiquities" (*Rechtsalterthümer*, Grimm 1828) and others as well pursued this interest in large part to understand earlier legal systems—including the commons (cf., Groth 2013). Remnants of festive events and language were found to be gateways toward piecing together legal history. There was and remains little research that looks at the present-day legal profession from the perspective of occupational culture, habitual speech, and writing practices, and their impact on social life—even though decisions with profound impact on social and cultural life are constantly generated by and interpreted through legal professionals. Transnational legal agreements of the type negotiated in WIPO's IGC on TK, GR, and TCE have a transnational impact. Thus, as scholars in ethnographically based fields, we must take up the challenge to "unlock" such diplomatic stages and to bring our kind of knowledge into the debate.

**Appendix:** The list of questions to be urgently addressed by the IGC at the 2006 meeting. The document "wipo_grtkf_ic_10_decisions.doc" is in the author's possession; like all IGC documents, it is also available on the internet portal of WIPO (2017).

## TRADITIONAL CULTURAL EXPRESSIONS/ EXPRESSIONS OF FOLKLORE ISSUES

1. Definition of traditional cultural expressions (TCEs)/expressions of folklore (EoF) that should be protected.
2. Who should benefit from any such protection or who holds the rights to protectable TCEs/EoF?
3. What objective is sought to be achieved through according intellectual property protection (economic rights, moral rights)?
4. What forms of behavior in relation to the protectable TCEs/EoF should be considered unacceptable/illegal?
5. Should there be any exceptions or limitations to rights attaching to protectable TCEs/EoF?
6. For how long should protection be accorded?
7. To what extent do existing IPRs [intellectual property rights] already afford protection? What gaps need to be filled?
8. What sanctions or penalties should apply to behavior or acts considered to [sic] unacceptable/illegal?
9. Which issues should be dealt with internationally and which nationally, or what division should be made between international regulation and national regulation?
10. How should foreign rights holders/beneficiaries be treated?

## TRADITIONAL KNOWLEDGE ISSUES

1. Definition of traditional knowledge that should be protected.
2. Who should benefit from any such protection or who hold the rights to protectable traditional knowledge?
3. What objective is sought to be achieved through according intellectual property protection (economic rights, moral rights)?
4. What forms of behavior in relation to the protectable traditional knowledge should be considered unacceptable/illegal?
5. Should there be any exceptions or limitations to rights attaching to protectable traditional knowledge?

6. For how long should protection be accorded?
7. To what extent do existing IPRs already afford protection? What gaps need to be filled?
8. What sanctions or penalties should apply to behavior or acts considered unacceptable/illegal?
9. Which issues should be dealt with internationally and which nationally, or what division should be made between international regulation and national regulation?
10. How should foreign rights holders/beneficiaries be treated?

NOTES

This chapter, published for the first time in this volume, was originally a talk presented in May 2010 in German at the Department of European Ethnology, at the University of Kiel, Germany. I have opted to translate it in the tone of an oral presentation in the hope that the issues presented might appeal to a broader readership—especially given that the cultural property conundrums are relevant to actors beyond the fields of cultural research.

1. In June 2017, as I am translating this talk, the IGC at WIPO is holding its thirty-fourth meeting.

2. The Convention of Biological Diversity, open after considerable negotiation in 1992 for signatories, and meeting for a first conference in 1994, is another site of international efforts concerning, among other things, questions of indigenous knowledge; WIPO is more directly concerned with ownership rights.

3. For an excellent analysis of the nature of negotiations in the IGC, see Groth (2012).

4. From an economic perspective, the minimal results are desirable inasmuch as the progress toward a potentially less profitable solution for Western stakeholders is delayed (Bizer, Gubaydulina, and Lankau 2010).

5. Author's field notes from November 11 to December 12, 2006.

6. Compare the appendix at the end of this chapter for the full list of questions circulated in the WIPO IGC at that session.

7. Compare Creative Commons. Accessed June 21, 2017. https://creativecommons.org/.

8. Compare Groth (2013) for a more comprehensive discussion of the commons and its ramifications for questions of cultural property.

9. Elinor Ostrom won the Nobel Prize in particular for her work on economic governance, especially the commons; in research which remained close to actors engaged in resource management based on a commons arrangement, she demonstrated that what could be shown to be successful in practice could also work in theory; while methodologically different from how ethnographers have approached commons arrangements (cf., Groth 2013), Ostrom's major study of 1990 is a work of high relevance for folklorists and anthropologists seeking support for practiced commons logics encountered in the field and applicable for new initiatives.

10. Lauer (2002) recounts the advent of authorial copyright from the perspective of media of distribution.

11. Writing in 2017, though, I am quick to acknowledge the disturbing, populist desire to withdraw into homogeneous cultural constructs and to negate the beauties and complications of choices.

12. Hafstein (2007) illustrates the additional complexities of "El Condor Pasa"—for its "communal origin" turns out to be filtered through a series of additional facets.

13. Many disciplines with ethnographic foci conceive of themselves as merely observing with an aim to foster understanding without influencing the systems they work on—an issue that leads time and again to rifts between "purely academic" and applied, public, as well as action-oriented branches of such disciplines. Kirshenblatt-Gimblett thematized this in 1998 under the heading "Mistaken Dichotomies," summarizing a lingering US-debate, and similar debates have taken and continue to take place in many other national and international contexts. This is not the place to pursue this history further, but it explains why many cultural researchers confront what is happening at the WIPO IGC with a mixture of desperation and anger, not least because they witness actors trained in normative fields such as law, economics, or public policy who handle issues of culture without the deference encoded in positions of noninvolvement.

## REFERENCES

Barth, Fredrik. 1969. *Ethnic Groups and Boundaries*. London: Allen & Unwin.
Bendix, Regina. 1985. *Progress and Nostalgia. Silvesterklausen in Urnäsch*. Berkeley: University of California Press.
Bizer, Kilian, Zulia Gubaydulina, and Matthias Lankau. 2010. "Die verborgene Effektivität minimaler Resultate." In *Die Konstituierung von Cultural Property*, Göttingen Studies in Cultural Property, vol. 1, edited by R. Bendix, K. Bizer, and S. Groth. 197–216. Göttingen: Universitätsverlag Göttingen.
Bourdieu, Pierre. 1977. *Outline of a Theory of Practice*. Cambridge: Cambridge University Press.
Cantwell, Robert. 1993. *Ethnomimesis. Folklife and the Representation of Culture*. Chapel Hill: University of North Carolina Press.
Comaroff, John and Jean Comaroff. 2008. *Ethnicity Inc*. Chicago: University of Chicago Press.
Dundes, Alison Renteln. 2012. "Folklore: Legal and Constitutional Power." In *A Companion to Folklore*, edited by R. Bendix and Galit Hasan-Rokem, 537–554. Oxford: Wiley Blackwell.
Eckl, Andreas and Bernd Ludwig, eds. 2005. *Was ist Eigentum? Philosophische Eigentumstheorien von Platon bis Habermas*. München: Beck.
Grimm, Jacob. 1828. *Deutsche Rechtsalterthümer*. Göttingen: Dieterich.
Grassmuck, Volker. 2004. *Freie Software: Zwischen Privat- und Gemeineigentum*. Bonn: Bundeszentrale für politische Bildung.
Groth, Stefan, 2012. *Negotiating Tradition. The Pragmatics of International Deliberations on Cultural Property*. Göttingen Studies in Cultural Property, vol. 4. Göttingen: Universitätsverlag Göttingen.
———2013. "Allmendgemeinschaften und Cultural Commons in der Disskussion um kulturelles Eigentum." In *Kultur_Kultur. Denken, Forschen, Darstellen*, edited by R. Johler, C. Marchetti, B. Tschofen, and C. Weith, 59–65. Münster: Waxmann.

Hafstein, Valdimar. 2004. "The Politics of Origins: Collective Creation Revisited." *Journal of American Folklore* 117: 300–15.

———. 2007. "Claiming Culture: Intangible Heritage Inc., Folklore ©, Traditional Knowledge™." In *Prädikat Heritage*, edited by D. Hemme, M. Tauschek, and R. Bendix, 75–100. Berlin: LIT.

———. 2014. "The Constant Muse: Copyright and Creative Agency." *Narrative Culture* 1 (1): 9–48.

Hayden, Cori. 2003. "From Karet to Market: Bioprospecting's Idioms of Inclusion." *American Ethnologist* 30 (3): 359–71.

Kirshenblatt-Gimblett, Barbara. 1988. "Mistaken Dichotomies." *Journal of American Folklore* 101 (4000): 140–55.

Lauer, Gerhard. 2002. "Offene und geschlossene Autorschaft. Medien, Recht und der Topos von der Geburt des Autors im 18. Jahrhundert." In *Autorschaft. Positionen und Revisionen*, edited by H. Detering, 461–78. Stuttgart: Metzler.

Lessig, Lawrence. 2004. *Free Culture. The Nature and Future of Creativity*. New York: Penguin Press.

Lord, Albert. 1060. *The Singer of Tales*. Cambridge, MA: Harvard University Press.

Ostrom, Elinor. 1990. *Governing the Commons: The Evolution of Institutions for Collective Action*. Cambridge: Cambridge University Press.

Robinson, Daniel F. 2010. *Confronting Biopiracy: Challenges, Cases, and International Debates*. London: Earthscan.

Shore, Cris and Susan Wright. 2011. "Conceptualizing Policy: Technologies of Governance and the Politics of Visibility." In *Policy Worlds. Anthropology and the Analysis of Contemporary Power*, edited by C. Shore, S. Wright, and D. Però, 1–25. New York: Berghahn.

Taylor, Charles. 1989. *Sources of the Self: The Making of Modern Identity*. Cambridge: Cambridge University Press.

Tschofen, Bernhard. 2007. "Antreten, ablehnen, verwalten? Was der Heritage-Boom den Kulturwissenschaften aufträgt." In *Prädikat Heritage*, edited by D. Hemme, M. Tauschek, and R. Bendix, 19–32. Berlin: LIT.

WIPO. 2016. World Intellectual Property Organization. Accessed June 17, 2017. http://www.wipo.int/tk/en/igc/.

# 12

*Patronage and Preservation: Heritage Paradigms and Their Impact on Supporting "Good Culture"*

## INTRODUCTION

The effort of UNESCO (United Nations Educational, Scientific and Cultural Organizations) to empower communities focuses on heritage holders. In emphasizing the need to involve such communities in heritage nominations, UNESCO lately draws attention to what I will loosely (and incorrectly) call communities of patrons—that is, individuals and groups who spearhead preservationist endeavors. They are, of course, generally not acting as a community, but rather are driven by a complex mixture of ideological, social, and economic motivations. Numerous case studies illustrate how individual actors or actor groups from within and/or outside of a community find a particular type of heritage worthy of preservation and set in motion a nomination process. Such actors serve as patrons, or intermediaries, for a community, assisting with the work of getting a particular heritage onto the world stage—a task that generally requires considerable resources. The term patron, in turn, provides a means to link the heritage-complex with the broader framework of sponsoring culture and the arts. Patronage (much as heritage-making) is an interventionist practice, and UNESCO, though economically quite impotent, is a well-positioned and globally recognizable icon that can alert financially mightier patrons to the goals of preservation. Patronage has a long history that helps to place the valorization processes at the heart of heritage-making within a broader context: the interdependence of (not only) financial support, and the sociocultural transformation of culture's value.

Sponsorship of arts and cultural expressions is by necessity selective and has thus brought forth and solidified hierarchies in what is considered "good culture" within a polity. It is worth asking how such mechanisms of selecting and supporting cultural practices and products are affected by the heritage regime: How do older, established regimes of cultural valorization figure in the present?[1] Heritage dynamics thus encourage one to ask what causes, motivates, and legitimates bestowing value on a spectrum of cultural expressions. How do broader sociopolitical and spatial shifts contribute to slow but perceptible changes in seemingly firmly established systems of valorization? Although the heritage regime fosters exclusivity—as not all nominations can be successful—heritage-making on the global level, as initiated by UNESCO, has brought some confusion or, more neutrally put, movement into historically established canons from what is termed "high" to "vernacular" arts. This may—as is suggested in the following—contribute to a successive flattening of distinctions based on aesthetic hierarchies so typical of earlier eras of what James Clifford has termed the "art-culture system," in and out of which indigenous arts may also travel (Clifford 1988, 224). The heritage regime renders cultural expressions globally into a kind of "aesthetic commons" that encompasses all social groups. While emphasizing community provenience, it temporarily obfuscates distinctions of class, ethnicity, and wealth out of which localized scales ranging from the vernacular to high art articulate(d) themselves. Heritage-eats-the-arts-system or heritage-levels-the-playing-field might be a description for the dynamic of support and sponsorship of expressive forms that motivated particularly the 2003 Convention honoring Intangible Cultural Heritage. UNESCO's heritage division is, after all, an effort not just to valorize but also to democratize the appreciation of world arts. This equalizing thrust in recognition brings about a seeming randomness in the politics and sponsorship of aesthetic taste—though perhaps randomness, chance, or luck were variables in how patronage of the arts came about in earlier times as well.

Heritage regimes in their evermore comprehensive anchoring are a particularly suitable place to reflect on how culture, associated with what

UNESCO terms communities, accrues value. Community can refer to
many different types of social groupings that actively practice or generate such culture at a particular moment in history.[2] As a complex and
costly administrative endeavor, UNESCO's various heritage lists assem-
ble excerpts of culture, intangible and rendered tangible, that may have
been valued at particular times with terms such as courtly culture or high
culture, folk or traditional or ethnic culture, and popular culture. Indeed,
the nomination texts posted by UNESCO will often use such adjectives
to refer to the "community" among whom a particular heritage circulates:
the royal ballet of Cambodia, inscribed in 2008, "has been closely associated with the Khmer court for over one thousand years" (UNESCO 2014);
inscribed in the same year, Guatemala's Rabinal Achí dance-drama tradition "is a dynastic Maya drama which developed in the fifteenth century,
and is a rare example of preserved pre-Hispanic traditions" (UNESCO
2014). Chovqan, a traditional horse-riding game in Azerbaijan, was
inscribed in 2013 for its strengthening of "feelings of identity rooted in
nomadic culture" (UNESCO 2014). From royal and dynastic to nomadic,
many such examples could easily be found in successful as well as failed
nomination dossiers. They illustrate location-specific connotations of culture valued for its group or class association.

The worldwide exhibition platform that is constituted by UNESCO's
lists broadens the privileges—or lack thereof—associated with cultural
manifestations in a local, historically circumscribed setting with the label
"of universal value." Valdimar Hafstein (2009, 102–14) traces in the instrument of heritage lists a transformation from exceptionality—as captured
in the earlier UNESCO designation "master piece"—to a representation
where all that is inscribed on the list is equally valuable, equally beautiful, and equally appreciated. The selection process also involves regional,
national—and finally—global competition, and one could argue that the
winners and losers in this process bring forth new hierarchies (Bendix,
Eggert, and Peselmann 2012, 18). However, the competition is informed by
rules and disciplined by concrete as well as diffuse guidelines, generating
new value-setting practices and an extensive paper trail. Together, this
makes for a pedagogy of how to value culture, and one can thus perceive
equally well UNESCO's heritage-making as a training ground for equalizing appreciation, restoration, and conservation of culture.

In the actual settings of cultural practice, the revalorizing processes commence as part of the heritage nomination and continue with successful inscriptions or placements on the heritage list. Whether it be safeguarding, protecting or even shielding from view, exhibiting, marketing, or a combination of some of the above, claiming and keeping heritage status carries a cost. Public and private sponsoring or patronage is thus essential to maintain the goals set out in a nomination file—and the question is how public institutions and private donors make up their mind regarding the financial support of heritage initiatives next to countless other local, regional, and national art and culture initiatives requesting funds to preserve, maintain, and/or innovate aesthetic expressions.

In this chapter, I am interested in the power of sponsorship or patronage in shaping the value of selected cultural practices and objects and thus seek to place the dynamics of heritage valuation and valorization into the broader framework of funding arts and culture. Value is measured idealistically and ideologically, and social as well as aesthetic, moral, and political contexts and convictions contribute to value judgments. But within a marketplace where such value has to endure, there is the need for capital—hence sponsorship or patronage. I begin with two examples illustrating what I term diversifying of value distinctions. Markets for art and entertainment as well as consumers contribute to a shift in the distinctions of high and low, arcane and popular cultures. From there I will turn to a brief characterization of patronage's history. These first two sections provide a basis for assessing the breadth of actors and groups seeking sponsorship and the mechanisms at play to assess value and decide for allocating funds. The contribution then concludes with observations on the heritage regime's potential impact on communities of sponsors.

## DIVERSIFYING VALUE SCALES: TWO EXAMPLES

After UNESCO's decision to welcome the "Gastronomic Meal of the French" onto the List of Intangible Cultural Heritage in 2010, the German weekly *Die Zeit* published this headline: "The World as Museum." The subtitle read "UNESCO now also protects French cuisine. Perhaps our life in its totality should become world cultural heritage?" (November 25, 2010).

Journalist Ijoma Mangold observed with some irony how nations and communities eagerly construct lists from healing knowledge and art to endangered dialects. To him, the bureaucratic ministrations of UNESCO transformed "everything that makes life worth living" and all things that "have their own dignity" (November 25, 2010) into a big mail-order catalog at the ratio of one-to-one. Mangold invoked the catalog distributed by Manufactum, a German mail-order business carrying the slogan "they are still available, the good old things" (cf., Manufactum 2016). He connects heritage-making with marketing cultural expressions to those with both upper-class tastes and a hankering for things traditional and handmade. Upper-class fascination with the handmade and traditional has, of course, a thick history since the nineteenth century. It has contributed to the foundation of museums and academic disciplines preoccupied with documenting and collecting the "old way of life," and is intertwined with earlier regimes of cultural protection (Bendix, Eggert, and Peselmann 2012, 17–18).[3] Bauman and Briggs (2003) have rightly argued that in the effort to point to folk and, later, ethnic difference, elite discourse has contributed to and solidified social and political inequality. Journalist Mangold, however, points to perceptible changes: The selection of difference from folk to ethnic to indigenous, marginal, aboriginal, subcultural, and so forth has gotten so broad, that the categories congeal into a vast sameness. Mangold is perhaps not just frustrated with the stranglehold of the heritage paradigm, but with the shifting ground of distinctions and the lack of clarity as to who has the authority, standing, and expertise to make pronouncements over canons of cultural expressions.

A second example is manifest in movie theaters all over the world. Since 2006, New York's Metropolitan Opera has offered live broadcasts of its performances in movie theaters. In the case of the midsize German city of Göttingen, a ticket costs between twenty-nine and thirty-five euros per showing, with a wardrobe service provided (but of course not for the movies that show simultaneously in this cinema complex). During the intermission, champagne and wine, juice, and fresh pretzels are on offer for the opera viewers who can, of course, also amble further down the hall and purchase popcorn, ice cream, and soda. A cartoon in the New Yorker captured the hybridization of entertainments and associated foods perfectly: A hotdog seller marches through the rows of seats during an opera performance, and one of the viewers says to his female companion: "There's no frank like an opera frank."[4] The hotdog is making its way from the sports stadium to the plush theater, the opera is spreading into the palace of popcorn. What was once considered a clear movement up and down the social ladder appears more like an increasingly exchangeable smorgasbord of choices—though certainly more so for those who can afford it than those who are limited in their budgets and mobility. Based on empirical evidence from the late 1950s to 1960s, Pierre Bourdieu (1984) asserted a clear association of taste and lifestyle with economic, cultural, and social capital. In the intervening decades, economic disparities may have grown larger, but cultural taste may no longer be a means to measure them. In the course of the past years, other beleaguered concert halls and symphonies, as well as ballet companies and even museums have taken to offering shows via movie theaters. They seek to broaden their audience and earnings, but they also fight to maintain a place among the plethora of entertainment available across media and screens ranging from televisions to computers, tablets to cell phones. Live broadcasts have been part and parcel of radio programs practically since the first radios were developed, and a further line of argument could be introduced on the role of mass media and media technology in bringing about a globalized, perhaps more democratic appreciation of the arts, and a corresponding lessening of the hold of historically grown canons of high culture.[5] Here, I will stay with the role sponsorship plays in the overall dynamic of establishing and shifting values accorded to cultural expressions. I used opera along with ballet and art museums as key examples of high culture that, until the early twentieth century, were firmly entrenched in upper-class taste, but now raise revenue in the palaces of popular culture.[6] Even the patrons and sponsors of the capitalist era—oil and car companies—are not giving sufficiently to maintain the art form. Apparently, the community of patrons has had increasing reason to give not simply to individual artists or institutions but to the preservation of all kinds of heritages. In the process, high cultural art forms such as opera and ballet increasingly mutate into endangered heritage—historically grounded art forms in search of resources and audiences.

These two quite different examples offer opportunity to reflect on what kinds of broader political and economic transformations might be discernible in the overwhelming drive to select and protect, evident in the heritage dynamic. Aesthetic productions such as opera and ballet could once rely on patrons; heritage-making is one among several forces pushing these elite arts to seek alternate forms of economic support and to simultaneously participate in the competition for patrimonial status.[7] In most states, from the federal down to regional and local levels, the public budget for "arts and culture" is small to nothing. Work and social services, defense, traffic, public works and urban development, health, education, and research are the top items in a state budget; the arts must always seek private support to sustain themselves. A category such as heritage brings further competition as well as confusion: actors can appeal to artistic, enriching qualities in their support of heritage both in its material and immaterial guise. In addition, however, they can invoke the significance of regional, national, and global reach and thus emphasize the political relevance of nominating and maintaining heritage—and both are costly. Heritage promoters thus increase the competition for scarce public and volatile private sponsorship.

## PATRONAGE—ITS IMPACT ON AESTHETIC VALUE AND TASTE

Gaius Cilnius Maecenas lived in the first century BC, and was so prominent, both as advisor to Augustus and as sponsor of the arts, that to this day, his name has become a term for private sponsorship. He extended patronage to young artists such as Vergil or Horace, and given his political association, such patronage also offered a certain degree of closeness to the ruling class. Lorenzo de Medici, unfolding his power in the second half of the fifteenth century, combined indirect influence or sponsorship in politics with patronage of artists. During his time, artists such as Leonardo da Vinci gave of their skill and vision to Florence. The flourishing of the arts through the Medici court has received art historical attention early on—not least because of the republican rather than monarchal political base (Thomas 2000). Examining Giotto's life and work two centuries prior, Julian Gardner (2011) recognizes in the painter's work evidence of the interaction between Giotto and different sets of patrons he served.

One could mention countless other cases where, through the patronage of architects, sculptors, musicians, ballet masters, and so forth, a shaping took place of the built environment, artistic performance traditions, and the public sphere as it is marked by artistry at large.[8] The power of patrons to imprint their aesthetic preferences on a given socio-spatial realm accounts for the emergence of "Culture" with a capital C and for the long-lasting distinctions between high and low arts. The intermeshing of artists and patrons was already recognized in the nineteenth century as an important area of study, when scholars called for systematic attention to how tastes in art and architecture took shape through the will and resources of patrons (McDonald 1973, 1). There was always a considerable impact on communities through the predilections of individual patrons. The cityscapes of Florence and Agra, Bangkok and Sydney would not be the same without the influential resources and tastes of particular patrons and investors. In an extension of UNESCO language, one could argue that generations of inhabitants of such cities have been enculturated into specific spatial-artistic experiences and continue to live with the economic opportunities deriving from the relationships of medieval to early modern patrons, colonial to postcolonial patrons, and their preferred artists.[9]

Earlier histories of patronage often focus on particular individuals and eras, intrigued by the power and importance of collecting, especially during times before there were museums and "systematic state-based custodianship of art" (Sachs 1971, 9). Individual patrons occasionally had close relationships to individual artists and in the process, gave opportunity to the unfolding of a given artist's creativity, a pattern well established for medieval court poets encouraged to praise their benefactors' deeds (Burgess 1981). However, what is most relevant for establishing a comparative view from earlier forms of patronage to present day mixtures of patrons, sponsors, and public support, is insight into the sociopolitical dynamic that engenders the flowering of particular types of arts and culture. In his scrutiny of cases of medieval literary patronage, William C. McDonald concludes that "one of the most important forms patronage may take is the creation of an atmosphere conducive to a literary flowering. This may be a time of relative calm ..., but can also be an era of struggle and feverish political activity" (1973, 193). As of the second half of the twentieth century, we have been living in an atmosphere conducive to "heritage flowering" with UNESCO mobilizing rhetorical conviction to engender public and private support to nominate, protect, and preserve.

Studies scrutinizing particular patronage cases from early modernity up to the twentieth century find an increase in the intertwining of individual patrons and state or communal leadership in the channeling of donations for aesthetic projects. Representatives of a growing bourgeoisie, for instance in Germany, formed art associations and founded museums; they engaged jointly and for the benefit of civil society in sponsorship—which simultaneously also enhanced their personal status (Frey 1999). Stephen Pielhoff (2007, 29) goes as far as to accord the most powerful role to intermediaries—individuals who convinced potential patrons to bestow gifts particularly for urban architectural and monumental projects; here, the recognition bestowed on artists through patronage found its parallel in the recognition sought by patrons for their gifts to civil society.[10] Pielhoff's attention to historical and political contexts helps to account not just for successes and failures in urban aesthetic projects, but also for different models in the negotiation and mixing of private patronage and public resources that emerge evermore strongly in the nineteenth and twentieth centuries. In the course of time, legal parameters further shaped and limited not just the extent of giving but also constrained individual patrons in exerting their taste and might (Mai and Paret 1993).

This dynamic, of course, concerns primarily tangible artifacts, but I would argue that the long history of living amongst buildings and sculptures generated in feudal and monarchal systems brought forth intangible sentiment, a sense of appreciation that would be necessary to extend the impact of private patronage into public preservation and restoration. The passage from a monarchal to a bourgeois-capitalist system also gave little time for reflection on what it means to preserve structures built through agents of former regimes. The bourgeois artistic taste seamlessly incorporated layers of older aesthetics. Communism broke this lineage, and did not accept past C Culture as natural heritage. The horror that Western states felt at the destruction of tsarist and Christian orthodox edifices and arts during the Soviet era exemplifies, however, some of the taken-for-granted heritage status of such works; the destruction of many Soviet-era sculptures and edifices post-1989 in turn spells out the displeasure at state sponsored, communist art and heritage construction, and affirms the apparent attraction of noncommunal, patronage-sponsored artistry within the capitalist realm. A peculiar case in point is the long discussion in reunited Berlin regarding the reconstruction of the city castle, damaged during WWII, torn down during the GDR era, replaced by the Palace of the Republic (a communist administrative building), which in turn, was torn down in 2007–08; now the city plans to reconstruct the castle—a discursive battle that was analyzed trenchantly by Beate Binder (2009).[11]

This brief historical sketch aimed to illustrate how preservation and protection firmed up incrementally to become a further goal for sponsorship or patronage. The preservationist impulse began with the maintenance of material culture of the upper classes, before it turned toward the preservation of folk culture through the efforts of homeland protection associations, the founding of open-air museums and similar initiatives.[12] As the value of past cultural manifestations increased, patrons had more opportunities to decide which aesthetic forms they wished to support: those representing the creativity and aesthetics of the past or those of the present and future. Naturally, this was the result of major shifts in political systems. Still, one might give some thought to understanding why preservation is so powerful an impulse within democracies, why its citizens are eager to maintain—indeed pay for the maintenance of—the splendors of their former suppressors.[13] If patrons were once publicly known, individual actors putting their imprint on a city or region, at present we face a more complex structuring of the financing of the arts. On the one hand, artists are expected to prove themselves in the market for creative goods. On the other hand, there are also generally limited public funds and foundations engaged in more or less competitive ways of selecting whom and what they will support. But there are also still patrons, from individuals to institutions such as banks or industries, that bestow some of their capital on the arts, potentially profiting in the process from a tax write-off (or forming a tax-exempt foundation for this very purpose). Artists in turn may opt to form associations that accept charitable donations—granting the donors tax write-offs for their generosity. Thus, there are certainly more actors involved in supporting and shaping a public sphere of art, as well as more democratic possibilities for individuals of widely divergent income and social status to participate in such sponsorship. Patronage can safely be called a cultural practice, and research on shifts in art patronage, sponsorship, and investment both historically and comparatively across the globe would seem to be an open field. It would certainly assist in understanding the place that safeguarding heritage occupies within this dynamic. It would also clarify the shifts in communities of patrons over time and from local to global settings and networks.

## GROWING CHOICES FOR SPONSORSHIP

The documentation and preservation of a cultural category such as Intangible Cultural Heritage offers opportunities for patronage or sponsorship beyond historically established and continually practiced types of arts. Heritage has been added into the spectrum of what is considered "valuable culture," and hence also culture worthy of investment. In English language discourse, highly valued art forms have been referred to, as stated earlier, as Culture with a capital C, tracing their provenience often to royal courts and accruing value not least from a long history of upper-class or bourgeois appreciation in contrast to vernacular, lower-class arts.[14] As public financial support for cultural activity through taxation has been notoriously low, the need to find patrons or sponsors has always been present.[15]

There were, not least due to the forces of nation-building, also some resources flowing into preservation of folk and ethnic culture. But comparing the private and public funds flowing into Culture (through the building, for instance, of museums and collections, national theaters and opera houses) to the resources available for the preservation of culture with a small *c*, the scales tip on the side of Culture—not least because small *c* culture was considered to be just there; it had not yet become a marked and market category. If anything, small *c* culture was for a long time considered vile and unrefined, something to be eradicated or improved on. In the late nineteenth century, but particularly as of the second half of the twentieth century, there were (and are) more resources flowing into vernacular cultures. We know the reasons for this, and can state them briefly: they range from decolonization and postcolonial claims, as well as global migration and increased heterogeneity supported by what Jean-Louis Tornatore (2012) has called, "Anthropology's Payback." What is of interest to me here, is the distribution of financial resources resulting from the shifting motivation of actors. They range from individual patrons to local institutions, nation-states, and international organizations, and have to deliberate where their limited funds should best go in the broad expanses of culture and Culture.

To put the argument into a schematic and thus overstated form, throughout early modernity, patronage defined, remained with, and thus solidified Culture. With the rise of national interest in preserving remnants of the vernacular there is also support for initiatives in the realm of culture. Behind this there are ideological shifts that would require further elaboration. Roughly stated, one might argue that there are three overlapping eras of patronage: medieval to early modern, early nationalists, and late modern paradigms. A medieval to early modern paradigm utilized the aesthetic power of the arts as an imprimatur for a particular political reign or court. Artistic skill and innovation thus received patronage. During an early nationalist paradigm, there was also support for the protection from innovation. The continuity and presumed lack of change in folk and ethnic traditions was considered a powerful resource for the growing idea of the nation-state and thus worthy of sponsorship. This brought about a split of expenditures between the continued patronage of innovative, skilled, individual genius and more state-sponsored support to preserve and protect worthy cultural forms. A late modern paradigm, finally, sees all aesthetic expressions as a resource and provides support depending on what the sociopolitical goal of patrons and creators might be. Economically, we have arrived at this heterogeneous stage, but politically this is not what can be expressed openly in most cases.

What is the impact of such shifts in sponsorship needs? I would argue that prestigious and innovative practices that once were constitutive of Culture find themselves successively integrated in the spectrum of practices requiring preservation. Expressive forms such as opera and ballet—not least through the global comparison enabled by UNESCO lists—have in the course of time become "traditional," much like the Cambodian royal ballet or the Peking opera (both on the Intangible Heritage List). Formerly sacrosanct, these arts must now compete ever more in the broader sponsorship market, as the competition from the realm of small *c* culture has grown enormously. Patronage—or individual sponsorship—remains important, but potential patrons have various options. They may gain prestige from sponsoring creativity, art, or aesthetic innovation, but they may also be inclined to let their resources flow into preservation, in order to participate where the action is. Patrons enable others, but their patronage reflects back on themselves and provides them with social and political capital.

Under the UNESCO mantle, heritage listings have become an arena of high prestige, and they are one among many factors contributing to the multiplication of cultures vying for both valuation and valorization (Kirshenblatt-Gimblett 2006, 189–91). Whether folk or ethnic, tribal, indigenous or fusion, outsider art, or classic Western high arts, they all need state and private support, they all work in one way or another with the market. Within this global dynamic, a continued separation into low and high arts, and low and high cultural creativity would appear mis-guided—if it were not for the power of historically established discourses of value. Aesthetic practices emerge(d) within a given time, place, and social context, and of course there are experts able to identify, date, and historically contextualize a given craft or practice. It is such expertise and old and new political discourses, coupled with issues of abundance and scarcity, that regulate the value of aesthetic practices. What has changed, however, is the number of communities and associated experts seeking support, be this public funds or private patronage.

The increase of expenditure for preservation is fostered and accompa-nied by a legitimating discourse. A habitualized bourgeois aesthetic taste for Culture has been joined by taste regimes encouraging the preservation and maintenance of small c cultures of folk, ethnic, tribal, and indigenous communities and histories.[16] The intent of such burgeoning discourses is to democratize value criteria—and by extension the access to sponsorship. The multiplicity of claims naturally brings with it governance efforts which in turn generate bureaucracy and hierarchy. This is particularly visible in the heritage field, where actors seeking to compile a nomination dossier to con-front the need to confirm and document (drawing on certified expertise) every criterion that supports an item's value. Yet, similar mechanisms are visible in any city council that needs to deliberate which arts initiatives are deserving of a bit of the already small budget set aside for arts and culture.

Heritage regimes tell us a great deal about the shifting value of culture, particularly its tangible and intangible aesthetic dimensions. But I would

also argue that understanding heritage regimes within the broader complex of cultural sponsorship and within the history of patronage elucidates
the resource nature of culture.

## CONCLUSION: ACTORS, RESOURCES, AND IMPACT

Placing the sponsoring of heritage preservation within the broader matrix
of cultural sponsorship allows one to see the resource nature of culture
particularly well. If we look at the history of patronage and sponsorship,
we see the continued entanglement of aesthetic, political, and economic
value potential. To accumulate value and unfold impact, the resource
requires sponsorship. Over time, there have been differently composed
communities of patrons recognizing the power of this resource in shaping
a polity. It is a community that is linked at best through competition: individual patrons or sponsors recognize each other's financial and political
position and their respective capacity to have an impact on the artistic
contribution to the public sphere.[17] Again, we can note that heritage-making is but one kind of selection and certification process within this arena
of cultural resource development and preservation, but we ought to ask
why it is appealing today and attracting many patrons.

Among heritage patrons, UNESCO is certainly the most prominent,
although not the most economically potent—UNESCO can funnel sponsors but is itself an under-endowed agency. Patronage is an interventionist
practice—but its goals are not always so clear cut, as aesthetic appeal and
the relationship between patron and client mix with the political potential
of works of architecture and art. Crucial to reflect for both UNESCO and
for heritage specialists on the ground is the fact that heritage policies are
embedded in the broader practices of cultural sponsorship. These have
local, national, individual and global histories.

The impact of UNESCO's heritage interventions ought to be reflected
further within these parameters. Sponsoring and protecting are twin
engines in generating cultural value. While it is groups, communities, or entire polities that may come to share and traditionalize such
values in the course of a given local history, there are communities of
patrons—overlapping with or separate from those sharing in such cultural

resources—that have and continue to play a major role in bringing about and/or preserving such cultural flowering. With all its efforts to coordinate and democratize this process, UNESCO is nonetheless also dependent on the patronage dynamic on the local and state level. What benefits do heritage investors reap vis-à-vis patrons of performing arts or sponsors of literature festivals? Which established and which newly created policies are there in a given state that encourage patronage and ease tax burdens? Questions such as these are important to pursue, not least because they integrate heritage in a broader socioeconomic and political matrix of bestowing value on particular aspects of culture.

NOTES

This chapter appeared originally in Nicolas Adell, Regina F. Bendix, Chiara Bortolotto, and Markus Tauschek, eds. *Between Imagined Communities and Communies of Practice*. Göttingen Studies on Cultural Property, vol. 8. (Göttingen: Göttingen University Press, 2015), 219–34.

1. On the interplay of cultural valorization and valuation, compare Kirshenblatt-Gimblett (2006); on the interface of old and new cultural protection regimes, compare Tauschek (2012).

2. For critical assessments of the terms group and community, consider Noyes (2003, 2006) and Hertz (2015).

3. The scholarship on this history is legion; some of it can be grouped with the anxieties of modernity and the discourses on folklore and authenticity (Bendix 1997); other components involve what Robert Cantwell (1993) has termed "ethnomimesis"—that which is at work in preserving and staging the purported folk.

4. The New Yorker, April 14, 2014, 54. Cartoon by Walsh.

5. I will pursue here neither Theodor Adorno's (e.g., 1963) arguments regarding culture and value, tied into his critique of the culture industry, nor the efforts within popular culture studies and media studies, to clarify the distinctions between taste and value cultures (e.g., Hecken 2012). But clearly, the creative industries' interests and the interests transported through patronage are evermore difficult to disentangle.

6. This is not to say that operas—and particularly operettas—were not also appreciated by other social classes, hence making it hard to see details of decor and dress, which remind of the appeal of the form. The social dynamic of opera and operetta appreciation is quite complex, and needs to be considered within the specifics of historical contexts, which in turn assists in understanding the decline of audience numbers (Honigsheim 1979, 91–5; see also Csáki 1998).

7. Italian opera singers are presently collecting signatures to nominate Italian Lyric Opera on the UNESCO list (Sempre Libera 2014).

8. Compare for example, Oevermann, Süßmann, and Tauber (2007).

9. Tim Edensor's (1998) study of tourism at the Taj Mahal would certainly confirm this; Davis and Marvin's (2004) assessment of Venitian tourism is more differentiated but also invokes this dimension.

10. Pielhoff works with sociologist Axel Honneth's theory of recognition; compare Groth (2015) for an application of Honneth's theory to the heritage dynamic.

11. Not enough is known of what was dismantled in Maoist China, and China at present is restoring or reconstructing some structures in order to participate in the opportunities and the prestige presented by heritage lists.

12. And, not to forget, a first impetus to imitate and then preserve folk housing came from the aristocracy as well, with the *Hameau de la Reine*, a village imitation built next to Versailles and given to Marie Antoinette in 1774 as a place to relax from courtly norms.

13. Compare chapter 5 of this volume, "Heredity, Hybridity, and Heritage."

14. Pierre Bourdieu offered a reading of class-based art appreciation in his *The Love of Art* ([1969] 1991). In German, one refers to the segment of valued cultural expressions ranging from literature to all the arts as *Kultur*—and entailed in this is the assumption that such high culture also denotes the desirable refinements within civil society, and introducing anthropological dimensions of the culture concept is thus all the more complex (Lindner 2003).

15. Industrialization has brought forth mass-produced art forms which added further complexity to the discourses on culture and value. The present chapter—at best—touches marginally on the role and debates about mass or popular culture, not least because their commercial base does not require patronage. However, as popular culture ages, it, of course, also enters into historicizing value practices, generates museum exhibits and the like, and thus is indeed also vying for funds from the limited pool of resources for "arts and culture." Recent research has sought to rectify earlier critiques of mass culture as a capitalist means of flattening the taste of and dumbing down helpless consumers. Kaspar Maase (2001, 2011) has carefully examined the politics of taste and class that contributed to scales of value. Research on the popular, in particular popular seriality, has convincingly focused on active reception of popular art forms and hence enabled a view onto creative processes and how they are valued in the intersection of commercial and vernacular practices (Jenkins 1992, 2006; Kelleter 2012).

16. Pierre Bourdieu's (1984) empirical study deconstructed aesthetic taste and its enduring power to express and enact distinction between social classes; while the study has not put an end to such distinction, its transfer in bits and pieces into the public sphere likely has contributed to the increase in aesthetic cultures asserting their claims for broader acceptance.

17. The newest form of (not only) arts and culture sponsorship is "crowdfunding"; it emerged in the first decade of the twenty-first century as an internet-based form of raising funds for initiatives, competing with other worthy endeavors to attract patrons. There is already a huge diversity of crowdfunding mechanisms, from Kickstarter, to credit-based and philanthropic versions (see Dresner 2014).

**REFERENCES**

Adorno, Theodor. 1963. *Eingriffe: Neun kritische Modelle*. Frankfurt: Suhrkamp.
Bauman, Richard and Charles L. Briggs. 2003. *Voices of Modernity: Language Ideologies and the Politics of Inequality*. Cambridge: Cambridge University Press.

Bendix, Regina. 1997. *In Search of Authenticity: The Formation of Folklore Studies*. Madison: University of Wisconsin Press.

Bendix, Regina F., Aditya Eggert, and Arnika Peselmann. 2012. *Introduction to Heritage Regimes and the State*, edited by Regina F. Bendix, Aditya Eggert, and Arnika Peselmann, 11–20. Göttingen: Universitätsverlag Göttingen.

Binder, Beate. 2009. *Streitfall Stadtmitte: Der Berliner Schlossplatz*. Reihe Kultur und Alltag. Cologne: Böhlau.

Bourdieu, Pierre. (1969) 1991. *The Love of Art. European Art Museums and Their Public*. Translated by Caroline Beattie and Nick Merriman. Cambridge, UK: Polity.

———. 1984. *Distinction. A Social Critique of the Judgment of Taste*. Translated by Richard Nice. Cambridge, MA: Harvard University Press.

Burgess, Glyn S., ed. 1981. *Court and Poet. Selected Proceedings of the Third Congress of the International Courtly Literature Society*. Liverpool: Cairns.

Cantwell, Robert. 1993. *Ethnomimesis. Folklore and the Representation of Culture*. Chapel Hill: University of North Carolina Press.

Clifford, James. 1988. *The Predicament of Culture. Twentieth-Century Ethnography, Literature, and Art*. Cambridge, MA: Harvard University Press.

Csáky, Moritz. 1998. *Ideologie der Operette und Wiener Moderne. Ein kulturhistorischer Essay zur österreichischen Identität*. Vienna: Böhlau.

Davis, Robert C., and Garry R. Marvin. 2004. *Venice, the Tourist Maze. A Cultural Critique of the World's Most Touristed City*. Berkeley: University of California Press.

Dresner, Steven. 2014. *Crowdfunding: A Guide to Raising Capital on the Internet*. Hoboken, NJ: Wiley.

Edensor, Tim. 1998. *Tourists at the Taj*. London: Routledge.

Frey, Michael. 1999. *Macht und Moral des Schenkens—Staat und bürgerliche Mäzene vom späten 18. Jahrhundert bis zur Gegenwart*. Berlin: Fannei & Walz.

Gardner, Julian. 2011. *Giotto and His Publics. Three Paradigms of Patronage*. Cambridge, MA: Harvard University Press.

Groth, Stefan. 2015. "Between Society and Culture: Recognition in Cultural Heritage Contexts." In *Between Imagined Communities and Communities of Practice: Participation, Territory and the Making of Heritage*, 59–81. Göttingen: Universitätsverlag Göttingen.

Hafstein, Valdimar. 2009. "Intangible Heritage as a List. From Masterpiece to Representation." In *Intangible Heritage*, edited by Laurajane Smith and Natsuko Akagawa, 93–111. London: Routledge.

Hecken, Thomas. 2012. "Pop-Konzepte der Gegenwart." *POP, Kultur und Kritik* 1: 88–107.

Hertz, Ellen. 2015. "Bottoms, Genuine and Spurious." In *Between Imagined Communities and Communities of Practice: Participation, Territory and the Making of Heritage*, 59–81. Göttingen: Universitätsverlag Göttingen.

Honigsheim, Paul. 1979. *Music and Society, the Later Writings of Paul Honigsheim*. New York: R. E. Krieger.

Jenkins, Henry. 1992. *Textual Poachers: Television Fans and Participatory Culture*. New York: Routledge.

———. 2006. *Convergence Culture: Where Old and New Media Collide*. New York: New York University Press.

Kelleter, Frank, ed. 2012. *Populäre Serialität: Narration—Evolution—Distinktion. Zum seriellen Erzählen seit dem 19. Jahrhundert*. Bielefeld: transcript.

Kirshenblatt-Gimblett, Barbara. 2006. "World Heritage and Cultural Economics." In *Museum Frictions. Public Cultures/Global Transformations*, edited by Ivan Karp, Corinne A. Kratz, Lynn Szwaja, and Tomas Ybarra-Frausto, 161–202. Durham, NC: Duke University Press.

Lindner, Rolf. 2003. "Konjunktur und Krise des Kulturkonzepts." In *Kulturwissenschaften. Forschung—Praxis—Positionen*, edited by Lutz Musner and Gotthart Wunberg, 75–95. Freiburg: Rombach.

Maase, Kaspar. 2001. *Prädikat wertlos: der lange Streit um Schmutz und Schund*. Tübingen: Tübinger Vereinigung für Volkskunde.

———. 2011. *Das Recht der Gewöhnlichkeit: über populäre Kultur*. Tübingen: Tübinger Vereinigung für Volkskunde.

Mai, Ekkehard, and Peter Paret, eds. 1993. *Sammler, Stifter und Museen—Kunstförderung in Deutschland im 19. und 20. Jahrhundert*. Vienna: Böhlau.

Manufactum. 2016. Accessed September 1. www.manufactum.de/home.html.

McDonald, William C., with collaboration of Ulrich Goebel. 1973. *German Medieval Literary Patronage from Charlemagne to Maximilian I. A Critical Commentary with Special Emphasis on Imperial Promotion of Literature*. Amsterdam: Rodopi NV.

Noyes, Dorothy. 2003. "Group." In *Eight Words for the Study of Expressive Culture*, edited by Burt Feintuch, 7–41. Urbana: University of Illinois Press.

———. 2006. "The Judgment of Solomon: Global Protections for Tradition and the Problem of Community Ownership." *Cultural Analysis* 5: 27–56.

Oevermann, Ulrich, Johannes Süßmann, and Christine Tauber, eds. 2007. *Die Kunst der Mächtigen und die Macht der Kunst. Untersuchungen zu Mäzenatentum und Kulturpatronage*. Berlin: Akademie.

Pielhoff, Stephen. 2007. *Stifter und Anstifter: Vermittler zwischen "Zivilgesellschaft," Kommune und Staat im Kaiserreich*. Göttingen: Vandenhoeck und Rupprecht.

Sachs, Hannelore. 1971. *Sammler und Mäzene. Zur Entwicklung des Kunstsammelns von der Antike bis zur Gegenwart*. Leipzig: Koehler & Amelang.

Sempre Libera. 2014. "Petizione all'Unesco per il riconoscimento dell'opera lirica italiana come patrimonio dell'Umanità." Accessed August 11, 2017. http://semprelibera .altervista.org/segnalazioni/petizione-allunesco-per-il-riconoscimento-dellopera -lirica-italiana-come-patrimonio-dellumanita.

Tauschek, Markus. 2012. "The Bureaucratic Texture of National Patrimonial Policies." In *Heritage Regimes and the State*, edited by Regina F. Bendix, Aditya Eggert, and Arnika Peselmann, 195–212. Göttingen: Universitätsverlag Göttingen.

Thomas, Anabel. 2000. "Fifteenth-century Florence and court culture under the Medici." In *Courts, Patrons and Poets*, edited by Daniel Mateer, 159–226. New Haven, CT: Yale University Press.

Tornatore, Jean-Louis. 2012. "Anthropology's Pay Back: 'The Gastronomic Meal of the French.' The Ethnographic Elements of a Heritage Distinction." In *Heritage Regimes and the State*, edited by Regina F. Bendix, Aditya Eggert, and Arnika Peselmann, 341–65. Göttingen: Universitätsverlag Göttingen.

UNESCO. 2014. "Lists of Intangible Cultural Heritage and the Register of Best Safeguarding Practices." Accessed December 18, 2017. http://www.unesco.org/culture /ich/index.php?lg=en&pg=00559.

INDEX

Abrahams, Roger D., 14n9, 92n28
aesthetic commons, 255
aesthetic cosmopolitanism, 202, 213
aesthetic identification, 100
aesthetic resources, 198, 202–204, 209, 212–214
Akagawa, Natsuko, 146
alpine transhumance processions, 30–32; audience, 32; display of cowherders and cows, 31–32
Anderson, Benedict, 2
*Annals of Tourism Research*, 18, 40n4
*Anne of Green Gables*, 82
Anne's Land, 82–83
Appadurai, Arjun, 3, 5–6, 179, 191n10; *Social Life of Things, The*, 5, 174
Appenzell Ausserrhoden, 183
*Association for Critical Heritage Studies*, 98
Association of German Heritage Sites, 130
*Atlas der deutschen Volkskunde*, 225
Austria, 107–108; calvaries (*Kalvarienberge*), 47; diaper-changing stations (diapering oasis), 52; Diaper Hiking Mile, 50–51, 53; Dwarf Park, 49; film industry and, 52; Gurktal, 49; Heidi Alm Falkert, 48; Magic Forest, 49; materialized narration of tourist sites, 47–53; royal fairy-tale wedding, 114–116; Schönbrunn castle (monarchal heritage), 108–111; Stations of the Cross, 47;
Stuffed Animal Zoo Experience, 49; Trebesing village, 50–51, 55
Austrian Magic Forest, 49–50

baker: craft of, 228–231; path to becoming, 230. *See also* German bakers
Barber, Benjamin, 106
Barbier, Carl, 31–32
Basque festival, 37
Bausinger, Hermann, 3
Beatles, 74
Belgian colonial museum, 104
Ben-Amos, Dan, 24
Bendix, Reinhard, 10
Benjamin, Walter, 79
bequest value, 176
Berlin, 62
Bern, 28–29
Billig, Michael, 201
Binche carnival, 136–137, 157
Binder, Beate, 263
biopiracy, 237
bioprospecting, 237
Blixen, Karen, 82
border zone, 4
Bourdieu, Pierre, 4, 13n1, 245
Bread Museums, 225
Broccolini, Alessandra, 220
Brown, Michael F., 162, 213, 244; *Who Owns Native Culture?*, 243

Bruner, Edward, 4
Budapest Declaration on World Heritage,
    2002, 163n1
Buford, Bill, 85
Busch, Wilhelm, 62
Byrne, Denis, 158

Cambodia, 148, 222; royal ballet of, 256
Canclini, Gabriel Garcia, 202
*Canta u Populu Corsu*, 201, 208
*canti corsu*, 203, 206, 208
Carinthia (Kärnten, Austria), 45, 48–49,
    51, 54–55; Experience Park, 49; Magic
    Forest, 49; theme parks in, 47; tourism
    promotion in, 46
China, 78, 222, 269n11
Chovqan game, 256
Clifford, James, 90n7, 255
Coca-Colonization of Austria, 53
Cohen, Erik, 90n7
Cologne cathedral, 133
Comaroff, John and Jean, 175
commoditization, of tourist narratives,
    81–85, 89n2
commons: aesthetic, 255; creative, 240;
    cultural, 7, 128, 157–158, 161, 171, 198,
    201, 241, 244, 248; tragedy of, 156
communal/community ownership,
    239–240
Convention Concerning the Protection of
    World Cultural and Natural Heritage,
    146–148
Convention for Intangible Cultural
    Heritage, 6
copyright, 6–7, 196, 237, 240, 244–245
costume, symbolic discourse of, 114–116
Cowherder's Festival, 28
crafts, study of, 230–231
creative commons, 240
Croatia, 220
crowdfunding, 269n17
cultural anthropology, 1, 10, 124, 126, 131,
    141, 174
cultural assets, 178
cultural commons, 7, 128, 157–158, 161, 171,
    177, 198, 201, 241, 244, 248

cultural displays, 23–40, 53, 104, 106, 109,
    119n11
cultural economics, 197
cultural essentialism in nation-building, 5
cultural expressions, 258
cultural heritage, 125, 130–132, 138–139, 146,
    154, 159, 170–171, 177, 190n1
cultural property, 6–7, 148, 159–160, 163n3,
    165n19, 196, 205, 213, 244–245, 248;
    economic anthropologic perspective, 248;
    legal anthropologic perspective, 248–249
cultural scholarship, 1–2, 4, 196, 213
culture, 264–265; bourgeois notion of, 4;
    commoditization of, 8, 38; community
    interest in, 7; expressive, 203–206;
    genuine, 4–5; honoring, 247–248;
    living, 244–245, 247; owning, 247; as
    a production, 178; as property, 8; as a
    resource, 158–162, 178–181, 187–190; value
    of, 5
custom bearers, 246

Dakota (hotel), 74, 76
*Denkmalschutz* (monument protection),
    99, 221
devaluation, 8, 11
de Staël, Madame, 23
*Die Piefke-Saga*, 87
Dietrich the Knight, 63, 65–68
Disneylands and Disney Worlds, 47

Ebert, Ferry. *See* Runzelschuh, Radomir
echoes program (Switzerland), 209–212
Eckl, Andreas, 239
educational journey (*Bildungsreise*), 79
education value, 177
Elizabeth of Wittelsbach (Sisi), 114–116,
    119nn10, 15
ethnic groups, 75, 89n3
ethnic purity, 113
ethnological knowledge production, 198
European Märchen, 64
expressive culture, 203–206

Fabian, Johannes, 11, 104, 202
fairy-tale activist, 63, 65–66

fairytale tourism, 20
fakelore, 3, 4, 24
folk atlases, 225–227
folklore, 2, 10, 203; vs folklorismus, 30; as verbal art, 203–204
folklorismus, 24, 30, 125
folkloristics, 1
folk music, as a cultural resource, 206–209
folktales of Runzelschuh, 44; materialization of tales and theming of landscapes, 45–47
food-related custom as cultural heritage: dumplings from Thuringia, 223; French cuisine, 220, 223; German bread, 217, 219–231; Mediterranean cuisine, 220
Foucault, Michel, 173
France, 220
Franz Josef I (Emperor), 107–108, 116
French cuisine, 220, 223
Frey, Bruno, 176
Frigo, Manlio, 159

Gates, Bill, 240
genetic engineering, 113
genetic resources (GR), 236
geographical indication (GI) system, 177, 191n11, 229, 232–233n10
German bakers, 199, 230–231
German bread, 199; as a cultural heritage, 217, 219–231
German Bread Registry, 218, 222
German Fairy Tale Street (Märchenstrasse), 20, 61, 68–70; Dietrich's narratives, 63, 65–68; historic figure of Baron Münchhausen, 65; Hofgeismar site, 65–66; Neukirchen's Märchenhouse, dramatic and visual stagings at, 64–65; Pied Piper of Hamelin, 63–64, 71nn3, 7; principle of, 62
German Research Foundation (DFG), 12, 226
global governance, morals and norms in, 164–165n15
globalized tourist economy, 20
Goree Island, 89n2
Göttingen University, 7, 12

Graburn, Nelson, 3, 18, 80
Grand Tour, 17
Grassmuck, Volker, 240
Greenwood, Davydd, 25, 37
Grimm, Jacob, 249
Grimm fairytales, 64
Grünberg, Gudrun, 64–65
Gstrein, Norbert, 87

habitus, 4, 92n23, 97, 127, 177, 212, 245, 248–249
Habsburgs, 111–112
Hafstein, Valdimar, 157, 242, 256
Hague Convention, 1954, 160
Hahn, Adolf, 65
Haider, Jörg, 116, 120n21
Half-Timbered Housing Street, 62
Hanau, 62
Handler, Richard, 24–25
Hann, Chris, 151
Hardermannli, 36
Harder-Potschete festival, 23, 35–37, 39; folkloristic displays, 36–37; impact on tourism business, 36; theme of forest spirits and fertility demons, 35–36
Hardin, Garrett, 156
Heimatschutz (homeland protection), 99, 221
Herder, Johann Gottfried, 208
heredity, 105–107, 114, 116–117; hereditary purity, 113, 120n18; Lippizaner stallions, case of, 111–114; royal, 108–111
heritage, 117, 118n2, 177; democratic preservation of, 109; differentiation between history and, 110; folk, 115; genuine vs fake, 130; Holocaust as, 110; ideology of, 106; meaning and usage of term, 105–106; memorialization of struggle, subjugation and violent victory, 110; nationalistic folk costume, 115–116
heritage conventions, 96–97
heritage-making/heritagization, 9, 96–97, 99, 124–126, 203, 214, 256; achieving and maintaining world heritage status, 130; actors approach, 129–132; aftermath of French Revolution, 154–155;

competition and quality control, 138; cultural practice, 132; as a cultural practice, 98, 100–101, 131–132; difference between image and economic value, 129–130; economic value-adding, 140; element of authenticity, 99, 125, 131; following interest in property by kin, 154; intangible heritage, 124, 136–137, 139–140; interpersonal and societal consequences, 132–141; local-global value exchange, 137; as meta-cultural production, 157; patronage issues, 133; selection of cultural heritage, 138–139; service-sector, impact on, 138; shaping of heritage goods, 126–129; UNESCO parameters, 129–130; valuation and valorization for, 152, 156
heritage nomination, 101
heritage police, 98
heritage scholarship, 9, 96, 98–99, 123
Hertz, Ellen, 12, 191n12
Herzfeld, Michael, 125
historical memory, 100
historical routes, 61
Hobsbawm, Eric, 2
Hochschild, Arlie, 138
Honko, Lauri, 14n2
host community and tourism, 38–39.
    *See also* Interlaken village
hostilities against tourists, 84
House of Wittelsbach, 115
human selfhood, 5
hybrid culture, 106–107
hybridity, 105–108, 113–114, 116–117
hyphenated landscapes, 61

*I Compagnoli*, 206–207
*Iliad* and *Odyssey*, 242
imagined community, 2
individual authorship, 243
inheritance, 146, 148, 163n1; blood relatives, 151; bridge between heritage and, 153–158; within family context, 153; of personal possessions and property, 150–153; restricted, 164n13; separation of dead individuals and, 152, 155–156; 'to inherit', 151; writ large, 153–158
intangible heritage/intangible cultural heritage, 124, 136–137, 139–140, 146, 158;

cooking crafts as, 220; safeguarding of, 160–161
intellectual property, 240
Intergovernmental Committee (IGC), 236–237, 249
Interlaken village, 23–24; alpine transhumance processions, 30–32; dairy farming, 27; folkloristic displays, 27–28; *Harder-Potschete* festival, 23, 35–37; health-related activities, 27; high-altitude nature of, 27; landscape, 26; native culture, 26; population, 27; reasons for public displays at, 37; staging of William Tell Play, 23, 32–37, 39; streets and waterways, 26; tourism and, 26–27; tourist profile, 27–28; Unspunnen festival, 23, 26, 28–30
*International Journal of Heritage Studies*, 98
*Invention of Tradition, The*, 19

Japan, 220
*Japanesen* play in Schwyz, 180, 184–186
Jeggle, Utz, 38
Jobs, Steven, 240
Johann, Erzherzog (Archduke), 116
Jules-Rosette, Benetta, 25

*Kalevala*, 204
Karen Blixen Museum, 82
Karl I, 111
Karl May open-air plays, 52
Kassel, 62
Kasten, Erich, 244
Kirshenblatt-Gimblett, Barbara, 90n7, 96–97, 130, 137, 152, 157, 159, 173, 176–177, 219; *Destination Culture*, 91n12
Klein, Barbro, 99, 212
knowledge society, 138
Korea, 220
Korff, Gottfried, 38
Köstlin, Konrad, 47
Kurin, Richard, 212

*Landscape and Memory*, 67
landscapes, 20
Leach, Edmund, 204
Lebendige Traditionen (Living Traditions), 189, 192n24

Lennon, John, 74
Lessig, Lawrence, 240
Lévi-Strauss, Claude, 141
Linnekin, Jocelyn, 24–25
Lippizaner stallions, 111–114
Löfgren, Orvar, 77
Lord, Albert, 242
Lowenthal, David, 105, 118n2
Ludwig, Ernst, 239
Luther, Martin, 134

MacCannell, Dean, 26, 48, 76
Manassas, 110
Mangold, Ijoma, 258
Märchenautomat (Folktale Automat), 44–45
Märchenpark, 53
Märchenwald, 53
Maria Theresia (Emperess), 116
Marquess, 207–209
Marx, Karl, 5
materialized narratives of Austria, 54–56; Carinthian sites, 48–49, 54–55; from children's books, 48–53; Disney-type environments, 49, 53; folkloristic endeavor of learning and knowing, 52; traditional narrative experience, 51–52
Mauss, Marcel, 19
Maxa, Rudy, 86
Mediterranean cuisine, 220
metacultural production, 96–97, 98, 127, 173, 190, 219
Metropolitan Opera, New York, 258
Modernity at Large, 3
Moser, Hans, 30
musealization, 110, 232n6
museum practices, 109, 119n11

Napoleon, Emperor, 28
National Front for the Liberation of Corsica, 201
National Geographic, 83
nationalism, 2–3, 29, 46, 105, 106, 107, 201–202, 204, 207, 265
nationalistic folk costume, 115–116
National Public Radio (NPR), 86
N'Dour, Youssou, 87

New York City's Central Park, 74–75; brief history, 75; features and areas, 75; John Lennon's memorial, 81; sculptures, memorials, and fountains, 75–76
Noyes, Dorothy, 162, 239

O'Keefe, Patrick, 159
Olmsted, Fredrick Law, 75
option value, 176
other, othering, 11, 247
otherness, 202
Out of Africa, 82
ownership rights, 7

Paghjella, 202, 206–207, 209
Parry, Milman, 242
patronage, 254; impact on aesthetic value and taste, 260–264; opportunities for, 264–267; role in valuation of culture, 257
patrons, 133, 254, 259–260
Peckham, Robert Shaman, 123–124
Peru, 220
pilgrimage, 17–18
Preah Vihear Temple, 148
preservation-oriented values, 221–222
prestige value, 176
Prince Edward Island (PEI), 82
printers' guild and rights to printing and distribution, 242
Pro Helvetia, 210–212
property, understanding of, 238–244; intellectual property, 240, 243; owning a property, 239; private property, 242
Prott, Lyndel, 159
public folklore, 7
public heritage, practices of, 153–158

Ranger, Terence, 2
reflexive modernization, 106, 118n3
Regev, Motti, 202
Regimes of Value in Tourism, 19
Rethinking Heritage, 123
rituals, 3
river routes, 61
Roman routes, 61
Romantic nationalism, 115
Romantic Street, 62
Rørøs, 136

royal fairy-tale wedding album, 114–116
Runzelschuh, Radomir, 44; folktales of, 44, 55

Savvy Traveler, 86
Schiller, Friedrich, 186
Schmitt, Thomas, 222
Schönbrunn castle, 108–111
SeaWorld, 47
semantics, 9–10, 149, 159–160, 163
Sennett, Richard, 153
sex tourism, 85
Shrove Tuesday celebrations, 184
Siebeck, Wolfram, 219
SIEF, 213
Silk Routes, 61
*Silvesterklausen* performances in Urnäsch, 180–183
Sisi, 108
Smith, Laurajane, 146
Sollors, Werner, 130
Spanish Riding School, 111–114
Spina, Carl Anton, 114
sponsorship of arts and cultural expressions, 255
stationers company, 242
Stewart, Susan, 78
Stocking Jr., George W., 2
Strawberry Fields, 74
Street of Mills, 62
Swenson, Astrid, 149
Swiss Association for Folk Music, 29
Swiss community, 246
Swiss Society for Folk Costume, 29
Switzerland, 179, 188–189, 203, 211, 222; *Japanesen* play in Schwyz, 180, 184–186; *Silvesterklausen* performances in Urnäsch, 180–183; tourism, 84, 180; Wilhelm Tell play in Altdorf, 180, 185, 186–187; Wilhelm Tell play in Interlaken, 23, 32–37, 39

tale type catalogues, 86; Aarne's Tale Type Index, 92n29; Thompson's Motif Index, 92n29
Tauschek, Markus, 101, 136–137, 157
Taylor, Charles, 243

Tell Play Association, 40n8, 186–187. *See also* William Tell Play
theater, 3, 33, 75, 128, 184–187, 258–259, 264
themed auto routes, 61–62; folktale employed in, 62; Hanau, 62; historical routes, 61; Kassel, 62
Throsby, David, 176
Thuringia, 135
tourism, 4, 9, 38, 170–171, 175, 177; affordable means of transport, 18; defined, 76; health as a motivation factor, 17; to heritage sites, 19; industry, 90n6; as leisure travel, 17; material satisfaction and needs of, 76–77; research, 18–19; role of image consumers, 25; scholarship, 18; study of, 18–19; touristic experience, 77–81; tourists *vs* travelers, 18; travel as a means to experience fiction and fantasy, 46
tourist art, 25
tourist categorization, 90n7
*Tourist The*, 18
tourist experience, 57n7
touristic experience, 77–81, 92n28; authenticity of, 79–80; component of longing, 78, 80; experience of a lifetime, 78, 82; hostilities against tourists, 84; narrative potential and its commoditization, 81–85; negative experiences, 80; reflexive narratives, 85–88; sense of endangerment, 80
tradition, 2, 19; invention of, 24–25, 38; traditionalized displays, 24
traditional cultural experiences (TCE), 236, 238, 244, 250
traditional knowledge (TK), 160, 236, 238, 244, 250–251; patenting of, 237
transaction costs, 176
*Travels in Hyperreality*, 47
travel storytellers, 84
Tschofen, Bernhard, 61
Turkey: heritage lists, 129; tourism, 84

Uffelmann, Dietrich, 65–68, 71–72n12
United International Bureaux for the Protection of Intellectual Property, 6

United Nations Educational, Scientific and Cultural Organization (UNESCO), 96–97, 108, 126, 136, 140, 146–149, 155–156, 159–161, 170–171, 175, 178, 189, 205, 223, 254–256, 265–266; Convention on Immaterial Cultural Heritage, 223; Convention on Intangible Cultural Heritage, 179, 220–224, 231, 255; Cultural Heritage Convention, 140–141; Intergovernmental Commission, 220

Unspunnen festival, 23, 26, 28–30, 39; aim to preserve traditional culture, 30; folk performers, 29; Napoleonic era, 28–29; sponsors and organizers, 29

valorization of culture, 151–152, 156, 159, 172, 190, 191n12, 231; development, 173–174; economic valorization of custom, 183; in heritage-making/heritagization, 152, 156; *Japanesen* play in Schwyz, 180, 184–186; political valorization, 173; *Silvesterklausen* performances in Urnäsch, 180–183; vocabulary of, 172–178; Wilhelm Tell play, Altdorf, 180, 186–187

valuation of culture, 257–260

value, 5–6; value culture, 11

value-related terminology in English and German economics, 10

Vede, Del, 50, 57n11

*Vielvölkerstaat*, 107

Vienna, 108–109, 112, 116

von Goethe, Johann Wolfgang, 79, 85, 90–91n12

Wartburg, 134–135

Weigelt, Frank, 160

Welz, Gisela, 91n18, 232n10

Werner, Amin, 224

Weverka, Jody, 80

Widbom, Mats, 212

Wiegelmann, Günter, 226

Wilhelm Tell Play. *See* William Tell Play

Willer, Stefan, 154

William Tell Play, 23, 32–35, 39, 180, 186–187; impact on tourist business, 33; theme, 34

working-class heritage, 98

World Heritage Convention of, 1972, 156

World Intellectual Property Organization (WIPO), 6–7, 148–149, 156, 160–161, 197–198, 205, 236–237, 249

xenophilia, 11, 247

xenophobia, 11, 247

Yúdice, George, 131, 203

*Zamballarana*, 208

REGINA F. BENDIX

is Professor of Cultural Anthropology/European Ethnology at
the University of Göttingen, Germany. Her books include *In
Search of Authenticity* and *Backstage Domains*. She is author with
Kilian Bizer and Dorothy Noyes of *Sustaining Interdisciplinary
Collaboration*, and editor with Aditya Eggert and Arnika
Peselmann of *Heritage Regimes and the State*. Together with
Ulrich Marzolph, she edits the journal *Narrative Culture*.

www.ingramcontent.com/pod-product-compliance
Lightning Source LLC
Chambersburg PA
CBHW022350280326
41935CB00007B/139